A CULTURAL HISTORY OF MEMORY

IN THE MIDDLE AGES

Edited by Gerald Schwedler

BLOOMSBURY ACADEMIC
LONDON • NEW YORK • OXFORD • NEW DELHI • SYDNEY

BLOOMSBURY ACADEMIC
Bloomsbury Publishing Plc
50 Bedford Square, London, WC1B 3DP, UK
1385 Broadway, New York, NY 10018, USA
29 Earlsfort Terrace, Dublin 2, Ireland

BLOOMSBURY, BLOOMSBURY ACADEMIC and the Diana logo are trademarks of Bloomsbury Publishing Plc

First published in Great Britain 2021
Paperback edition first published 2024

Copyright © Bloomsbury Publishing, 2021

Gerald Schwedler has asserted his right under the Copyright, Designs and Patents Act, 1988, to be identified as Editor of this work.

Cover image: © Leemage / Getty Images

All rights reserved. No part of this publication may be reproduced or transmitted in any form or by any means, electronic or mechanical, including photocopying, recording, or any information storage or retrieval system, without prior permission in writing from the publishers.

Bloomsbury Publishing Plc does not have any control over, or responsibility for, any third-party websites referred to or in this book. All internet addresses given in this book were correct at the time of going to press. The author and publisher regret any inconvenience caused if addresses have changed or sites have ceased to exist, but can accept no responsibility for any such changes.

A catalogue record for this book is available from the British Library.

A catalog record for this book is available from the Library of Congress.

ISBN: HB: 978-1-4742-7338-1
       PB: 978-1-3504-0858-6
       Set: 978-1-4742-7384-8

Series: The Cultural Histories Series

Typeset by RefineCatch Limited, Bungay, Suffolk
Printed and bound in Great Britain

To find out more about our authors and books visit www.bloomsbury.com and sign up for our newsletters.

CONTENTS

LIST OF ILLUSTRATIONS		vi
GENERAL EDITORS' PREFACE		viii
Stefan Berger and Jeffrey Olick		
	Introduction	1
	Gerald Schwedler	
1	Power and Politics	17
	Jean-Marie Moeglin	
2	Time and Space	41
	Joel T. Rosenthal	
3	Media and Technology	57
	Anna Adamska	
4	Knowledge: Science and Education	73
	Lucie Doležalová and Tamás Visi	
5	Ideas: Philosophy, Religion, and History	91
	Farkas Gábor Kiss	
6	High Culture and Popular Culture	107
	Caroline Horch	
7	The Social: Ritual, Faith, Practices, and the Everyday	123
	Rainer Hugener	
8	Remembering and Forgetting	147
	Kai-Michael Sprenger and Gerald Schwedler	
NOTES		163
BIBLIOGRAPHY		177
NOTES ON CONTRIBUTORS		207
INDEX		209

ILLUSTRATIONS

INTRODUCTION

0.1	*Liber confraternitatum recentior*	4
0.2	Multiplicity of persons and acts to be remembered in Holy Mass	6
0.3	Erased tomb and inscription of a knight. Cloister of San Giovanni in Laterano	10
0.4	Johannes Romberch, *Congestorium artificiose memoriae*	11

CHAPTER 1

1.1	Jean Froissart, *Chroniques*	29

CHAPTER 4

4.1	*Confession Before a Monk and a Deacon*	77
4.2	*Mourning Christ*	78
4.3	*Crucifixion* (1420)	79
4.4	*The Three Living and the Three Dead*	80
4.5	*The Three Living and the Three Dead*	81
4.6	Maimonides' autograph with a passage crossed out	85

CHAPTER 5

5.1	Memorial aid for remembering the parts of the sermon	92
5.2	Memorial aid manuscript, Biblioteka Kórnicka	93
5.3	Johannes Romberch, *Congestorium artificiose memorie*	94
5.4	*Ars memoriae*	95
5.5	John of Głogów, *Questiones librorum de anima magistri Johannis Versoris*	101

CHAPTER 6

6.1	*Bust of Otto I of Bamberg*	109
6.2	Tomb of presbyter Bruno, Hildesheim Cathedral	110
6.3	Atzmann lectern, Church of St Kilian	112
6.4	Bayeux Tapestry	113
	a. *Edward rex*	113
	b. *Hic Willem dux*	114
	c. *Hic dederunt Haroldo coronam regis*	114
	d. *Hic Haroldus rex interfectus est*	114

LIST OF ILLUSTRATIONS vii

6.5 Cappenberg head of Barbarossa 116
     a. Front view 116
     b. Rear view 116
6.6 Gravestone of the Counter-King Rudolf von Rheinfelden 117
6.7 Charlemagne, equestrian statuette of Metz 119
6.8 Memorial image of the "Covenant of Nuns", *Hortus deliciarum* 121

CHAPTER 7

7.1 Front cover of the Barberini diptych 126
7.2 The Reichenau confraternity book 129
7.3 The *liber viventium* of Pfäfers 130
7.4 A drawing in the *liber vitae* of New Minster 132–3
7.5 The first chapter office book of Saint Gall 135
7.6 The necrology of Petershausen 137
7.7 The second chapter office book of Saint Gall 141
7.8 The anniversary book of Uster 144

CHAPTER 8

8.1 The *damnatio memoriae* of King Theodoric 154

GENERAL EDITORS' PREFACE

STEFAN BERGER AND JEFFREY K. OLICK

Any project titled *A Cultural History of Memory* begs a number of questions from the very beginning. For instance: What does it mean that this project is a *cultural* history, rather than some other kind of history? (What other kind of history might it have been?) In turn, what makes memory a feasible and interesting topic for such a history? (It certainly isn't immediately obvious that it would be.) Finally, why a cultural history rather than *the* cultural history? (After all, with forty-eight chapters spread over six volumes, how many more cultural histories of memory could one imagine?)

CULTURAL HISTORY

A Cultural History of Memory is but one entry in a series of cultural histories already and soon to be published by Bloomsbury, including cultural histories of Animals, the Human Body, Food, Gardens, Women, the Senses, Dress and Fashion, the Theatre, Work, Law, Money, and Hair, among many others. The publisher has taken a light hand in prescribing the orientation of these projects, leaving the definition of cultural history to each project's senior editors. And this is very well, as there are many different ways to inflect the idea of cultural history, and different approaches are likely appropriate to the different subject matters. In turn, we have not imposed any particular definition on the editors of the six volumes in this current project, nor have they on the authors of the forty-eight chapters that comprise the total product. That being said, we have relied on a broadly shared understanding of the purposes and tools of cultural history in framing this particular entry in the series, and it is clear that its many authors have as well, though perhaps with occasional divergences.

Namely, contemporary cultural history, at least as it has been practiced in and on the West (and this is one of the important limitations on the project we will discuss below), has defined itself in contrast to at least three other approaches (on the historiographical developments sketched in the following pages see in greater detail Berger, Feldner, and Passmore (2020)). First, there is a broadly defined "traditional" political historiography, dominant in the nineteenth century, that wrote the story of states, their leaders, and their wars. These "high politics" approaches, of course, fully advanced the claim to "objectivity," particularly since the matters they studied—states, their leaders, and their wars—have been quite well documented. These approaches, nevertheless, not only studied the world of nation-states and their high politics but were often part of defining the claims of those states and glorifying the achievements of their leaders, so their claims to be value-free and scientific were obviously dubious ones.

Following this, though at different times in different parts of the world, and only partly under the influence of Marxist perspectives, there developed a vibrant interest in "economic" and "social" history alongside, and sometimes in contrast to, the traditional political histories: the stories not of the "great men" and the great achievements, but of economic processes and social structures. Like political history, this was often presented in national containers and sometimes served the purpose of highlighting the particular "achievements" of nations in the economic and social spheres. Only later did a nascent Marxist historiography, often relatively weak in the universities before the 1970s, come to understand this study of history to be part of a struggle not merely to interpret or understand history, but to change it, as Marx famously put it in his eleventh thesis on Feuerbach.

A stronger concern for ordinary people in social history, however, only occurred with the turn to "history from below," sometimes also referred to as history of everyday life, micro-history, or historical anthropology. This was largely a development that gathered momentum from the 1970s onwards. "History workshop" movements that often became supporters of this new, more human-agency centered understanding of social history, critiqued older forms of social history for being too focused on structures and processes and thereby for ignoring human agency. Furthermore, these approaches criticized the adherence of much of social and economic history to modernization theories and teleologies of progress that appeared to many practitioners of historical anthropology as outdated. The interest of these historians in the everyday had made them turn to anthropology and, inspired by anthropological methods and theories, they set out to change understandings of the social and cultural. As Robert Darnton has put it, "The anthropological mode of history [. . .] begins from the premise that individual expression takes place within a general idiom" (quoted in Hunt 1989: 12). In other words: history had to start from individual human agency and then locate it within a wider collective field.

More difficult to understand is the next form of "traditional" historical interest that was always a lesser strand when compared to political and economic/social history: namely, intellectual history or the history of ideas. Like "traditional" forms of history that focused on states, wars, and high politics, intellectual history has often focused on a narrow slice of life as well: the thoughts and ideas of other great men than politicians (though sometimes them too), mainly artists, scientists, philosophers, and others whose writings are seen to have captured, defined, and led the "spirit" of an age. To be sure, intellectual historians are quite interested in the contexts and structures that enabled the great thinkers to produce their great works, as well as in how those great works affected the less great thoughts of the cultures and societies that produced them. The recent influence of the so-called "Cambridge school" around Quentin Skinner and J.G.A. Pocock is a good example of such contextualization of great thinkers. Internationally even more influential has been the "history of concepts"—shaped seminally by the German historical theorist Reinhart Koselleck. Conceptual history is now a truly global undertaking and one that takes seriously the belief that we need to thoroughly historicize our key concepts in order to understand how people made sense of the world and how they consequently acted in the world.

Next to political history, economic and social history, historical anthropology, and intellectual history, cultural history now forms one of the great traditions of historical writing, reaching back to the very beginnings of professional historiography. Jacob Burckhardt and Johan Huizinga are just two examples of classical representatives of cultural history that can still be read with great pleasure and benefit by contemporary cohorts of students. However, older cultural history often had a strong emphasis on studying "high culture" and thereby distinguishing what was "true" and "worthwhile" culture from "popular culture" or simply "trash." When a "new cultural history" began to conquer history departments in the 1980s, it democratized older forms of cultural history by redefining culture in broader and more inclusive terms. Furthermore, many of its practitioners were much influenced by the "linguistic turn" and theories associated with poststructuralist approaches (Toews 1987: 879–907). Like historical anthropology the new cultural history was dissatisfied not only with an older political history interested mainly in "high politics" but an older social and economic history reducing the past to structures and processes. Unlike an older intellectual history, it was also not so much interested in "great ideas" but instead in ordinary thoughts and practices. Whilst the initial interest in language led cultural historians to study discourses, many soon realized that discourses had to be related back to practices. Furthermore, practices had much to do with things and objects, in other words, materials that needed to be considered to have an agency of their own in history. The history of material culture could thus build on the linguistic turn and practice theory, but it carved out a niche of its own in a field of cultural history that became increasingly compartmentalized as we enter the new millennium after 2000.

Marxist social historians like E.P. Thompson and Geoff Eley spearheaded new understandings of the history of society that took on board many of the insights of the new cultural history without ever abandoning an appreciation of the Marxist understanding of social developments. Thompson, for example, focused not only on the economic condition that made the English working class, but on "the way [. . .] material experiences are handled . . . in cultural ways" (Merrill 1972: 20 f). This happened, according to Thompson, through "cultural and moral mediations." In turn, however, Gareth Stedman Jones moved the discussion even farther afield from economic reduction when he declared that "We [. . .] cannot decode political language to reach a primal and material expression of interest since it is the discursive structure of political language which conceives and defines interest in the first place" (Stedman Jones 1983: 21-22). For the "new cultural historians" in this tradition, then, what they, in part following Emile Durkheim among others, called "representations" became of primary interest. And, as Roger Chartier put it, "The Representations of the social world themselves are the constituents of social reality" (Chartier 1982: 30). This is because, as Lynn Hunt writes, "All practices, whether economic or cultural, depend on the representations individuals use to make sense of their world" (Hunt 1989: 19). The goal of cultural history is thus, as again Chartier defines it, to show "how, in different times and places, a specific social reality was constructed, how people conceived of it and how they interpreted it to others" (Chartier 1998: 4). In this, Chartier followed Lucien Goldmann, who had defined worldviews—the true subject for intellectual historians who were interested in culture more broadly—as "the whole complex of ideas, aspirations and feelings which links together the members of a social group [. . .] and which opposed them to members of other social groups" (Goldmann 1967: 17). And this is indeed the approach that most of the authors in these six volumes have taken, though in an obviously wide variety of ways in and for a wide variety of contexts.

MEMORY

The turn toward memory, especially understood as a collective or cultural phenomenon, can in fact be seen as—though not only as—another inflection of the new cultural history (Berger and Niven 2014). Its interest in representations and discourses encouraged an interest in memories as constituting those representations and discourses. Whether it was written in pursuit of a nostalgic longing for a great national past, as is evident in some of the contributions to Pierre Nora's seminal seven-volume study on the realms of memory of France (Nora 1981–7), or whether it was conducted in the search for understanding and possibly overcoming the consequences of traumatic events in the past, like genocides or wars, memory history has linked contemporary memories to processes of sense-production in the present that gave rise to very different and always contested understandings of the past.

It should already be obvious, then, that the cultural history of memory undertaken in the forty-eight chapters that follow is not just about recall or other basic cognitive processes. Though the concept of memory employed across these six volumes is sometimes the lay understanding of memory as what and how people can recall in different times and places, the majority of the chapters take memory to be something broader. Memory may seem to take place within individual minds, yet for most of the last century numerous scholars both within and beyond cultural history have understood memory more broadly (Olick, Vinitzky-Seroussi, and Levy 2011). Individual memory always takes place within social contexts, with social materials, from social positions, and in response to social cues. So whatever neurological or mental processes it involves, these are obviously deeply embedded in structures and contexts that extend far beyond the individuals whose minds engage in remembering, traditionally understood. Individuals, moreover, employ many technologies of memory—for instance, chanting or writing—which exist outside of themselves and are not part of their brains, and which vary across social settings and in their impacts on individual mnemonic processes. In this way, it becomes perhaps clearer why memory is such a rich terrain for cultural (and other!) forms of history.

However, many of the chapters that constitute this cultural history of memory take yet another step beyond the mind—that is, beyond what Maurice Halbwachs, one of the key figures in contemporary thinking about memory, called the social frameworks of memory, to see memory as an inherently social activity (Halbwachs 1950). We often—even most often—remember together. Social psychologists understand that there are significant differences between remembering alone and remembering in a group, whether this is a matter of simple recall (e.g. when a group of individuals can reconstruct memorized lists more completely than the sum of individuals alone via cuing and other social processes) or in narrative process (e.g. when a family retells a story of an experience they have shared, and the complete narrative emerges from the many voices involved, which bring different pieces than everyone necessarily would have recalled). However, some scholars argue that groups themselves remember; for instance, they build libraries and fill them with materials, they curate representations of the past in museums and elsewhere in ways that transcend the resources of individuals, and they preserve knowledge that very few individuals recall (Assmann 1992). As such, scholars often refer to social, collective, or cultural memory—the forms and traces of the past that transcend the capacities or even interests of individuals—and many do not believe these forms of memories are merely metaphors (see Erll 2008). The field of memory is thus a vast one, and it is clear that understanding all the different forms of memory—from the neurological to the museological—requires, and is an appropriate subject for, all the resources of cultural history.

Having said that, the development of memory studies since the 1980s has been characterized by the gradual constitution of a new discipline that was self-consciously transdisciplinary. Of all the disciplines that constituted this new field, historians were arguably in a minority. Literary scholars and sociologists were far more numerous, and, as all six volumes in this series demonstrate, a cultural history of memory cannot do without referencing a range of literary, sociological and other disciplinary approaches to memory.

Apart from its characteristic transdisciplinarity, which had a major impact on memory history, however, the latter also remained, for quite some time, tied to the national container that, as we have already discussed, had been so strongly established in the historical sciences in the century roughly between 1850 and 1950. The move of memory history to *transnational* forms of memory has only been a relatively recent development, following a general trend in historical studies to criticize "methodological nationalism" and move to more transnational forms of historical writing, emphasizing interlinkages, adaptations, and transfers. However, as a perusal of any of the hugely successful conferences of the Memory Studies Association will show, most scholars today still focus on national memory.[1] Transnational, let alone global memory is not practiced very widely,[2] which also reflects a major difficulty for a cultural history of memory; there are simply not enough scholars who can truly synthesize vast amounts of work on a particular theme in a global perspective. Here we can only trust that our failure will be an inspiration to future generations of scholars to move to more global perspectives on memory history.

Where our six volumes have hopefully been more successful has been in moving histories of memory away from their fixation with trauma, especially national trauma. The huge body of work on the memory of genocides, in particular the Holocaust, and the equally massive amount of work on the memory of wars, especially the two world wars, but also the Vietnam war and a range of civil wars, is an indicator of to what extent memory scholars have homed in on traumatic events in the past. Undoubtedly, much of this work has been incredibly valuable and inspirational, but the six volumes that we introduce here, whilst not ignoring genocides and war, also intend to highlight a range of other areas in which memory history can be usefully applied.

If *A Cultural History of Memory* tries to escape memory history's bias toward "methodological nationalism" and toward traumatic events in the past, it also deliberately—and structurally—seeks to introduce a longer-term perspective and to show how memory history is a relevant and intriguing exercise for older periods of time. Once again, looking from a bird's eye perspective over the field of memory history, we see a massive concentration of work in the modern period, basically from the late eighteenth century to the present day. But the first four of our six volumes underline to what an extent the history of memory benefits from considering older time periods. As general editors, we particularly hope that modernists (of whom we are culpable examples) may delve into the writings on pre-modern times, as it will reveal not only substantial differences, but also, and certainly more striking to us, amazing similarities when considering the role of memory for cultural sense-production.

A CULTURAL HISTORY

Finally, what of the definite article "A" Cultural History of Memory. In the first place, across a work as extensive as this one (or these ones), it is obvious that there are many different approaches to the subject matters. Though all contributing to this cultural history, the authors come from numerous different disciplines and specialties, have different foci, bring to bear different interests and expertise even within this "one" work. We do so, moreover, from numerous different countries, languages of origin, and periods of study, though the list, however extensive, is still limited in significant ways. In the second place, however, much as the publishers did not lay a heavy hand on the forms of cultural history to be employed, they did determine that all the volumes should have the same structure. Hence, we came up with eight themes that had to be the same across all six volumes. In choosing broad themes—power and politics, media and technology, knowledge: science and education, time and space, ideas: philosophy, religion, and history, high and popular culture, the social: rituals, practices, and the everyday, and remembering and forgetting—we sought to give the volume editors the space to adapt those themes to the particular foci appropriate to different times and geographies. As any reader of the six volumes will realize, the editors made good use of that leeway, but this also leads to the phenomenon that different authors have put the emphasis of their respective chapters differently and usually in line with their own specialisms.

The publisher also dictated the epochal labels we employed, and they determined that the eight topics addressed in each chronologically constituted volume should be nominally the same as the topics in the other volumes. Much as we appreciated the reasons for this—for instance, so that a particular theme could be followed across the epochs, or that someone interested in a particular epoch could recombine the history of memory we have produced for that epoch with the history of something else addressed in other entries in the series—this constraint did raise concerns for us and our colleagues. For instance, no single chronology labeling applies uniformly for different areas of the world (e.g. not every society or culture identifies the same antiquity, or an antiquity at all). And the present chronology is a very Western one indeed. Moreover, the application of these labels can be anachronistic. After all, the people whose forms of memory we are studying in a particular age did not understand themselves as having that particular place in history (e.g. the people in the antiquity we have studied did not think of themselves as inhabiting an ancient world). Finally, had we not understood the imperative of recombination of themes and periods, the editors of each epochally-defined volume might have wanted to label the eight chapters differently from the editors of the other volumes, since the same relevances did not necessarily obtain in the same ways in different periods.

Nevertheless, much as the ground we have collectively covered here is vast indeed, we might still hope—if not for other, at least for additional work in this vibrant field on this fascinating subject. We hope that, despite the additional works that might be possible—and that we hope will be produced—what we have to offer here will be of use to as many as possible. The field of memory studies is a relatively new one. But the sophistication of the chapters (and volume introductions) we have the pleasure of presenting here shows that much as the field has a long way to go, it is well on its way.

Introduction

GERALD SCHWEDLER

Man without memory is not. There seems to be general agreement that memory is an essential element of human existence. Memory enables the acquisition of language and patterns of social interaction. Mnemonic capacity bridges past and present, absent and transcendent, personal and public, time and space. In the Middle Ages, *memoria* was conceived as an open concept that allowed diverse approaches and perspectives. Written and material testimonies of the Middle Ages document the awareness that memory and its complementary counterpart, oblivion, affected all spheres of human life.

An introduction to the cultural history of memory in the Middle Ages has to consider this multiplicity of perspectives and the fact that memory and oblivion become evident in a wide range of medieval practices and phenomena: Memory was vital in the legal sphere, as regulations and norms had to be remembered before they could be enforced or adapted. Memory was relevant for contracts and prices in the economic sphere, information that had to be remembered to give stability in economic life—and replaced and forgotten, when market situations changed. Memory was important in the educational process for the formation of knowledge and intellectual capacity. Selection and alteration of memorized contents as well as forgetting opened the field for creativity and innovation. The most explicit cultural force of memory was developed in cultic and religious practices. The "command to remember" is present in almost all religious groups. In Christianity, the central ritual in the Mass is being introduced with the words "this do in remembrance of me" (Lk. 22.19 and 1 Cor. 11.24: *hoc facite in meam commemorationem*). As a cue for remembrance in Islam, we find the act of *dhikr* (arab. ذكر), and in Judaism the biblical command *Zachor*! (זָכוֹר), which is explicitly dealt with in the book of Deuteronomy (Deut. 25.17). In general, cultic practice, for which memory and commemoration served as motors of cultural production, proved to be the most creative field of human expression in the Middle Ages (Angenendt 2013).

From a modern perspective, "memory" has become a term under which almost all social and cultural practices can be subsumed. Memory, by some scholars spelt with capitalized "M," was ambitiously addressed as a "total social phenomenon" and later has been claimed to replace the concepts of "Society" or "Culture" as analytical categories (Algazi 2014: 25). It is indisputable that memory has a strong influence on individuals, groups, and even societies, yet this needs to be analyzed with a set of theories from different disciplines and in its individual and social function (Assmann 2006). Besides the most productive approaches from sociology, cognitive science, or psychology, memory has also been analyzed fruitfully from the perspectives of anthropology, material culture, and history. The interdisciplinary field is best described with the term "memory studies" (Olick 2011). Various approaches have proven useful within the field of medieval studies and led to an impressive research output.

Not all phenomena that are treated in research under the term "memory" are related to one another. The medieval usage of the Latin term *memoria* already encloses many diverse, even contradicting meanings. The basic connotation of *memoria* is remembrance and commemoration. As can be seen from the usage of the word over the centuries in the Middle Ages, *memoria* refers to the process of mentally storing information as well as the preserved material itself, be it mental or physical (Niemeyer 2002: 872; Prinz 1966). Yet there are also specific medieval connotations. *Memoria* indicates the memory of the words and deeds of Jesus Christ as well as their use in cultic practice. In the sense of cultic practice, *memoria* also referred to the memory of saints and martyrs. In this sense, *memoria* has a liturgical and even performative connotation. Furthermore, *memoria* denotes a material side of remembrance, i.e. it could be used for the tomb, altar or relic of a saint (Raesaenen, Hartmann, and Richards 2016). Referring to the act of commemoration, *memoria* could further mean celebrating mass for the dead and played an important part in monastic life (Niemeyer 2002: 873; Prinz 1936–66: 665–84). *Oblivio* is mostly seen as a counterpart of memory. It is generally used in a negative sense, where loss of information or knowledge is being regretted. However, various authors praised oblivion as it enabled (monastic) concentration on essentials: prayer and the *officium divinum*. Metaphors for *oblivio* were found in the fading of writing or the flowing away of memories as in the ancient River Lethe (Weinrich 1999; Oexle 2009).

The concept of *memoria* is represented by different words in modern languages. The English term "memory" encloses the Latin multiplicity of meanings. The less frequently used term "remembrance" only refers to the active storage, while its verbal form distinguishes between "remember" and "remind." Yet the process may better be understood if one uses the term "recollect" which indicates activity and human will (Carruthers and Ziolkowski 2002: 1). French *"mémoire"* is paired with *"souvenir"* which has a distinct material connotation and in German there are different terms to indicate *"memoria,"* "Erinnerung," "Gedächtnis," "Gedenken," and most specific *"memoria"* in the meaning of "commemoration" (Welzer 2010: 1–3). Similar to English, where the multiple concepts of *memoria* are enclosed in one single word with the same root ("memo-"), Slavic languages denote memory with words based on the root "pam-," cf. the terms "Pamię" in Polish or "память" in Russian for "memory."

It seems convenient to introduce the cultural history of memory in the Middle Ages by showing its enormous value in medieval everyday life and then continue towards the theoretical reflections by medieval writers. Therefore, the first section is an outline of different forms of the medieval practices, demonstrating how and where memory became evident in medieval life. The second section presents various positions on memory in medieval thought. It is divided into two parts, the first dealing with the tracts on artificial memory, the *ars memoriae* in particular and the second part with the most relevant theoretical reflections on memory in general. A third section is a brief survey of the main fields of memory studies in the Middle Ages.

PRACTICE OF MEDIEVAL MEMORY

The practice of *memoria* can be seen as a general cultural phenomenon, which touched all fields of social life. Medieval traditions and practice of commemoration ("Erinnerungskultur") linked the commemoration of the dead, the cult of the saints and relics, the cult of images and most central, the *cultus divinum*, to which these practices were orientated. It will be useful to deal with the facets of individual and cultural practice of memory first before treating practices in the field of civic life and administrative culture.

Memoria mortuorum

Caring for the dead is an anthropological principle, where memory played an important part. Organized memory and social rites of commemoration can be found in all belief systems, although their specific customs vary during the passage of time. Forms of caring for the dead could influence and imitate each other as becomes evident in comparative perspectives concerning for example Christian and Ashkenaz rites (Schur 2008; Borgolte 2014). Through death rituals it was possible to demonstrate which place the dead should take in social life in the future and how they would be regarded in physical, spiritual, emotional, social, and cultural terms. Some fundamental dogmatic conventions served as structuring principles and should be indicated to understand the enormous extent, to which the Christian tradition used resources for the commemoration of the dead. A prerequisite for Salvation and eternal life were good deeds on earth. On the basis of John 11.25: "He that believeth in me, though he were dead, yet shall he live." Belief and good deeds during one's lifetime were important. Already Tertullian (after 150–220) spoke of a *refrigerium interim,* a temporary position for the soul before final salvation at the End of Days. It was the explanations of Augustine that brought together various facets of afterlife, mass, commemoration, and intercessory prayer. He distinguished between different post mortal degrees. The Saints needed no intercessory prayer as they immediately shared God's eternity after their deaths due to their holy lives (the *valde boni*). Those who had destroyed all hopes of salvation due to their evil deeds on earth (the *valde mali*) intercessory prayer would not help. But for the large group of persons in-between, post mortal deeds such as prayer and donations could help to relieve their duration in the *ignis purgatories*—the living were able to help the dead. According to Augustine, the most effective way was the commemoration of the divine office, which was performed and supported by the surviving members of the community and by relatives. In other words, the dead needed the living, as only they were able to perform intercessions and pious works (Oexle 1996: 44). Most striking is the possibility for the interaction of the individual and the group: memory had a communal character of commemorating the dead and the individuality of the deceased. Memory was a social practice, exercised by individuals through their personal and at times highly emotional relationship to the deceased. Commemoration in families, communities, and confraternities touched on all group members, constructing social cohesion.

A special form of commemoration of the dead was the genealogical memory, where living and dead family members were entangled. Extensive genealogies of aristocratic families demonstrate the relevance of past recourses for the legitimation of the present (Oexle 1995a; Moeglin 1993). Although such a representative veneration of noble ancestors provided stability, this form of genealogical memory forced living family members to live under the "shadow" of their deceased ancestors (Klapisch-Zuber 2000). This form of family memory blended historical memory into liturgical *memoria* that was outsourced to monasteries for efficient and sustainable remembrance of the names of the family. The inclusion into the *Libri memoriales* or *Libri vitae* and the commemorative practice to recite the names on the anniversaries developed from the ninth century onwards. It gave the past a presence in present social life.

Monastic *lectio divina* aimed to uproot merely personal, historical memories, and replace them with a new "memory" of "universal" experience as expressed and memorized in the Scripture and the Church Fathers (Coleman 1992: 166). Commemoration of the dead was combined with the Saints and ancestors and extended to the commemoration of

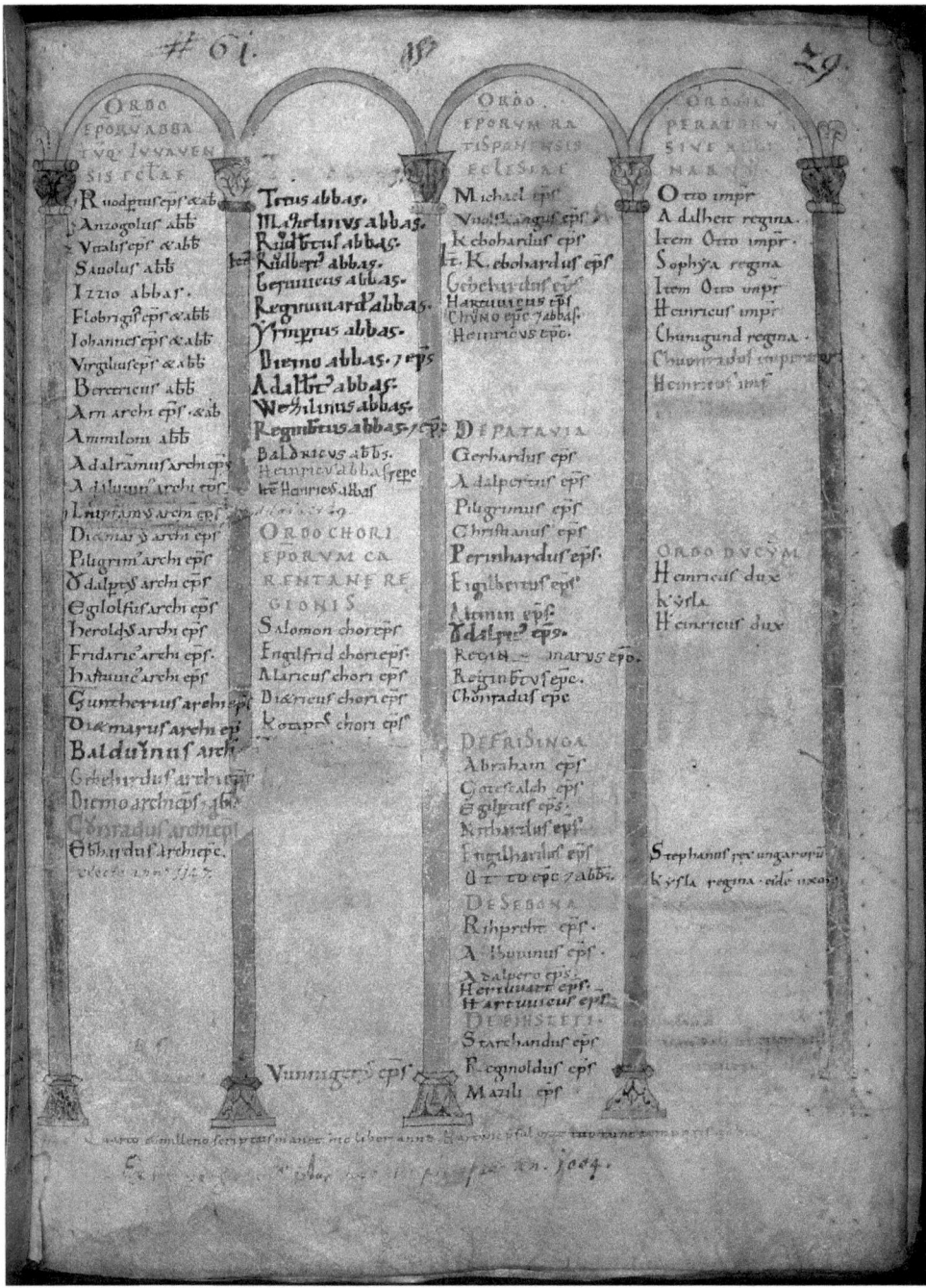

FIGURE 0.1: *Liber confraternitatum recentior*, St. Peter Book of Memory (Salzburg, Erzabtei St. Peter, Hs. A 1, p. 29), including lists of bishops and rulers. Some names are erased. The manuscript is listed in the UNESCO Memory of the World Register. © Martin Haltrich, Erzabtei St. Peter Salzburg.

Jesus Christ. In the late Middle Ages not only parishes but most specifically confraternities organized solidary commemoration. For the humble, intercession would provide the assurance of a standard burial and intercessory prayer the immediate family could not guarantee. For those of higher status, a confraternity could involve the representation of social power. More abstract forms of commemoration included lists of names that were commemorated in other communities and monasteries, as well as in the special form of medieval necrologies as memory books.

Since the early church, Christian communities and to a much greater degree monasteries offered forms of organization for such donations for the dead. The donations made for the salvation of the soul (*pro remedio animae*), made during lifetime or through relatives were used for pious work, such as caring for the poor. The high Middle Ages developed an institutionalized frame for such foundations specialized on memory. Above all, the monastery of Cluny attracted enormous economic and political attention through their special practice of commemorating the dead (Oexle 2009). Further examples show the engagement of the living for the souls of the dead. Piero de Medici prepared an extraordinary arrangement for the intercession of his father involving 12,000 masses in fifty-three different ecclesiastical institutions (Gordon and Marshall 2000: 5). This extensive reciprocity and exchange between the living and the dead has led some historians to portray the dead as integral to the contemporary construction of community (Oexle 1996: 50).

The *lieu de memoire*, the grave, is also essential for the commemoration of the deceased. For Augustine, graves are mere signs of memory that indicate that the remembrance of the dead should not be forgotten. As stimulus for memory and commemoration in the context of the Holy Mass, it was useful to place the grave as close as possible to the altar, where the mass was celebrated. Yet this place became reserved for Saints and high-ranking clerics. Laymen were allowed this exclusive place if they founded the monastery or church (Moeglin 2005). Although in a Carolingian Capitulary from 813 burials in churches were no longer permitted, the practice never really ceased over the course of the Middle Ages. However, the importance was not only attached to the deceased's name, but also to the date of his/her death, which became part of the grave inscriptions (Scholz 1998: 275). Exceptional tomb constructions were of esthetical value and the construction of grave monuments occupied leading artists (Horch 2001).

"This do in remembrance of me." Liturgy and remembrance

Christianity is a religion of commemoration and remembrance as the memory of the deeds of Christ is the core of Christian belief. In mass, the biblical sentence "Do this in my memory" became the essential functional axis of the service. Memory of God is decisive for the relationship between God and man. Above all, memory or oblivion of God determines salvation or damnation. The act of memory (*anamnesis*) constitutes the community of the faithful anew every time (Lk. 22.19 and 1 Cor. 11.24). Celebration of memory in the form of the liturgy of mass is the representation of the salvation history. Theological interpretations during the Middle Ages even saw the act of commemorating Christ in mass as the convergence of times and spaces. This can be seen in the theologian Honorius Augustodunensis' (1080–1151) work *Gemma animae* (Ohly 2005; Jungmann 1958: 1.154).

Another late medieval development was the emphasis on personal preparation for death through prayer and pious works and also through a more personal exploration of the own conscience (*memento mori*). In 1336, Pope Benedict XIII confirmed the notion of the individual judgment and the importance of individual confessions of sins. In the decades to come this would lead to a change of religious practice, prominently represented in the *devotio moderna*-movement, where on the basis of Thomas of Kempen's *De Imitatione Christi* new forms of internal practice of belief prevailed. Such focus on one's own sins and the rise of indulgence, specifically testaments and individual legates/bequeaths yet again lead to a change of the forms of *memoria*. Masses for the dead were no *missa publica* anymore that required the presence of the public; they were *missae speciales* exclusively for the memory of the dead.

FIGURE 0.2: "This do in remembrance of me" (Lk. 22.19 and 1 Cor. 11.24). Multiplicity of persons and acts to be remembered in Holy Mass, Cistercian Gradual, Prague 1410, Luzern (CH), Zentral- und Hochschulbibliothek, P 19 fol.1r. © ZHB Luzern (www.e-codices.ch).

Memory, orality, literacy

Memories need to be stored and stimulated so that they can be used constructively. In the diction of the *artes memoriales* it was the *loci* and *imagines agentes* that initiated the act of memory. Both can be material and immaterial, each having a different influence on the acts of memory. It has proven useful to highlight differences and specific qualities of material aspects and analyze the media used for memory closely. Certainly, there has never been a clear division between oral and literate culture, although both had distinct potentials and areas of application. Vast parts of cultural life were "stored" in oral tradition. In the Middle Ages, the great majority of men and women were unfamiliar with the practice of writing and used spoken language, as well as gestures to stabilize memories. Sagas, laws, and history were anchored in oral tradition. There were conventionalized stimuli to make things remembered such as the ceremonial transmission of a stick or a hand full of earth to symbolize the act of transferal of property—and even more so the ritual slap into the face of boys as a reminder to respect property boundaries (Schmitt 1993: 37). The overestimation of the role of memory in the written form derives from the fact that it is a comparatively stable medium of memory. Trusting the written word has a long tradition. Cassiodorus (485–c. 580), statesman, court member of Theoderic the Great, and prolific Christian writer praised the advantages of papyrus in contrast to the uncertainty of human memory in his text collection named *Variae* XI.38: "It keeps a faithful witness of human deeds; it speaks of the past, and is the enemy of oblivion. For, even if our memory retains the content, it alters the words; but there discourse is stored in safety, to be heard for ever with consistency" (Cassiodorus: 160). For the learned, especially in a clerical and monastic context, the predominant practice was to read, comment, and spread penned knowledge, ranging from the Bible, liturgical books and chronicles to memory aids such as accounting books. Every recording, which contains references to the past, can be understood as part of memorial tradition, including charters, letters, inscriptions, synodal protocols, norms etc. The history of record-keeping shows how close the ties between literacy and medieval state formation were. Again memory—in particular in the form of administrative writing—shows its relevance for the consolidation of social formations.

To a certain degree, the particular reverence of intellectual authorities may be seen as a sign of *memoria*. The important compilations of the high Middle Ages referred to the sources by name such as the *Decretum Gratiani*, the *Glossa ordinaria*, the theological or encyclopedic *summae* or the "Books of Sentences" of Peter Lombard (Rischpler 2004).

History and the past

Memory as a form of history and a representation of the past appeared in manifold forms. Historiography of the Middle Ages frequently combined reflected analysis of past events with forms of social memory on the basis of religious and liturgical commemoration. The notion in the preface of Bede's *Historia Ecclesiastica* to write only *gesta . . . memoria digna*, deeds that are worthy of memory, is made more explicit in Gervase of Canterbury (1141–c. 1210), who clearly distinguishes between ordinary memorabilia and the memories that are worthy of remembrance: *Non tamen omnia memorabilia notare cupio, sed memoranda tantum, easicilicet quae digna memoriae esse videntur* (Gervase of Canterbury, Gesta regum anglorum, I.89). This also extends to genres such as *gesta episcoporum* or *gesta abbatum* as well as narratives of the foundation of institutions or lists with the names of abbots, bishops, popes, and kings. The act of recalling them positively in these texts demonstrates that they deserved memory. While in biographical and hagiographical writing, commemoration corresponded to a high degree with historical memory, there were many texts recalling the past, where the intention of analysis, distraction or teaching a lesson (*historia magistra vitae*) prevailed. Yet already in the eleventh century, the monk Otloh of St. Emmeram (Geary 1994b: 17) perceived that history was just like hedges in the field. From time to time it was important to cut the branches, in order to have the ways and paths freed from overgrowing.

Memory was also an important topic in the genre of visionary literature. The most elaborate work in this field is the *Divina Commedia* by Dante Alighieri (1265–1321), who composed a panorama of deceased from all epochs, creating a sort of "world memory" (Ohly 2005: 30). He recalled their names in his book and thereby brought them back to life, back into the memory of the reader. He ascribed a place to each of them in heaven, purgatory, or hell according to their deeds. The different places of punishment or wellbeing represented their individual sinful or positive pasts, from then on inscribed into eternal memory.

The strong conception of post mortal punishment lead to the emphasis of memory as a moral authority. Those who did not contribute to the values of the community or even appeared inimical or destructive were expelled from the liturgical community of the living and the dead (Sennis 2004). Memory was not celebrated for unrepentant criminals, suicides, traitors, or heretics. They were excluded and at times even barred from the basic rites of burial and commemoration. The most extreme situation was the so-called *damnatio memoriae*, practiced in Antiquity. Mainly emperors, but also state officials, were declared enemies of the state after their deaths. All death rites and memorial practices were prohibited, inscriptions and other memorabilia destroyed (de Vincentiis 2004; Fried 2001). The paradox of *damnatio memoriae* consists in the fact that although all positive memory was erased a person was never completely forgotten. This has to do with the second effect of *memoria*, a life-practical function. Persons who underwent a *damnatio memoriae* still served as negative examples in order to deter acts against the community. In the Middle Ages, parts of this practice survived, however under different social conditions and representations of media (Scholz et al. 2014).

MEMORY AND OBLIVION IN THE *ARTES MEMORIALES* AND MEDIEVAL THOUGHT

The elementary medieval understanding of memory dates back to the elaborate conceptions of Antiquity. Through the selective process of the *interpretatio Christiana* the ancient inheritance was appropriated, adapted, and enriched with biblical and patristic thought. Evidently, some spheres of reflection on memory were more prone to revision than others. Conceptions of how to train personal memory, the *artes memoriales*, underwent less change, yet all fields relating to the human soul and Christian understanding of the transcendental were adapted in a more diverse and complex manner by various authors. To deal with the two major semantic fields, it is useful to begin this section with the oratorical traditions of the *artes memoriales* and show their continuity throughout the Middle Ages. A second step will be a condensed overview of the medieval reflections on memory and oblivion in medieval thought as proposed by influential theologians and philosophers.

Artes memoriales

Medieval reflections on artificial memory are based on the elaborate antique texts on the *ars memoriae*. These tracts derived their importance from the function of memory for the delivery of speeches in ancient public life. To produce an elaborate and convincing discourse memory was important and thus had a firm position in the organization of civic affairs. The essential medium of public speech was the basis of social interaction. Memory was one part of the five stages in developing and presenting a speech: *inventio, dispositio, elocutio, memoria,* and *actio.* Cicero saw *memoria* in *De inventione* as the "firm perception of words and things in the act of invention."[1] The *artes memoriae* offered devices and training to enhance the orator's mnemonic powers. The most accessible text in the Middle Ages was the treatise *Rhetorica ad Herennium* (3.28–40) which medieval scholars attributed to Cicero, although it was probably written by Cornificius in the first century BCE. Three other works explain the principles of artificial memory: Cicero's work "On the Orator" (*De oratore*, 2.86–90.350–60), the "Marriage of Philology and Mercury" by Martian Capella (5. 538–9) and the *Institutio oratoria* of Quintilian (11.2.11–51). The basic assumption of the enforcement of artificial memory was that it was important to conceive places (*loci*) in one's mind. Usually they take an architectonic shape, such as rooms, palaces, or cities. Memorizing works by connecting existing with mental places and structures. In the mental place or map one needs to locate images (*imagines*) that can be associated with the subjects one intends to memorize in a metaphorical or metonymical way. Recalling these subjects requires walking through these places and reconsidering the images one has located there one by one in a well-preserved order (Hajdu 1936; Blum 1969; Neuber 2001; Berns and Neuber 1993; 1998). Oblivion in the context of oratorical mnemonic practices is seen as the involuntary loss of the connection between *loci* and *imagines*, the need to improvise arguments and formulations.

The inheritance of the *artes memoriae* from Ancient Rome was copied selectively and adapted in Christian surroundings, above all in ecclesiastical and monastic centers. They were not copied or developed further in Islamic schools or manuscript culture, nor in rabbinic tradition (Visi 2010). In Christian life, artificial memory only played a minor role compared to what was called *memoria* in the sense of commemoration. Over the course of the Middle Ages, various authors reflected on the *artes memoriales*. Hugh of St. Victor (1096–1141) elaborates on the *Rhetorica ad Herennium* in his own work *De tribus maximis circumstantiis*. He not only sees memory as a treasure-house and explains the need of artificial memory for public speaking and preaching, but also establishes memorizing as an instrument for self-perfection, leading to a moral change in humanity. The combination of mnemotechniques and a theological connotation derives from Augustinian thought, where the source of morality is knowledge coming from Divine Wisdom which can be found in human memory (Heimann-Seelbach 2000, 374–80; Carruthers and Ziolkowski 2003, 18–9; Carruthers 1990: 46–79). The Italian rhetorician Boncompagno da Signa (*c.* 1170–after 1240) reflected on artificial memory and stated that any creature or object on earth could serve as a structural memory aid, be it an architectural form, a painting or a sculpture. Memory was not a sole technical aid to recall contents but also to serve as basis for ethical considerations. He stated that the whole world and all its objects had a memorative function, as the world was created to show and help remember its creator God (Carruthers 1996: 44–64). Tracts on artificial memory were especially important in the field of preaching. In his work *De memoria artificiali adquirenda* Thomas Bradwardine (*c.* 1290–1349) also focused on the importance of

FIGURE 0.3: Erased tomb and inscription of a knight (sixteenth century). Cloister of San Giovanni in Laterano (Rome). © G. Schwedler.

memory for the act of preaching. Mnemotechniques were elaborately explained in the "Art of Preaching" by the Franciscan writer Francesc Eiximenis (*c.* 1340–*c.* 1409), who dedicated a chapter to the topic of memory (Carruthers 1992; Heimann-Seelbach 2000; Rivers 2010). Furthermore, personal mnemonic capacities were trained in the field of jurisprudence. Memory was important for the procedures at court itself, but it was of far greater importance for the apprehension and storage of legal knowledge. The law compilations in canon and civil law made it necessary to know substantial laws by heart, at least the initial words of decretals or laws by which they were quoted. In his widely read and copied *Dictionarium Iuris tam Civilis quam Canonici*, Albericus de Rosate (1290–1360) explains how the *ars memoriae* based on the *Rhetorica ad Herennium* could be used for enhancing one's mnemonic capacity for legal texts. He recommends *imagines* such as eagles, lions or horses, but also places like a palace with many rooms and streets with adjacent houses in order to memorize structures and details.

A new turn in medieval *artes memoriae* occurred in the fifteenth century. The Humanist reverence for Antiquity combined the lecture of ancient mnemonic tracts and new techniques (Heimann-Seelbach 2000; Carruthers 1990). All over Europe, one could perceive a new interest in artificial memory and the number of tracts on artificial memory increased significantly. The *Liber ad memoriam confirmandam* ascribed to Ramon Lull (1232–*c.* 1315) most probably dates from the early fifteenth century (Yates 1966). A text

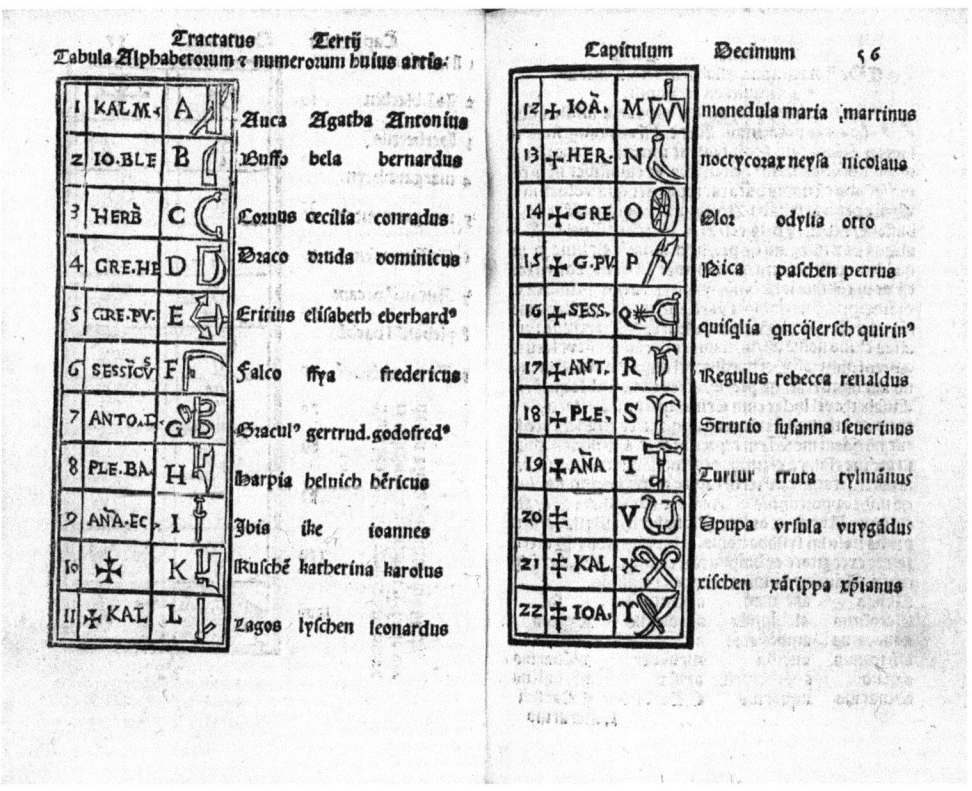

FIGURE 0.4: System of numbers, symbols, and names as *ars memoriae*, Johann Romberch de Kyrspe (*c.* 1480–1532), *Congestorium artificiose memoriae*, Venezia 1533, p. 55–6. © Creative Commons (Public Domain).

by the Venetian writer and physician Giovanni di Fontana (c. 1395–c. 1455) is of special interest. His *Tractatus de instrumentis artis memorie* (written in cryptographic letters) is dated 1430 and deals with technical memory aids (Kranz and Oberschelp 2009). Starting out with a stone, placed on the door handle to prevent forgetting certain things, he explains how mechanical aids could enhance the natural memory. He proposes a mechanical device consisting of several wheels and numbers. Each combination represents a new *locus* that could/should stimulate the memory to something else. It was not only able to store information but could also encrypt texts. The specific perception of memory within a technical context as practiced in Giovanni Fonatana's text prefigures the Renaissance fascination of complicated devices and voluminous texts on the *ars memoriae* with the air of hermeticism and dubious practical value.

Memory and oblivion in medieval thought

After this selection of medieval responses to the *artes memoriae*, it is useful to demonstrate the more differentiated development of the concept of *memoria* in theology and philosophy. Many positions derived from the ancient inheritance. Research tradition on medieval philosophical reasoning generally highlights the two ancient poles, the more "psychological" tradition embodied by Aristotle and the more "idealist" tradition of Plato. Platonic and Neoplatonic notions determined memory as the capacity to recollect and thereby convert opinion into knowledge. They were based on Plato's claim that true knowledge consisted of recollection. As early Christian tradition and patristic literature favored a Christianized Platonic position (Neoplatonism) the more idealist perspective prevailed until the high Middle Ages, when the Aristotelian concept gained influence.

One cannot underestimate the influence of Augustine (354–430), who formed the Christian understanding of memory, on the early Middle Ages. He accepted many aspects derived from ancient mnemonic and philosophical tradition. However, he emphasized the importance of memory for the individual soul. To Augustine, who started out as a trained *rhetor* and was familiar with the *artes memoriae*, was more than just a technical capacity in the rhetorical tradition. In a Christianized context, the term *memoria* additionally contained the liturgical and ritual facets of commemoration. The objects of remembrance were not only the words and deeds of Christ, but also those of saints and martyrs (cf. Sermo 64: *memoriam martyrum celebramus*). Augustine's most elaborate reflections on memory can be found in his Confessions. He refers to memory as an "independent storehouse" (Conf. 11.8), a "vast hall" and "treasure-house" (Conf. 11.8), the "stomach of the mind" (Conf. 10.21 and 11.13). To him, memory is a "vast and infinite profundity. Who has plumbed its bottom?" (Conf. 11.8). He acknowledges the uncontrollable nature of memory with dark and mysterious aspects as things may remain hidden to our consciousness and asserts that it is "the abyss of human consciousness" (Conf. 10.2), as "Memory's huge cavern, with its mysterious secret, and indescribable nooks and crannies" (Conf. 11.8). Augustine uses many spatial images to convey the vast capacity of memory. Other than the Aristotelian tradition, memories are images—and ideas—formed by the senses based on material experience. The human memory stores impressions received from the senses and allows them to be organized and recalled. The mind also stores other kinds of "images" that are not physical: purely abstract concepts like mathematics, or human emotions, which do not exist outside the individual human mind (O'Donnell 2004: 1252). Memory is the power of the mind or soul that can summon the past into the present. Past, present, and future can be united in the soul. Therefore, memory is the place, where the individual soul has the internal capacity to perceive, to locate, God: "But where," asks Augustine "in memory can you be lodged, Lord, where lodge you there?" (Conf. 10.35: . . . *sed ubi manes in memoria mea, domine, ubi illic manes?*). Augustine sees *memoria* as a faculty that contains what both "is" and "is not" at the same time. The nature of memory is real and seems to offer a link to the past as well as to transcendent experience. However, as the *imagines* are not actually the things remembered themselves, the process of recalling these images is susceptible to error. Augustine created the strong position of memory in Christian thought. Due to its transcendent nature, it was the place to expect divine experience: through memory the mind ascends to God. It remained deeply rooted in Christian theology over centuries. It was, for example, accentuated by the influential Franciscan theologian St. Bonaventure (1221–74). He developed the belief that *memoria* was the place to perceive God, as it was the function to retain and represent the present, the corporeal and temporal, the successive, past and everlasting things all at the same time (Bonaventura, Itin.3.2. ed. Hayes).

Next to Augustine, there was another highly influential writer who saw the close connection between memory and the divine, Isidore of Seville (*c.* 560–636). In his widely read encyclopaedic work *Etymologiae*, written *c.* 630, he treats *memoria* in relation to the term *anima*. He uses Augustine's notion that *memoria* is an essential feature of the soul. However, he emphasizes the character of memory as a process: "while it [*anima*] reflects, it is *memoria*" (*Isidori Hispalensis Episcopi* 1962, XLI.13.: *dum [anima] recolit, memoria est* . . .). Isidore even goes one step further. According to his etymological method, he derives *mens* from *anima* and *memini*. Forgetting means being unmindful: "The mind is called thus because it excels in the anima, or because it remembers. This is why one calls 'forgetful people' (*immemoris*) 'mindless' (*amens*): Forgetfulness is un-mindfulness. And, therefore, it is not *anima*, . . .".[2] Forgetting, the absence of memory, is associated with the absence of the mind. Consequently, forgetting also meant the absence of the soul.

In the Carolingian era, the concept of memory was reflected upon intensively. An exponent of Carolingian thought on memory was Alcuin, Charlemagne's most important counsellor (730–804). In his tract, *De rhetorica et virtutibus* ("On Rhetorics and the virtues"), he explained and compared *De Inventione* of Cicero and the tract on rhetorics by C. Julius Victor in form of a dialogue between Charlemagne and Albinus (for Alcuin). Commenting on the antique tracts, he has Charlemagne say that *memoria* was the noblest part of rhetoric. This high esteem of memory certainly echoes the Augustinian perception of the divine capacity of memory. It is therefore not surprising that he does not repeat antique mnemonic tricks for artificial memory. If memory was the place for human-divine encounter, he recommended only external circumstances to affect one's own memory: regular practice of learning by heart and writing, studying and above all, avoiding drunkenness (*ebrietas*) which endangers the integrity of the mind.[3]

Another telling Carolingian position on memory can be found within the work of Hinkmar of Reims (806–82). On the basis of Augustine, Hinkmar argued that memory was inseparably unified with human intellect and human will. He metaphorically explained this with the similarity to the Holy Trinity, consisting of Father, Son, and Holy Spirit. They are discernible but still unified.[4] In the same way as Augustine perceived it, memory represented a functional part of the soul and the perception of God. Hinkmar maintains the importance of memory in respect to God and adds two other genuine individual human resources, *intellectus* and *voluntas* on the same level. This indicated a new focus in theological thinking, where *memoria* lost importance compared to the other human capacities. By the time of scholastics, *ratio* was considered a crucial human function.

In his works the Cistercian abbot Bernhard of Clairvaux (1090–1153) turned the positive connotation of the term *memoria* into the opposite. In a sermon addressed to members of Paris University, he aimed to vilify the strife for scientific knowledge in contrast to the knowledge of God. He turned all traditional positive connotations into the opposite. Instead of the *aulae memoriae*, where information is stored, he spoke of a cesspit or sewer, where novelties accumulate like sewage.[5] Yet he did not use the metaphor of the book, where memories are written with divine ink, he used the image of parchment, onto which spilled ink made memories irretrievable—even more, as any attempt to clean the page would lead to the destruction of the page. Instead of the positive classical metaphor of memory as the stomach he spoke of the stomach filled with bad memories leading to stomach ulcers (Schwedler 2014: 244). Bernard of Clairvaux concludes that memory is negative, especially in the context of acquisition of knowledge at university. "Novelties" should be forgotten and replaced by genuine Christian behavior such as the seven biblical Beatitudes.

A less negative position on memory can be seen in the work of John of Salisbury (1115–80). To him, memory was not only the personal capacity of the mind but the possibility to retrieve information from the past through external media, above all books that preserved the literary heritage. Memories in the written form can and must be used as a basis and stimulus for the education of the young. Memories are essential to reflect on human weaknesses and develop remedies against frailty and contingency of human life (von Moos 1996: 560).[6]

The Dominican theologians Albertus Magnus (*c.* 1206–80) and his pupil, Thomas Aquinas (*c.* 1225–74) were engaged in the discovery of Aristotelic thought. Both wrote commentaries on Aristotle's *De memoria et reminiscentia* and they combined it with the tradition of Augustine and Isidore in recognizing the essential function of recollection for the soul. In both texts they reacted to the Aristotelic conception of the location of memory. Based on Aristotle, they conclude to consign the place of memory directly within the soul. Albertus agreed that mnemonic places were entirely pragmatic. He considered them to be like cognitive schemata rather than real objects. They could resemble existing things but they were not real themselves. Albertus Magnus and Thomas Aquinas alike drew from Aristotle's work on memory that recollective association proceeded by convention and not by necessity. Remembering the color white, the attached image could be milk or snow. Both memories could be "true" (Carruthers 1990: 277). The novelty of their perspective was that they considered *memoria* not as part of rhetoric but as part of ethics, where it was grouped with the other virtues of prudence (Coleman 1992: 69). Here, memory only served to take the ethically right decisions by providing information.

In the following decades, scholastic reasoning ascribed *memoria* a merely auxiliary importance within the human capacities, focusing on *ratio*. A good example is the reflection of Jean Buridan (*c.* 1301–*c.* 1359/62) on Aristotle's concept of memory. In fact, many philosophical and theological tracts did not consider *memoria* as primary human faculty for interaction with the inner self at all (Ohly 2005).

MEMORY AND OBLIVION IN MODERN RESEARCH

Memory and oblivion in the Middle Ages have been studied from different perspectives. The most distinct field of research focuses on the *artes memoriae*. An initial study on mnemotechnics is the rarely quoted but important work of the literary historian Helga Hajdu (Hajdu 1936; 1967) followed by the comprehensive books of Frances Yates (Yates

1966), Janet Coleman (Coleman 1992), and the productive research of Mary Carruthers (Carruthers 1990; 1998; 2002). She emphasized that the study of memory should not only focus on mnemonic tracts that stressed functions and explanations of memory but that medieval memory had to be studied in its general cultural context (Carruthers 1990: 13). The close relationship between the development of mnemotechnics and science as well as literary and cultural phenomena has since been subject of many studies, thereby developing the topic (Doležalová and Visi 2010, Rivers 2010). Research on tracts on the *ars memoriae* in the later Middle Ages especially showed that they were not only written as technical texts in the field of rhetoric, but as a genre to reflect on ethical phenomena (Heimann-Seelbach 2000).

An intensive field of research, centered on the term *memoria,* is the study of commemorative practice. Most prolific was the so-called "Freiburger Schule." All manifestations where death and oblivion were overcome through specific and mostly communal acts of memory were the focus of this research. The aim was to analyze the social functions of collective commemoration, liturgical memory, forms of genealogical and dynastic memory, foundations and reflections in writing such as necrologies, memory books etc. (Oexle 2009; Hugener 2014; Faini 2008; Spiegel 2002). Monasteries, graves, books, and communities became places of commemoration in the terms of Pierre Nora's concept of the *Les lieux de mémoire* (Moeglin, 2002). Furthermore, organized procedures of commemoration needed material background and had to be managed, which led not only to the consolidation of monastic and social formations, but also to the production of administrative writing beyond the actual commemoration books, the so called *Libri vitae* (Hugener 2014; Jussen 2002).

Research on writing as a basic operation of memory has a long tradition. Of great impact were the works of Michael Clanchy and Brian Stock. Growing literacy in the High Middle brought about changes in social organization and thought (Clanchy 1979, 3rd ed. 2013; Adamska 2000). Literacy opened up new perspectives of group formation. The perspective of "textual communities" made it possible to search for shared knowledge and memory (Stock 1983). The relevance of script for memory was stressed again in *Phantoms of Remembrance* by Patrick Geary, as he underlined that creation of memories usually followed utilitarian purposes. Monuments or lists of names tell us more about the successors and heirs than about the things or people remembered (Geary 1994b). An analysis of the processes of selection and deselection in the context of writing and medieval historiography has since proven to be a most fruitful approach to the phenomenon of memory in the Middle Ages (Bouchard 2014).

Yet it is still debated if impulses from the field neuroscience can be made fruitful for the study of medieval memory. Johannes Fried has been criticized for combining results of modern psychology with his results that most events in the early Middle Ages are not well documented and sources get lost over the course of time (Fried 2012). Reviewers argued that "Memorik," as he calls his approach, does not help to explain the difficulties in understanding the discrepancy between an event or personality that is badly documented by contemporaries but had an important impact on later events in medieval history. The force of memory consists in the ability to construct and shape stimulating images for each new generation. Hence St. Benedict or the forged charter of the Donation of Constantine were *imagines agentes*. As resources of the past they were used, shaped and re-shaped in the construction of contemporary identities (Gantner, McKitterick, and Meder 2015; Mostert 2008). Texts frequently underwent adaption to contemporary needs, the so called *réécriture*.

As in recent research the qualities of media, time and space became more central, focus shifted towards the specific forms and situations of memory (Pethes 2008: 9–11; Rivers 2010; Tracy 2015). Answers to the question, what the "objects to remember with" were, included myths, names, manuscripts, specialists, women, monks, canon lawyers—depending on the specific situation, where memories of the past were "needed" and adapted for the present. This leads to the question of transmission of memory and above all, the question of control of media and censorship. Forgetting is no longer seen as a mere deficit of memory, but as a partially passive and a partially active procedure. The notion deriving from psychology and cognitive science accepts that oblivion is a cultural factor with its own value (already Reik 1920, cf. Butzer and Günter 2004: 9; Eco 1988). To see memory as a process and not as a product as the terms "collective memory" or "cultural memory" suggest leads to Niklas Luhmann's redefinition of memory: "The main function of memory is forgetting in order to avoid blockage of the system through the coagulation of results of earlier perceptions."[7]

CONCLUSION

Memory and oblivion in the Middle Ages concern fundamental fields of thought and action of individuals and groups. Memory and oblivion enable the correlation between the inside and the outside of beings with the dialectics of storage and selection. And last but not least, memory and oblivion are two faces of the same process, adaption of knowledge for the present. In the same way as they address many facets of the *conditio humana* they need to be addressed from a multitude of perspectives such as theology, liturgy, philosophy, sociology, and psychology, bundled under the perspective of memory studies. The historical approach tries to emphasize the aspect of change and development and to see recollecting and forgetting as continuous processes.

To understand memory in the Middle Ages, it is important to take the aspect of material transmission into account. The concept of memory cannot be retrieved through an analysis of the end products such as single monuments or texts, although these frequently happen to be the only available sources. Important media of memory such as texts and images, monuments, rituals, historiography, poetry, and prose need to be seen in their context and their social position. Nonetheless, the objects are not mere souvenirs of the past. They only present knowledge of the past in a doubly deformed way. First, the media of memory was created or encoded semantically with specific intentions for recollection. Monuments and texts referring to the past were created intentionally to influence the future. Secondly, media of memory have different durability and depend on the circumstances of transmission. Often, memory depends on accidental or contingent transmission of the medium—and above all, the interest of later generations to include it in their memorial practice.

The knowledge that common memories have a strong impact on group identities has often been exploited for the shaping of groups and social coherence. The erection of monuments, commemorative ceremonies, literary memory, censorship, or deletion of monuments or places of memory are a few of the many possibilities available to form a social group's memory. To analyze these social practices will continue to be an interesting and telling field for historic research and will remain relevant in order to understand the specific forms of medieval culture.

CHAPTER ONE

Power and Politics

JEAN-MARIE MOEGLIN

"So that the honourable enterprises and noble adventures and feats of arms, which became the wars of France and England, may be notably recorded and perpetually remembered, so that brave may have an example of encouraging each other to do well, I want to deal with and report on a history and matter of great praise" (Froissart, *Chroniques*, ed. Kervyn de Lettenhove II, 4). These first words of the prologue to one of the most famous medieval chronicles, the *Chronicles of France and England* by Jean Froissart (second half of the fourteenth century) perfectly define the purpose of historians of the Middle Ages: to put history into "perpetual memory." In the Middle Ages, history is fundamentally conceived as the confinement of time that runs in a written, definitive and intangible memory. It is therefore important to show how historians have proceeded to create this memory and what constitutes the issues involved in this process.[1]

THE HISTORIAN AS A CREATOR OF A MEMORY OF THE PAST

Isidore of Seville (d. 636) gave his definition of history in his *Etymologies*, the great encyclopedia that transmits important facets of the ancient culture to the Middle Ages: "History is the story of past events; it is thanks to it that the facts of the past are known" (*Etymologiae*, ed. Lindsay, cap. 41). History was the true account of events that had occurred and thus opposed the fable (*fabula*). Hughes of St. Victor (d. 1141) later defined precisely the four questions to which the historian reporting facts had to answer: who, what, when, where? (*Didascalicon de studio legend*, ed. Buttimer, 113–14).

To be a historian was therefore to record the "facts" and transmit them to posterity. Richer of Reims specified in his prologue at the end of the tenth century regarding his intention in writing a history of the Gauls/French: "my particular purpose is to recall the wars that were often fought by the French, the various disorders they experienced and the various sources of their affairs" (*Monumenta Germaniae Historica Scriptores*, henceforth *MGH SS*, 38, 35). More than two-and-a half centuries later, the author of the *Annales gibelines* of Piacenza echoed this: "we considered it worthy and useful to bring to mind the wars, tribulations, anguish, sedition and torments that occurred in Lombardy during the time of the Holy Roman Emperor Frederick, with the sole aim of reporting and narrating the truth" (*MGH SS*, 18, 469). A good century later, Jacques de Guise (d. 1399), author of the *Chroniques du Hainaut*, in turn indicated to his readers, why he gave the date of the death of Louis the Pious: "and so that the memory of the event would be known to all, Louis, son of Charlemagne buried in Aachen, died in the year of the Lord 840" (*MGH SS* 30, 1, 136).

This memory of the past created by the historian was a written memory. The written word is indeed the only means to preserve facts and illustrious people from the permanent danger of oblivion. The author of the life of Emperor Henry II reports how the same came to Monte Cassino and was miraculously healed by St. Benedict from his gallstones. He points out that this miracle was recorded in Monte Cassino so that the men of the present would commit to memory God's deeds and to not be forgotten by the men of the future because of "the antiquity of time" (*MGH SS rerum Germanicarum,* henceforth *MGH SS rer. Germ.,* 69, 83). At the beginning of the twelfth century, Hughes of Fleury dedicated his ecclesiastical history to the Countess Adèle of Blois, expressing the hope that she would contribute decisively to the illustration of her name, preventing her from being corrupted by the passing of time which is generally the enemy of memory conservation among the men of the future (*MGH SS* 9, 357). Lambert of Wattrelos in his *Annales de Cambrai,* written in the third quarter of the twelfth century, had a particularly important event to report on concerning the date of 1156, "we must remember what is destroyed and forgotten because of old age" (*MGH SS,* 14, 481).

"To ask for memory" and to "restore to memory" what is "worthy of memory," is therefore a means of saving from oblivion the achievements of the past by recording them in writing. Indeed, the lively memory of humans is not always perfectly reliable. It is of short duration; it can only go back as far as an estimated 100 years, with which the utmost limit of human memory is reached. This is indicated by the author of a continuation of the *Gesta* of the Archbishops of Magdeburg who reports that in 1491 the Archbishop of Magdeburg celebrated the liturgy in Halberstadt according to the old customs whose memory no one had preserved, that is to say that no one had seen them practiced over the last 100 years (*MGH SS,* 14, 481). It is, at last, perishable because it disappears with the man who preserved it. Thus, what is accomplished in time also perishes with time and is erased from the memory of men, if its commemoration is not immediately ensured through writing as Albert Behaim, after and before many others, emphasizes in the middle of the thirteenth century: "what happens in time must be diligently put in writing if one does not want its remembrance to perish with time and disappear from the memory of men" (*MGH Epistolae* (*Briefe d. spät. MA*), 484–5).

Only the written word can therefore produce a long, reliable, and stable memory, one that would in some way permanently feed the temporary and fleeing memory of future generations of the subsequent centuries as Adalbert, Dean of Bamberg, author of the *Life of Emperor Henry II* around 1150–70, wrote: "about this same chalice, what we have heard from religious men in truth, we considered it worthwhile to note for the memories of the men of the future" (*MGH SS rer. Germ.,* 69, 306). This universal memory was the memory of "all faithful to the holy Church of God, present and future" as we read in the chronicle of the monastery of Scheyern (*Chronicon Schirense*) in the first half of the thirteenth century (*MGH SS,* 17, 615). It is apparently due to this universal memory that the many authors who explained that they wanted to "commit to memory" (*memoriae mandare, memoriae tradere, memoriae commendare, memoriae transmittere, posterorum memoriae commendare*) did so only with those events of the past they considered worthy of being preserved, so as to make it an "eternal memory" (*memoria aeterna*) or perpetual—as Froissart said—a memory that would last "for ever and ever" (*in secula*).

However, historians knew that they were engaging in a difficult and uncertain struggle against the force of oblivion that is able to carry away and to erase everything: "the old age of time has left many facts to be forgotten and has entrusted only a few to memory," deplores the author of the *Vita Bertulfi Renticensis* (*MGH SS,* 15, 2, 633) at the end of the eleventh century. "Because the course of time has removed the memory of past events from the men of the present," states the author of the *Chronicon Affligemense* (*MGH SS*, 9, 407) around 1120–40. In a historical note written at the beginning of the thirteenth century at the Bavarian monastery of Niederaltaich, the author complains: "because actions, even when they have been accomplished magnificently, are totally erased from the memory of men by the course of time if they have not been put to the perpetuity of writing" (*MGH SS*, 17, 374).

In fact, historians had too often been guilty of negligence, a scandal that Reginon of Prüm denounces, for example, in the prologue to his chronicle written at the beginning of the tenth century; he noted with indignation that while Jewish, Greek, and Roman historians and other peoples have transmitted the facts that had been accomplished in their time through their writings to this day, there is a "perpetual silence" about much more recent facts of our time "as if nowadays, either humans had stopped acting, or they had not done anything worthy of being committed to memory or, if actions worthy of remembering had nevertheless been carried out, no one would have been able to preserve them in writing" (*MGH SS rer. Germ.*, 50, 1). More optimistic, however, was Jacques de Guise, who at the end of the fourteenth century drew up a long list of all the historians, from Moses to Gislebert and Martin of Troppau, who had written the history of the kingdoms so that "if it were to disappear from the memory of men, it would remain at least in books" (*MGH SS*, 30,1, 81).

The role of the historian was therefore to choose and report what, in the past and the present, qualified as worthy of being remembered (*dignum memoria*), worthy of the "memory of the men of the future" (*posterorum memoria*) and to select the "most worthy facts of memory" (*gesta memoria dignissima*), so that what was important to commit to a perpetual memory would not be forgotten. "In the year of the Lord 1214, the 6th day of the calends of August, a memorable event occurred on the bridge of Bouvines near Tournai," this is how the author of the account of the Battle of Bouvines in 1214, known as the *Relatio Marchianensis*, begins his account (*MGH SS.* 26, 390–1). As a historian it was his hope that this work of building a perpetual written memory, which he compiled with so much effort, would never be lost. Saba Malaspina urges his future readers at the end of the prologue to his *Chronicle of the Affairs of Sicily*, written in the 1280s, to be indulgent with the weaknesses of his work but to ensure that it is not forgotten "but is preserved by a lasting memory" (*MGH SS*, 35, 90). Thirty years earlier, another historian, Vincent de Beauvais, had even sought, in what is undoubtedly his first historical work, to constitute by compiling and abbreviating the earlier authors in what he himself calls a "memorial of all eras" (*Memoriale omnium temporum*) "because it contains a short memory of all times" (*MGH SS*, 24, 157). In the first quarter of the fourteenth century, another author, Jean de Saint-Victor, wrote a *Memoriale Historiarum* fashioned as a memory of all histories (Guyot-Bachy 2000).

To become a historian and to preserve in writing the memory of achievements was thus a duty without which the memory of important or even essential events would be lost. Thietmar of Merseburg highlights this at the beginning of the first book of his chronicle around 1010–20: As Bishop of Merseburg it is his task to restore in memory the history of his once famous and now almost forgotten bishopric (*MGH SS rer. Germ. Nova Series (N.S.)*, 9). Around 1075, Adam of Bremen initiated the project of writing down the acts of the Archbishops of Hamburg-Bremen by noting that this work had not been done yet, which may prompt a hostile mind to conclude that either they had done nothing worthy of being remembered, or, if they had nevertheless done something notable, that no author had wanted to keep it in mind (*MGH SS rer. Germ.*, 2, 1). Sometimes however, it was too late: in the first half of the eleventh century the author of the *Gesta* of the bishops of Cambrai noted with bitterness that he had wanted to give the names of the founders of Cambrai and Arras but their memory had not been preserved in any history and that he therefore preferred to remain silent rather than invent fables (*MGH SS*, 7, 403).

WRITING DOWN THE MEMORY OF PAST TIMES

In the twelfth century, the author of the annals of Genoa clearly states: "Because the facts of the present are open and known to the people of the present, as soon as they belong to the past, they will no longer be known to future men, therefore it is good and useful to tell the truth of the current facts" (*MGH SS,* 18, 25). The fundamental principle of the historian's memorial work is thus to put down in writing the current facts as he has witnessed them, to set down in writing their memory and transmit them to posterity before they are lost. This provides the guarantee of truth in the historian's narrative and the memory he creates. Eginhard, for example, already put forth that the fact of having been a witness guaranteed the truth of his account: "I was well aware that no one could tell more truthfully than myself, the things in which I myself had participated, those that I know for certain by having seen them with my own eyes." (*Eginhard, Vie de Charlemagne*, ed. Sot, 90). The living experience of the historian directly feeds the written memory he creates, which will enter the collective memory that, according to the historian, is timeless, intangible, and eternal as long as those who constitute it have not departed from the right path of truth, that is, from the faithful transcription of the lived experience of the present, simply as it really happened. These might have been the words of the chroniclers of the Middle Ages long before Leopold von Ranke.

Yet quite naturally a historian cannot have witnessed all that is important to commit to memory; when telling something that exceeds what he has witnessed, the historian will then rely on the testimony of persons of indisputable authority; Helmold of Bosau (d. after 1177) declares only to report the facts "that he has heard from men of great age or that he has seen with his own eyes" (*MGH SS rer. Germ.*, 2). Rudolphe of Saint-Trond, author around 1114–15 of the deeds of the Abbots of Saint-Trond, states in the same way: "From Adelard II up to myself, everything I report, I either saw or could see it; and what I did not see, I learned from the accounts of those who saw it" (*Rodulfus Trudonensis, Gesta Abbatum Trudonensium*, ed. Tombeur 5). Otto of Freising also declared in the middle of the twelfth century that after having relied on Orose, Eusebius and their successors, he would now rely on his own experience and that of reliable witnesses: "we will tell the following, because these are events of our recent memory, relying on what has been transmitted to us by reliable men, or as we have seen and heard it ourselves" (*MGH SS rer. Germ.,* 323). In the same manner, John of Salisbury declares in his *Historia Pontificalis* of 1164: "In what I am about to say I will write nothing else, with the help of God, than what I know to be true by my own sight and hearing, or only what has been supported by the writings and authority of reliable men (*Historia Pontificalis*, ed. Chibnall 4).

As for the times that the historian has not experienced himself, if he wants to write their history, he will have to refer to the works of his predecessors who wrote the history of their times by respecting the criteria that were provided through the directly lived experience or the accounts of reliable and honorable men. For this reason, for example, Benedict of St. Maur, in the middle of the twelfth century, claims to have favored the history of the destruction of Troy (*De excidio Trojae*) by Dares the Phrygian (probably written in the sixth century CE) and the Ephemeris of the Trojan War (*Ephemeris belli*

Trojani) by Dictys the Cretan (undoubtedly from the first century CE) to Homer's account, since Homer had lived 100 years after the events. On the other hand, Dares, mentioned in the *Iliad* as Hephaestus' priest in Troy during the siege, and Dictys of Crete, who allegedly participated in the siege, were regarded as eyewitnesses. They were, therefore, similar to judicial procedures, more credible than the others. Based on their lived experience, they provided the *veritas historiae* while the others only relied on fictions. In the same way, the *Historia Karoli et Rotholandi*, also known as the chronicle of the Pseudo-Turpin, which has been written in the middle of the twelfth century but was considered to be the work of Archbishop Turpin of Reims, a faithful of Charlemagne. It tells of the imagined campaigns conducted by Charlemagne in Spain against the Saracens and was considered as a true and trustworthy account as it had been written by a witness of the events and contemporary of Charlemagne, Archbishop Turpin; it was thus a considerable success in the Middle Ages.

Hence, an author writing a history of both the past and the present will affirm, usually in the prologue addressing his future readers, that, when referring to past events, he has only relied on the information of the most credible authors, and regarding the times of the living "memory" (about 100 years), he has written only about what he himself had seen or heard from reliable witnesses. In the prologue to his *Gesta Normannorum*, William of Jumièges, for example, dedicates the same to Duke William the Conqueror: "For the beginning of the story up to Richard II, I drew on Dudon's *Historia*, a skillful man, who diligently sought what had to be transmitted in writing to posterity, from Count Raoul, brother to king Richard I. I myself account for the rest that I have learned it either from people who are trustworthy both because of their age and their experiencing of the events, or that I have acquired a solid knowledge of them myself as a witness" (*Gesta Normannorum*, ed. van Houts 4–6). As for Otto of Freising, in his prologue he ask not to be accused of lying because of what might perhaps appear strange in his account as he has only relied on his predecessors for what predates his own time: "Let no one want to accuse me of lying for facts that according to the norm of our time might perhaps seem strange because up until the events of our recent memory, I have used nothing else, and of it only very little among many things, than what I have found in the writings of honorable men" (*MGH SS rer. Germ.*, 45, 10).

The historian, eager to transmit a true memory of the past to posterity, will therefore be the compiler of the good authors of the past who have written about the events of their time as they saw them and heard about them themselves or having received them by reliable witnesses (Guenée 1985). He will select in their stories the passages that interest him, and he will carefully arrange them as any good compiler must do. Then, in turn, he will tell the story of the present, and he will transmit to his successors the written memory of the past that he has thus updated, and they will act in the same way, compile his work and pursue it from when the feather fell from his hands. Henry, Archdeacon of Huntingdon, who wrote a *Historia Anglorum* from 1120 to 1154 relied on and continued many authors mainly the Venerable Bede and the *Anglo-Saxon Chronicle* of the tenth century. There are at least six compilations of this work, each of them the result of a revision and proof of Henry's work. The tenth and last book, reports on the civil war that broke out between Etienne de Blois and Mathilde and Henry II. It concludes with the coronation of Henry II in December 1154 and the last sentence reads "and now a new book must be dedicated to a new king" (*Historia Anglorum*, ed. Greenway, X, 40, 776). Perhaps Henry intended to write this book himself, at least to start it, but it is quite likely that he knew, given his already advanced age, that a new historian would have to follow his work. Medieval historians hence identify as members of a chain in which each one refers to his predecessors, adds to the building before handing over to his successors, all dedicated to the immense work of creating a memory of the past.

WHAT DOES THE MEMORY OF THE PAST COVER?

The medieval historian consequently had the essential task of writing the history of the past to build the memory of the men of the future, *ad memoriam futurorum*. But what exactly did this memory of the past the historian compiled for his contemporaries and for posterity cover?

History could be conceived and written in two different ways; in the manner of chroniclers and annalists, which consisted of reconstructing, in the most concise possible way, the chronology of events essentially by simply answering the questions Hughes of St. Victor had precisely defined, who, what, when, where. Secondly, according to the principles of *historia*, i.e. by establishing the sequences, causes and effects, the particularities of past events, by focusing on the meaning of history without paying too much attention to events and dates.

These two methods of historiography had been defined in ancient times, but the ancient authors placed them in a hierarchy. Cicero had indeed theorized this reflection on the distinction between two modes of historiography. In Book II of his *De oratore*, he reports that the writing of history in Rome began with simple annals that priests compiled each year to ensure the preservation of events, to commit them to a "public memory" (*memoria publica*). Many others then followed this tradition by leaving simple memorials (*monumenta*) of dates, peoples, places, and facts without giving their narrative a rhetorical form. They mainly wanted to write down the events. A quite different model was proposed by Greek historians such as Thucydides and Herodotus who, thanks to an ornate style using all the resources of rhetoric, had made a coherent narrative of history instead of merely reporting on it. Until then, Roman historians had remained the narrators of events (*narratores*) and not *exornatores rerum* able by the power of rhetoric to provide the *ratio rerum* (Cicero, *De Oratore*, II, 12, ed. Sutton 52–6). After Cicero, Aulus Gellius made the distinction between history and annals by quoting in his *Noctes Atticae* (second century CE) the tribune and historian Sempronius Asellio (*c.* 159–91 BCE): "According to Asellio, in the annals it is simply given what and in which year something had happened; the historian, on the other hand, provides reasons [*ratio*] for what happened and exposes the deliberation [*consilium*] that is at the origin of what happened. Due to this, the annals are absolutely incapable of motivating the people to defend the *res publica* or to give them lessons that would allow them to overcome evil" (*Aulus Gellius, Noctes Atticae,* V, 18). Writing simple annals was, he argued, like telling fables to children and not writing history.

In the eyes of ancient authors, annals or the chronicles or *Chronographia* were therefore defined as a historical genre characterized by a brief mentioning of the events occurring in a defined unit of time (usually a year), the absence of rhetorical format and an established link between those events, the choice of a continuous chronological thread and no concern for coherence. They were thus clearly distinguished from the genre that was recognized as superior, i.e. great histories in the manner of Herodotus and Thucydides, and later Sallust, Livy, or Tacitus, who gave the impetus, the beginnings and ends of the actions of the agents of history, but were not necessarily concerned with their exact dates.

The Middle Ages recognize this distinction but added a new perspective, that of Eusebius of Caesarea of the 320s. In his great effort to embody a Christian vision of history that broke with the ancient traditions, the latter, in fact, had at first undertaken to develop a universal chronology by writing his "Chronological and Abridged Canons of the Universal History of the Greeks and Barbarians" which aimed at incorporating the history of the Jewish people, the "chosen people" of the Old Testament, into the history and universal chronology of all the peoples and kingdoms of the world. The first part of the *Canons* of Eusebius was not known to the Latin West, but the second part was known owing to a Latin translation, adaptation and continuation given by St. Jerome between 379 and 381. However, this second part of Eusebius' work effectively gave a universal chronology in "world years" (*annis mundi*) in the form of synchronic tables: parallel columns made it possible to map the events of the Old and New Testaments with those of the kingdoms and empires that had developed since if not the origins of the world, at least from Abraham and Nineus onwards. St. Jerome had given his translation the name *Temporum liber* before quoting it in 392 as *Chronicon omnimodae historiae*. St. Augustine mentioned the *Chronica* of Eusebius and Jerome.

Eusebius had not only established a universal Christian chronology, he also showed that this history had a meaning that Christians had to be able to decipher and know in order to strengthen their faith based on a theological conception of history. Shortly after his *Canons*, he wrote a second book on history in which he gives a detailed account of the history of the Church from the incarnation of Christ to his time; it was a *Historia ecclesiastica*, a history of the Church portrayed as a history of the path of God's chosen ones toward eternal salvation. Written in Greek between 305 and 324, it was translated into Latin in 402/403 by Rufin of Aquileia and continued until the death of Theodosius I in 395 which made it accessible to the Middle Ages. With this ecclesiastical history, Eusebius wanted to create a founding memory of identity for his readers, Christians and posterity, to enable the "community to become aware of its identity by knowing its past."[2] Eusebius' goal was to establish a link between the apostles and his time. It was necessary to show that the economy of salvation was realized in history, to reveal the true meaning of the history of the Church, a history that reveals "the merciful benevolence of our Saviour for all of us" but also played its part in the creation of the "Evil," source and origin of all heresies and deviations, and that of the persecuting emperors—its instrument. It is the confrontation of God and the Devil, of truth against error that Eusebius retraces in history.

Eusebius had the feeling that he was moving along a ground that no one had yet cleared: "I am the first to try this work, to move forward on a desert and unspoilt path, so to speak" (*Eusebius of Caesarea, Historia ecclesiastica*, I, 1, 1–2). While he wrote this at the beginning of his *Historia* when defining his project as a historian, he stated later: "I once gave a summary of these events [referring to his Chronological Canons] but I have now decided to give a detailed account of them" (*Eusebius of Caesarea, Historia ecclesiastica*, I, 1, 6).

In Eusebius' eyes, therefore, the opposition of the two "genres" the ancient theorists described, was no longer a difference in essence but a simple difference between a summary and a detailed account of history. Christian history consists of two inseparable aspects: First the Christian chronology of history had to be established, to put into order the great events that mark the journey of the Church of the chosen ones toward eternal salvation; then the profound meaning of this chronology had to be clarified by showing that history is, in God's eye, an eschatological achievement, a struggle between the good and the wicked, good and evil, and of how the Church of the chosen, under the gaze of providence, continues to grow and overcome obstacles and adversaries. For this reason, it was necessary to show, just like Orose did after Eusebius remarkably in his *Historia adversus paganos*, how God leads his people, brings them back on the right path when they deviate from it by sending them calamities and disasters as warnings—always just as many as men needs to correct his conduct (van Nuffelen 2012).

Mainly due to the example Eusebius of Caesarea gave, the distinction between history and chronology was transmitted to the Middle Ages with an example for each of these historical "genres." Hughes of St. Victor, for example, wrote that Eusebius of Caesarea had written both a chronicle and a history. But at the same time, Eusebius had removed from this distinction both its conceptual rigor and the value judgment that accompanied it. Medieval historians were taught a lesson by Eusebius: there were two possible ways of writing history, both of which contributed to giving substance to a Christian vision of history, one was the chronologic way of giving priority to facts and dates, the other was the historical way of reconstructing causes and effects, ins and outs, and seeking to rediscover the meaning of history fulfilled under God's gaze. Historians of the Middle Ages were able to orient towards the first or second, but overall all practiced a mixed genre that variably associated chronicle and history.

The memory of the past that historians were responsible to establish was the memory of the Church's march of the chosen ones towards Parousia. As Bishop Frecalf of Lisieux wrote in the prologue to the universal chronicle he wrote in the late 820s to Helisachar, former chancellor and still close to Louis the Pious, that the latter had asked him to "record all the events worthy of memory that had taken place in the different parts of the world" (*Frechulf,* ed. Allen, 17).

The genre of a universal chronicle/history was thus the historical genre par excellence in the Middle Ages and, from Eusebius and Orose to Werner Rolevinck's (d. 1502) *Fasciculus temporum*, countless chronicles and universal histories were written during the Middle Ages. Several models were implemented to organize them, from the synchronic history scheme of Eusebius to the parallel arrangement of popes and emperors of Martin of Troppau. However, within this universal history, it was possible to identify a more restricted history: that of a man or a line of men, a resounding event or of a given people or country. Particular histories resulting in a particular memory with an own autonomy could thus be detached from a universal history.

THE FUNCTIONS OF A MEMORY OF THE PAST

It follows that the historian chooses and organizes in narratives what he considers has to be "committed to memory," what is "worthy of memory," and shall not be forgotten. This choice is naturally determined by a certain idea of the function and use of building a memory of the past. Yet again, medieval historians proposed a reorganization of the legacy of antiquity.

Entertainment, *delectare*, is the first function of a historical narrative. The attention and interest of the readers has to be retained; it has to refrain from retelling every detail in order to not bore his readers, as Henry of Livonia writes: "Many glorious events occurred in Livonia at the time of the conversion of peoples to the faith of Jesus Christ, but they cannot all be recorded and transmitted to the memory for fear of boring the readers." But this desire to entertain, except for a few mediocre historians, cannot be the sole aim; it has to support the historical narrative, by holding the reader's attention, to fulfil its truly important functions.

These essential functions are first and foremost the functions of teaching and instructing. *Historia magistra vitae*, this famous Ciceronian maxim "history as witness of the centuries, light of truth, life of memory, mistress of life, messenger of ancient times" (*Cicero, De*

Oratore, II, 9, 36) was always present in the Middle Ages. It might be subsumed that Cicero referred to the idea that what happened once in history has an ever-present value because it is always likely to happen again, and the experience of the past therefore teaches us good conduct for the present; the future Pope Pius II, Enea Silvio Piccolomini, described this lesson in a different way in one of his many historical works: only experience can teach. However, humans only live for a short time and therefore can only collect a limited experience, therefore only history—retraced by the line of the mentioned historians—provides the whole duration of human experience, in the field of ecclesiastical history as well as in the field of lay history (*MGH SS rer. Germ.*, N. S., 24/2, 237).

History first served the use of providing the memory of divine warnings administered in the past in the form of prodigies heralding famine, death and other plagues; Robert of Torigni (d. 1186), abbot of Mont-Saint-Michel and passionate historian, declares "that they must be committed to written memory so that, if they happen again, sinners who remember having provoked God's wrath at some point, will easily confer to the remedies of penance and confession that will enable them to appease God" (*Chronicle of Robert of Torigni*, ed. Delisle I, 92). In the middle of the twelfth century, Richard of Cluny echoed this by declaring that he had included in his chronicle all kinds of extraordinary events so that in the future humans will be able to better understand their meaning if they happen again: "wonders or famines or eclipses of the sun and moon, or what illustrious men have lived under what rulers, or if it is revealed that something like this has happened in some place, that too I have transmitted to memory so that if something like this happens again one day, the non-ignorant posterity will know how to judge these things through a comparison with the past" (*MGH SS*, 26, 76).

Broadly speaking, reading about history teaches people to imitate virtue and seek good, to avoid vice and to abhor evil. At the end of the twelfth century, Gervase of Canterbury wrote in the prologue to his chronicle that humanity is confronted with three fearsome dangers: Demons, the world and the flesh; however, fortunately there are three weapons that allow him to resist them: "prohibition, precept and example" (Gervase of Canterbury, ed. Stubbs, Rolls Series 73, 1, 85). But Gervase also notes that "there are a lot of those whose minds are more easily inclined to avoid evil or to do good by example than by prohibitions or precepts," even if, alas, Gervase notes, there will always be people who "enjoy doing evil and exult in the most evil actions" (Gervase of Canterbury, ed. Stubbs, Rolls Series 73, 1, 86).

After and before many others, Robert of Torigni observes in the prologue preceding his chronicle that it is thus important to the historian to highlight the example of virtues that will give rise to imitation, while that of vices will help to avoid them: "to propose to the imitation of men of the future the good life and commendable morals of those who preceded them, to describe on the other hand the examples of bad, not so that we imitate them but so that they are avoided" (*Chronicle of Robert of Torigni*, I, 92). Imitating virtuous actions, fleeing reprehensible and shameful actions was ensured because of the memory of the past that historians constituted. The author of the *Gesta archiepiscoporum Magdeburgensium* writes, probably in the middle of the twelfth century: "lest the actions worthy of memory of the elders be poured into the cloud of oblivion, it seems to me useful and honest that a sure memory of them be transmitted to contemporaries by the quill of durable writing so that good people take an example from the virtue of good actions and that they learn in a salutary way to refrain from bad actions" (*MGH SS*, 14, 376). At the same time, Cosmas of Prague praised the achievements of a Bohemian Duke to its readers and gave them an example "particularly remarkable and worthy of memory, and an example to be imitated by posterity" (*MGH SS rer. Germ. N.S.*, 2, 107). Also, when, in the middle of the twelfth century, Benedict of Sainte-Maure told the story of how young Richard I of Normandy had to defend his duchy against the King of Western France, he used the pernicious conduct of the French as a pretext to explain his conception of history. The story warns the readers of the fiend "we must take an example, know, perceive and hear how the French have always practiced great felony towards those of Normandy," because the history of the ancestors is a true mirror "where mankind can see itself and reflect itself." According to Henry of Huntingdon, it was necessary to follow the example of Moses—who, in the Middle Ages, was considered as the first historian who wrote the book of Genesis following God's dictation—as *secretarius Dei*—and to report on the virtues as well as the vices (*Henry of Huntingdon, Historia Anglorum*, X, 25, 750). This had often been the first justification that, for example, John of Winterthur offered in the writing of his chronicle: "because a reliable and faithful written relation to past events brings to successive future generations a usefulness that is not slight but rather important, I, Brother John" (*MGH SS rer. Germ. N.S.*, 3, 1) a use derived from the examples of virtues to be imitated and the vices to be avoided alike, such as the abominations that John reports about three Begines that were uncovered in Constance in 1339 and that he wished to transmit to his readers: "so that the sin of the latter may not be erased in this chronicle but may be perpetually transmitted as a damned memory" (*MGH SS rer. Germ. N.S.*, 3, 249).

This view of the memory of past events did not only encompass a moral dimension; it was also of political significance: the *De excidio Britanniae* of Gildas, written around 540, aimed at showing how moral corruption and the vices of Breton leaders had caused the ruin of Brittany; an example not to be followed! It is therefore a lamentable story (*flebilis historia*) that Gildas wrote, like the prophets of the Old Testament, warning and averting the dangers to come. (*De Excidio Britanniae,* ed. Winterbottom, ch. 37, p. 36). History can become a reliable mirror for the prince as it offers models of conduct in the account of the deeds of their ancestors; Freculf, Bishop of Lisieux, addresses the Empress Judith in the prologue to the second part of his *Historiae*; following his direction, her son, the young Charles, will be able to recognize in it as a mirror "what must be imitated and what must be avoided" (*Freculf*, 436). In 1047, the Imperial Chaplain Wipo wrote in dedication to Emperor Henry III about his *Gesta Conradi* that he had wanted to preserve for him "like in a mirror," the glorious achievements of his father for whenever Henry had to act himself. Even three centuries later, Levold of Northof states in the preface to his History of the Counts of La Marche that his account will allow the present count to follow in the footsteps of his ancestors and to learn to rule his land and his subjects in justice and in the fear of God: "for the perpetual memory of men of the present as well as those of posterity, especially those who are zealots for the honour and rank of this county, I have decided to write this little book about the Counts of La Marche, your ancestors, their origin, their achievements and successes, how they behaved, how they grew and prospered, how and with what valor they have expanded their land and lordship to this day; I write it as I learned and received these facts, partly on the basis of old ancient writings, partly according to the statements and reports of the elders, partly drawing on what I experienced myself or learned from my parents in my time, partly relying on what I saw and knew, so that you may learn to govern properly in justice and fear of God your land and your subjects" (*MGH SS rer. Germ. N.S.*, 6, 1). It is not only the prince who will be able to use the exemplary mirror provided by his ancestors; the principality's officers will also be able to model their actions on the example of their glorious predecessors who worked for the development of the principality and whose memory must therefore be particularly preserved.

At the beginning of the fourteenth century, William of Nangis, at the beginning of his *Gesta* of King Louis IX, more generally stressed the importance of the work of historians reporting on the achievements of past rulers, thus preventing them from erasing themselves from human memory: "when in fact such deeds are recited to contemporary kings and princes, it cannot be but a brief and silent exhortation that the latter should make themselves magnanimous by similar actions and conform to their (past) morals and lives" (*MGH SS*, 26, 632).

Preserving the memory of the events and men of the past was therefore a highly beneficial work to the education of the men of the future. However, this did not exhaust the usefulness of the memory that historians had to constantly nurture. Retaining the memory of illustrious men was also a means of immortalizing them; and it was a well-deserved reward for the virtues they had demonstrated during their lifetime.

This idea of the preservation of memory as a guarantee of immortality played a significant role in ancient times. Cicero confirmed that it was the love for glory that had led the ancient Romans to so many illustrious actions and many other Roman authors agreed. Valerius Maximus, author between 24 and 31 CE of the *facta et dicta memorabilia*, a book of considerable success in the Middle Ages, invoked, for example, Aristotle's authority to declare that the desire for glory was quite normal. Certainly, with the advent of Christianity, Sulpicius Severus (around 360–first quarter of the fifth century), criticized in the preface of his *Life of Saint Martin*, the habit of pagans to believe in the immortality of reputation, of *fama*, instead of focusing on the immortality of the soul ("they believed they could perpetuate themselves by the sole memory of men, whereas the office of man is rather to seek the perennial life than the perennial memory" (*Sulpicius Severus, Vie de Saint Martin*, 252). Yet he immediately evaluated, if not canceled, this criticism by declaring that it was legitimate and useful to write about the life of St. Martin because it would provide a remarkable example worthy of being chosen as a model to future generations. Writing the lives of great men and perpetuating their memory was therefore useful, provided that the glory sought was not profane glory but that due to the actions accomplished during his lifetime in the service of faith, the salvation of men and the Church. Medieval historians had learned the following lesson: by telling the stories of legitimately illustrious people and highlighting their glorious deeds, they inspired their readers to imitate these stories. Moreover, the author of a rewrite of the life of St. Conrad, Bishop of Constance, wrote in the twelfth century: "If these [great men] enjoy an eternal memory in heaven before God, why should their merit be ignored on earth?" (*MGH SS*, 4, 436). In fact, around 1160, the author of the life of Bishop Meinwerk of Paderborn (d. 1036) indicated that Charlemagne would enjoy after his death "the glory of eternal life and a perpetual remembrance among future men because of his multiple and incessant efforts to promote and extend the borders of the Christian religion" (*MGH SS rer. Germ.*, 59, 4).

Doing justice to the memory of great men after their death was hence a duty that could and should legitimately be done to those who had earned it by their actions during their earthly life. Eginhard already wrote in the preface of his *Life of Charlemagne* that he considered himself too indebted to the emperor "to prefer to leave out himself rather than not doing justice to the memory of such a great man" (*Eginhard, Life of Charlemagne*, 94). This theme was never again forgotten in the Middle Ages. Chaplain Wipo once again justified in his biography of Emperor Conrad II his intention "to attach with the bonds of writing the fleeting memory of things" by stating that "it ensures to those who have administered [the Roman Empire] well in this life a certain form of glory of immortality" alongside providing an example to their successors (*MGH SS rer. Germ.*, 61, 4). The contemporary of Conrad II,

Archbishop Bardo of Mainz, perhaps not considered the most brilliant successor of St. Boniface, but after his death, a monk wrote a glowing praise for his deeds and concluded it with a vibrant cry for "his memory not to be erased and his name to be invoked from generation to generation" (*MGH SS*, 11, 342). As for Empress Cunegunda, wife of Henry II, "her eternal memory compensated for the brevity of her life" (*MGH SS*, 4, 823).

Every man should legitimately aspire to be qualified after his death as a person of "memory to be maintained" (*recolendae memoriae*), "good and commendable memory" (*bone et laudabilis memorie*), "glorious memory," "illustrious memory" (*clare memorie*), "pious memory," of "happy memory" (*felicis memoriae*), or even "blessed memory" (*beatae memoriae*), "venerable memory" (*venerande/venerabilis memorie*), "holy memory" (*sancte memorie*) as well as "very holy memory" (*sanctisime memorie*), "divine memory," "perpetual memory," "eternal memory," or "immortal memory." In opposition were those who were "of damned memory" (*damnatae memoriae*) or "of sinister memory" (*pessimae memoriae*).

The celebration of the memory of great men and their noble deeds did not only have an earthly dimension but did also work as a means of providing access of the deceased to eternal salvation. Thietmar of Merseburg (d. 1018) reported that he had not been able to write all the deeds of King and Emperor Henry I, known as the "bird-catcher," but he hoped that the memory of his actions would be recorded in the Book of Life because in heaven the deeds of the good were recorded on silver tablets while the demons recorded the deeds of the evil in their own books. The historian thus rose to the rank of a collaborator similar to the celestial powers when writing the Book of Life, which would constitute the basis for eternal judgment. On the other hand, the memory of bad people would be destroyed. Eudes (or Odo) de St. Amand (d. 1162) recounting the miseries of the crusaders during the Second Crusade refused to explicitly name Manuel Comenos, who was considered responsible for the miseries of the crusaders, because his name did not appear in the Book of Life. The memory of the villains disappears immediately without trace as it is written in the Bible, "their memory perishes with them" (*Periit memoria eorum cum sonitu*, Psalm 9:7), a formula often used by medieval authors.

To preserve and celebrate before God the memory of virtuous deeds and good people and to contribute to their inclusion in the Book of Life, was on the other hand an important justification, if not the main justification for the work of a historian, because the celebration of the memory of the deceased before God is a duty, especially toward his benefactors, his friends, and relatives. For those who have rendered this service on earth to him, this service will prove worthy during their intercession before God. In his chronicle, Thietmar of Merseburg clearly states: "I would welcome, if it could happen that due to my humble efforts the memory of all excellent men could revive and shine with contemporaries as well as with men of the future, even if it will not delight them but because of their mercy, they will remember me before God the Almighty" (*MGH SS rer. Germ. N.S.*, 9, 203). It is indeed because he substantially fulfilled his duty to commemorate the dead that he can hope to gain access to eternal life: "I, although almost already dead because of my sins, will live, I hope, in the clear contemplation of God, healed because of the merits of the latter, and if I have accomplished little good in this century, I have at least constantly celebrated the memory of the dead" (*MGH SS rer. Germ. N.S.*, 9, 218).

This duty of *memoria* was one to friends; Richard of Cluny thus ends the prologue of his chronicle dedicated to his abbot by assuring him that he will work to preserve his memory in his chronicle: "I will not stop placing your memory in our leaflets so that your name may live and be loved by people of the future" (*MGH SS*, 26, 77). Yet it was particularly a duty of monks that they owed their founders and benefactors, often buried within their walls, and to whom they had a debt to repay by celebrating their *memoria*, through liturgical ceremonies but also by preserving the memory of their deeds and their exemplary life. This explains why in a monastery, the cantor, head of the liturgy, is also often the one with the title historiographer of the monastery. This was the case at the monastery of Saint-Denis, the necropolis of the kings of France in which, at least since the beginning of the twelfth century, it had been the objective both to religiously celebrate the liturgical memory of the deceased kings and to write the account of their lives, reign by reign.

The role of historians in establishing the reputation and posthumous glory of the living was in any case decisive and indispensable because, as the author of the *Chronicon Polonorum* wrote at the beginning of the twelfth century: "the fame of the knighthood of the Romans or Gauls would never have been so popular in the world if it had not been preserved by the testimonies of writers for the memory and imitation of the people of the future" (*MGH SS*, 9, 464).

FIGURE 1.1: Jean Froissart, *Chroniques*. Luxuriant page illumination and illustration of the episode of the English King Richard II meeting the army of peasants, 1381. Bibliothèque nationale de France, ms. Français 2644, fol. 154v. © Historic Images / Alamy Stock Photo.

The historian Jean Froissart wrote at the end of the fourteenth century; his work exemplified a largely secularized vision of the ideal order of society; the pivot of this order is in his eyes the memory of the prowess of which the historian is in charge "because the memory of the good and the reminder of the valiant obviously arouse and ignite the hearts of the young baccalaureate" (*Jean Froissart, Chroniques*, I, 5). As a matter of fact, he synthesizes the official functions that medieval historiography had assigned to memory: the narrative of past prowess pushes men of the present to accomplish new ones, probably because the example of virtue provokes imitation, but also because these men of the present see the immortal glory that prowess has given to heroes of the past; they also want to take part in the ensured immortality. Froissart went so far as to accordingly rearrange the ancient theme of the three orders of society: Society, he writes in one of his prologues, is divided into three parts: the nobles who perform actions of brilliance; the people, who speak about them and admire them; the clerics, that is to say historians and men of letters, who ensure the survival of the memory of the actions of brilliance (*Jean Froissart, Chroniques*, ed. Luce I, 5).

THE INSTRUMENTALIZATION OF THE MEMORY OF THE PAST

Consequently, historians had proclaimed themselves clerks of the memory of the past, *memoria temporum*, starting from a Christian vision of world history, according to which it was just as important to establish a precise chronology of all the great events and persons who had been important milestones in the long journey of humanity since the creation of the world towards the return of Christ and the end of the world as to give meaning to these events and to situate them in God's plan of leading the Church of the chosen towards the coming of the Kingdom of God (*civitas Dei*). Furthermore, the work of these historians creating a memory of the past was necessarily a contribution to the establishment of a universal and global history of the world from its creation by God to the apocalypse, Christ's return to earth and the final struggle between God and Satan. On this basis, the long chain of historians had undertaken to create the stable and shared memory of a community united by a past and common memories, *memoria temporum, memoria rerum gestarum*. This memory had not lost its religious dimension at the end of the Middle Ages, but it had become much more inclusive because its role in maintaining the stability of society had been recognized.

For their task historians had to provide facts adhering to two criteria; truthfulness and an exemplary moral significance, so that they could faithfully fulfil their ultimate mission to preserve an authentic memory of the actions of brilliance as well as of evil deeds carried out under the gaze of God, in order to allow their contemporaries and successors to guide their behavior according to good examples, so that they would choose the right path that led to heavenly life, but also to ensure on earth the immortality to which they aspired in heaven.

Naturally, this work made them select from the diversity and abundance of events, or from the stories of their predecessors, according to the principle of what they considered "worthy of memory" and to integrate this into a coherent narrative. It was never a perfectly objective work; this memory of the past that they created could not be a transparent mirror of historical reality; the writing of the history of the past and the present was necessarily a rewriting by a historian. It has to be noted that the instrumentalization of the memory of the past was equivalent to the writing/re-writing of the history of the past and the present.

Moreover, it was not only inevitable but even legitimate as the historian's responsibility to establish before God the true merits and to guide the action of his contemporaries authorized him, incited him or even forced him not only to ignore one fact or to highlight another, but even to change the narrative of the events he told, i.e. to sometimes say how things should have happened rather than how they had actually happened, even if by accident. The gap between "what should have been" and "what actually happened" was intended to disappear within the historical narrative. This was necessary all the more because a historian never took up writing simply as a pastime, but because he or his client was aware that it was necessary, in a given place and on a given date, in given circumstances, to draw a mirror of the past before the eyes of his contemporaries that would convince them to act in the right way. The present and the future were in fact in natural continuity with the past. The memory of the past and present was therefore not constituted for itself; its meaning was obligatory for those of the future; it had to be an instrument of action and intervention on the present and the future; its configuration depended on the fulfilment of the expectations assigned to them.

The instrumentalization of the memory of the past, or rather, the use of history for higher purposes, was therefore a constant in the writing of history throughout the Middle Ages and led to the creation of partisan and conflicting memories. Nithard, for example, a first cousin and a determined supporter of Charles the Bald, already in his *Historia* written in 841 referred to the order given to him by Charles the Bald to preserve the memory of the struggle against Lothar: "As you know perfectly well, my Lord, you and your brothers have already suffered persecution from your brother for almost two years, although it is by no means deserved, before we entered Châlons-sur-Marne you ordered me to commit to memory with a pen the events that have occurred in your time" (*Nithard, Historiarum Libri*, IV, 2). The confrontation of the brothers, Lothair, Louis, and Charles who succeeded their father Louis the Pious, was not just any war, it was a persecution by Lothair against Charles and it was imperative to recount it, to establish his memory not as that of a normal and ordinary war but as an unjust persecution by the bad against the good. It seems all too obvious that this recollection of the event was that of Charles the Bald's supporters, or even Nithard himself, and not that of their opponents; a memory that was therefore manipulated and recomposed.

Hence, it must be recognized that drawing on the openly claimed functions—to delight, educate and build, commemorate and remember—and through the true and exemplary historical narrative as the founder of an intangible and perpetual memory of the past, the use of history and the instrumentalization of the memory of the past in the service of political goals were inevitably intertwined. Due to the impossibility of applying the inferences of this new understanding on the entire history of medieval historiography and the immense effort made by medieval historians to constitute a memory of the past, I would like to sketch the overall evolution and to provide with the help of a few selected examples an illustration of some of the main forms of the instrumentalization of the memory of the past that we encounter during the Middle Ages, even at the risk of being somewhat schematic.

In the first important period up to the twelfth-thirteenth century, history had been written almost exclusively by bishops, canons, and especially monks in cathedrals, collegiates, and monasteries; the construction of a historical memory of the past is thus predominantly in the service of these institutions, their members, their patrons, and protectors whose role, function, and merits were influenced by their service in light of the Church's march toward eternal salvation. Established by the universal histories such as the Chronicle and Ecclesiastical History of Eusebius of Caesarea and the *Historia adversus paganos* of Orose, this constituted the landmark of these chronicles and histories. This is not to say that only chronicles and universal histories were written during this period, but the authors who wrote history felt, even when dealing with only one particular topic, that they contributed to situating the agents and events of contemporary history within a universal historical memory, thus giving purpose to their respective topic and period of time. The establishment of the Germanic peoples within the Roman Empire and the constitution of new kingdoms led to the emergence of different chronicles and histories which, in various different ways, sought to integrate the history of these peoples within the framework of the universal history provided by Eusebius of Caesarea and Orose. We can draw on the example of the *Historiae* of Gregory of Tours and the ecclesiastical history of the English people of the Venerable Bede.

Bishop Gregory of Tours, from a Gallo-Roman senatorial family of many previous bishops, was convinced that his function as bishop, his ancestors, and the fact that he was the successor of St. Martin of Tours, the apostle of Gaul, made him the authoritative interpreter of God's will and his purposes for men through the signs they address to men and which only the men of God, i.e. the bishops, comparable to the prophets of the Old Testament, knew how to decipher (Heinzelmann 1994). It was therefore important that those who ruled Gaul in the second half of the sixth century, the Frankish kings and the aristocracy, surrounded themselves with bishops and followed their advice. Unfortunately, this was not always the case, especially with the king of Neustria, Chilperic I (d. 584), a kind of new Herod or Nero who obstinately sought to thwart the will of God as it was expressed by the bishops. Gregory therefore undertook to write his *Historiae*, a universal history from creation to the end of the world, and to reveal, just like Eusebius of Caesarea and Orose as his role models, the order of the world by God according to the methods of the exegesis of the four senses of Bible scripture that made it possible to establish this history: Gregory set himself the task to create memory, *memorare*.

His Ten Books of Histories (written between 573 and 593) are therefore not a detailed account of historical facts, but a reconstruction of the role they played in the plan of God, although this might not be apparent to naïve readers: the march of God's people, the Church as a community of saints, toward the end of the world and the coming of the Kingdom of God, a march sometimes favored, sometimes hindered by those, kings, who govern Gaul and who fulfil their mission well or badly according to whether or not they let themselves be guided by the bishops. The organization of the books devoted to contemporary history shows how Gregory adjusts his account of history to this purpose: Books V and VI focus on the action of the evil king par excellence, Chilperic; Books VII to IX answer to them by concentrating on the "good king," Guntram. Book X announces the Last Judgment. The chronology is furthermore not the only apparent guiding thread of Gregory's story, rather, it is the theme of the march of the Church of the chosen ones and the struggle of good and evil that is the guiding principle of his story. The episodes that provide the material for the different books are both selected and told according to their deeper meaning.

The understanding of the meaning of these episodes is ensured by a typological approach that recognizes in the events of the present the replications of events of sacred history told in the Bicle: a son of a king (Chramn, son of Clotaire I) rebels against his father and perishes; he is a second Absalon, Solomon's unfaithful son; the subjects of the good king Guntram suffer because they do not have a Christian way of life, it is a repetition of the sufferings of the subjects of the good king of Israel, Ezechias. God's interventions in history—as described by Gregory of Tours—support the accuracy of his interpretation of history; they reveal the fundamentally evil nature of a mode of royal government such as that of Chilperic, who would like to exclude bishops from the affairs of the kingdom; they do, however, demonstrate the accuracy of that of the King of Burgundy Guntram who involves bishops in the government of the state.

Gregory of Tours addresses the kings of the Franks to tell them how they should behave and his brotherly bishops to tell them what their role is, and he warns them by instrumentalizing the memory of the past: in the past God has punished and he will punish in the present and the future those who do not respect his laws and commandments. He particularly punishes those who do not show their respect for Saint Martin and his church in Tours.

A few decades later, the Anglo-Saxon monk Bede, known as the Venerable (d. 735), wrote his history at the monastery of Wearmouth-Jarrow in Northumbria in a similar way—the decoding of history is an exegetical work—but from a very different perspective than Gregory's because he felt the strong feeling of belonging to the Anglo-Saxon people. He is the author of important exegetical treatises but also of several historiographical works in which he deciphers and interprets the history of the world as well as providing the hidden meaning behind the biblical text. Bede wrote two chronicles, the *Chronica minora* and their amplified version, *De ratione temporum* ("About the calculation of time") or *Chronica maiora*, in which, after demonstrating how the lunar calendar can be established and the date of Easter calculated, he retold the central milestones of universal history since the creation of the world. But Bede, like Eusebius of Caesarea, whose model he uses, did not only establish the chronology of universal history; in a complementary way, he wrote a *Historia ecclesiastica gentis Anglorum* in five books. In applying the Eusebian principle to the history of the church and to the Anglo-Saxon peoples, he puts forth his conviction that human history is not arbitrary but obeys a plan of divine providence that sought the integration of the Anglo-Saxon people into the church of the chosen.

His ecclesiastical history (Bede, *Historia ecclesiastica gentis Anglorum*) is clearly presented as a memorial undertaking; remembering as the essential task of the historian. He reports in the preface to the book that he drew from the materials transmitted to him by his informants which were "worthy of memory" (*quae memoria digna uidebantur*) and he urges his readers to pray for the salvation of those who only compiled events "which I had thought were worthy of memory and pleasant to the people" (*quae memoratu digna atque incolis grata credideram*). Behind the apparent modesty of the subject, Bede presents himself as the one who knew how to give meaning to the events of history whose memory it was necessary to preserve, to commit them to an ordered memory by making them appear as the implementation of designs of divine providence, i.e. the conversion of the Angles and Saxon peoples. Even though the Bretons tried to prevent them from converting to true faith, divine providence, never intending to abandon its people, took on the task of implementing this conversion.

However, this memory of the conversion of the Anglo-Saxon people to the Christian faith he established for eternity is deliberately selective: the memory of the bad kings does not deserve to be preserved and they are legitimately removed from it: "from the unanimous consensus of all, it has been established that the name and memory of the apostates should be totally erased from the catalogue of Christian kings, and that no year should be used for the memory of their reign" (*Historia ecclesiastica gentis Anglorum*, ed. Lapidge and Monat III, 9). Telling the story of Bishop Aidan's life, he writes that he will briefly tell without further comment what was not to his credit but that he committed in detail to memory what was to his praise and would serve to enlighten his readers, in accordance with the historian's mission: "as a true historian, I have simply reported the facts that have been accomplished through him or by him by praising those worthy of praise among his actions, and by commemorating those that serve the usefulness of the readers" (*Historia ecclesiastica gentis Anglorum*, III, 17), "We thought it wise to commit to memory" (*Historia ecclesiastica gentis Anglorum*, IV, 14). Bede introduces the account of an event to which he had a true relationship and which appeared of notable importance. Again when reporting on a battle, he declares that he will retell a particular episode because it will be beneficial to the salvation of many: "it happens that a memorable event has been accomplished there, which consider worthy of not being ignored because it will, if reported on, be beneficial to the salvation of many" (*Historia ecclesiastica gentis Anglorum*, IV, 22).

Since the beginning of the Middle Ages saw the establishment of the Germanic peoples in the Roman Empire, it was important to establish for the benefit of contemporaries and posterity a memory that obliges and highlights the straight path God had traced for contemporaries, the one that the bishops and monks were responsible of showing. This work of inserting a specific memory of the events, episodes, and actors of contemporary history into the course of universal history has been pursued in the following centuries by many authors, bishops, canons, and monks; it is inseparably linked to an instrumentalization of history in the service of a vision and political goals, whether they are specific to the authors, or those of the institution to which they are attached, or those of the patrons of the institution and/or the sponsors of their stories. It is especially moments of crisis that have been conducive to the engagement of historians when it appeared that offering a mirror of the past and present was likely to favor in the present and the future a specific policy and their respective promoters.

A good example for this is the *Chronica* of Sigebert de Gembloux (d. 1112). While the Gregorian movement of church reform deeply shook the world order and provoked a gigantic confrontation between the supporters of the old world order and those of a new order, reshaping the memory of the past and placing the course of events of the present in the background of this memory was more than ever a decisive issue because it made it possible to legitimize the politics that one supported or advocated in the present by showing that it was part of the God's plan since the origin of the world.

Sigebert, a monk in Gembloux close to Liege, was a determined supporter of the Empire, which he considered to be the framework established by divine providence for the realization, guided by the emperors and assisted by the Pope and the bishops on the one hand, of the great laity on the other, of the march of women and men towards the end of the world, the return of Christ and the arrival of the heavenly city. In his chronicle he aimed at showing that this lesson, which was at the heart of the fate and troubles of the present, was legitimized by the entire history of the past since the creation of the world. The chronology of universal history, in the form of a synchronic history of all the empires and kingdoms of universal history since Nineus established by Eusebius of Caesarea in his *Chronicon*, provided him with the framework that he only had to repeat and follow. He powerfully revealed and described how, throughout the course of history, the *regnum* or *imperium Romanorum* constituted the fourth and last universal empire as announced by the prophecy of Daniel, which saw the advent of peace and the conversion of all to the true faith before the return of Christ and the end of the world (Chazan 1999).

At the same time, the crusaders had taken Jerusalem; the memory of such a resounding event, which seemed to be an important milestone in the history of the Church of the chosen ones towards the advent of the City of God, had to be preserved (Lobrichon 1998; Schuster 2000). Several authors claimed to be eye-witnesses in order to highlight its eschatological significance and to ensure its memory: "Now, therefore, the pen must be used so that the story of those who have taken the path to Jerusalem what has happened to them and how their business and labor, with God's help, have shone brightly and flourished becomes known soberly and clearly to those who ignore these events. This is what I, Fulcher of Chartres, as I saw with my own eyes when walking with the other pilgrims, have diligently and carefully gathered together to make it a memory for the men of the future" (*Recueil des Historiens des croisades, Historiens occidentaux*, III, 327) wrote for example Fulcher of Chartres, first a member of the entourage of Etienne de Blois before becoming a chaplain of Baldwin of Boulogne, in his account written before his death, probably in 1112.

For a long time, at least until the twelfth century, establishing the memory of a people or a man made it necessary to situate oneself within the history of the world from its origin to its end, constituting the horizon for all the adventures that affected the march of humanity towards the arrival of the heavenly city. Gradually, however, this horizon faded into background even if, retrospectively not for a long time. The particular histories of a kingdom, a royal or princely lineage, a war, an event, or a man were developing increasingly independently somewhat freeing themselves from the shackles of universal history; they open up to a diversity of constructions and memory strategies developed by those who want history to be used to demonstrate the accuracy and truth of the ethical, moral, or political positions they defend.

A striking example is that of the historians, increasing in numbers from the twelfth–thirteenth centuries, who want to provide a memory for a kingdom and to the dynasty that govern it in order to exalt its prestige and power. Their histories, which can be called territorial or even "national," retrace the history of a country whose foundation is placed in a past as old and prestigious as it is steeped in legends. They were developed along the guiding principle provided by the uninterrupted succession of kings who, since time immemorial, have followed each other as the heads of a country.

The sources and methods of formation of these territorial and/or national histories are varied. They often relied on an ancient account (*origo gentis*) of the people whose heirs were the inhabitants of the country. For others, the necropolises of the dynasties at the head of the country, through which the *memoria* of the deceased buried in the monastery was ensured and by which their genealogical traditions were preserved, were the first source of their elaboration. Providing the materials and already developing a dynastic and territorial protohistory, they were able to outline the transformation of the uninterrupted succession of kings and princes who ruled the kingdom into a vast genealogy of the members of a "house" chosen by providence to rule the respective kingdom and its inhabitants.

We can thus see how an ancient memory was created and written to show how a new people situated itself in God's plan as well as a lineage and dynastic memory. It was created in a monastery at the service of both its interests and that of its patrons and synthesized and rewritten to become both the memory of a kingdom and a people, and the memory of a princely house and the achievements of its members, all in the service of the transformation of this country into a powerful and prestigious kingdom.

This process can be illustrated with two examples, those of the formation of a national history in France and Bavaria during the last centuries of the Middle Ages. In the French kingdom, the first laboratory for the creation of a national memory was the monastery of Saint-Denis, the great royal necropolis north of Paris, where the proximity to royalty made it mandatory to preserve the memory of the kings of France. This historiographical work carried out in Saint-Denis began with abbot Adam (predecessor of Suger) at the beginning of the twelfth century, in response to the serious alert that the monastery experienced when King Philip I was buried in 1108 in Fleury-sur-Loire and not in Saint-Denis. Thus, in 1108, abbot Adam initiated a solemn commemoration of Dagobert, the legendary founder of the abbey, on January 19, who was considered the first king to have been buried in the monastery. Saint-Denis first acquired the *Historia Francorum* of Aimoin of Fleury (d. after 1008), written at the turn of the tenth to the eleventh century, which reported the glorious history of the Frankish people becoming French until 654. In the first half of the twelfth century and due to the impetus of his abbot Suger, the monastery undertook to write the history of the kings of France itself, taking up and continuing the history of Aimoin, which had become the foundation of French national history, and rewriting the *vita* of the rulers who succeeded the throne from father to son. At the same time, the monastery of Saint-Germain-des-Prés, which could also claim to be an ancient necropolis of the kings of France in the person of several Merovingian kings, also produced a number of historical works on the kings of France.

At the beginning of the 1270s, it was then possible for the monk Primat of Saint-Denis (d. after 1277), following the order of his abbot Mathieu de Vendôme, to take up and adapt all these materials and stories in French to write the *Roman des Rois*. As Bernard Guenée recently showed by rigorously analyzing the lexical system implemented by Primat, the *Roman des Rois* is much more than a mere translation of the Latin compilations produced at Saint-Germain-des-Prés and Saint-Denis into French, it expresses Primat's own interpretation of the past of France and its kings. Regarding the past of the kingdom of France, Primat describes that what he uses to develop the model to follow in the present. Writing history means acting on the present and the future. Having been continued and reworked, reoriented in other directions, the "Novel of the Kings" became known in the centuries of the "Great chronicles of France" (i.e. the fourteenth and fifteenth century) and became the first French national chronicle, the first history of the kings of Francia and France. It had established itself above all as the written memory of France, which was itself an important element of the kingdom's cohesion and power. At the end of the fifteenth century, Louis XI wrote the following in the *Rosier des guerres*: "It seems that in order to lead and confirm this present *Rosier*, it is quite appropriate to remember things that have passed since the name of France began to flourish" (Krynen 1993: 487).

Taking the example of Bavaria Hermann, abbot of Niederaltaich, was the one who, in the third quarter of the thirteenth century, built Bavaria's first memory in universal history, which merged with the history of the Roman Empire with thenceforth German sovereigns as rulers (Moeglin 2012). In Hermann's view, the legitimate world order remains the Roman empire governed by Catholic emperors with undeniable and unchallenged authority. Bavaria, the *ducatus Noricorum*, is nevertheless an intangible political entity within the "kingdom of the Germans" (*regnum Teutonicorum*) itself being the heart of the Empire. While Hermann witnessed the order of the world deeply shaken by the emperor's unholy conflict with the popes and the unsettling of disorder everywhere, he drew a mirror of a history in which contemporaries could see the legitimate order of the world to be restored. It is in this context that he implements a history of the Duchy of Bavaria into the history of the Roman Empire as written by Frutolf from Michelsberg at the beginning of the twelfth century, thus creating a historical memory of Bavaria. Frutolf had taken up the contemporary chronicle of Sigebert of Gembloux from Liège, who in turn had relied on the chronicle of Eusebius-Jerome, the guiding principle of *contemporalitas regnorum* in the course of universal history that was graphically translated into paintings. With the Christians began the sixth age, which was the age of the Roman Empire, the last universal empire. Certainly, the Germanic peoples emerged as a new element in history, but they did not found a new empire or even a new kingdom, but remained an integral part of the Roman Empire. After the fall of the Western Roman Empire, the Eastern rulers continued the list of rulers from Augustus until they were replaced by Charlemagne as the seventy-third emperor of the Roman Empire. If it is important to present the *origo* of the German peoples, even if they have not founded a new kingdom, it is because they are, the Franks and the Saxons, the ones for whose benefit the transmission of the Empire was intended.

It is this historiographical scheme that constitutes the backbone of Hermann's annals; originally ending in 1106, he first extended it to 1146 with a copy of the chronicle of Otto of Freising, then with extracts from *Pantheon* by Godefroy of Viterbo. By taking up historiographical traditions that had previously appeared in other monasteries, he reconstructed the history of Bavaria since Duke Theodo and his people returned to Bavaria in 508 and carefully established the succession of these Dukes of Bavaria from Theodo I to the contemporary Dukes of Hermann, Louis of Upper-Bavaria and Henry of Lower-Bavaria. This construction of a historical memory legitimized Hermann's request by his monastery to restore the legitimate order of the world—a powerful Duchy of Bavaria within an empire of undisputed legitimacy and authority.

Half a century later, a canon of the collegiate church of St. Mang in Regensburg, Andreas of Regensburg, resumed the work of building a historical memory for the inhabitants of Bavaria. In his chronicle of the princes of Bavaria written in the 1420s, first in Latin and then translated into German by Andreas himself, he relies on the accounts, few of them true, of the Bavarian history written in the twelfth and thirteenth century and links it—being his main innovation—to the thirteenth century drafts of the dynastic memory of the Dukes of Bavaria Wittelsbach, that had been masterfully taken up and reworked, probably at the end of the fourteenth century, at the monastery, the ducal necropolis in Scheyern. This dynastic memory showed that the Wittelsbachs directly descended from the great emperor Charlemagne and it legitimized the development of a notion of *reditus* of the Duchy of Bavaria to the Charlemagne ancestry with the inauguration of Otto I of Wittelsbach in 1180.

The guiding principle of the chronicle of the Bavarian princes of Andreas of Regensburg is provided by the reconstruction of the uninterrupted succession of the dukes of Bavaria since the first of them, the Armenian Bavarian. From Charlemagne's time onwards, this genealogy tended to merge with the Wittelsbach genealogy. The chronicle of the Bavarian princes of Andreas of Regensburg was widely distributed through manuscripts. In the last quarter of the fifteenth century, various authors, above all Hans Ebran von Wildenberg, Ulrich Fuetrer, and Veit Arnpeck, used and reworked it to form great histories of Bavaria and its princes. They highlight the indissoluble link between a princely lineage, a country and its inhabitants.

Yet Andreas of Regensburg knew that Bavaria was a duchy located within the Holy Roman Empire, the fourth and last universal empire, and he had previously written in a traditional form the history of this Empire since the end of the thirteenth century as already put forward in the *Chronicon* of Martin of Troppau, a chronicle of the popes and emperors. At the origin of Andreas' work lies in fact the desire to build a memory of the events he attended—*memorie digna litteris sunt mandanda*, he wrote several times—and for him it was primarily the Hussite shock and its terrible repercussions in Germany, whose events he carefully noted from his point of observation, namely his collegiate church and the city of Regensburg. For him, the intended historical memory for his contemporaries and especially for posterity only made sense when placed in the whole duration and depth of a history, that of the Holy Roman Empire and that of the Duchy of Bavaria within this Roman Empire.

In this work of constructing a memory, the historian's vision of the present had a decisive role; the construction of a historical memory was an instrument of action on the behavior of men of the present and the future. As we have seen, this memory could reach from the origin of the world to the most contemporary present. Andreas of Regensburg is thus an excellent example of medieval historians who were aware that the work of building a historical memory led to placing themselves in a chain: to take up, that is, to perform a work of compiling histories that others had written before them which then constituted the memory of the past, and to extend it with the account of the time they had lived, before giving way to other historians who would in turn take their place in this chain tending towards the construction of a memory of the past.

However, other historians were so fascinated by the novelty and importance of the events they had experienced that they despised to integrate their work of building a historical memory within the depths of the past; this is the case for Froissart, the first chronicler and in a way inventor, yet without the name of course, of the Hundred Years' War which had begun when he was just born, probably in 1337.

Drawing his initial inspiration from the chronicles of the Liège canon Jean Le Bel, Froissart was the first to present the war of the kings of France and England as a long-lasting confrontation between two kings, two countries, and two peoples. The beginning is precisely dated by Froissart with the end remaining uncertain at the time.

This war also had a meaning and a there was a lot at stake. In the prologues to the various essays in Book I, Froissart takes up and extends the idea, already developed by Chrétien de Troyes at the end of the twelfth century, of the translation of chivalry and knowledge from east to west, from Athens to Rome and Paris. The question was whether the knighthood, "Prouesse," would continue its journey westwards and settle permanently in England or return to France? This is the challenge, according to Froissart, of the fierce struggle waged by English and French kings and knights, of which Froissart intends to give his readers a true and objective account without favoring either party.

To write this true story, Froissart assures his readers, that he only writes and places into lasting memory what he has seen himself or heard from reliable witnesses. He willingly reports on the investigations he carried out with agents from both sides in the conflict so that his account accurately reflects the truth of the facts. He certainly knew and visited many of the important agents of the war, but the confrontation of his account with the other chronicles of the time and especially the comparison of the different essays of Froissart's four books reveals a historian in fact far removed from the model of the "great reporter" with whom he has often been compared. In Froissart's case, the concern for the coherence of the story takes precedence over the truth of the story and even leads to a reconstruction of historical reality and establishes a perfect story far removed from the reality of events. Thus, Froissart was the first to assign a beginning to the wars of France and England: the challenge of the French throne by Edward III reportedly transmitted to Philip VI in Paris by Bishop of Lincoln and which was immediately followed by the launching of military operations by Walter Manny. This challenge by the Bishop of Lincoln has become part of France's historical memory. However, the Bishop of Lincoln had never actually been to Paris and Froissart dates this so-called challenge which he variably changes within the different essays of his Book I. The most widely circulated edition places it in 1339, whereas another edition dates it to 1337.

The chronicles therefore offer a carefully composed account of the war in which truth and falsehood are inextricably intertwined, but never compromising on its coherence (Moeglin 2006; Croenen 2018). As a brilliant author and composer of a colorful narrative, Froissart was able to convey what is largely a historical fiction of the course of history; he provided a narrative of the Hundred Years' War subsequent historians considered to be based on the truth.

Regarding the authors of "memoirs," they write as private persons of generally high social rank who want to share with a selected audience the experience they have acquired during their careers. In a way, the seneschal Jean de Joinville, a friend of St. Louis, is an early example of this with his Life of St. Louis written at the beginning of the fourteenth century. Philippe de Commines is the most famous example of the end of the fifteenth century: after a long career as an influential political advisor and ambassador, particularly to Italy where he had an important network of contacts, he retold his experiences, combining the writing of the memory of an era and the lessons that posterity can learn from it. The *Commentaries* of Pope Pius II (d. 1464) are another fine example of one of the great agents of the era and of the merged desire to remember and learn from lived experience.

CONCLUSION

The author of the *Rosier des guerres*, who is known to have composed his work almost following a dictation by King Louis XI, wrote around 1460: "the good deeds... last only as long as those who see them live, but what is written for the common good is forgivable" (Krynen 1992: 405). Creating a written, stable, and perpetual memory of past and present time had been the work to which all historians throughout the Middle Ages had devoted themselves by forming a long chain in which each one passed something on to his successor when death forced him to.

The work of historians was in fact guided by their own precise ideas and conceptions, those of the institution(s) to which they belonged, or those of their sponsors. The written constitution of historians' intangible and perpetual memory was obviously only a myth that could not have been abandoned, however, without undermining the legitimacy of the work of chroniclers and historians. The present inevitably changed the memory of the past and following the convenience offered by referring to a memory of time that supposedly passes engraved for eternity, it was in fact the main issues of the chronicler's own time that guided his pen and led him to seek to impose his memory of the past and the present, without being able to prevent others, yet again, from recovering and diverting his work in an attempt to impose on posterity "their" memory of the past and the present.

However, the question arises that when talking about the memorial work of medieval chroniclers and historians it might be more suitable to talk about a "prevented," "manipulated," or "forced" memory in order to take up Paul Ricoeur's notion of misguided memories. Without totally rejecting the legitimacy of this question, the answer might be too simplifying because it ignores the fact that the memory of the past, a decisive source of prestige, legitimacy, and authority, was a fundamental issue in ancient societies and thus cannot be reduced to the point of making it a simple copy of the historical reality as it apparently unfolded. This is what underlies and in a certain way justifies the strategies of forgetting, selective recollection and rewriting of the event, of mixing fiction and reality that characterize memory or rather the memories created by medieval historians; and it is also what makes it interesting for readers and current historians.[3]

CHAPTER TWO

Time and Space

JOEL T. ROSENTHAL

While memory is a basic element of human consciousness, "social memory" is a construct, a specific form or application of the larger concept (Halbwachs 1952). In this essay "social memory" will be used to apply to various kinds of remembrances and recollections that were spoken in a social context or dictated into a written version. On some occasions when the memories were offered by more than one speaker, they cross a line and can be thought of as "collective memory," though their link between the speakers' past and present is much the same. Read together they form what Peter Burke, in the volume on Cultural History of Memory in Early Modern Times calls a "memory community."

As we use the term social memory, we refer to recollections offered in a place, and at a time, and in social setting, when others of the speaker's world could share that memory, or at least know that it was being offered. If the memory was an individualized one—not shared by others in a social setting or context—it at least had to be socially credible; acceptable as reasonable (if not "true") by those who shared in hearing or reading it. The memory was framed or limited by the social setting of the person who offered it—some fragment of the past, whether it was that individual's own past now being enunciated and shared or some impersonal past (such as the memory of a royal death). To be social memory it had to be bounded by time, by life experience, and usually by comparable memories of one's peers. But within these limits social memory can be offered as a window into experiences and recollections of experiences being enunciated by people unlikely to leave any other footprints in the historical record.

The concept of memory and/or recollection was an issue of great interest to medieval thinkers (Carruthers 1990; Herrmann and Chaffin 1988). As was so often the case, they took and then expanded the legacy of classical thinkers, beginning with Plato, going on to Aristotle, and then into medieval Christian thinking—all well covered by modern scholarship (Carruthers and Ziolkowski 2002). Classical education linked training in memory with training in rhetoric and this made Cicero a figure in the links between the ancients and medieval contributors to the discussion. In the Middle Ages some of the writings on memory and recollection developed numerous visual schemes, with diagrams and charts, to illustrate how memory (and the brain) worked (Carruthers and Ziolkowski 2002).

Beyond medieval theories about memory there is the important issue of the transition from a world heavily reliant on orality to one basing its records—and therefore the preservation of memories—on the written text. This was a great change in culture and mnemonics and it is one we can track through the course of the high and later Middle Ages (Clanchy 2013; Stock 1985; Connerton 1989).

PROOFS OF AGE

We turn now to what we offer as social memory in action. The memories we call up were offered as testimonies at Proof of Age proceedings in late medieval England. A Proof of Age proceeding is what its name indicates: memories elicited at a hearing to "prove" that an heir was of age because jurors remembered an event from the time of his or her birth and/or baptism. The editions of the Proofs of Age are to be found in volumes of *Inquisitions Post Mortem* that have been published since 1970, running from the reign of Richard II (1377–99) through the middle years of Henry VI (the 1440s). References in the text are to volumes and item numbers (not to pages). The convention in editing the Proofs of Age is to translate the vital memory passage but to omit the standardized language of inquisition.

When the heir claimed to be of legal age (twenty-one for men, fourteen for married women, sixteen for unmarried women) a royal official, the escheator, was instructed to convene a jury of twelve free men of the village who would offer memories regarding why/how they remembered the time of the birth or baptism. These social memories, offered under oath and in the company of one's peers, are a link between that dramatic events (and date) of some years ago and the now of the Proof—the past being folded into the present. They are a dip into what has been referred to as a sharing of narratives (Rosenthal 2018).

There are many Proofs of Age from the late fourteenth and fifteenth centuries. Between 1377 and 1447 we have 134 such proceedings, with an almost full quota of social memories (minus a few damaged documents). They give us a view of what ordinary people thought memorable; no other source draws on so many social memories of so many men of the village. These are mostly voices and memories that would be otherwise unheard. We can organize the multitude of memories into three basic groups. The largest is those memories that center around that critical baptism (or the birth). These, as we shall see, touch on the many aspects of the event, running from fetching the midwife when needed to her churching, some weeks later. For ease of organization, the many variations on these memories can be lumped together as baptism-related or baptism-centered, focused on the heir more than on the juror himself. The second group focuses on the juror himself: a birth or marriage or death in his family, or some secular transaction. Lastly, there are memories of external events, things that happened to others but which remained vivid and were offered by the juror. Recalling the sacking of the town or the hanging of a thief are good examples.

One feature of all these memories is that they are all men's memories (Harris-Stoertz 2015). No women were ever called before the escheator, though many of the men's memories actually rested something learned from a woman. His wife might have told him of the baby's birth, or he saw the midwife carrying the baby to church. But regardless, it was never her memory; social memory was men's memory. To redress this imbalance toward the end of this essay we turn to the will of a wealthy fifteenth century widow—discussing her testamentary clauses and bequests as a form of social memory now as enunciated by a woman.

Though a Proof of Age proceeding was a pro forma affair by the later Middle Ages, it was official business. As such, the escheator would begin by putting the basic question to each juror, being "asked how he remembers this after so long a lapse of time" (16/1053). The twelve men have been "questioned and separately examined [. . .] as to how they know this [the heir's age, and], they all claim to have seen the parson write the day of

Philip's birth in a church Bible" (22/530). And regardless of the memory being offered, the responses were always accepted as sufficient for the purpose, as "proof" that the heir was of age. Sometimes it was the collective social memory of the villagers, summed up by the twelve men selected to speak for all. The jurors affirmed that "moreover, her age is well known by common report [. . .] and he [the juror] has seen and heard it reckoned up in the parish [. . .] by known persons who are her kinsfolk and friends" (15/656). The village might speak as one, and after the first juror had offered his recollection sometimes "all the other jurors believe and know it by testimony of their fellow jurors and of very many other trustworthy persons [. . .] who were present at the time" of the baptism (15/658). The collective nature of their common social memory might be made explicit: "the jurors collectively say that John was 21 [. . .] and individually they give the following reasons for being sure" (17/275). Their collective social memory summed the common wisdom of the community, had they been asked, and we have a Proof stating that "the jurors had other notable evidence if it were necessary to produce it" (19/901) (Bedell 1999; Holford 2008).

The escheator needed twelve memories from his twelve jurors. These might be offered one by one; twelve memories from twelve men. In one jury, the men stated their ages as 50, 49, 60, 50, 47, 60, 48, 49, 50, 47, 45, and 60 at the time of the Proof, and their memories related to having fetched the god-mother, a death, a birth, and other such ordinary matters (22/230). Common or joint memories were frequently offered—testifying to a common social setting or experience and resulting in a common memory. It might be tersely expressed: "they all say that they were in the church at the time of the baptism and saw William raised from the font" (25/336). But all twelve in unison was a bit unusual; mostly the number who bonded for a common memory was six or fewer, though we can offer one collection of ten (of the twelve) who had "congregated in the church to hear a sermon by master Robert Thomas, doctor of theology, and they saw the chaplain write the date and year in the church's missal" (24/560). In the jury that had talked of "other notable evidence," there were four groups of memories (19/901). In one jury, the men had been examined separately and then split into two even groups; six recalled having seen the baby lifted from the font and the other six had congregated a week later for a wedding and learned what had happened the previous week (17/148). In the sort of common activity that catches the pace of village life, a common memory from five men saying that one had been "enfeoffed by charter of a carucate of land" and the others had been with him at the time (15/655).

When a juror was called to step forward, he began by stating his name and age. Though a man's age per se may not seem to be part of his social memory, that he always began by stating it contributes to the idea of serious record keeping and to the power of memory. That these men could state their age (with some presumed measure of accuracy) reinforces the idea that they held on to events of the past and the passing of the years in a regular fashion. Social memory here, too, as each juror gave his age in the presence of fellow villagers who had presumably known him through life. A birth cohort meant a group of men (and women) with similar life experiences at roughly the same stages of life: confirmation and first communion, marriage, parenthood, going off to war, and the like.

The heir's age might be recorded in a service book at the baptism, as we shall see, but for the jurors, no indication of how their own years had been recorded and tallied. Most jurors stated an age that placed them somewhere in middle age, at least by the gauge of modern longevity, while the youngest jurors would have had to be of at least legal age at the time of the baptism some twenty-one years ago. A few men were quite old and this must have been a credible claim. There is no indication of why our twelve jurors were singled out for jury duty but it seems unlikely, given the spread of their ages, that age in either direction was a factor. Most juries were composed of a mix regarding jurors' ages, though some were tightly bonded in this regard. In a jury in 1428 the jurors claimed to be 80, 70, 71, 75, 84, 77, 72, 70, 73, 77, 76, and 76 (23/141), and in one in Somerset they said they are 80, 87, 63, 60, 60, 59, 81, 69, and 80, and then three men, stating to be 61, 61, and 73, offered a common memory (20/272).

A few more general considerations. While a Proof was a solemn affair, and the results were important for the village, both the sacramental and the celebratory aspects of the baptism were likely to remain well fixed in village memory. The baptism and all that surrounded it was remembered as a time of general rejoicing, for much eating and drinking, for decorating the church, for noting the arrival of celebrities, for rewarding those who ran errands, etc. No wonder these memorable events still stood out, over the years, amidst the ebb and flow of daily life; they did not happen often (McGlynne 2009).

One sign of the way memories went back to the festivities is the occasional juror pegging his recollection on celebrity-spotting. Given that the heirs were all from families of note, it is hardly surprising that we hear of men and women of exalted status who had been present at the baptism, often having come to play a role and often to give out gifts of note to babe (and mother). One juror remembered the presence of Elizabeth Despenser as the godmother, along with the bishop of Worcester and the abbots of Evesham and of Pershore, plus John Beauchamp of Holt of the Beauchamp clan. Beauchamp had come "carrying two clothes of gold with the arms of King Richard" (18/885). In a jury in Yorkshire in 1433, one juror remembered Lady Margery Fitzhugh as a godmother, plus the "kin and friends of the late Lady Fitzhugh," along with Lord Fitzhugh and William Montagu (24/129). This had been the baptism of the Darcy heiress—and she being a Fitzhugh granddaughter—and so the presence of these notables was to be expected. The baptism of the Le Straunge heiress drew the earls of Arundel and of Salisbury (18/944). Jurors with these memories had probably been telling their stories for years.

BIRTHS

The dynamics of memory-selection are what they are; each juror offered whatever he (or his fellows in a common memory) chose out of the vast storehouse of recollection with which everyone lives. In most Proofs some of the memories are usually aligned around a common theme while others go off in other, and individualized, directions. But given the large number of memories under discussion, the genres of memory, the basic themes of recollection, are mostly limited to a few basic categories. When one theme tied together a number of the memories, we wonder if it had been suggested or even rehearsed in advance—a sort of "let's talk about the day when . . ."—or whether it was a case of one juror's memory jogging another's, or whether it really was just coincidence. A memorable happening of twenty-odd years ago was a good hook on which to hang a number of memories, given the nature of village life and culture.

In the "theme Proofs" we might find about half of the memories running along much the same line, the same category of memory. In a Proof from Surrey, five men pick up what we can call the family theme, though the memories vary: a sister's death by drowning, the birth of a daughter, a father's death, a juror's marriage, and a sister's marriage (15/665). Good will for the new mother of the heir might be the theme, as jurors recalled having given her twelve partridges, six pheasants, eight capons "because of her recovery from the birth," and four fat geese to "congratulate her with other neighbours because of her recovery," along with "a barren doe" (26/351). Some of the theme memories were less sanguine, and we have related memories of purchasing a black horse that died, six oxen (one died), twelve worthless cows, twelve pigs (two died), and 100 sheep (two died) (20/267).

As the heir's birth and baptism were the point zero for the memories, it is logical that we have more jurors' memories related to some aspect of the ceremony than to any other event or milestone. In the many chapters of the baptism scenario, the memories cover the wide spectrum of baptism-related activities, running from fetching the midwife to the churching of the mother. From this mosaic of social memory, we can reconstruct the spiritual and the social acts of this "rite de passage" as they are recalled in the collective social memory of the village.

THE MIDWIFE

The theater of birth and baptism opened, as village memory went, with the memories of fetching the midwife (Harris-Stoertz 2015). This was urgent business and being chosen for such an errand meant a degree of importance for the messenger. The last-minute nature of preparations for the birth come across in a memory of a man who had been "in bed with his wife Agnes on the day of the birth when Thomas Taberwell came at dawn to ask her to be midwife to Elizabeth the mother" (19/996). An experienced midwife came prepared: "Isabel Harper was midwife and she brought a comb for Joan as soon as she saw her born because she had a hairy head" (25/522). Nor were the risks only those run by the new mother, as we learn from the juror who told of when he "went to the manor with the mid-wife who was carrying Joan. A great oak [. . .] suddenly fell, a branch hit the mid-wife and she only just escaped with her life" (23/136). But she might also carry the good news: "Joan Glyn, mid-wife to John's mother Elizabeth, came to John Clyvedon's court at Zeals and announced that William Stourton had had that day at dawn a beautiful first-born son for which he praised God" (21/876). And while birthing was women's business the occasional memory hints at the near-presence of a man, as with a Cornwall juror who remembered because he "was at Tremadart when Anne mother of John was in labour and he heard her crying. Before he withdrew, she gave birth and he saw messengers sent to seek the godfathers and godmother" (25/129). Such an experience left a strong memory: "in the night of 12 August 1411 [. . .] [he] heard Margery, then wife of John Sumpter, labor and cry out especially for her child's delivery, and early in the morning of 13 August he knew through Joan, then his wife, that Margery had that night been delivered of an infant afterwards named Christine" (22/829).

BAPTISM

Given a safe birth, fetching those needed for the baptism was next on the agenda, along with seeing that the church was prepared and the paraphernalia needed for the ceremony were at hand. It might be a matter of fetching the godparents, who, as people of consequence, were often remembered by name. We have a Yorkshire juror who had gone "to fetch William Boynton, Christopher's god-father, so he would come to the baptism. He went at the command of Christopher's father" (25/611). In a Devon Proof, one juror had himself been a godfather and another was married to the godmother who gave the baby 40d (i.e. 40 pence) "from Brian's goods that Sunday" (25/524). While being asked to be a godparent was an honor, there were memories of odd problems. One man recalled declining; he had "excused himself for a secret reason which he told him [the father]" (20/269). Another begged off, saying "although he wished to be a godfather he refused because such a spiritual relationship could in the future be an impediment to marriage," such being the wide boundaries of spiritual kinship (23/309). Feelings might run high, as a common memory tells us: "There came Lady Katharine [. . .] proposed to ride to Shute and expecting to be godmother of William. There she met Edward Dygher, a servant of William Bonevile, whom half seriously she reproached for being merry and talkative. He asked where she was going. To which she replied quickly that she was going to Shute to make her nephew a Christian. Grinning he answered in his mother tongue 'Kate, Kate, ther to by myn pate comyst ow to late' because the baptism is performed. Mounting her horse again she rode home very angry not seeing the child's mother again for 6 months. And this all the jurors know" (20/130). Another possible quarrel was quickly resolved, as the juror recounted: he had "heard Anne's god-mothers arguing about Anne's name [. . .] they agreed to name her Anne because she was born on the feast of that saint" (26/352).

It might not only be necessary to send someone to fetch the priest at the last moment, but this might apply to the father as well, as some jurors recount those distant events. Roger Goldham told of being "sent to Holkham to fetch Richard Prat, chaplain, for the baptism. [. . .] Richard baptized William on the same day in the presence of Roger [the juror]" (23/592). Two men recalled when they "were sent that day to the vicar of Brampton to warn him for the baptism and they were present in the church." Perhaps they were to make sure the vicar did as requested (19/663). It was imperative that a cleric with a double role be on the spot, as Walter Tateshale remembered having been sent "to find John Marhan, chaplain, who was to be god-father" (and the performing priest) (18/886).

Men who had carried the good news might well remember being rewarded for their errand. A Somerset juror recalled that "after hearing about the birth of a son to Margaret, wife of John de Sancto Mauro, [he] rode with all haste to the manor of Merssh to tell Ella, lady St. Maur, mother of John father of John, about the birth. She gave him two gold nobles—such things he had never before had—and he afterwards went to Beckington church before the baptism" (23/602). Several jurors told of the news, well received in the village: "he met many men and women coming from the church [and] they told him that Thomas had been baptised, which gave him great joy" (23/724). It was a time for open-handedness and one man recalled when he had "carried two silver platers to the church, holding gold and silver for throwing to bystanders when Richard was baptised" (25/131).

The actual ceremony of baptism can be thought of as a drama with numerous scenes; personnel, main roles and supporting ones, various props, choreography, even scenery. Some jurors had played an active role, though mostly, as we have said, it was really as spectators, though even a small assigned role was worth recounting. Perhaps he had "carried a silver basin and ewer [. . .] to give water to the godfather and godmother for washing their hands after raising Thomas from the font" (23/724). Critical for the social aspects, if not the sacramental: one juror had carried "two pewter pots and clary wine and malmsey and four silver goblets," while another had carried a torch "and held it during the whole of the baptism." Another juror recalled having "carried salt in a silver salt-cellar, and a towel" to the church (23/136). Village memory lived in the recollection of when there had been "12 silver pots [. . .] full of red wine [were] to refresh the god-fathers, the god-mother, and other bystanders" (25/128). As the day of the baptism was a festive one, the parish church had to be dressed accordingly. Some jurors recalled having been sent to see that all was ready: "he found it [the church] adorned with cloths of silk and gold, and the font hung with cloth of gold decorated in red" (23/139). This was obviously an expected standard, and one man had been pleased to report that "the font [was] suitably decorated with ten white, silver cloths," upon his inspection (23/596).

The baptism itself—the priest performing the ceremony and the baby being lifted from the font—was an obvious event to recall, and sometimes it came with an incident or twist out of the ordinary, as well as the occasional mention of the juror's own role. But mostly it was just the memory of having seen the baptism, the juror as spectator. Though one of his fellows had carried a chrism to the font, it was hard to top the juror-cum-spectator who had seen "Henry V raise Henry Grey from the font on the day of the birth and baptism" (25/612). In a Proof of 1442, eight jurors couched their memories in the "I saw" style: the godmothers lifted the baby from the font, the father held a book before the rector, someone else carried bread and "two pots full of sweet wine to give to men and women present at the baptism." In addition, "the holy-water clerk broke the lamp before the high altar and the oil fell on his head" (26/142).

Baptism as spectacle or theater could leave vivid memories. One garrulous juror said he had heard the priest celebrate a "mass of St. Mary at the Holy Trinity altar" and afterwards he and a companion "saw John Mitford [the baby] carried to the font for baptism. Robert Kirkeby asked him whose son this was, to which he [the priest] responded that it was the son of William Mitford. The priest said to him 'deo gracias' because William Mitford has an heir of his name" (22/358). Closer to the action was a juror who recalled meeting "many men and women joyfully coming from the church and among them there was a woman carrying John. He asked them who that child was and they reported that he was the son of William Mitford" (22/358). Though the ceremony was a familiar one, there was always the chance of an odd happening, as with the man who remembered the ritual because he "saw Humphrey urinate in the font at his baptism" (23/311). Another had been in the church, "reading the third morning lesson and [he] heard William cry out at the font," which here was attributed to "the cold water" on the font (18/673 and 24/565). Nor was cold water that serious as compared to the time when "John fell from the chaplain's hands into the font and [. . .] John's godfather then said to the chaplain, 'Prest, prest, fond be thi hened'" (22/358).

Not infrequently, given the centrality of the parish church, the juror had been there for some other purpose but happened to see the baptism; the coincidence of time and place. Two men had gone "with master Ivo la Zouch, chancellor of Cambridge University, to the church, and after the baptism to the house of the friars minor to hear the preaching of holy scripture" (18/310). In a Proof with some joint memories, six men had been at the baptism because they had come for a wedding—"they with many other neighbours were present at the marriage and saw the baptism"—while the other jurors had been in church for the chaplain's first mass, which they attended with "many other friends of his [who] made offerings because of friendship with him and they saw the said heir at the church door to be baptised" (16/78). Other roles, in a sense, for the parish church itself. Two men in Cumberland had been "at the church for a love-day concerning various disputes between John Lambert and Thomas Hudson. They brought them to agreement and saw William carried from the church after baptism" (26/334). Less dramatic, the jurors had been in church on their way to a cock fight, or when going to sell wool and lead, or to meet a kinsman arriving from overseas (22/365).

One kind of memory that stands out is that of seeing the date of birth or baptism set down in writing, usually in a service book and usually by the priest. The act of writing made an impact, long remembered (Clanchy 2013; Stock 1985). When a priest wrote the critical date, it was often at the explicit behest of the father or godfather and the juror's remembrance seems to confirm the special status accorded the written record. From a common memory we learn that the jurors "know his age by inspection of a book of martyrs in the church in which the birth was noted" (18/309), whereas in a Proof from York, the jurors differed slightly from each other. One recalled seeing the chaplain "writing the day and year of the birth in the calendar of Elizabeth's great primer," while for his fellow it was seeing "the day and year put into a psalter" (18/997), for whatever the distinction was worth. In these book-related memories the idea of the durability of a written text seems to have been accepted as a special memory. We have the four jurors who "heard the rector order the clerk of the church to enroll William's name and the time of his birth in the book of the benefactors of the church as a perpetual memorial of the birth" (26/335). This would seem to tie the baby into the culture of village and parish as well as of his own family.

The last act in the protracted drama of birth and baptism relates to the mother's churching, with gifts to her being the usual memory (Cressy 1993: Harris-Stoertz 2015). A juror in Sussex recalled that he was present with his father when the baby was born and then "when the mother was churched [. . .] [he] saw the wife of Richard Mansey present Margaret a cock" (22/359). It was the gift-giving at the time that evoked most of these memories: "that day he gave a pipe of red Gascon wine to John ap Harry, Hugh's grandfather, for the day of churching of Elizabeth, Hugh's mother" (24/267).

THE JURORS' OWN LIVES

While memories centering around birth and baptism are the most pertinent and the most common, given the purpose of a Proof, many jurors fell back on a recollection of something more personal that roughly coincided with the critical time. These memories offer us rare and valuable snippets of autobiography: the birth of a juror's child or a burial in his family, or perhaps a physical assault on the juror. Each man's memory was his own, to cherish and to offer up in segments as he chose. But it was also a social memory— memory that had to be credible in terms of his own life and the context of his society.

LIFE-CYCLE EVENTS

The memories of life-cycle events or milestones for the juror were easy to recall and to align chronologically with the birth of the heir and the collective memory of the village. Births in the juror's family, pegged around the time of the heir's baptism, were not hard to recall. They were usually phrased in a simple fashion: he "knows because Joan his wife gave birth to a son named Nicholas," or he "knows because George his son was born 25 July after the birth of Ralph [the heir]. George is now aged 21 and more" (23/717). On the other hand, the birth memory might be a grim one, still much in his mind: he "knows this because on that day Joan his wife died pregnant of a son, Christopher, which Christopher is aged 22 years and more" (17/955).

Jurors' marriages were less frequently the memory offered. But for some it was the coincidental event that served to link the juror's life with that of the heir: he "married Margery, daughter of John Arte, on the feast of the Circumcision 1418, the day of the birth, in the same church" (25/303). The links of the chain might be spelled out towards the day of the Proof: he "married his wife in that church at that time and they have lived together for 22 years" (19/784). But some men recalled a wrinkle in the fabric: he had been "with Edmund Brit in the church to arrange his marriage to Christine, Edmund's daughter, and as they could not conclude owing to her absence, [they] arranged to meet the next Sunday" (19/997). We get no indication of whether it was worked out to mutual satisfaction.

Death in the family seems to have left more vivid memories than marriage, as it did for two men on a Norfolk jury; "John his brother was buried in the churchyard of Heacham church," and, then in the same vein from a fellow juror who had "buried his kinswoman Alice Frebern, at Fakenham" (23/138). Some jurors chose to tell more: "on that day, for lack of care by her nurse, his daughter named Walkelina suddenly died of thirst in her cradle. For this reason, he came to the church [. . .] to ask the parson to say divine service for his daughter's soul and saw the parson writing while Philip was baptised . . . the memory of this misfortune has never left him" (22/530). More sad tales: "on that day Weburga then his wife gave birth to two boys and died instantly after their birth, on which day he came to the church to have the cross and holy water placed and sprinkled on her body. He went straight to the parson asking that he come to say the divine service for the soul of his late wife." In a memory linking birth and death, a man in Essex knew the dating of the heir's birth "because his wife Margaret, after the death of their daughter Isabel, was Robert de la Doune's nurse, and Isabel died on the feast of the nativity of the Virgin following Robert's birth" (26/156). A family death could well remain a vivid memory: he knew the date "because on that day Reynold his son fell into a well in Miston and died and lay there for three days" (18/672). Stark and memorable was the laconic tale of the man who "knows because Joan his daughter died of plague on the day that Philip was born" (24/562).

CASUALITIES AND VIOLENCE

Memories did not always hinge around the milestones of life and all sorts of other memories were offered and, were we to tally them, there were probably more instances of "bad news" than of "good news" in what the jurors recalled. We have men who spoke of being injured in an accident and men who had been victims of a criminal assault. In a world in which most people engaged in some form of physical labor, accidents—sometimes fatal—were not unfamiliar, and one man remembered the key time and event because he then "was hunting in the forest of Rach on that day and was run down by a deer. He broke his left arm" (25/297). A less common fate, no doubt, than that of the juror who "fell from his horse and broke his right shin on the Thursday following" or his fellow who had been "playing football with associates on the Sunday following and broke his left arm" (25/351). Still a vivid memory, there was the man who had fallen "from a tree that day collecting apples in his father's orchard and had such a fall that he lay in bed for a month" (26/156). What must have been a fatal accident was still the tale one man offered: "his brother was working as a plumber on the said church and fell to the ground and broke his back" (15/297). Recovery might be slow, at best, as in the memory of the man who had been "riding in fog, his horse was startled and stumbled on a stony broad. He fell to the ground and only by the grace of God escaped death. He often suffered from that injury afterwards" (22/530). Misfortune was never far away, as when "a ruinous stable in which he was standing was blown down [. . .] and a beam fell and broke his head almost to the brain. So a fortnight later he came to the leech [. . .] to have his head cured, and saw the said Mary at the door of the church prepared to undergo the sacrament" (15/656).

Being victimized by violence in a criminal assault was also something likely to be well fixed in the memory. One memory, with perhaps a rare touch of humor, was the recollection of having been in church "when William was baptised and money was taken from his [the juror's] purse" (23/718). But others were less fortunate, as was the juror who recalled that "John Forster insulted, assaulted, wounded and badly treated him" (21/674). "Merry England" was not always so merry, as for a Devon juror who remembered the baptism because it coincided with when "John Rake and several strangers ambushed him at Bigbury on that day, in an assault that left him with three maimed fingers in his right hand" (25/296). Or even a toothache: (22/827), "so bad he could not possibly forget the pain," or being mauled by a cat (22/674).

But against these more dramatic and traumatic tales there are the less fraught memories touching business dealings—the give-and-take of daily life by men of some modest standing. The main focal points of these memories were transactions involving land or animals and many jurors dated the baptism by its coincidence with the time of their involvement with one or both. Dealing in animals could be risky: one juror recalled the day on which he had "bought 100 ewes from John Holdefast of London and within seven days they all died of murrain" (26/148). Maybe land was a safer bet, as in the memory of a juror who "knows because of the date of one part of a charter in his possession by which he enfeoffed John Myll of 1 acre land in Trusham" (26/144). Some men wanted to tell more, "John Gorgeys, father of Joan mother of Joan daughter and heir of John Wybbury bought a parcel of meadow and land in Chagford from him, to give to John Gorgeys and his heirs and assigns in fee simple. The charter was sealed in the church ... in the presence of Robert Cary and others who were trustworthy. He [the juror] was there when Joan was baptized, and saw a monk write her age in a missal" (25/298). One memory dredged up an old grievance, the juror recalling that he had made "a wax candle weighing 2 lb. on that day to burn and hold in the church at Thomas's baptism for which he has not yet been paid" (22/359). Much sweeter, of course, was to recall the profit side of the ledger: "John asked why he had been summoned. John Gorgeys said it was to buy one of John's horses, of a color called 'Greyameler', to ride on pilgrimage [...] John sold the horse for 8 marks, paid then and there. He subsequently entered the church and saw a monk write Joan's age in a great book. He said that the horse was the best and most sure-footed that he ever had" (25/298).

A final theme of the autobiographical memories shines light on a more cheerful aspect of village life. These memories center on the pride of recounting the entry of kinfolk—usually a son—into the church. A good bragging point: "Robert celebrated his first mass in the church" (24/132). A little more prestigious, perhaps: "John his first-born son took holy orders at London that day and was ordained in the priesthood by the then bishop of London" (22/189). Even more so may have been entry into an order, as when his son: "professed as a monk ... on the day that Elizabeth was born" (23/722). The special event was still remembered; he told of when he had ridden "with his brother [...] to Chalcombe abbey to see his wife's brother Thomas Blysworth, one of the canons, made abbot on 12 February 1400" (921/872). On a different note, we have the memory of a juror at Redbourne: "Thomas Trent, [...] says that Joan his daughter, then a nun at Nun Coton, Lincolnshire, died on 22 September 1402" (22/827), but there was good news to balance the bad, as when "in the same year his daughter Katherine became a nun in the house of Katesby and was professed there" (15/159).

MEMORIES AND THE EXTERNAL FRAME OF REFERENCE

Some jurors chose a memory that rested on something beyond their own family and doings, let alone the baptism itself. Though mostly these external memories are of fairly pedestrian events, some are of quite striking matters and we may wonder why others on that same jury did not offer a similar memory. Perhaps the man who offered the memory was deemed as deserving of his own moment in the sun, since the vast majority of memories indicate that most jurors were comfortable with offering their tried-and-true recollection of an ordinary event (Holford 2008).

Most of the external memories revolved around village life, though they went to its odd moments and its unusual happenings. There are memories of extreme weather, of fire, and of flood, leaving vivid memories of their effect on daily life. There was the juror who recalled that "immediately after the baptism there was a flash of such bright lightning that a young girl playing in the road lost her eyesight" (22/223), a memory much like that of when "there was such loud thunder at the time of Walter's baptism that a small boy in the church lost his sense" (24/269). Fires were a constant threat to property and even to life. One juror "knew because his home in Cockermouth went up in flames. While working to extinguish the fire with his neighbours he saw Ralph carried to the chapel for baptism" (23/314). Windstorms were also a threat—fierce and unpredictable. It might be the time when "such a wind blew up on 8 May 1418 that Richard Ace was blown from the bridge [. . .] into the water where he drowned. It was said when the coroner viewed the body [. . .] that John, son of Joan, had been born and baptised that day" (24/398).

Another common thread that ran through village memory was the parish church as a building, it being very much the center of village life and a collective village responsibility. We have seen it as the site for love-days and as a rendezvous place for all sorts of secular gatherings, and the building itself figured in village memory. A juror in Gloucestershire remembered the baptism because "John clerk of the church broke the church's great bell by ringing it the same feast day that Ralph was baptised" (23/269), while another juror talked of when "an ash tree fell on the belfry of Sprotborough church at the time of the baptism" (21/147). As the upkeep of the nave was a village concern, we have jurors who "on the same day they and others began to make and fill in the foundations of the belfry of the said church" (15/652). And the worldly aspect to church affairs might be recalled, as in the memory of two jurors who went back to when "they rendered accounts of goods, etc., bequeathed to St. Mary [. . .] at divers times, as is enrolled in the missal there" (15/449).

Few memories relate to sexual scandal. Though such matters must have set tongues wagging when they were fresh, in their recounting but few jurors went this route, whether through reticence or to avoid shaming the village. While Robert Fullere remembered when "Margaret Morys of Loddon was then pregnant by Thomas Holm chaplain, and for shame took her goods on the following morning and left the town," his fellow jurors were more inclined to fall back on memories of a marriage, a birth, and perhaps the purchase of three horses from the Fakenham fair (19/783). Against the main current, there was the memory of one man who now recalled when "John Homne, who survives, then town bailiff, placed Alice Blast on the tumbrel in the vill, called 'a Gumscole,' for many defaults and transgressions perpetrated by her to the harm of the whole vil of Kidderminster (22/673). It was a joint memory of three jurors taking us back to when, "on the same day [as the baptism] a certain priest called Sir John Launcy went round the church, by way of penance, with a woman called Joan Wynkman, and they saw it" (16/341). In these memories the jurors named names, as the fires of gossip had no doubt kept these details warm over the years.

On the idea that the woes of others are always of interest, numerous jurors offered memories of crimes committed by or upon outsiders, of violence wreaked or suffered, of punishments, and dramatic deaths. At a Proof in 1434, a juror took the bad-weather memory to the limit: he "swears that such a wind blew up on 8 May 1413 that Richard Ace was blown from the bridge of Sherington into the water where he drowned. It was said, when the coroner viewed the body [. . .] that John, son of Joan, had been born and baptised that day" (24/398). Crime was memorable and punishment perhaps even more so. A Norfolk juror remembered that on "that day an unknown thief was arrested at Loddon with 10 sheep stolen at Norton Subcourse and he was taken to Norwich castle," while a fellow juror could continue in this vein: "Alan Morel a common thief was arrested for felony on that day, taken to Norwich castle, and remained there until he was hanged" (19/783). Some crime was more picturesque, the king's bailiff "arrested Norman Durston [. . .] suspected of counterfeiting [. . .] and charged to this effect with the multiplicity of silver and gold, against the statutes" (23/139). Norman's subsequent fate was probably not a happy one. Suicide was a crime, and there clearly was a ghoulish interest in the matter. We have the recollection that "on the day of her birth Thomas Trumpet feloniously committed suicide with a knife worth 1 d." (24/268). It seems to have had elements of a spectator sport, at least for the juror who remembered the time of the baptism because it was when he learned that "John Hertwode hung himself with a noose [. . .] He [the juror] came to see John hanging and on his return met a woman carrying John [the baby] to Bosham church for baptism" (23/143). One simple memory was he "knows [the date] because John de Thurleby hung himself" (25/526).

Some men offered a memory quite removed from local doings and along lines of memory but rarely traveled. In a sense, it is these unusual recollections, offered before one's peers and in the context of collective behavior that we see how "social memory" is the result of yoking "social" with "memory." The longest of all the out-of-the-loop memories is that of one John Kempe, accounting a pitched battle between Lollard heretics and the good men of Essex and linking it to the baptism. He says "that on that day and year above said [. . .] many Lollards gathered with insurgents against the church's power and privilege and, like disturbers, destroyed the king's peace, proposed that the young be not baptised, to the prejudice, destruction and scorn of the entire church. Thomas Malgrave [. . .] afraid that Richard [the baby] would be killed unbaptized, ordered many armed men, [. . .] to destroy the force and their diabolic intention. They fought the Lollards on the same evening [. . .] and two hundred of them were thrown to the ground and killed. Richard was born and baptised on the same day and this battle happened twenty-two years ago" (24/566). It seems striking that none of Kempe's fellow jurors offered their take on this memorable event.

Two men on a York jury offered their versions of a striking event. One remembered the baptism because "there was an earthquake throughout all England when Edward was born in May 21 years ago" and his fellow remembered an equally striking happening: "Edward was born in the year after the rebellion of the commons of England at London, which was in the summer 22 years ago" (18/854). Again, the other jurors stuck to the familiar and day-in-day-out sort of recollections. One loquacious memory did touch on a family affair: "the translation of St. William is celebrated on 8 June in the province of York and on the day of William Ingilby's birth a miracle took place after prayers and divine service in honour of St. William. One of Richard's boys called Wilfrid was exhausted by fever to the point of death but he was saved by St. William on that day" (23/309).

So, these many social memories shed a bright (and believable) light on the rhythms of daily life. The jurors who recalled memorable events of twenty-one (or fourteen, or sixteen) years ago talked of the presence of their social betters, looked back on family and personal milestones, and occasionally told of a great windstorm or the devastation caused by Welsh rebels. The memories were almost all secular, even though their focal point was a basic sacrament of Christian life. The testimonies were all and always offered in the presence of one's peers and, indeed, it is not unlikely that memories may have been freshened or sharpened by the comparable recollections of those peers. The many common or joint memories seem to argue for this as likely, if not always the case. But for the most part, juror after juror and jury after jury, individual and private memories were enunciated and shared in a social setting.

SOCIAL MEMORY OUTSIDE THE PROOFS—A WOMAN'S WILL OF 1450

Other sources beyond the Proofs of Age give us a different slant on the style and voice of social memory. The voices and the memories of the village women were totally excluded from the Proofs. We now offer redress by looking at the will of an affluent woman, wherein she could enunciate and thereby impose her social memory upon those affected by its many clauses and conditions (Burgess 1987a). When Joan Buckland, widow of Richard Buckland of Edgcott, Northamptonshire, wrote her will in 1450 she was remembering people, institutions, and material objects, all tied to her in life and now remembered in death. She created a social universe through her exercise of social memory—the clauses and benefactions and conditions of her will. Her will follows the conventional arrangement of bequests: the burial church, other ecclesiastical institutions, various people, were both clerical and lay, who specifically identified family members, instructions and bequests to executors, disposal of the residue of the estate. And yet, it is a highly individual document, a statement of how Joan's life was tied into her death.

The writing of the will linked Joan Buckland's past to her present and, as the conditions were to be fulfilled, into the future. The will was dated May 6, 1450 and since it was not probated until June 1462 it is likely that she lived for a long time after the document had been written, though there are no indications of any changes made during the intervening twelve years. She wrote a long will, really fulfilling the common place of "I will remember you in my will." Whether Joan ever spoke these words, she honored them; the implementation of her social memory long outlived her as a person. Judging by her will she had no close family; one god-daughter is all we find identified as kin. Were there other close kin we can assume she would have mentioned them, since wills—monuments of social memory—were documents of inclusion rather than of exclusion. Given that we are correctly reading the absence of near-kin, Joan's death also meant the breakup of a household of significant size and wealth as indicated by her many domestic bequests.

Even for a wealthy widow, Joan's will is long and detailed. It spread the wings of benefaction widely, with numerous beneficiaries simply designated as "my servants" or "residents of the village." After opening with the conventional bequests to her burial church Joan singles out people and items or sums in a will that runs to more than seven pages in print. With her memory of people, things, and places as our guiding beacons, in the bequests to the burial church she included a number of service books, with sufficient familiarity to distinguish among them: "a masseboke, the first worde of the second leaf dei dixit," and "ji Grayle, the first worde of the secunde leaf vel hoc." In these details she could show off her literacy and her affluence.

Once her primary obligations to the burial church had been discharged, Joan turned to other ecclesiastical beneficiaries, some for individuals, some for a house (as for the four friaries at Oxford and at Northampton). Her memory, like her geographical reach, was broad; the hospital of St. John at Banbury, the vicar of Doncaster, the vicar of Blakesley, among others. The bequests to ecclesiastical recipients were mostly of domestic items, hardly distinguishable from those to her numerous lay beneficiaries. The rector of Edgcott was remembered for "j good ffetherbed with j large matrasse filled with white canuase & a bolster, a paire of the best blankettes [. . .]" and more of this sort, as she ended the long list by giving him "the grettest panne that is in my kechyn" a peculiar bequest to a priest who presumably held a living with an established domestic arrangement. The various clerics may have held livings that were in her gift.

Most of the will was concerned with the distribution of comparable household items to eleven men and eight women singled out by name, alongside those unspecified servants, friends, and tenants. Some of Joan's female beneficiaries are identified in terms of their husband: "Elizabeth Richard Clarell wyff, j violet gowne furred with Amysee grey." Joan's god-daughter—so named and further identified as Richard Clarell's niece, being one of the few where the connection is noted, was to receive the only significant cash bequest: "j parie of shetis of ij leuys and dim. & x li. to her marriage and i. bolle pece of siluer." Some of those remembered were rewarded for what must have been a long record of good service. Horses and grazing stock were to be distributed rather widely. In a rather open-ended bequest Joan said, "he that keepith hem at that day [of her death] haue the best & j Cowe the best." Alison Swayn was down for "ij kyne & xij ewen," and Henry Cheyny was to receive "j of the Carthorses & j cowe." It is hard to gauge the generosity behind a bequest like "a pece of Arasse with the Salutacion" for Isabel Knyghtley, or the 'j speven red and green paled" for Walter Mantel. Various groups were to be recipients of a common or a collective bequest, a practice found in other comprehensive wills where numerous servants, retainers, and tenants were to be remembered. Joan instructed that "euery tenaunt of myn in Ochecote haue dim. quarter of wete [one quarter] and dim. quarter of Malt . . ." and then she names eight more towns to share in "all the remenauntz of whete and Malt that it be departed . . . and [in] other poor townes that be here abowte." This was recollection and largesse befitting the "lady of the manor" and Joan made a number of bequests that also brought some of those generic village poor in her net.

Most of the many bequests are of a fairly ordinary sort, at least by the standards of a rich woman. Whoever Richard Clarell was, her bequests to him occupy two paragraphs of the printed will. Items for a chapel—altar clothes, a chalice "that I haue at London," "silver candlesticks for the aulter and 23 of my best spones that ben here" plus other items of liturgical hardware. Then Joan went on to leave curtains and cloth and carpets, sheets and towels, and more from the linen closet. Comparable in scope were her bequests to Robert Carleton, master of St. John hospital at Banbury, and again it was domestic rather than ecclesiastical items. So much detail, so many items to pass on, so many people to remember.

When we looked at the memories offered by jurors at a Proof of Age we noted that only a few focused on something outside the realms of ordinary experience and the common twists and turns of village life. Similarly, most of Joan's will followed the most conventional paths of benefaction with but a few beyond the usual list of recipients and items. But again, there are some that catch our attention and that indicate how her "memory" was running as she thought beyond her own future. It might be a bequest to an individual: "to my Skryvener at London a flat pece gilt vncouered which is in a standard at London at saint Thomas of Acres." Or as in the last bequest of all: "Item, to the poer men of ffyshmonger Craffte in London to be departed after the discrescion of myn Executours xx li." She remembered as she chose to remember.

EPILOGUE

Social memory, whether we retrieve it from the recollections of the many jurors of little individual stature or from the last will of an affluent lady, may manifest itself in most diverse forms. In either case we see how experiences, memories, and the ties of social and kinship bonds from the past were called up to be recounted in a social context in the present. It could be before one's peers and a royal official or might be as last wishes as enunciated and (as yet) to be implemented. In either case, it was social memory that bound past to present. The "future" also was a player at the table; the now-of-age would inherit, Joan's executors would, presumably, carry out her last wishes. As no one, supposedly, is an island unto oneself, so none of the many parties who offered the memories we have summoned up from the vasty deep stood apart from their society. Social memory was a powerful ligature that bound and helped define society, whether it was for some ecumenical movement like a crusade, or at the village level for a baptism and all that entailed. It might be individualized, as in the will in which Joan Buckland created her own community of beneficiaries, her social universe, composed of men and women unified in no other way. It might be as one of a jury of twelve and recalling a common and unexceptional experience, known to and perhaps shared by the others. In either case, the memories that encompassed those within made them into a social universe tied together and, in many ways, actually created by social memory.

CHAPTER THREE

Media and Technology

ANNA ADAMSKA

MEDIEVAL MEDIA OF MEMORY IN THE SCHOLARLY DEBATE

As the days of man are short, and his age fails with time as a shadow, human need requires that the memory of the deeds of present men, faithfully stored away in writing, be providently transmitted to those who come afterwards.

—CDM I, n. 119

This preamble, dating from 1290, is one of the countless introductory formulae in medieval charters expressing the impermanence of human life and the need of turning to the written word to protect the memory of events and of people's achievements. Dramatically opposing *memoria* (memory) reinforced by writing, and *oblivio* (oblivion), these commonplace *formulae* resonate with the preoccupations of many medieval authors about the limited abilities of human recollection (Fichtenau 1957; Minnis 2005: 265).[1] They also strongly influenced the ideas of modern scholars on how memories were stocked and transmitted in the Middle Ages. According to the paradigm of our modern literate mentality, which assumes the superiority of the written word over orality, many scholars see the Middle Ages as the period of a radical passage "from [oral] memory to written record" (Clanchy 2013). Although this passage did indeed take place, in this chapter we will argue that it was not that simple, and certainly not as radical as one used to think. Michael Clanchy, the author of the seminal monograph on the development of administrative literacy of the English State after the Norman conquest, noticed that "the growth of literacy did not occur in a cultural vacuum. It replaced non-literate ways, which seemed equally natural to those who were accustomed to them. The most difficult initial problem in the history of literacy is appreciating what preceded it" (Clanchy 1993: 41). Thus, although we will acknowledge the importance of the written word as a medium of medieval memory, we will also present arguments in favor of the thesis that memory was, in fact, a "multimedia" phenomenon. It engaged a broad scale of communication tools: speech and sound, images and graphical signs, concrete physical objects as well as acts of performing religious and legal rituals. The use of the written word, certainly growing during medieval times, by no means caused other media to be abandoned. The length of the historical period under consideration and the complexity of the source materials make it impossible to provide a detailed survey of *all* media of memory. It is interesting nonetheless to seek an answer to the question how entrusting memories to written texts interacted with other ways of retaining and transmitting information about the past.

Posing this kind of question became possible thanks to the remarkable development of research on social communication and literacy in pre-modern Europe. Several conclusions can be drawn from the investigations of the last thirty years (Mostert 2012). Scholars have definitively gone beyond the comfort zone of certitudes based on simple either/or distinctions: either orality or literacy; being either literate or illiterate; either possessing basic literacy skills or not; either knowing Latin or not, etc. In the first place, it has become clear that medieval communication was *not* a bipolar, static structure, but rather a multi-dimensional, dynamic phenomenon encompassing orality, literacy, aurality (relating to the ear), and visuality (relating to sight) in permanent interaction. Secondly, participation in written culture could take place in different registers and on different levels of literacy, depending on the *genre* of text and its language. And there has come about a growing awareness among scholars that one and the same person may be "literate" in one register and merely semi-literate or illiterate in another register. These scholarly realizations result in a pressing need to revise traditional opinions about the skills of individuals needed for participation in written culture, to whatever stratum of medieval society they might belong.

We are becoming ever more convinced that the lack of the technical abilities of reading and writing did not exclude individuals from contact with the written word—even if active use of the written word could considerably change attitudes to writing. When investigating the literate behavior of an individual or a social group, medievalists are learning to pay attention not only to active and personal participation in written culture through different forms of reading and writing, but also to its passive forms, for instance by listening to texts read aloud or the delegation of technical literacy tasks to professionals, semi-professionals or "occasional" scribes.

We should also realize that, considering the media of "medieval" memory we are talking about a period of roughly 1,000 years, which witnessed profound changes in the tools and technologies of social communication. From the perspective of literacy, a person living in the twelfth century would probably be more likely attuned to the fully literate ways of life of contemporary Western society than to those of the—medieval—seventh century. Which is not to deny that one also meets fully literate people in the seventh century. Three moments in the history of medieval media have been indicated as turning points that made possible the growth in the use of writing. The first of them was the introduction of word separation in the seventh and eight centuries, which gradually supplanted the antique practice of *scriptio continua* in the Latin script. Secondly, the ninth century not only saw extraordinary developments of the use of the written word in all domains of social life in the Carolingian realms, but also developed a model minuscule script which until our times has remained the touchstone of script in the West (McKitterick 1989): the letters you read on this page are the direct descendants of this graphical revolution. Finally, in the so-called "long thirteenth century" the written word started to be commonly used in everyday life for administrative and economical purposes (Bertrand 2015). We are therefore justified to speak about "many medieval cultures of writing in which the general idea of a single culture of writing was more—or less—realised" (Mostert 2011: 74), always bearing in mind the changes wrought by time which strongly influenced the role of the written word as a technology of memory as well.

One final preliminary observation has to be made. Most of the vehicles and technologies of memory, which we perceive as "medieval," were not invented in the Middle Ages but were inherited from Antiquity. Historical accounts, commemorative inscriptions, depictions of persons and events, dedications of buildings in memory of remarkable people as well as religious and secular public rituals (e.g. the festive entries of rulers), had for centuries proven to be highly efficient media of memory in ancient Mesopotamia, Egypt and Persia, in Greece and, finally, in Rome. Watched and admired by generations of "barbarians", they were copied, imitated, and creatively adapted inasmuch as the cultural resources of the early medieval successor states of the late Roman Empire allowed (cf. Pohl 2008). Later on, with the various "renaissances" of classical culture in the ninth, twelfth, and fifteenth centuries, their efficacy was merely reinforced by the ever-vivid memory of Rome as the golden standard of cultural achievement (Kytzler 1993; McKitterick 2015: 225).

THE SOCIAL CONTEXT OF THE MEDIA OF MEMORY: WHAT SHOULD BE REMEMBERED? AND FOR HOW LONG?

How do societies remember? How do individuals remember? The answers given to these crucial questions have resulted among other things in the distinction that is often made between collective and individual memory (a.o. Connerton 1989; Brenner, Cohen and Franklin-Brown 2013: 4–5). These forms of memory are important for our subject. They help us to indicate those persons or groups of people whose memories have been preserved, and also those who used and controlled the available media and technologies. Scholars generally agree that in the early Middle Ages these media transmitted rather the products of the collective memory of various groups in the society than those of individuals, even if the concept of "collective memory" itself is subject to discussion (cf. Foot 1999: 187–8). It most certainly cannot be seen as the simple arithmetical sum of the memories of individual persons: both personal and collective memories were permanently undergoing processes of selection, valorization, construction, and reconstruction, under the influence of challenges of a present faced by communities and individual persons alike (Schmitt 2013: 17–8).

In both cases, preserving and transmitting memories had to serve the same double goal: to allow one to know what had happened in the past, and to experience once again certain events deemed crucial from an individual or collective perspective. This is most clearly illustrated by the essential memory strategies applied by the Christian Church: oral tradition and the written word both transmitted knowledge of the life and deeds of Jesus Christ from one generation to another. At the same time, every act of reading aloud his words as recorded in the Gospel made his sacrifice happen in the "here and now" for every Christian throughout the centuries. Moreover, by developing the idea of the *communio sanctorum* (the community of the living and deceased), early Christianity took on itself the permanent duty of remembering the names of the deceased members of their community or of people that were somehow important to it (for instance benefactors), in order to be able to pray for their souls (see Hugener in this volume).

As far as worldly matters are concerned, a distinction used to be made between *memorabilia* (things that *might* be remembered, because they were curious, extraordinary, or weird) and *memoranda* (things that *necessarily* had to be remembered) (cf. Wallis 1995: 81). *Memorabilia* might be transmitted in a casual, sometimes in an almost accidental way, for instance in the form of stories and anecdotes, and it is here that we can hear most clearly the voices of individuals. What *had* to be remembered, possessed a much more serious character and did not vary all that much from one social group to another. Each group (an ethnic, religious or urban community, a dynasty, a family) had to preserve the memory of its origins as well as of decisive events from its past. Answers to the questions: "where are we from?" and "what made us special?" were supposed to lead to an answer to the crucial question: "who are we?" Memories of remarkable predecessors and events helped to define identity and to reinforce the coherence of any social group, be it religious or secular, and gave it a legitimation for the future. Moreover, to be able to function well, every community had to know its legal order and find ways to pass this knowledge on to future generations. A system of inheritance, a penal code, and knowledge of the consequences of the legal actions undertaken by a community's members were as important as practical procedures of settling disputes and controversies (Davies and Fouracre 1986).

In traditional societies all these crucial matters were transmitted mainly by word of mouth. Modern scholars emphasize the important role of women played in the process of forming oral "commemorative chains" (Geary 1994b: 48–80; Van Houts 2001: 8) and in the transmission of "things which *should* be remembered" from one generation to another, almost exclusively in the form of oral counsel and stories. The predominance of the oral mode of communication should not surprise us. Even in the late Roman Empire, so familiar with the use of writing in many domains of life and enjoying relatively high levels of alphabetization, written texts were usually presented as the written rendering of the speech (e.g. Mostert 1995; Small 1997). The political turbulence and the great migrations in the fifth and sixth centuries not only swept away the old infrastructure of educational institutions, but also reinforced for a long time oral culture, as consequence of arrival of peoples living outside the boundaries of the old Roman Empire (the Roman *limes*) who were called "Barbarians" by the old historiography. For centuries, the Church was to remain the chief depository of written culture, as written texts were the foundation of its religious message and of canon law. Secular society had to delegate scribal work (in the purely technical sense of the word) to a relatively restricted group of literates: to people who knew how to read, how compose different genres of texts, and how to write them down.[2] Most professionals and semi-professionals of the written word were bound to ecclesiastical institutions (for instance to the monasteries and episcopal seats); some of them served to the lay elites.

The relative scarcity of writing personnel and technological issues (such as the problem of accessibility to writing supports and tools) often made decisions of what *should* and what *might* be written down into a first moment of selection of what would be remembered or forgotten. From early medieval times, the Church cared about writing down the deeds of her illustrious sons—saints, bishops, and missionaries spreading the Christian faith. This interest led to such textual genres as lists and biographies of popes and bishops, diptychs, hagiographical accounts, annals, and universal chronicles which showed the history of the Church as the fulfilment of God's plans with his Creation (Sot 2003; Bartlett 2013: 19ff.; Foot and Robinson 2012).

As far as lay society was concerned, the first need was to establish and reinforce the collective identities of ethnic communities through developing accounts of their origins and history. A long series of "ethnic" historical narratives has come down to us, starting with those concerning the various branches of the Goths in the fifth century and ending with the different branches of Slavs in the early twelfth century. They usually include two crucial elements: the story of their (most often mythical) ancestors and that of their conversion to Christianity (Plassmann 2007; Garipzanov 2011; Innes 2012: 547–58). In this way, every new "nation" entering the expanding orbit of medieval Latin civilization could be included in the universal and, at the same time, sacral history of Christendom.

In one expert's opinion, the barrier between "oral" and "written" was very soft: "Oral tradition might be called on to validate or interpret written tradition, and written tradition might incorporate much that had been oral" (Geary 2002: 111).

Entrusting the memory of legal actions to the written word was a more complex matter. Especially beyond the boundaries of the old Roman Empire, the Church was the first institution to develop the awareness that it might be useful to have written proof of the pious donations and liberties given by lay people—to start with those of the rulers. Such records might have the form of elaborate charters, but equally often they were merely simple notes (*notitiae*) about who transferred (*tradidit*) his property to whom and under which conditions. Toward the end of the first millennium, many ecclesiastical beneficiaries of such donations started to order them in dedicated books called *libri traditionum* and cartularies (Declercq 2000: 148–9).

On the question as to what extent early medieval lay society saw recording legal actions in writing as useful, a variety of scholarly opinions have been voiced. Positivist historians took it for granted that the use of the written word for legal (and for practical purposes generally) almost disappeared in the confrontation of the Roman Empire with the oral legal culture of the "barbarian" successor states. They held that its revival took place only with the development of canon law and Roman law from the late eleventh century onwards. Nowadays, the concept of the "Dark Ages" has been revised (Wood 2013). Ever more serious arguments are now provided to adjust the positivists' judgment. What had to be remembered were first of all the property rights to the land. Everywhere in Western Christendom, in the centuries following the disappearance of the Roman administration, the interest in recording in writing the transfer of property rights, persisted, especially of purchases and sales of land made by lay people, including women (Brown et al. 2013). At the same time, it is becoming ever more clear that, until the end of the medieval period, producing a written evidence of a legal action was only one of many ways of ensuring its remembrance: issuing a charter could be part of an act of "performance" of law which included also the spoken word and ritual behavior (Geary 1999; Mostert and Barnwell 2011; Koziol 2012).

Two fundamental changes concerning the implementation of the written word as a medium of memory came about, gradually, after the year 1000. The development of urban settlements in the medieval West, and the simultaneous growth of new forms of the economy, from the late eleventh century onwards resulted in the emancipation of new social groups. These town dwellers, including merchants, adopted the written word not only for solemn purposes, but also to retain the memory of the actions of individual people in their daily life. This "individualization" of the use of script, which at the same time was getting an ever more "pragmatic" character, was most clearly visible in the towns, especially among the merchants. But the remarkable intensification of the use of the written word for administrative purposes also marked the everyday management of ecclesiastical and monarchic estates (Bertrand 2015). The town dwellers gradually started to use the written word as a working tool of the money economy, especially of trade (Denzel et al. 2002). This means that in the later Middle Ages it became necessary to remember new kinds of matters—business matters, profits, and the expenses of individual persons. They became as important as legal rules, remarkable events, and deeds of extraordinary men. Equally interesting is the fact that the memory of these new matters was most often kept by the actors themselves in the economic life: literate town dwellers held the pen to keep their own accounts, and they also started to perpetuate in writing the memory of their ancestors and to express their social identity (Mostert and Adamska

2014a, 2014b). At the end of the period under discussion here, in certain parts of Europe the growing practice of using the medium of script for transmitting *memoranda* important for individuals reached even peasants. Although they might lack the technical skill of writing, some Tuscan and French peasants, involved in the local money economy, asked persons they knew to be able to write to enter their transactions in booklets of expenses (Adamska and Mostert 2010).

We observe both individualization and democratization of the use of script in its function as a tool of memory. One other phenomenon should be mentioned here, the development of "archival memory": entrusting the memory of actions and events to writing made sense only when one intended to keep the records afterwards, and to use them again when needed, usually before the court. Considering a piece of parchment or paper to be as trustworthy as the memory of a living witness (Schulte et al. 2008; Barbier 2014), however, required an essential mental shift on the part of the users of the written word, which supposed an understanding of how the writing actually works. The conscious keeping of written records and the emergence of archives, starting with those of the ecclesiastical institutions, can be considered as an important mark of a literate mentality (Adamska 2004), even if the efficient management of information contained in the archival records posed a considerable challenge (Declercq 2000; Guyotjeannin 1997; De Vivo 2010). The archival collections of the earlier Middle Ages may have been vulnerable to natural disasters and to premeditated destruction. But in general records were intended to be kept "in perpetual memory of a thing": forever (Bedos-Rezak 2016: 9). A revolutionary change in this respect occurred in the later Middle Ages, from the thirteenth century onwards: the new imagery of temporariness which resulted from the development of urban life and "urban" occupations, stimulated an awareness of short-term legal actions (Bertrand 2015: 52–3). If such actions were registered in writing, there was no reason to preserve their records forever, but only as long as the records might really be needed. The emergence of the short-time preservation of records (which belonged to the register of pragmatic literacy), is usually seen as a sign of the "desacralization" of writing. It can also be perceived as one of the first signs of a modern attitude towards remembrance and oblivion, as a "license to forget."

TECHNOLOGIES OF WRITING

There is no doubt that the choice for one or another medium of memory depended on the resources and practical skills of those who made such a decision. At first sight, the implementation of the written word in this function seems relatively simple, as in the production of written texts all kinds of materials might be used. In practice, the goal of the message as well as the intended (long or short) preservation, together with its intended accessibility, determined the purely technical aspects of the whole enterprise. Another important determinant was the availability of writing materials and tools.

Writing materials and tools

The most obvious difference was that between hard and soft writing surfaces. In the Middle Ages, the ancient practice of carving inscriptions in stone and putting them on public display was continued. Such inscriptions commemorated great persons and events, whose memories were meant to last long and to be generally known (Favreau 1997; Zajic 2014). In the early Middle Ages, this practice was also well known in areas outside the

Roman *limes*, especially in Scandinavia, where a considerable number of post-glacial stones carrying commemorative inscriptions in runes can be found. In this monumental epigraphic literacy, originating from a memorial tradition (Williams 2008: 285; cf. Zilmer 2012: 141), the medium and the message reinforced each other, literally, under the very eyes of the reader, who could experience the substance of the material and read that the memory of the people and events recorded would last as long as the stone itself (Harris 2010: 127ff). This type of memorial records developed in parallel to the use of other kinds of hard materials as writing surfaces, such as (precious) metals, ivory, or wood. Because of their much more modest size, individual inscriptions usually supposed a smaller circle of users, but the numbers of these inscriptions might be larger, supposing their large-scale use by individuals. A good example of the use of wood is the wooden rune-stick, in use in early medieval urban settlements in Scandinavia (Spurkland 2004: 333). Producing a text on a hard support had little to do with "writing" as we usually imagine it. This was rather the physical labor of carving, demanding special tools and skilled craftsmen, who themselves might not be able to read the texts they were carving (Zajic 2014: 394).

Among the soft writing materials on which one rather "painted" letters (*pingere*) with ink applied by a pen made from birds' feathers, the most popular became parchment, produced from animal skins (mostly of sheep, calf, and goat). Similar to papyrus, it originated from the Middle East and started to be produced on a large scale in the Hellenistic period. With the extension northwards and eastwards of the frontiers of Christendom, it proved to be much sturdier than papyrus, as parchment was able to survive in the humid climes of Transalpine Europe. Moreover, parchment also lent itself better to the new form of book which developed from the second century CE onwards, as it did not crack when folded. The *codex*, the form of book which we still use today, more convenient in daily use and from the beginning associated with the new expansive "religion of the Book," gradually replaced the ancient roll (*rotulus*) (Diringer 1982: 162ff). Using parchment, however, was dependent on livestock and on mastering the technical complexities of its production (Rück 1991; Meyer 2013). This caused parchment to be considered precious—or simply expensive.[3] The cost of the production of some manuscripts might be prohibitive. A large Bible might require the skins of 200 to 400 animals (Thomson, Morgan, Gullick, and Hadgraff 2008: 76), and the cost would be considerably augmented by the inks used, and the pigments used in the colors of illuminations. Those who made the decisions about writing things down that should or might be remembered, had to make considerable financial efforts (Schutz 2004: 117). Texts written on expensive soft supports required more careful measures to prevent physical destruction and theft, and their accessibility was therefore much reduced. There is rich evidence for the practice of considering manuscript books and parchment charters as valuable objects, and of keeping them under lock and key as any other treasure (Steinmann 2013).

The physical fragility of parchment and paper could be counterbalanced to some extent by some measures, which may be surprising from a modern point of view. To guarantee the durability of records of legal actions, for instance, the texts of charters were copied in gospel books or manuscripts serving the Church liturgy, giving them a quasi-sacral value. And special formulae (maledictions), enumerating supernatural punishments for those who dared to transgress the stipulations mentioned in legal documents, were included in the texts (Little 1975). From the eleventh century onwards, with the progress of pragmatic literacy, these semi-magical safety measures gradually made room for legal measures such as seals and subscriptions, which could guarantee the authenticity of records.

The cost of writing materials ceased to be the crucial determinant of decisions about writing things down when paper was introduced in Europe by way of the Islamic Middle East and of the Caliphate of Cordoba in Spain. It came to be used on a large scale from the thirteenth century onwards. When paper mills started to make an appearance north of the Alps at the end of the fourteenth century, paper became more than ten times cheaper than parchment of the best quality (Bresc and Heullant-Donat 2007: 381–2). Produced from rags, it did not eliminate parchment as the main support used in book production. It rather became the support of choice in the diversified domain of pragmatic literacy with its administrative documentation, bills, accounts, etc.—text which, as we have seen, to some extent became the object of short-time preservation.

Before the "paper revolution," texts meant for the temporary use were produced on another traditionally well-tried, locally abundant, and cheap material. Wooden tablets, covered with a layer of wax, have been used without interruption from the Roman period until the late fifteenth century by the professionals of the written word (especially by notaries and scribes) as well as by schoolboys (Lalou 1992; Bertrand 2015: 58ff). Their remains are found everywhere in Europe. This is in contrast with texts recorded on pieces of birchbark, known almost exclusively from north-west Russia, most probably thanks to the physical conditions of their preservation in the soil. This "birchbark literacy" had a predominantly practical character. Scholars have found hundreds of business agreements, confirmations of payments, lists of goods, and short letters, mainly from the twelfth century, produced by the inhabitants of the Great Novgorod region. They show a flourishing practical, private literacy and confirm opinions about the impact of widely accessible writing materials on the spread of writing in matters of daily life (Schaeken 2012).

Although towards the end of the medieval period the offer of affordable writing materials and tools—together with their accessibility to people who knew how to use them—was widening considerably, their spread was by no means equal throughout the various social groups. For inhabitants of the towns, even those of a low social position, it was rather easy to find a rudimentarily equipped occasional scribe or a jobbing clerk who could write down matters important to them. In the countryside, however, the difficulty of getting the necessary scribal materials can be illustrated by sixteenth-century evidence from the case of a peasant from Cambridgeshire who, in 1578, asked a surgeon from the next village to write down his last will. To fulfil this demand, the man had to look for pen, ink, and paper among all his neighbors (Spufford 1971: 30).

The type of writing material, its price, the technical skills of the scribes, and the availability of adequate tools certainly influenced the length of the messages written and the shape of the letters. The labor and time involved in carving in stone or wood might stimulate a preference for short messages. In the case of longer texts, one often decided to abbreviate some (often repeated) words, especially the dignities of the persons mentioned, conjunctives, and the repetitive elements of nouns and verbs. The practice of abbreviations, originating in Antiquity and developed in the Middle Ages into complex and locally diversified systems of abbreviation (Bischoff 1989: 80ff) can be found also in texts written on parchment or paper. Here, however, the main reason for them would rather seem to be the economy of valuable materials or greater speed of writing.

Letters carved in stone or in metal or wood usually had a distinctive shape: they were frequently majuscules (placed between two lines) and "thin," as carving round forms could be challenging. The ultimate example of a script fitting to material pre-conditions is formed by the Scandinavian and Anglo-Saxon runes (the *Fuþark*). The sixteen basic signs of the writing system were all vertically oriented and possess almost no round or curved elements (Spurkland 2004: 334; Page 2014: 414). Soft writing materials did not pose such limitations: Not only the placing of all characters between four parallel lines, resulting in a distinction between majuscule and minuscule script was possible, but also the development of horizontally oriented, round forms. On the other hand, the comparative study of the developments of the epigraphic and "bookish" Roman script, conducted in parallel by the scholarly disciplines of epigraphy and paleography, allows the conclusion that the developments were indeed parallel: The influence of the Carolingian reform, focused on legibility of writing, is visible also in inscriptions, just as the later "Gothicization" (sharpening) of forms of letters (Favreau 1997; Derolez 2003). These parallel developments kept the scripts intended for the writing down of memories legible to those who had learned to read.

Alphabet and language

The choice of alphabet could be an integral part of the decision to use the written word as a tool of memory. The modern predominance of the Latin (Roman) alphabet in Europe can put one on the wrong track when considering the period before the twelfth century. Latin script, spreading as the instrument of the textual culture and language of the Roman Church, had to coexist with Greek script in southern Italy, and, even more importantly, with well-developed runic literacy (sometimes called "runacy") in Scandinavia, Britain, and maybe even in Hungary. The model of the Christian mission elaborated by the Western Church supposed that Christianized ethnic groups would adopt the Latin alphabet together with Latin as the language of literacy. When vernacular literacy started to grow, the practice developed to augment the Latin alphabet with additional characters, to render the peculiar phonemes of several languages (e.g. Shaw 2013). However, there was a very interesting exception from these patterns. This came about through the missionary activity of the Byzantine Church, interested in the conversion of eastern Europe. In the second half of the ninth century, on the eve of the mission among the Slavs, a new script was invented to meet the peculiarities of Slavic languages (Ilievsky 2002–3; Kuznetsova 2006). Despite some exceptions, the Slavic languages, written with their "own" characters, did not became the *lingua quarta* (the "fourth sacred language") of Western Christendom, after Hebrew, Greek, and Latin. Nonetheless, the Glagolitic alphabet (and subsequently its revised version, the Cyrillic alphabet) dominated the development of literacy among Slavic-speaking people who accepted the forms of Christianity propagated by Eastern, or Orthodox Christianity.

The choice of alphabet, or at least of the specific features of the script in which a commemorative text was to be written, was determined by the choice of language. Generally speaking, in the first millennium, in Ireland (where a distinctive, so-called uncial script was developed), in Anglo-Saxon England, in Scandinavia, and in Croatia (which cordially embraced Glagolitic writing), Roman characters were "reserved" for the Latin language and one's "own" script for the vernacular. However, commemorative texts were not necessarily monolingual. In Anglo-Saxon charters, for instance, containing the proof of legal actions, one switched easily between languages and scripts within one and the same text (Tinti 2018). From the eleventh century onwards, the growth of vernacular literacies vehiculated by the Latin alphabet is clearly visible, for instance in Norway (Spurkland 2004: 334). In the following centuries, this alphabet was to become the most important carrier of written vernaculars almost everywhere in Europe. Nonetheless, the close coexistence of various writing systems, variously called "multilateralism" (Bredehoft 2011), "digraphia" (Larsson 2013) or "biscriptality" (Bunčić et al. 2016), was to remain one of the features of literacy until the end of medieval times. This marked especially those areas where Latin culture and the Roman Catholic faith bordered on those of Byzantine Christendom or with Islam, for instance in the Latin kingdoms in the Middle East, in the Norman kingdom of Sicily, or in the Grand Duchy of Lithuania. At the crossroads of religions and cultures some fascinating linguistic and graphical hybrids could be found. Some charters from the kingdom of Cyprus, for instance, were composed in Latin, but this language was recorded phonetically and, most probably, pronounced in the "French way" (Richard 2002). And from the eastern edge of late medieval *Latinitas* come some texts written in Cyrillic script, but their language is Latin and Polish (Janeczek 2014: 29).

Along the long path from the intention to entrust the memory of people or events to writing the final text, the choice of the language of the message would be one of the final decisions to be made. But which choices were available? As the frontiers of medieval Europe were spreading, Latin gradually ceased to be the mother tongue of an ethnic group as any other.[4] Due to its function of one of the main languages of the Gospel and as the main tool of communication of the Roman Church, Latin obtained the position of a sacred and authoritative language. From the point of view of sociolinguistics, it occupied a "higher," more noble and more respected position than the vernacular tongues, which occupied the "lower" position in this system of "diglossia," where two languages were in use by single language communities (Ferguson 1959). Contrary to almost all vernaculars before the end of the eleventh century, Latin possessed everything that was needed to make a language "writable" and ensure the legibility of the texts written in it: stable spelling, a rich vocabulary in various domains, and clear punctuation (Maierù 1987). If, therefore, the need arose or there was a will to set down in writing the recollection of an event, a state of ownership, or of a legal action, memory was so to speak "translated" from the realities of vernacular life into the framework of a written text, more often than not in Latin. This also adjusted vernacular realities to the rules of one or another textual genre, because "written language is something more than only [the] transcript of the speech" (Burke 1991: 20). The best examples of such transformations during the process of recording things in writing, are the quite numerous depositions of witnesses that used to be made before ecclesiastical and secular tribunals throughout Europe. These sources are very much appreciated generally by historians, as they offer a possibility to investigate the processes of remembering and managing the personal memories of individuals, both men and women, who at the same time were members of their communities. However, irrespective of the character of the case at hand (which could be connected with canonization, heresy, political, or criminal matters), the words spoken by the living witnesses were not only translated by the clerks into a language of records, but also adjusted to the rules of the narrative. Most often there was a list of questions prepared in advance (Marchal 2001: 564–5; Klaniczay 2004; Everard 2001).

In the twelfth century, languages other than Latin started the process of becoming writable. This complex process, which in some cases was to be accomplished only in the first half of the sixteenth century, has been discussed frequently by scholars (Boitani et al. 1992–2006). It will suffice here to point out that the chronology of the passage from Latin to the vernacular varied according to the register of literacy. Vernacular legal documentation, for instance, emerged much later than literary and historical texts (Brunner 2009; Adamska 2015). Because of its prestige, Latin remained a language to consider when making decisions about writing commemorative texts even after the medieval period. Both in post-Conquest England and in the Netherlands as well as on the southern shores of the Baltic Sea and in East Central Europe, authors and commissioners of texts often had to choose between one of the several vernaculars present in these multilingual parts of Europe. The final choice may have been motivated not only by such obvious factors as the goal and the intended public of the written message, but also by the competences of the scribes and by political reasons (a.o. Hlaváček 2004).

THE PRINTING PRESS: THE GREATEST TECHNOLOGICAL INNOVATION OF THE MIDDLE AGES?

From the middle of the fifteenth century onwards, the first evidence reaches us of the spreading, from Rhineland, of a new technique for the making of multiple copies of written texts: the printing press. Thanks to the experiments of Johannes Gutenberg and other craftsmen of the period, the copying of texts by the press with movable type (cf. Mosley 2013), fairly early on got industrial dimensions. Printing contributed to the definitive separation between the act of composing of a text and that of producing copies of it. It also changed the process of decision-making about entrusting memories to the written word. Quickly a group emerged of (mainly secular) professionals of the new technology: printers, publishers, and booksellers, active most often in urban environments. They introduced into the world of the written word concepts that are familiar to us: of profit, publicity, and distribution strategies (Jacob 2007: 24–5).

The impact of the invention of the printing press on the development of literacy in late medieval Europe remains an emotional subject among historians. Some of them perceive it as something like a "Big Bang" which inspired, almost from scratch, the rise of modern written culture. This attitude is inspired by the Enlightenment's convictions about the superiority of literacy over orality and of the printed word over the handwritten word. It has been reinforced in the second half of the twentieth century by the seminal works of Marshall MacLuhan and Elisabeth Eisenstein (MacLuhan 1962; Eisenstein 1979) and has been uncritically repeated ever since. Recent research has nevertheless introduced new important perspectives. Strictly speaking, the real technological development in the production of written texts did not take place when the first printing presses were introduced, but only around 1500, when a new sort of paper came into use. It contained a smaller amount of gelatin and was more suitable for printing than the older type of paper, which had been difficult to fold and proved liable to crumbling in the process of printing (Barrett 2013: 126). In many parts of Europe, therefore, the considerable growth in the production of cheap printed books (many of them in the vernacular) is visible only from the early sixteenth century onwards. Before this period, the main body of printed texts were leaflets and forms for certain types of documents, for instance letters of indulgences which were widely used in the pastoral practice of the Roman Church. Moreover, although the technical innovations of the printing press and of resilient paper were very important in the long term, they did not result mechanically in the abandonment of other tools of social communication, nor in mass alphabetization and literacy (Tóth 2000; Walsham and Crick 2004). The introduction of print on a large scale resulted in the idea that all copies of a text should be identical to one another. However, the physical apparition of the book remained essentially unchanged, and the medieval grammar of legibility was not abandoned.

THE MANAGEMENT OF INFORMATION RECORDED IN WRITING

In this chapter, until now we have been mainly discussing the various technical issues influencing the decision taken by communities or individuals about entrusting things to be remembered to the written word. After the commemorative aim of the message had been established, the suitable material and tools had been provided, and the alphabet and the language agreed to, yet another set of decisions had to be made. Those who shaped the written text had to make decisions concerning the organization of the material.

If a community wanted its history to be written down, in which order should the events be described? The chronological order of the successive years, obvious to our modern literate minds, might be very difficult to retain, as the memory of people living in a predominantly oral culture would associate events with memorable moments recurring every year, such as religious or customary holidays, or with the rhythm of agricultural life, rather than with an "abstraction" such as a year's number. In many medieval historical narratives based on oral tradition, a "relative chronology" of events, the result from a cyclical perception of time[5] is clearly visible. The old Roman habit of using the years of the rulers' (or, later, the popes') reigns as a time frame also continued to be popular. The use of the idea of Christian era, which grew from the eighth century onwards (in great part thanks to the Anglo-Saxon Venerable Bede), reinforced the linear perception of time (Greenway 1999). But navigating the succession of the years remained the privilege of the literates, and the growing precision of chronological information in the late medieval accounts had much to do with the development of literacy and changes in the imagery of time. Dating events precisely remained a difficult operation, and in different parts of medieval Europe there were many alternative ways of starting the year. The possibilities included a.o. Christmas; January 1, when the Circumcision of Christ was celebrated; Easter, the date of which moved from one year to the next; and at the feast of the Annunciation in March. These few examples show that, for medieval professionals of the written word, the strictly chronological organization of historical knowledge presented a permanent challenge.

Recording in writing the shared past also required a decision on when to start the narrative. The common-sense answer "from the beginning" quite often meant "from the Creation of the world." This led to the phenomenon of universal chronicles, which included local and ethnic stories into the grand narrative of the History of Salvation (a.o. Marsham, 2012).

Entrusting the memory of the ownership of land and goods to written records inspired similar questions of how to organize the matter. Monastic scribes trying to impose some order on the written donations to their communities in the cartularies they put together at the turn of the second millennium, often chose the geographical order, as if they were taking an imaginary walk through their (sometimes far-flung) possessions, from one estate to the next. Next to this geographical framework, which might have had some mnemonic value, they also could copy documents in the order of the dignities of their issuers: first came the papal, imperial, and royal ones, and next those of bishops and minor rulers. The issue of the management of written information became even more poignant in cases of surveys and inquests concerning legal, economic, or political matters. Such texts became ever more popular in the central and later Middle Ages, including such ambitious enterprises as the Domesday Book. For this survey, the geographical order was chosen, in connection with a more or less uniform questionnaire, prepared in advance (e.g. Roffe

2016: 298ff; Andrade 2011; Dejoux 2014). The same problem of organization vexed the creators of the early state archives which developed from the late thirteenth century onwards. To retrieve a charter containing requested information, royal clerks tried putting the records in cupboards in chronological or in topographical order, or *ad personam*, according to the persons involved. All attempts at order had their disadvantages. The late medieval period also saw the development of the use of signatures on individual records. At an early stage, they were mainly pictorial or textual (using memory props), but from the fifteenth century onwards we can see the growing use of "modern" alphabetical and numerical signatures (Rück 1971; De Vivo 2010). This allowed the verification of a document's authenticity.

The internal organization of written texts also brought with it another issue. Especially in historical accounts, each author had to decide which matters should be emphasized as more important than others. Their choices were not always those of modern historians. For instance, scholars used to reproach Gregory of Tours (d. 595), a great historian of the Merovingian period, for the seeming disorder of his narrative: to modern readers, he jumped casually from one subject to another. For others, Gregory was the master of juxtaposition and of building up of a complex narrative through careful organization of his material (Martínez Pizarro 2003: 55). Moreover, every medieval author had to decide which matters to include in his narrative, and which were doomed to oblivion because he did not mention them at all. Only once in a while we encounter chroniclers who hint that they deliberately omitted information. The anonymous author of the first account of Polish history summed up the description of a sensitive political conflict with the significant words: "Let us leave this question open, and tell [something else]" (Knoll and Schaer 2003: 97).

FROM ORALITY TO LITERACY—AND BACK

The concerns about the management of information mentioned above were matters only for literate people, as they involved dealing with ever larger amounts of written information, the authenticity of individual documents, and the problems involved in finding them back. Those who did not possess technical skills could come into contact with the written word through listening. The practice of collective reading aloud embraced not only various kinds of narratives—would they be religious, historical or purely "literary"—but also charters and even accounts (Coleman 1996; Geary 1999: 174; Duffy 2001). However, in general perspective, the confrontation with written texts would lead to differences not only in the way people thought about writing, but also about the content of the texts, and, by implication, about memories of past events. Literates could develop ideas about the past which were quite different from the other people living in the same community. Literate monks might be aware of incompatible stories about how their monastic community had acquired certain landed territories. Aimoin of Fleury, writing in the first years of the eleventh century, related how his fellow monks believed that their monastery had acquired a village as an expression of gratitude for being cured by the monastery's patron saint, St. Benedict. After this story, he mentioned that he found charters which showed the donor to have been a traitor, who had been dispossessed by the king, and that it was the king who had given the village to St. Benedict. He wisely refrained from deciding the matter, as he had to continue living with his fellow monks, but it is clear that he believed the evidence of the charters (Mostert 2008: 42). Even in an intellectual center such as Fleury, some monks' minds were more tainted by literacy than others.

Believing a story without written evidence that might be adduced to prove it occurred both in predominantly literate and predominantly oral milieus. What were the media of memory available to non-literates? They could not actively check documents themselves, and of necessity had to trust their physical memory. Their memories were in need of memory props if they were to become part of their community's social memory (cf. Connerton 1989; Fentress and Wickham 1992). There were quite a few available to them (De la Roncière 1983). Objects, unique ones or in daily use, might attract stories to cluster around them. Seeing such an object would trigger the memories of those who had heard the story before. The rituals involving the transfer of property could involve the handing over, before witnesses, of objects symbolizing the property: knives, twigs (Sroka 2011: 269), or sods. Knives and twigs might be attached to the charters that were drawn up to keep the memory of the transaction alive. Many a knife came off later on, and the story it was supposed to help remember was lost forever. The archives, as the case of Durham proves (Clanchy 1993: 38–40), nevertheless kept the unstuck knives, in memory of their function. Memories might also be linked to rituals, liturgical invocations, memorable names, or old customs. In the case of the resolution of a border conflict between the county of Holland and the duchy of Brabant, in the last quarter of the fourteenth century, one made certain that the event would be remembered by roasting a whole ox and doling out the meat to the witnesses. For good measure, a boy was also thrown into a well on this occasion, to make sure he would not forget the event to his dying day. According to a document drawn up in 1383, another boy, presumably of the same age, remembered this instance of conflict resolution vividly (Van der Gouw 1980). It would not be difficult to find other examples of the use of memory props to help non-literates remember what they had witnessed. They were not exclusively used in the Middle Ages either. Symbolic objects occur, for instance, in the Old Testament as well. The Book of Ruth states quite clearly that "a man plucked off his shoe and gave it to his neighbour; and this was a testimony in Israel" (Ruth 4: 7). This is to be expected, as medieval non-literates were no different from non-literates in other times and places in the kind of memory props they might use to make sure their version of the past might endure.

We do see, however, gradual changes in the way the non-written supports of oral memory were regarded. In England, at the end of the thirteenth century, it was decided that only written evidence was henceforth admissible as proof of transactions involving landed property, and the lawyers arbitrarily put the maximum age of those documents at 100 years. Documents older than the year of accession of King Richard I (1189) would be impossible to check. This measure would in time make for increased trust in writing. But in 1289 the story was given credence of the Earl of Warenne, who stormed into the room where the legal emissaries from the king were studying charters, and showed them the rusty sword with which his ancestor had fought side by side with William the Conqueror as his "charter" (Clanchy 1993: 35–43). The learned lawyers no longer could accept symbolic objects such as rusty swords as evidence. Remnants of arguments reminiscent of oral memory have had a long life, however. Until the end of the twentieth century, a prospective house buyer could be held to the promise to buy he had inadvertently made before witnesses to the vendor. The witness's oral testimony to the promise was enough. This was changed, so that today only a document signed by the buyer is deemed sufficient.

More important still was another change. Nowadays, we write things down so that we do not need to keep them in our physical memory. In the Middle Ages, however, things were written down so that the details could be remembered by the people who had decided that it was necessary not to forget them. Just as other memory props, written texts were meant to activate memories that might be activated, in this case by asking those in the community who knew how to read, to render the visible characters on the page audible, by reading them aloud. The mention of a battle in a chronicle may once have been the point of departure for an evening's entertainment (Plummer 1892–9: 2, XXI). And there are those who consider the value of sealed charters in a primarily oral society to have primarily resided in the seals with their legend, with the charters attached to them merely functioning as another memory prop. At some moment written texts could begin to substitute memory; when this happened exactly, is a matter for further research.

CHAPTER FOUR

Knowledge: Science and Education

LUCIE DOLEŽALOVÁ AND TAMÁS VISI

In a renowned essay Norbert Elias (1991) argued that the same mechanisms of socialization that produce the "we-identity" of individual human beings are also responsible for the creation of the "I-identity," that is, the individual focus of one's identity.[1] In traditional societies, Elias argues, the "we-identity" is stronger than the "I-identity," which means that people have a very strong loyalty to their community, they subordinate their individual preferences to the values and norms of the community, and they tend to see their fate more as something directly linked to the fate of their community than as an outcome of their individual decisions. However, this may change when social structures change. In such situation a "tilting of the we-I balance in favor of the I" may occur, and consequently people will perceive themselves more often as individuals responsible for their own decisions than as a community sharing a common fate (Elias 1991: 217).

Personal memories are more likely recorded and transmitted to others in societies that appreciate or cultivate individuality at least to some degree. Jacob Burckhardt (1818–97) notably argued that the "birth of the individual" took place in the Italian Renaissance (Burckhardt 1878: 70–88). Charles Homer Haskins (1870–1937) no less notably argued that other renaissances took place several centuries earlier: the Carolingian Renaissance, the Ottonian Renaissance, and most importantly, the Twelfth Century Renaissance (Haskins 1927; on the historiography of this concept, see Novikoff 2016: xv–xxii). Following upon Haskins' ideas it has been argued that the "birth" or "discovery" of the individual was an achievement of the Twelfth Century Renaissance (Bolgar 1954; Morris 1972) or of the so-called Renaissance of Islam in tenth-century Iraq (Kraemer 1986). It is not our purpose to address these medieval renaissances here; it is sufficient to point out that the individual may have had several births in the Middle Ages. In other words, a "tilting of the we-I balance in favor of the I" may have taken place in several different historical and cultural contexts throughout the Middle Ages, and for that reason, a clear-cut periodization and a continuous and linear history of medieval personal memory is hardly possible.

Modern neuroscience recognizes several independent memory systems—short-term and long-term memory, declarative and explicit (memory that can be put into words), and procedural and implicit (memory of a way to do something, e.g. drive a car). Of the various types of memory recognized today, we have virtually no access to medieval short-term memory, sensory memory, and procedural memory. It is only declarative memory—one that may be consciously recalled—that is accessible in some ways. Declarative memory is commonly divided into semantic (memory of the facts) and episodic (memory of personal experience). The Middle Ages may seem to have valued the semantic memory more than episodic memory: There are very few personal accounts as opposed to a great number of fact-oriented writings. Yet, on the other hand, the concept of the created world as a brief passing stop included the idea that all should be aware of their individual deeds in order to reach salvation. Personal episodic memory played a crucial role in this. Since Augustine (*De trinitate* X, 11), memory was, together with intelligence (*intelligentia*) and will (*voluntas*), recognized as one of three components of the soul,[2] and thus fundamental in making moral judgments.

This study focuses on medieval persons' memories about themselves or about other persons and stresses aspects that had special importance for self-fashioning, rather than discussing, e.g. eyewitness reports of historical events, which were highly regarded in medieval historiography (cf. Damian-Grint 1999: 68–83) but are covered in the study by Jean-Marie Moeglin in this volume. Memory is divided here primarily into intentional and unintentional. The first section addresses personal voluntary (intentional) memory and focuses on the interplay of semantic and episodic memory in contexts specific for medieval culture, namely memory training, casuistry, confession, the Passion, and the art of dying. The second section surveys personal involuntary (unintentional) memory, namely love and trauma. The final part shows how these two types of memory, one cultivated and exercised, the other suppressed, co-exist and interact within personal conception of oneself: It addresses the role of memory in self-fashioning. Special attention is given to nostalgia, as well as the relation between personal and community memory. Although shaped by the particular interests of the two authors, the examples were selected to point to patterns of wider relevance.

THE INTERPLAY OF SEMANTIC AND EPISODIC MEMORY IN PERSONAL VOLUNTARY MEMORY

Exercising and organizing memory

Due to its crucial role in salvation, it was important to keep memory in a good shape, and while different people were gifted with different natural memory, there were artificial means of improving it, too: in addition to the art of memory, a complex strategy which was nevertheless much more widespread than one would expect today (see Gerald Schwedler's introduction and the contribution of Farkas Gábor Kiss in this volume), there were advice and tips for improving memory, many general recommendations as well as medical recipes (Carruthers 1990, Rivers 2010, Carruthers and Ziolkowski 2003). Many of the medieval observations are still valid today. For example, a late medieval treatise on the way of studying (anonymous *De modulo studendi*, written *c*. 1450s–1460s, perhaps in Olomouc), points out, among other things, that in order to remember the matter well, one should always learn not too long but intensively and from the same textbook, and avoid disturbances and alcohol (Odstrčilík 2013).

At the same time, there were, of course, limits and restricted capacity of memory. Remembering too much would have been considered unnatural, a *hubris*, and thus it might be linked to the devil. For example, in 1446, there was a nineteen-year-old man from Spain traveling in German lands who had such incredible memory that he was considered a disciple of the Antichrist. A Benedictine monk from Sankt Gallen, Gallus Kemli, copied a lengthy account describing in detail his incredible memory and concluding:

It is written about him to our universities, that he knows everything there is to be known and everything that there is to be done. That is why some people consider him good, others bad. Some say that he was taught by the devil, others [that he was taught] by God. Therefore it seems to many that he is the predecessor of Antichrist or one of his disciples, or that he is either an angel or a devil in the form of a man. Because no one ever heard of anyone similar in this world, nor it seems possible that he could have learnt and have commended into his memory so much, even if he was older or very old.[3]

As Mary Carruthers persuasively showed, the aim of exercising memory was not rote memorization or simple passive retention, memory was seen as a strong active and creative power, belonging to ethics. Also, the art of memory treatises always stresses that what suits the memory of one person is not useful for another and therefore advises everyone to design their own memory images. Furthermore, it was recognized that information linked to strong emotion imprints itself more deeply on the mind.[4] Thus, although it is primarily semantic memory that these treatises are directly concerned with, it was recognized that semantic memory depends on episodic memory, individual capacities, and personal predilections, and its ultimate purpose was seen as personal moral improvement.

Memory control in casuistry

Following Aristotle, medieval thinkers reflected on the processes of transforming episodic memory into what we call semantic memories. At the beginning of his *Metaphysics*, Aristotle claimed that "science and art" originated in "experience," while experience was produced from "memory." Paraphrasing Aristotle, St. Thomas Aquinas wrote in his *Sententia libri Metaphysicae*: "For an experience arises from the association of many singular [intentions] received in memory. And this kind of association is proper to man, and pertains to the cogitative power (also called particular reason), which associates particular intentions just as universal reason associates universal ones."[5]

In other words, knowledge, both theoretical and practical, was believed to be something universal, or universal-like, something which went beyond individual experiences. Such knowledge was believed to have been distilled from particular memories. On the other hand, medieval thinkers were fully aware of the need to learn to apply the general knowledge to particular cases. As Aristotle remarked, "for the physician does not cure man, [. . .] but [he cures] Callias or Socrates" (*Metaphysics* A.1 981a18–19). This meant, for example, that the patients' episodic memories of the symptoms of their diseases had to be interpreted in terms of the physician's semantic memory of medical theories and his procedural memory of therapeutic practices.

Professional records of cases preserve personal memories through an interplay of semantic and episodic memories. Recollections of medical, juridical, astrological, or penitential cases all exhibit this pattern: the episodic memory of an individual is recorded in terms taken from the semantic memory of professionals paying extra attention to those elements which are vital for the evaluation of the situation from the point of view of the given profession.[6] Casuistry was an essential component of several medieval discourses, including law, medicine, astrology, and penitential literature, and personal memories of medieval individuals were thus sometimes recorded in writing and transmitted to posterity in casuistic texts.

Such emergence of personal memories is heavily influenced by these particular contexts which bring up only selected issues and may include determining circumstances like tension, fear, or hope. These memories are shaped by the fact that they often come forth in a dialogue with authority, as right or wrong (i.e. rewarded or punished) answers to concrete questions. Recent studies show how personal memory is easily manipulated through language and how false memories appear (e.g. Straube 2012). This can be documented in the Middle Ages, for example, through inquisition records; a notable example is Jacques Fournier's register of the French village of Montaillou in the early fourteenth century (Ladurie 1978).

Confession

The most "medieval" subtype of this kind of professional casuistry is probably penitential literature which attempts to describe the sins of individual Christians recording all the key elements which provide the priest with the basis for determining the appropriate penitence for the particular sin. In 1215, the Fourth Lateran Council prescribed that every Christian believer must confess his or her sins to a priest at least once a year. The text of the ordinance (canon 21 of Lateran IV) includes some instructions for the priests, too:

> But let the priest be discreet and cautious, and let him, after the manner of skilled physicians, pour wine and oil upon the wounds of the injured man, diligently inquiring the circumstances alike of the sinner and of the sin, by which [circumstances] he may judiciously understand what counsel he ought to give him, and what sort of remedy to apply, making use of various means for the healing of the sick man.
> —Watkins 1920: 748–9

In other words, the priests were supposed to help confessors by inquiring about those circumstances that defined the essential characteristics of the sins according to Christian moral theology. Thus, the personal memory of the confessor was constructed in a dialogue with the priest who used his knowledge—or semantic memory—of Christian theology for the purpose of directing the episodic memory of the confessor.

Since the success of the penitential process was believed to be a precondition of salvation, it was crucial for all to be able to inspect their memory and consciousness in order to identify their sins to confess and repent efficiently (and be eventually saved). Personal recollection thus became gradually rooted within Christian religion in the Latin West. This recollection was oriented primarily toward the negative (Christians are not asked to recall and indulge in their good deeds) and, toward the end of the Middle Ages it became clearly structured. Christians were asked to recall their sins first by going through the individual vices in their minds, later by considering the Ten Commandments (Casagrande and Vecchio 1994; Bossy 2002). This thorough and oft repeated exercise not only made people remember the Decalogue very well, it also organized and shaped their memories, and, consequently, their new experiences would be immediately stored in these ready categories, too. It is possible to get a glimpse at confessions primarily from handbooks for preachers and moral treatises. In the thirteenth century, Bonaventure (1221–74) gave detailed advice on how to remember in order to confess properly in his *De modo confitendi et de puritate consciencie* (On the way of confessing and purity of consciousness):

> In order to be able to confess in a better way, you should try, at least once a day, to examine how you spent the time, and run through individual hours wondering about places where you were, with which people, what you thought, what you said, what you heard, what you did, so that you realize the easings of the tongue, the heart and the senses, in which aspects and how many times you committed an offence or gave others

reason to commit one . . . and repeat [these things] orderly in your mind, and do not be lazy to exercise this type of examination . . .[7]

Bonaventure, and many anonymous authors after him, invited the sinners to recall their whole day using primarily chronological order and location, followed by anything else they were able to remember, not only deeds but also thoughts, not only their sins but also leading others into sin. Exercising such memory frequently was encouraged. The close association between personal memory and the confession in the Middle Ages is manifest in literary texts, too, as it was shown recently by Kisha G. Tracy (2017) on the example of Middle English literature (Langland, Gower, Chaucer and the Gawain-Poet.

Meditation—personal Jesus

The interplay between episodic and semantic memory worked in a very different way in another genre of medieval religious experience: the meditations over the Passion of

FIGURE 4.1: *Confession Before a Monk and a Deacon*, Dirc van Delft, *c.* 1400, Walters Art Museum, MS 171, fol. 112v. © Creative Commons (Public Domain).

Christ. In this case the Christian believer's point of departure was his or her semantic memory of the Gospel. It was believed that a mere knowledge of the Savior's life was not sufficient: the believers were expected to flesh out their knowledge with imaginations, emotions, and sensual perceptions which were to transform their knowledge into a kind of personal experience. In other words, the enterprise was to create episodic memories of the life of Christ on the basis of the semantic memories that one could learn in the church or from books.

These "memories" spread especially in late Middle Ages, the time from which many guides to such meditation, as well as several resulting personal meditations, survive. Although these texts are rather stereotypical, they provide information both on some patterns that would be deeply stamped into the minds and on ways of structuring and helping memory: There is frequently a spatial organization, ordered stops for the mind to consider, and aspects applying to the senses: colors, smells, tastes, sounds and physical feelings. Although the life of Christ is certainly a learned fact and thus it should be labeled as semantic memory, the late medieval meditations on the Passion are shaped as rich personal memories: they abound in sensual details and make the meditating individual a direct witness of the action—he or she not only sees but also smells and tastes and hears and feels—for example the dropping blood from the cross (Arvay 2011; McNamer 2009; Hale 1995).

FIGURE 4.2: *Mourning Christ* (*c.* 1415), the follower of the Master of the Calvary of Týn, polychrome wood relief. Museum of Religious Arts of the Plzeň diocese © Creative Commons (Public Domain).

FIGURE 4.3: *Crucifixion* (1420), Master of the Rajhrad Altarpiece, National Gallery, Prague. © Creative Commons (Public Domain).

Thus, semantic memory is transformed into episodic memory and Christ becomes truly internalized and strongly linked to deepest personal emotions. Texts of this type abound in both Latin and vernacular in late medieval West.[8] This concept of "personal Jesus" is a good example of the alterity of medieval memory culture: It is not natural to us to consider remembering the Passion as episodic recollection, and yet this is what it was in the Middle Ages.

The personalizing of the life of Jesus lies both behind personal devotion and much of hagiography.

Literary conventions of hagiographical texts shaped the ways saints were remembered and they even provided models of behavior for religious persons who had aspirations to be respected as spiritual leaders or even venerated as saints. Thus, e.g. Jeff Rider shows how several prominent victims of murder in the twelfth century all followed an established pattern in their behavior in order to be categorized as saints (Rider 2000). Similarly, an early narrative of the death of Jan Hus at the stake in Constance in 1415 are much inspired by the Gospel narratives of the Passion—Hus is described as climbing up the Calvary, praying the same Psalms as Christ etc. It is a question whether this imitation is primarily the work of the author, or whether Hus himself followed the Gospel model in the last moments of his life (Fudge 2011, Doležalová 2014).

Prospective memory—readiness to die

Unprepared death, i.e. death without confession, in the state of sin, was considered one of the worst possible events because it would cause eternal damnation according to

FIGURE 4.4: *The Three Living and the Three Dead*, mural painting (fifteenth century), St. Jodok church, Überlingen. © Creative Commons (Public Domain).

Catholic belief.[9] This concern led Christian thinkers to the prospective memory of death, that is, keeping on one's mind the necessity to be prepared for death which might come at any moment. Thus, a whole genre, *ars moriendi* (the art of dying) was dedicated to preparing oneself for death and keeping death on one's mind. Among other things, these texts provide detailed guidelines on blocking out worldly concerns and idle thoughts and turning one's mind to God and penitence in the last moments. The priest assists the dying one to search in his or her memory and find all sins to be confessed (Bayard 2000; Campbell 1995; Laager 1996; Borst et al. 1993).

This topic appears in literary texts too. For example, Petrarch's fictional dialogue with St. Augustine begins with the latter's reproaching the former: "What are you doing, wretched man? What are you dreaming about? [. . .] Do you not remember that you are mortal?"[10] Augustine urges Petrarch to remember his sins, his miserable human condition, and his approaching death several times in this dialogue. Petrarch's "forgetfulness" (*oblivio*) is the main target of this fictional Church Father: "You wouldn't be so surprised if forgetfulness had not overcome your mind. Indeed I must now remind you of a number of unpleasant things, however briefly."[11] Augustine comments on various events of Petrarch's life; thus, remembering death opens a unified perspective on the latter's life-story in its entirety.

Neuroscience distinguishes between retrospective and prospective memory, that is, memory of the past and "memory of future", i.e., remembering what should be done. The medieval "art of dying" can be considered a very special case of prospective memory. Unlike normal prospective memories, which have a certain deadline after which they become irrelevant (e.g. remembering to catch a train the next morning), the prospective memory of approaching death is relevant and pressing at every moment. Meditation, confession, and the memory of death must have resulted in one's mind in what neuroscience calls priming—the oft-repeated words and ideas become readily available on one's mind and shape new memories and even identity.

FIGURE 4.5: *The Three Living and the Three Dead—Roman de la rose*, Bibliothèque nationale de France, Cod. 378, fol. 1r. © Creative Commons (Public Domain).

PERSONAL INVOLUNTARY MEMORY

While describing the process of recalling a particular piece of information from memory in his *Confessions*, Augustine includes an observation on other pieces offering themselves:

> When I go into this storehouse, I ask that what I want should be brought forth. Some things appear immediately, but others require to be searched for longer, and then dragged out, as it were, from some hidden recess. Other things hurry forth in crowds, on the other hand, and while something else is sought and inquired for, they leap into view as if to say, "Is it not we, perhaps?" These I brush away with the hand of my heart from the face of my memory, until finally the thing I want makes its appearance out of its secret cell.[12]

Involuntary memory is exactly what Augustine describes here: Memories offering themselves unrequested, imposing themselves, pushing themselves forward in one's mind. They are impossible or difficult to control. The strongest of those, as the authors of treatises on artificial memory know and repeatedly mention, are linked to strong emotions.

Love

The image that love captures and empowers the whole person was familiar already in Classical Antiquity and was taken over in the Middle Ages, too. The memory of the beloved is constantly imposing itself in the mind of the lover and distracts his or her attention from other concerns. Love was often described as a kind of disease which affects one's brain and may even cause death. Abu Bakr Muhammad Ibn Abi Sulayman Dawud al-Isfahani (868–909), an important scholar in Baghdad, summarized the matter in the following way:

> Galen said that passionate love ['*ishq*] is an activity of the soul and it is hidden in the brain, in the heart, and in the liver. In the brain there are three places [i.e. ventricles]. Imagination is in the front [ventricle] of the head, thinking is in the middle, and

memory is in the back part [of the brain]. And nobody loves in the true sense of the word unless, when the one, whom he loves, departs, [the beloved one] does not disappear from his imagination, thinking, and memory as well as from his heart and his liver. And [such a person] is prevented from eating and drinking due to the troubled state of the liver, and cannot sleep due to the troubled state of his brain, [due to] his imagination, memory, and [due to] the thinking that is in him. All the places of his soul will be in a troubled state. But when he is not troubled at the time of the separation [from the beloved one], then he no longer loves [him], and when he meets him, then all these places [of the soul] are free [from the imprint of the beloved person].
—al-Isfahani 1932: 18

Similar ideas are echoed, for example, in the *Epistolae duorum amantium* (Letters of two lovers). The dating of this text has been debated—it survives in a manuscript written in the late fifteenth century by Johannes de Vepria, but seems to have been authored much earlier. There has also been disagreement whether it is a formulary of model letters or a real exchange, and it was even suggested that it is correspondence between Peter Abelard (1079–1142) and Héloïse (1095–1164) from the time of their love affair. For instance, the man in the collection writes: "Never do I wake so suddenly that my mind does not find you already in it."[13] The simple clause stresses the omnipresence of the thought of the beloved who is here not a memory that needs to be recalled but becomes part of the identity of the loving one. Along the same lines, the man continues in other letters, e.g.: "To his most beloved lady, whose remembrance no forgetting can obstruct, from her most faithful one. May I forget your name only when I no longer recall my own."[14] Or: "Farewell, my supreme hope, in whom alone I take pleasure, whom I need never recall to mind, because I never forget."[15]

From the rhetoric of love letters, love poems, and similar sources, it might seem that love was a positive experience. Yet, there is a connotation of the loss of control of one's mind, which might be perceived as thoroughly undesirable: a common image is that of love-sickness. From the Middle Ages, especially noteworthy in this respect is the correspondence between Abelard and Héloïse, following Abelard's autobiography. Here, they both recall their past love affair, each with different emotions. Abelard has moved on, transformed carnal feelings for a woman into spiritual love for God and insists that Héloïse does the same:

> Let us make good use of our austerities and no longer preserve the memories of our crimes amongst the severities of penance. Let a mortification of body and mind, a strict fasting, continual solitude, profound and holy meditations, and a sincere love of God succeed our former irregularities.
> —Hughes 1818: 154; cf. Bayle 1713: 194

Héloïse cannot forget and the thought of her beloved constantly disturbs her:

> . . . I ought to apply myself to extirpate my passion. How much better it were to forget entirely the object of it than to preserve a memory so fatal to my peace and salvation? Great God! shall Abelard always possess my thoughts? Can I never free myself from those chains which bind me to him?
> —Hughes 1818: 141; cf. Bayle 1713: 181

The involuntary memory imposes itself on her and all Abelard's advice for austereness is useless.

A century earlier Ali b. Ahmad Ibn Hazm (994–1064), a significant Muslim scholar of Andalusia, wrote that love should never be forgotten, even if it causes enormous distress. Forgetting was considered a reprehensible thing, a token of ignoble character. A noble person, Ibn Hazm argued, patiently endures all the pains of love, but forgets nothing "though in his heart there is a pricking anguish more painful than the stab of a stiletto" (Hazm 1981: 245; English translation Arberry 1953). Ibn Hazm's work was never translated to Latin and there is no evidence that Abelard and Héloise were aware of it.

This approach to love, shared by Jewish, Christian, and Muslim littérateurs, influenced theological literature too. A major Jewish theologian of the twelfth century, Moses Maimonides (1138–1204) pointed to love sickness as a possible model for the passionate love of God:

> What is the correct form of love? It is in the man who loves God with a love so great, abundant and mighty that his soul is bound to the love of God, and he devotes himself to it continuously, whether he is in repose or active, eating or drinking. Stronger than this is the love of God in the hearts of those who love him and devote themselves to the love of him continuously, as we have been commanded, "with all your heart and with all your soul" (Deuteronomy 6:5). And this is what Solomon meant metaphorically when he said, "I am lovesick" (Song of Songs 2:5). In fact, the whole book of the Song of Songs is an allegory of the subject.[16]

However, as the continuous remembering of the beloved one becomes an ideal to be imitated, it is no longer perceived as a symptom of a disease or uncontrollable passion, but as a norm to be followed. In Islamic (Sufi) mysticism continuous remembering of God is a central goal that is to be achieved through chanting the various names of Allah, and other rituals, which are all referred to as *dhikr*, that is, "remembering." Remembering God is more properly classified as "voluntary memory."

Intrusive thoughts

Intrusive thoughts are unwelcome, involuntary thoughts, images, or unpleasant ideas that may become obsessions, are upsetting or distressing, and can be difficult to get rid of and manage. They may be based on memory of an actual experience (may result from a trauma which might be repressed with more or less success) but also of an imagined event. Medieval examples are not easy to search for: autobiography is not a prominent genre in the Middle Ages, and, in general, there are few descriptions of personal negative experiences. If such descriptions occur, they are more likely to be found in letters, such as the following remark of Maimonides about the tragic death of his brother, David, in a private letter he wrote in Fustat (Old Cairo) in 1185:

> The greatest misfortune that has befallen me during my entire life—worse than anything else—was the demise of the saint,[17] may his memory be blessed, who drowned in the Indian sea, carrying much money belonging to me, him, and to others, and left with me a little daughter and a widow. On the day I received that terrible news I fell ill and remained in bed for about a year, suffering from a sore boil, fever, and depression, and was almost given up. About eight years have passed, but I am still mourning and unable to accept consolation. And how should I console myself? He grew up on my knees, he was my brother, [and] he was my student; he traded on the markets, and earned, and I could safely sit at home. He was well versed in the Talmud and the Bible, and knew (Hebrew) grammar well, and my joy in life was to look at him. Now all joy

> has gone. He has passed away and left me disturbed in my mind in a foreign country. Whenever I see his handwriting or one of his letters, my heart turns upside down and my grief awakens again. In short, "I shall go down to the nether world to my son in mourning" (Genesis 37:35).
>
> —Goitein 2015: 207

It is remarkable that Maimonides' intrusive memories were triggered by certain objects, namely, letters in the handwriting of the deceased brother. One may also observe that a biblical quotation is used by Maimonides to sum up his personal experiences. The usage of shorter or longer citations from sacred or classical texts as apt expressions of one's personal feelings is widely attested in medieval literate cultures.

Intrusive memories may also result in sleep disorders and repeated nightmares. One such occasion is known from a copy of a brief medieval letter in which a certain Sommer, priest at St. Michael's in Prague describes to a certain Roiko that he has been unable to sleep because of Jan Hus who is calling him to himself:

> I spent almost the whole night without any sleep, an image of Jan Hus was constantly showing itself to my eyes. I spent the day with the usual work, now I wish to rest, but I cannot. Because Hus calls me from the council of Constance and presents accusations, so I humbly pray to be granted that it [i.e. the council] brings a decisive judgement according to right and equity, and consequently I could sleep in peace.[18]

Here, there is involuntary memory of Jan Hus being examined in Constance—undoubtedly linked to bad conscience—which forces itself on Sommer and prevents him from resting.

There have been attempts at tracing post-traumatic stress disorder resulting from experiencing wars in the Middle Ages (see, e.g. Heebøll-Holm 2014) but the surviving sources do not provide conclusive evidence.

At the same time, it is not sure that the medievals would perceive any of the above discussed examples of "involuntary memory" as belonging to the category of memory at all. If a person or an event is constantly on one's mind, one does not have to enter the process of recollection, and thus one does not actually remember but simply thinks. The distinction between memory (recollection) and thinking (cogitation) was made by Aristotle in his *De memoria and reminiscentia*, a treatise that was much commented on throughout the Middle Ages. Thus, during the Middle Ages, memory was linked to effort that needs to be made in order to recall a stored image.

However, Ibn Rushd or Averroes (1126–98), a very influential medieval commentator of Aristotle, reinterpreted memory as the capacity to recognize individual objects and thus he "downplay[ed] the idea that memory is principally concerned with our awareness of the past as past" (Black 2017: 455). Averroes would be happy to know that while neuroscience came up with many distinctions and definitions of memory, it did not (yet?) find any solid distinction between the act of remembering and the act of thinking.

SELF-FASHIONING

Episodic memories can serve as building blocks in more sophisticated narratives about one's own life. However, when such an autobiographical narrative is constructed, episodic memories may be reshaped to fit the narrative pattern. As a person remembers his or her life in a new way, certain memories may be marginalized, forgotten, or suppressed, and thus, new regime of remembering is installed in his or her mind. In some exceptional cases we may observe the process of mnemonic take-over.

SCIENCE AND EDUCATION

Maimonides provides an interesting example again. Due to various historical circumstances, a relatively great amount of his autographic manuscripts, letters, and other documents have been preserved, which allow us to access some information which he may have not wished to share with us.[19] In one of his legal responsa, Maimonides addresses a Jewish mystical text, entitled *Shi'ur Qomah*, which purports to describe the mystical body of God. At the time he wrote this responsum, Maimonides firmly held the opinion that it is absurd to attribute any kind of corporeal existence to God. In fact, the incorporeality of God was a corner stone of Jewish theology in his thought. Therefore, he could not but condemn the mystical book in question as heretic that deserved to be burned. Interestingly, Maimonides emphasized that he had never ever been of a different opinion:

> I never thought that it was one of the works of the Sages of blessed memory [= Talmudic rabbis], and far be it from them that this [book] should have come from them. It is but a work of one of the Byzantine preachers, and nothing else. Altogether, it is a great *mitsva* to delete this book and to eradicate the mention of its subject matter; "and make no mention of the name of other gods" (Exodus 23: 13), etc., since he who has a body [*qomā*] undoubtedly is [to be classed among] "other gods."[20]

Despite Maimonides' claim we do have clear evidence that he did accept the mystical book in question as an authentic text when he was younger. In his commentary on the Mishnah, which he finished in 1168, when he was about thirty years old, Maimonides

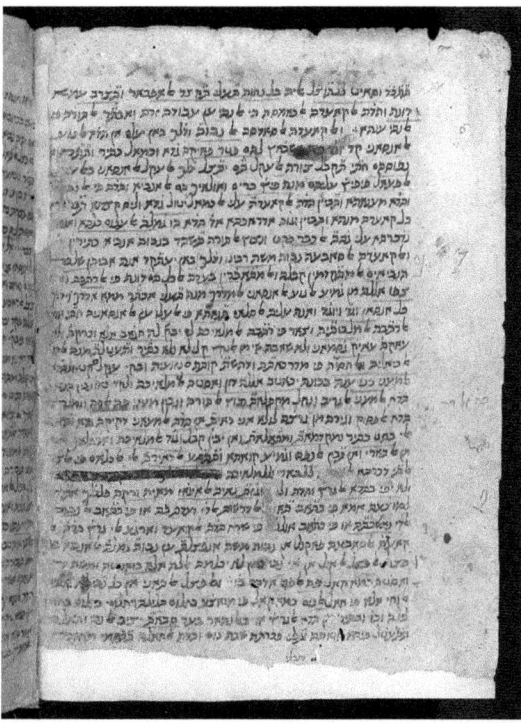

FIGURE 4.6: Maimonides' autograph with a passage crossed out, which expresses an idea he later denied to have ever believed. Oxford, Bodleian Library, MS Pococke 295, fol. 60v. © Bodleian Library.

included the *Shi'ur Qomah* in his list of the holy texts of Judaism.[21] However, in a precious Oxford manuscript (Bodleian, MS Pococke 295 (Neubauer, no. 404)), that was in all likelihood Maimonides' personal copy of the commentary on the Mishnah, the clause concerning *Shiur Qoma* is crossed out with a "bold stroke of deletion" probably by Maimonides himself.[22] When Maimonides changed his mind about the mystical text, he erased the relevant words in the autograph manuscript of his work, and later he plainly denied that he ever held this opinion.

Gathering personal memories into a single narrative leads to an important literary genre: autobiography. In medieval Latin tradition there are few autobiographies—coherent narratives that would offer an insight into personal life as a whole. It is surely partly due to the belief that one's life cannot be really grasped before it ends. The few autobiographies are linked to exceptional personalities and, in many cases, they have a clear agenda. Thus, the autobiography of Charles IV (*Vita Caroli*), may not only have been at least partly written by someone else, but it also clearly stresses only selected aspects—those that contribute to an image of a great ruler (Nagy and Schaer 2001; Antonín 2017). Abelard presents his autobiography *Historia calamitatum mearum* (The history of my misfortunes) as a private consolation to a friend.[23] Yet, it is generally agreed that Abelard meant it to become public and the text indeed abounds in self-defense and boasting that would be superfluous in consolation.

Autobiographies were more frequently written by Muslim intellectuals than by their Christian or Jewish peers.[24] Perhaps the oldest Arabic contribution to this genre is actually a translation from Middle Persian: Burzoe, the physician of the Sassanian emperor Khusraw Anushirawan (r. 531–79) related the history of his life in the introduction to his translation of the *Panchatantra*, an Indian collection of fables, which would be known in the Arabic tradition under the title "Kalilah and Dimnah." The original Middle Persian is lost, but its Arabic version by Ibn al-Muqaffa' (d. 755–6) survives and is considered the first masterpiece of Classical Arabic rhymed prose.

Building on this and other precedents, such as Galen's treatise about his own writings that was translated to Arabic by a Nestorian Christian medical writer, Hunayn Ibn Ishaq, autobiography became an important genre of Arabic literature. As a remarkable collective study on Arabic autobiographies states:

> In the late eleventh and twelfth century, there appears to have been a flowering of autobiographical writing and personal record keeping, which, if these did not constitute full autobiographies as such, were widespread enough for biographers such as Yāqūt to draw on extensively in compiling their biographical dictionaries. [. . .] Two lengthy, independent autobiographies from the beginning of this period, those of Ibn Buluggīn and al-Ghazālī, were composed within a few years of each other (c. 1095 and 1107), the former being a political family history, in which the author's life occupies well over half the work and the second a systematically organized account of the author's spiritual crisis, exploration of differing schools of religious philosophy, and eventual acceptance of Sufi teachings.
>
> —Reynolds et al. 2001: 53

Most of the medieval Arabic autobiographies focus on the studies and intellectual career, and they do not reveal much about the inner life of their heroes. Hilary Kilpatrick has identified "autobiographical fragments" in biographical collections that provide more colorful details. For example, the poet and singer Nusayb (d. 729) who lived in Egypt during the Umayyad times, relates some experiences that we would call today "racial discrimination": since he was black, some of the influential persons of contemporary Muslim society, including ʿAbd al-ʿAziz b. Marwan, the son of the caliph Marwan I, and governor of Egypt, were reluctant to admit his poetic achievements (Kilpatrick 1991: 5f). Another important example is the aforementioned Ibn Hazm (994–1064). In his treatise on love, Ibn Hazm relates several episodes of his romantic life including a longer narrative about his unhappy love with a slave girl in Cordoba during his adolescent years (Martinez-Gros 2013: 87–9).

Nostalgia?

Among fictional autobiographical narratives, one of the most famous is the prologue to the Wife of Bath's Tale. Chaucer's heroine has a complex, unique, and well-argued self-perception. Remembering her own past fills her with joy:

> But Lord Christ! when it all comes back to me,
> Remembrance of my youth and jollity,
> It warms the cockles of my heart. Today
> It still does my heart good that I can say
> I've had the world, what time's been mine to pass.[25]

There is other evidence of nostalgia, i.e. ameliorating one's personal memories, especially the memories of youth, in the Middle Ages. For example, evoking the memories of a beloved woman who left the poet is a standard element in the basic genre of Classical Arabic poetry, the *qasidah* (el Tayyib 1983: 43–52). Similarly, meditations about Time as a power that gradually dissolves everything important in human life is a frequent topic of medieval Arabic and Hebrew poetry (Tobi 2004: 219–46). As opposed to modern society, though, there is usually little nostalgia about childhood.[26] The concept of childhood was different in the Middle Ages, above all, due to health, material and social resources and especially mortality (e.g. Orme 1995). In addition, Christians believed that no one would remember anything from the first period of their lives because the memories would be washed away by the water of baptism.

Nostalgic memories may concern either personal or social situation. For example, in medieval Bohemia, there is a rich literary tradition of carefully crafted nostalgia about the reign of Charles IV and the time before the Hussite revolution; there are many more of such nostalgic narratives praising the wonderful past than there were contemporary praises (e.g. Kadlec 1986). This, however, does not necessarily mean that the nostalgic memories are false memories but simply that the past was better grasped in contrast with the present. In any case, looking back at one's life with sadness about the time gone forever seems to have been as frequent in the Middle Ages as it is today.

Individual and community memory

Ethnographers described "floating gaps" in African oral societies' knowledge of their past: memories of past events become more and more confused as time passes and they usually reach back to no more than fifty to eighty years (Vansina 1985; cf. Assmann 1997). Such "floating gaps" can sometimes be identified in medieval personal remembering too.

A fine example is the death of Jan Hus (in 1415 in Constance) giving rise to the Hussite movement, which, by backward association, became connected to communion under both kinds (*sub utraque specie*, that is, giving both bread and wine to laics at communion):

By the 1470s, it became a common belief that Jan Hus was burnt at the stake because he was promoting communion under both kinds. That was never the case. Similarly, there was a sun eclipse on June 7, 1415, the second day of Hus' investigation in Constance. It was an important event; the members of the council went to watch it together. Yet, later on, community memory emerged that the eclipse took place on the day of Hus' burning, July 6—clearly by association with the darkness accompanying the death of Christ according to the Gospels. In 1477, Kříž z Telče (Crux de Telcz, 1434–1504), at the time a preacher in Soběslav, later Augustinian canon of Třeboň (Wittingau), sent a letter to a utraquist priest in Tábor, consulting him exactly on these two issues—whether Hus was burnt because of the communion or for some other reason, and whether there was the eclipse at the time of his burning, or at some other time.[27]

This shows that the false memory, although it seemed doubtful to an intellectual, was deeply rooted in community memory sixty years after the event. The real controversy about Hus' teachings and the exact chronology of his trial and execution were not retained in the personal memory of most people; consequently, retrojections and fabricated memories could spread across various segments of society without much resistance.

CONCLUSION

This study has shown that there was a variety of reasons for recording personal memories in writing during the Middle Ages. A major source of motivation was religion: Personal recollections for religious purposes often stressed guilt, death, and, in case of Christianity, the unattainable model of the Passion of Jesus Christ. Remembering death entailed a unified perspective on one's life from birth; a gloomy view that centered on sins and miseries, but, nevertheless, allowed contemporaries of the Middle Ages to see themselves as individuals and masters of their own fate at least to some degree.

Also, memories were recorded in casuistic literature for professional purposes, including legal, medical, and penitential cases. Such personal memories were results of "directed remembering": A professional lawyer, physician or priest oriented the remembering subject to recall certain circumstances at the expense of others. Autobiographical narratives reshaped episodic memories frequently on the basis of narrative models learned from hagiographic or classical literature.

But remembering was not always a disciplined and controlled process. Love sickness (which included perpetual remembrance of the beloved) is more widely documented than other traumatic experiences, although also medieval writers occasionally reported how they suffered from intrusive memories. Loving and remembering God was sometimes compared to love sickness and it entailed forgetting this world for the sake of a transcendent reality.

Semantic memory played some role in articulating and recording most of the types of personal (episodic) memories: the individual's experiences were described as instances of generalized theories or imitations of sacrosanct models. Connecting the individual experiences to the pre-existent models was an essential component of the "know-how" of personal remembering in the Middle Ages; in this sense personal remembering was an "art of memory." This art was, however, not exercised in every sphere: there was, for example, no theoretical framework that encouraged recording personal traumatic memories, and consequently they occur infrequently in medieval sources.

Imposing pre-existent models on remembering helped the contemporaries of the Middle Ages to make sense of their memories, but it also put limitations on their recollections. Events or experiences that did not match the given models were likely to go unrecorded, and thus they remained inaccessible to posterity. And even the personal memories that were actually recorded may have easily been distorted in some respect in order to fit literary conventions or theoretical preconceptions.

CHAPTER FIVE

Ideas: Philosophy, Religion, and History

FARKAS GÁBOR KISS

The understanding of memory has never been static. In the last three centuries of the Middle Ages, several aspects of medieval memory practices started to change. Two examples should illustrate these transformations here: Around 1500, a Franciscan friar in Poland devised three images which were supposed to help the memorization of his sermons, which he appended to his manuscript containing mnemonic advice (Kiss et al. 2016). The first one represents Christ with a dagger and a flute, a cartwheel, a candle, and a jar attached to his two hands and legs, whereas he wears a cross on the top of his head. These kind of images with Christ and a dagger etc. are not a rarity by the end of the Middle Ages: The verses of the Gospels have been similarly depicted and summarized in a series of curious illustrations that have been copied in manuscripts and later on printed with the title *Figurae Evangelistarum*.[1] The following two drawings reveal a more startling aspect of the late medieval understanding of memory. The contents of two sermons—probably held in front of a Franciscan community—are summarized by the images of two devils, one of them sitting, the other standing naked upfront (Figures 5.1 and 5.2).

How was it possible that the Christian message of the sermon, stored in the form of mnemonic symbols on the five body parts of Satan could be reconciliated with Satan itself? The advice of rhetoric is well known—one should conceive striking and occasionally alarming images because they help memory.[2] However, is it not somehow forbidden to combine a virtuous message with a devilish image? Is not the mind contaminated if it retains devils just in order to be able to deliver a sermon? Should not virtuous messages be remembered by virtuous mental images? Or is immoral imagination allowed if the general purpose is morally good?

The second change that needs to be addressed can be illustrated by an early print, the *Congestorium artificiose memorie* (Compilation about artificial memory) of Johannes Romberch, a German Dominican from Cologne who wrote it at the beginning of the sixteenth century, but the text was published in Venice only in 1520 (Romberch 1520). Romberch's work has been justly called a final stage of late medieval art of memory, as the author compiled a number of memory aids which were circulating in manuscript form in the fifteenth century into one single collection (Yates 1966). It is a treatise on memory as a part of rhetoric practice. Nevertheless, the first image contained in the book (see Figure 5.3) is not an *imago agens*, an "active image" that would be typical for a medieval art of memory.

Instead, it displays an anatomical head marking four senses out of the five, and depicting the internal structure of the brain, starting with common sense (*sensus*

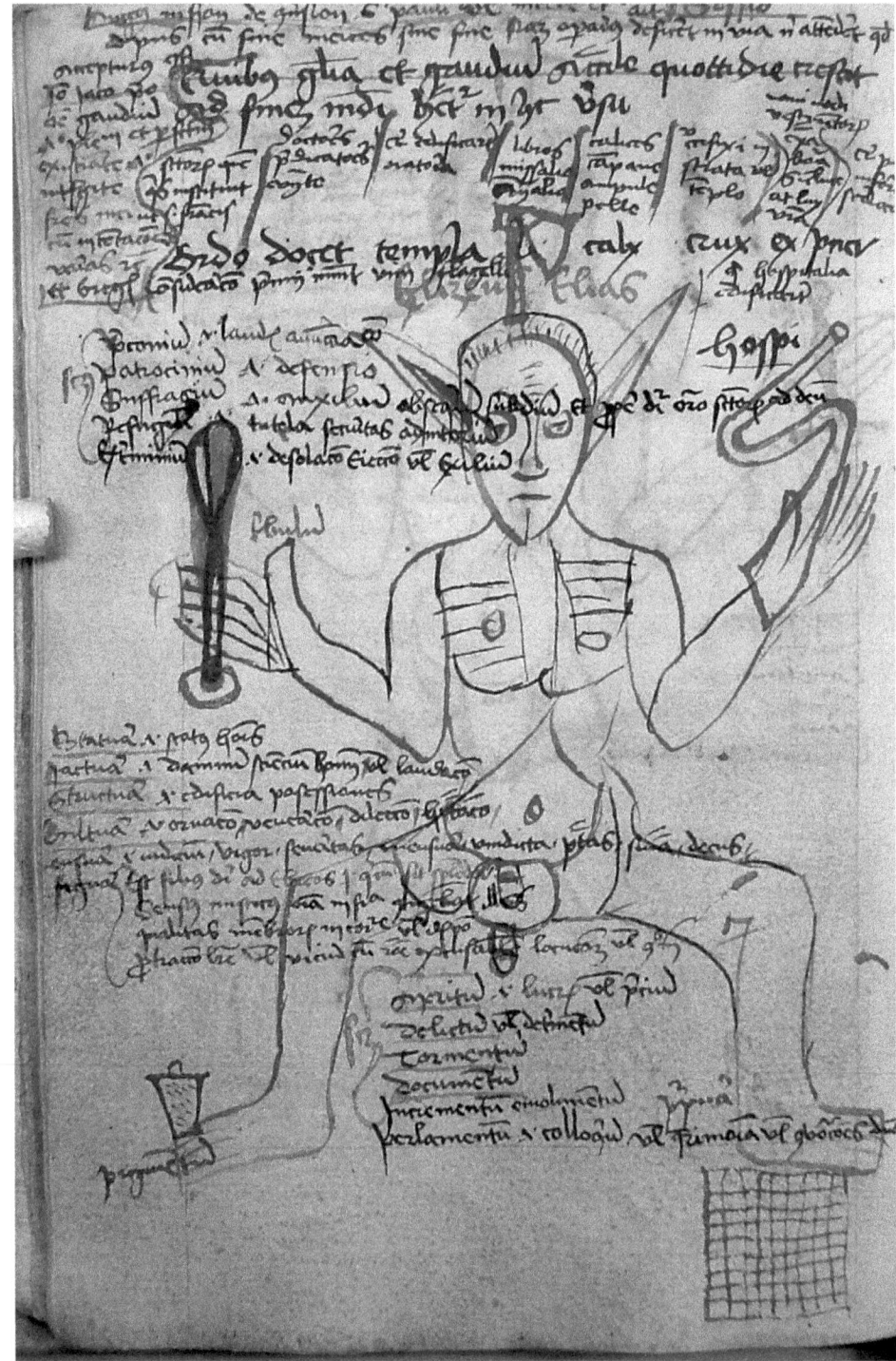

FIGURE 5.1: Memorial aid for remembering the parts of the sermon. Miscellaneous manuscript containing various sermons and tracts for observant preachers, fifteenth century. Biblioteka Kórnicka, ms. 1122. 24v. © Biblioteka Kórnicka, Poland.

FIGURE 5.2: Biblioteka Kórnicka, ms. 1122. 25r. © Biblioteka Kórnicka, Poland.

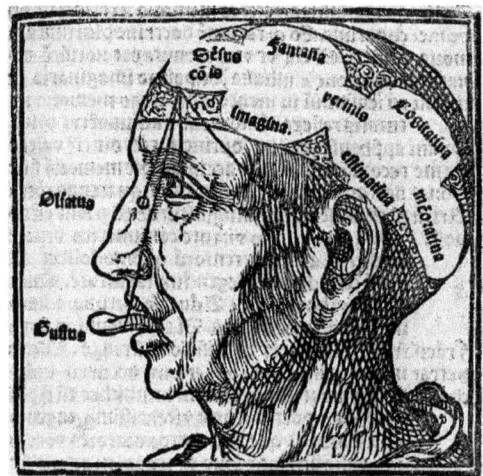

FIGURE 5.3: Johannes Romberch, *Congestorium artificiose memorie* (Venice: Georgius de Rusconibus, 1520), B1v. © Creative Commons (Public Domain).

communis) on the front, where all sensory nerves arrive, continuing with imagination, phantasy, cogitation/intellect, estimation, and finally arriving to memory, the *vis memorativa*. This image type is well-known from medieval sources, basically representing Avicenna's theory of the faculties of the soul (see Hasse 2010). But how is it connected to the rhetorical aspect of memory that is otherwise the main subject of Romberch's treatise? Such images of the brain also occur in meditational manuscripts—for example, as in a mid-fifteenth manuscript containing mnemonic texts from the Benedictine abbey of Melk (Stiftsbibliothek, cod. 1835, p. 186) (Kiss 2012).

Did these anatomical drawings of the internal structure of the brain help the users to meditate and memorize? How did the conceptualization of memory processes change their attitude to the practice of memorization? Was there some more intrinsic connection between late medieval memory practices and the medical knowledge about the brain structure?

In this chapter, I will argue that the metaphors of memory processes provide an invaluable clue to trace these changes. It is well-known that human cognition relies on metaphor systems in the process of thinking and metaphors have a fundamental role in human perception and understanding by allowing the mind to construct complex social, cultural and psychological realities.[3] Metaphoric descriptions of the mental processes of reminiscing and memorization have radically changed from the late Antiquity to the late Middle Ages, and the twelfth century marked a turning point in this process, closely reflecting the revival of Greco-Arabic medicine, meditative spirituality, and dialectic thinking. Examining these modifications in the metaphoric descriptions of memory processes will greatly contribute to our understanding of the possible connections between the increasing importance of a medical conception of memory and the morality of memorization in the last centuries of the Middle Ages.

What are the metaphoric constructs that characterized memory in the Middle Ages? In the late Antiquity and the early Middle Ages, the primary quality of human memory was its weakness and frailty. When the Roman senator Cassiodorus extolled the virtues of

PHILOSOPHY, RELIGION, AND HISTORY 95

FIGURE 5.4: Mid-fifteenth manuscript containing texts on the *ars memoriae* from the Benedictine abbey of Melk (Stiftsbibliothek Melk, cod. 1835), p. 186. © Stiftsbibliothek Melk.

memory in the name of Theoderic the Great on the occasion of the appointment of a new member of the administration, a certain Capuanus in 523/526[4] wrote: "There is a great benefice in not having the defect of oblivion, and it is almost like being among the Gods to have everything always at present, what has ever happened in the past."[5] His words suggest that good memory—one that befits a newly selected archivist—is a rare, unique, and almost divine asset; it is the faculty of knowing all the events that took place in the past, and of keeping track of it, as if one was God. Cassiodorus invested memory with a supernatural quality that can be paralleled to Boëthius' contemporary aim of considering the events of the world *sub specie aeternitatis*, from the perspective of eternity. Boëthius' advice in the *Consolation of Philosophy* was not to lose sight of the divine perspective, the eternal horizon, by focusing too much on the material and earthly side of existence. Instead, the wise philosopher avoids public action and leads a life of contemplation (*vita contemplativa*) in order to get closer to divine vision (Boëth. *Cons*. 5, 2 and 5).[6] This contemplation observes the turns of fate, the machinery of the world, the causes and effects of events with serenity and tranquility. In comparison, Cassiodorus' divine perspective is different. It records the events instead of considering their causes, and its main aim is to avoid oblivion.

Cassiodorus' eloquent praise of memory was prompted by a rather unusual circumstance: Capuanus, the subject of Cassiodorus' letter was a stammerer, as it is clear from the euphemistic description that he as the head of Theoderic's administration provided.[7] As he wrote, although his oratorical skills may have been less advanced than desirable, and he may not have sounded as fluent in speech as others, his memory was prodigal. By a rhetorical turn, Cassiodorus made a virtue out of Capuanus' hampered speech, and claimed that he could retain more archival knowledge than others, and that he could be justly called a treasure house (*thesaurus*) of memory: "That memory, which is justly called the thesaurus of orators, is so firmly incorporated in him, that whatever he heard once, you would think that he has hidden it in writing."[8] The metaphors of memory imply two important background concepts here: an enclosed and heavily guarded space, as a treasure house, and recondite knowledge that is retained from the curious public not only by the stammering Capuanus, but also by the very nature of memory, its mental seclusion from the physical world.

The diffusion of these ancient ideas in the Middle Ages was secured not only in manuscript copies of Cassiodorus' text, but also by their reappearance in arengas of charters, i.e. the specific narrative section in the preambles of charters. This provided a constant field of reception to the idea of the memory as a fragile carrier of things in the past that can nevertheless be guarded in a safe storeroom. Cassiodorus' claim about Capuanus' memory, for example, found an unexpected audience in the early thirteenth century in Hungary, where the sentence about the benefices of good memory was quoted in letters and arengas of charters, as it justified the use of writing in the field where it was most needed, the administration of official documents. The idea that "there is a great benefice in not having the defect of oblivion, and it is almost like being among the Gods to have everything always at present, what has ever happened in the past" was reused in completely unrelated matters, once in a tithe transaction, and once in a donation of an estate to a bishopric.[9] Taken out of its original context, where it referred to the unwritten knowledge of a state archivist, the sentence started to circulate praising the virtue of writing as a tool of immortalizing the memory of deeds, and at the same time recorded the concept of memory as a frail human faculty, as opposed to writing. The circulation of this commonplace also demonstrates how the memory's frailty was generally perceived as an obstacle to fulfilling human mental capacities, which led to the medieval revival of the *artes memoriales*, the artificial drills for memory improvement which aimed at intensifying one's mnemonic capacities. In fact, the broad dissemination of the idea that human memory is frail, instable, and broken—which was considered a result of limited access to writing—might have stimulated the growing interest in these memory techniques in the Middle Ages.

METAPHORS OF MEMORY

An examination of collocations (as Firthian linguists call the sequence of words and terms that often co-occur) dealing with memory would definitely reveal a lot about the changing perceptions of mnemonic practices throughout the Middle Ages. Using the arengas of charters as a kind of repertoire of common place knowledge of the high Middle Ages, it seems that the conceptual field of memory included several facets. First and foremost, it was unstable and fragile, whereas its counterpart, writing—as we have seen above—was seen as firm. Perhaps one of the most popular starting phrases of the preambles of high medieval charters is the sentence "human memory is unstable" (*labilis est hominum memoria*),[10] one that was probably memorized by the clerks as it could be used on any occasion of putting something into writing. In fact, this idea has been so widespread that its presence was deemed to be insufficient to prove the influence of one scriptorium on another, or the use of one collection of model charters in another center of learning (Iwanami 2004).[11] Beside the ever recurring phrase *labilis est hominum memoria*, one often finds the adjective *fragilis* attached to memory, which refers to the fragmentation of past events because of its weakness. The metaphoric constructs of lability and its opposite, stability, of firmness and changeability, evoke the concept of memory as a container, a treasure house or a building. Another related variant calls memory fragile, *fragilis*: "Because memory is fragile, and cannot hold too many things."[12] Indeed, if we look for the origins of this phrase which was so widely used in arengas composed in the thirteenth and fourteenth century chanceries, we find that it stems from Seneca the Younger, who openly claimed that "memory is a very frail vessel, and is not strong enough to hold a mass of things; it must necessarily lose to the extent that it receives, and the newest impressions crowd out the oldest" (Basore, trans. 1935). Seneca's fundamental concept of memory, as a "vas fragile," a frail vessel, is responsible for many of the metaphoric expressions and collocations associated with memory. In comparison with writing, unwritten memory is unstable. Since memory is fragile, and—going a step further—even infirm, almost sick, it is necessary to confirm it by written witnesses, in order to remedy its weaknesses. The presence of the adjective sick/weak (*infirmus*) or unstable (*labilis*), or the idea of bringing remedy to this situation (*remedio succurratur*), already prognosticates the medical treatment of memory, that become the subject of numerous treatises from the late thirteenth century onwards, as for example that of the popular *De bonitate* by Arnald of Villanova (1235–1311).[13]

One further concept closely attached to memory is the question of dryness and fluidity. Memory is often called fluid in charters: it *flows* (*defluit, elabitur*) into oblivion, it has to sustain the *flow* (*fluxus*) of time. To quote one example from Bremen in 1235: "The finger of the mighty Nature has inscribed into human minds, that those things which are carried out by mankind in the course of time, should be ripened by human diligence, and put into writing when they are mellow, so that they *would not flow into the depth of oblivion with time as time flows by*."[14] The background of these metaphors is more than a simple similarity between the quick flow of time, and the passing of memory: As we will see, according to the humoral pathology of Galen, the best conditions for memory were cold and dry, as it was imagined as a kind of storage place. Just like memory's fragility and instability is an unwanted circumstance, in the same way fluidity can lead to oblivion.

"MEMORY CELLS"

However, a new popular imagery of memory started to emerge around the twelfth century which did not have any roots in Antiquity and was not focused on its weaknesses. Rather, it described the process of memorizing using a specific terminology, referring to the *memorial cells* in the brain. Just to quote the preamble of a charter from the early fourteenth century as an example: "Because the capacity of memorial cells does not suffice to store in memory the diverse prolixity of contracts, it is necessary to immortalize the circumstances of events by a series of letters."[15] The popular references to memorial cells, or brain cells from the twelfth century onwards, peaking in the thirteenth and fourteenth centuries, suggest that by this time the rhetorical concept of memory as a tool of performance started to be at least partially complemented by a medical one. Perhaps the most important influence on the evolution of a fresh concept of memory, one that is less fluid, less corrupt, and that can be manipulated and directed, was a new, medical understanding of the functions of the brain, which reached the Latin West in the twelfth century.

It was Nemesius of Emesa, a Christian philosopher of the late fourth century, whose writings were instrumental in transmitting the ancient theory of a tripartite division of the brain. Working under Platonic influence, he identified three cerebral ventricles, which he held responsible for phantasy (or imagination), intellect and memory, respectively. The *Peri physeos anthropou* was translated into Latin with the title *Premnon physicon* by Alphanus, the archbishop of Salerno in the late eleventh century.[16] Whereas this early translation was not very influential, a new translation was prepared by Burgundio of Pisa in 1159 (Verbeke and Moncho 1975), who dedicated his work to Emperor Frederic Barbarossa, and attributed the original to no lesser an authority than St. Gregory of Nyssa.[17] Burgundio's attribution was widely taken up by the readers of the text in the late twelfth and thirteenth century, which contributed to its popularity with philosophers such as Albert the Great or Thomas Aquinas. According to Nemesius, vision receives the freshly incoming images, memory stores them, and the mind connects the sensory experiences with the items stored in memory.[18] Nemesius, following the Aristotelian tradition, differentiates between memory and reminiscence, the latter of which he defines as "it is called remembrance when oblivion mediates memory."[19] Reminiscence is the restoration process of corrupt memory, which extends not only to sensory experiences and knowledge, but also to ideas as e.g. the existence of God.[20] The organ, which retains these images, is in the back of the brain, the "posterior ventricle," and the "*animalis spiritus*" which is inside it.[21] Nemesius proves the existence of these differing brain functions by the example of various brain lesions which have an impact on the sensory experience, the intellectual capacities and the memory according to the location of the injuries.

The word *cellula*, little cell, does not appear in either of Nemesius' translations, as Alfanus translates it into Latin as *venter*, belly, and Burgundio as *ventriculus*, ventricle, instead. Nevertheless, the idea of brain cells gained widespread acceptance around 1200 by works which popularized the ideas of Nemesius (and were falsely attributed to the authority of St. Gregory of Nyssa!) and complemented it with the humoral pathology of

Galen through Arabic intermediaries. The ventricular conception of the brain was a central element in the psychology of Avicenna,[22] and he discussed the anatomical separation of the soul's faculties in the brain in his medical *Canon* (1.1.6.1–6),[23] which in turn became influential for popular Latin medical handbooks as the *Speculum medicinae* of Arnaldus of Villa Nova (Bazell 1993). Galenic theories on the brain and the memory processes were transmitted among others by Ibn Al-Jazzar, whose treatise on forgetfulness and its treatment was translated into Hebrew and paraphrased in Latin, as well.[24] Nevertheless, the first Latin texts to combine the theory of humors and brain ventricles seems to originate from the Salernitan medical school from the twelfth century. The *Anatomy of master Nicholas, the physician*,[25] which might be a written version of a lecture at the Salernitan school, described the memory cells in detail:

> [The brain] is divided into three cells, the cellula phantastica in the anterior part of the head, the cellula logistica in the middle, the cellula memorialis in the posterior part. In the cellula phantastica imagination is said to have its seat, reason in the cellula logistica, memory in the cellula memorialis. The first cell is hot and dry, having much spirit and a little marrow; the second is hot and moist, having much spirits and much marrow; the third is cold and dry, having little spirits and much marrow [medulla!].
>
> [. . .] The cellula logistica is hot and moist for the following reason: just as among the natural forces there is digestion of what has been received, and separation of the purities from impurities of the diet, by the action of heat and moisture, so also among the functions of the mind there is a property of discrimination brought about by heat and moisture, by which things received into the cellula phantastica are distinguished, for instance, the true from the false, the honest from the dishonest, merriment from sobriety, and other contrasting things. [. . .] The cellula memorialis is cold and dry, for the following reason: Just as among the natural functions, there is first an attraction of nutriment by heat and dryness, and digestion by heat and moisture, and then there must be retention by means of cold and dryness; so likewise among the functions of the mind, besides the attraction of ideas to the cellula phantastica by heat and dryness, and the separation of the true from the false, and so forth, in the cellula logistica, by heat and moisture, there must be also retention, and this is carried out in the cellula memorialis by the action of cold and dryness. For this reason that cell is called treasure house of the memory. It has much marrow, that it may be easily stamped with the impressions of diverse ideas, but not much spirits, which might flow about and remove the impressions of ideas.
>
> —Corner1927

These ideas found their way not only into various revisions of this anatomical text, as the Salernitan *Anatomia Cophonis*,[26] or the *Anatomy* of Richard the Salernitan. Richard of Salerno, or Richardus Anglicus as he was often named in manuscripts, coupled the idea of the cells with the image of the brain as a temple:[27]

> Furthermore, the brain is called a temple of the soul, or of wisdom, or of science. Because as there are three principal parts in a temple, the vestibule, the consistory and the repository (apotheca), the same is true for the brain. Hence, various forms are conceived by the soul in the phantastic cell, as if in a vestibule; in the logistic (rational) cell a decision is made about the imaginative forms as in a consistory, and in the memorial cell, as if in a repository, reason selects those things which were taken up by the imagination, and sends them to the memory for conservation.

The very same idea was taken up by William of Conches in the mid-twelfth century in his encyclopedic dialogue called *Dragmaticon*,[28] and then by Vincent de Beauvais in his *Speculum maius*, written in the second half of the thirteenth century.

> Furthermore, the physicians propose that the brain is a temple or a seat of the soul, and mostly in respect to the part of the soul, which is rational. Because as there are three principal parts in a temple, the vestibule, the consistory and the repository (apotheca), so the phantastic, logistic and memorial cell are the principal parts of the brain. The soul receives by the imagination various forms with the phantastic cell, it decides about the imagined things in the logistic cell as if in a consistory, and it conserves in the memorial cell–as if in a repository–those things which the imagination received and the reason discerned.[29]

As the *Speculum maius* of Vincent de Beauvais was the most extensive and perhaps the most widely used encyclopedia of the late Middle Ages,[30] it transmitted the ventricular conception to other handbooks and preaching aids, as e.g. the *Aureum Rosarium* of the Hungarian observant Franciscan Pelbárt of Temesvár at the end of the fifteenth century.[31]

On the other hand, philosophical commentaries on Aristotle's *On the Soul* (*De anima*), a standard work commented on at all faculties of arts from the thirteenth century onwards, also became instrumental in transmitting the doctrine of brain ventricles. Whereas Aristotle's *On the Soul* did not contain references to the physical distribution of brain functions, these commentaries already have combined the practical medical knowledge derived from Galen and its Arabic successors with the Aristotelian theory of the soul (see Martino 2006; Martino 2008; Nikulin 2015). Two examples will suffice here. In the anonymous commentary *On the Soul* of a probably English master, written in Italy around 1250, and preserved in a single Siena manuscript,[32] the theory of brain ventricles is interspersed with references to *Metaphysics* of Al-Ghazali,[33] which described in detail how the three virtues, or powers of the brain (the phantastic, the logistic/rational, and the memorative virtue) can communicate with each other by identifying the sensory experiences in the storehouse (*archa*) of forms and intentions. As the commentator quotes from Al-Ghazali: "this cogitative virtue once turns to look for those [forms] which are in repository (*archa*) of forms, and once it turns to look for them in the repository of intentions."[34] Thus, the cogitative virtue acts as a kind of merchant, commuting and exchanging forms between the two repositories. The repository of intentions is located in the frontal part of the posterior concavity of the brain, where the estimative virtue is located, whereas the memorative virtue is placed in the back part of the posterior concavity, retaining whatever the estimative virtue has perceived about the non-sensory intentions. Relying on Avicenna, the author claims, that memorative virtue is related in the same way to the estimative virtue as imagination is related to common sense (*sensus communis*).[35] Thus, due to Al-Ghazali's and Avicenna's influence, anatomical knowledge about the brain became part of the discussions of the soul's virtues by the thirteenth century.

Another example, which clearly demonstrates the infiltration of medical ideas into the commentaries on Aristotle's *On the Soul*, is a late fifteenth century work of a professor of Cracow, John of Głogów.[36] As he published a commentary on Johannes Versor's widespread summary of Aristotle's teachings on the soul, he discussed in detail the question "whether there are only five interior senses" (John of Głogów 1501). Noting the differences between the various divisions of the brain ventricles by philosopher on the one hand, and by physician on the other, he finally accepts the views of Avicenna on that

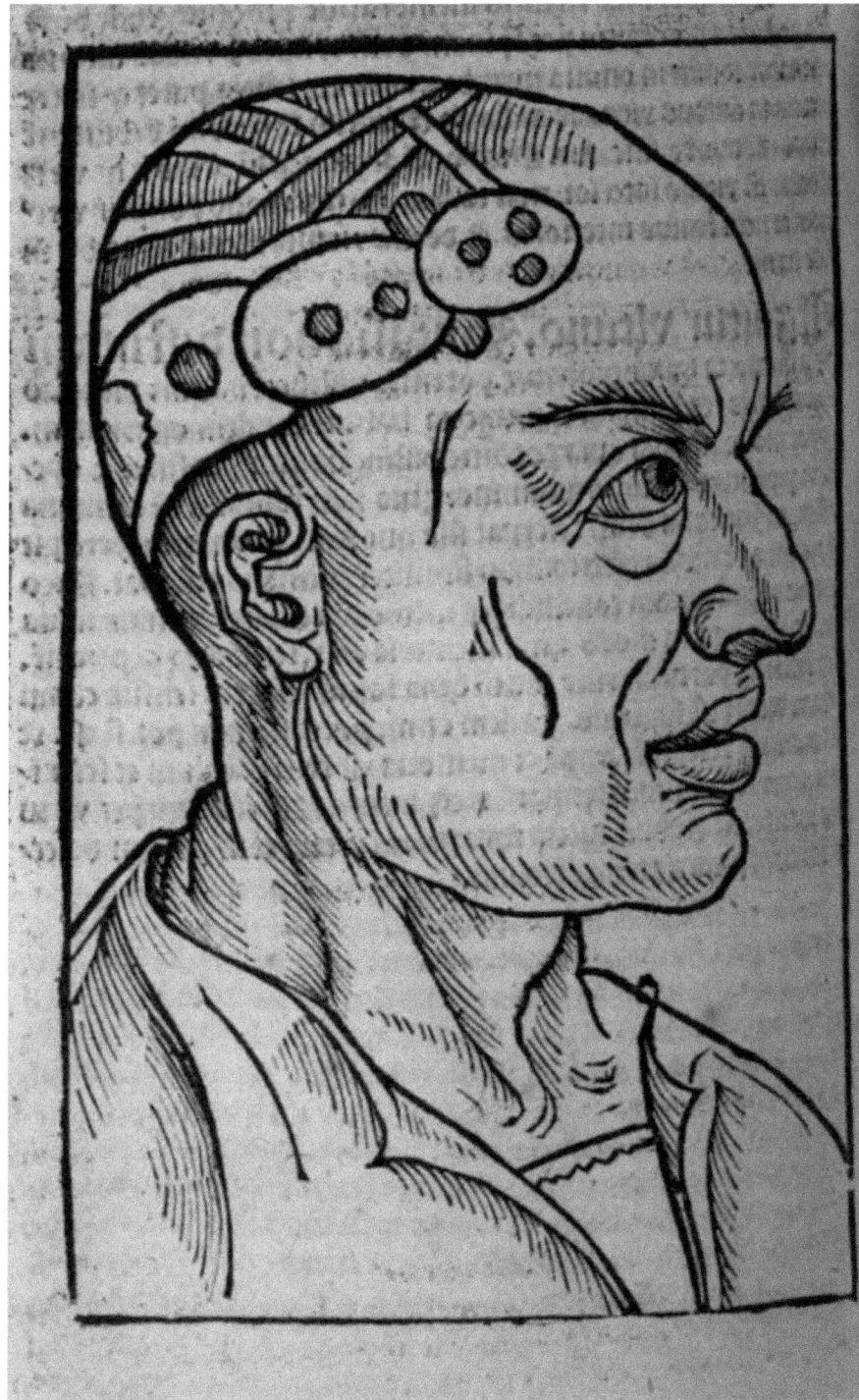

FIGURE 5.5: John of Głogów, *Questiones librorum de anima magistri Johannis Versoris*, impensis Johannis Haller, Metz, Caspar Hochfeder, 1501. © Creative Commons (Public Domain).

question and also distinguishes five interior senses altogether (John of Głogów 1501). Nevertheless, when discussing these philosophical questions, he frequently refers to the medical anatomy of Mundinus (Mondino de Liuzzi), a physician of Bologna, who wrote his *Anathomia* in 1316.[37] Moreover, John of Głogów inserted an image depicting the brain ventricles after his questions about the interior senses, and added a longer text with the title "Explanation of the physical head" ("*Declaratio capitis phisici*").[38]

Such images of the brain ventricles became omnipresent in introductory handbooks on philosophy by the fifteenth century, as, for example, in the *Parvulus philosophiae*, sometimes attributed to Albert the Great, but probably composed by Peter of Dresden in Prague,[39] or even in general introductory handbooks to the arts course, as the *Margarita philosophica* of Gregor Reisch (1503). The case of John of Głogów's university textbook shows that not only standard introductory handbooks to the arts course, but also specific philosophical treatises on the powers of the soul were deeply influenced by the medical and anatomical knowledge of Arabic medicine by the fifteenth century. The philosophical conception of memory was directly exposed to the medical interpretation of the brain's functions, and the two approaches were aligned to each other in an "interdisciplinary" manner.[40]

The influence of these medical doctrines on the imagery of memory cannot be measured exactly, but a few telling signs indicate that they had a tremendous impact on the conceptualization of memory even outside the circles of medical doctors and philosophical lecture rooms. Unfortunately, there exists not a single medieval Latin linguistic corpus which would incorporate all memory-related words and expressions from all over Europe, but it is possible to test the database of the Patrologia Latina in order to retrieve the occurrences of memory cells or *cellula memorativa* in Latin works before 1200, the end date of Father Migne's collection. The only examples this database yields are from the *De disciplina scolarium*, and the *Moralium dogma philosophorum*, which are actually false hits, as they are not the works of Boëthius and Honorius of Autun to whom they were attributed in Migne's outdated edition.[41] Thus, we may rightly suppose that before 1200, only William of Conches' *Dragmaticon* and medical works contained references to memory cells, and the theory of brain ventricles started to be employed widely in a metaphorical sense only afterwards.

A good case in point is the *De disciplina scolarium* (*Scholars' discipline*), attributed widely to Boëthius in the Middle Ages, but actually written in Paris around 1230 or 1240, as an introductory textbook to student life at the Faculty of Arts (Weijers 1976). It was one of the most popular introductions, which included advice to teenage students on how to study and provided some general terminology which might have come in handy at the beginning of their studies, e.g. the theory of human complexions. At least 111 manuscripts transmit this work, and Olga Weijers could identify thirty-two commentaries on it in the 1970s, so it had an extremely broad dissemination all around late medieval Western and Central Europe. Its condensed and flamboyant style often leaves the reader perplexed, as we will see from the following examples. The literary canon is characterized using these words: "The tradition of Seneca, the incompleteness of Lucan, the prolixity of Vergil, the urbanity of Statius, the coarse translation of Horace, the even coarser publication of Persius, the derogatory insult of Martial, the discretion of Ovid all have to be investigated, and transmitted to the memorial cell."[42] As the *De disciplina scolarium* employs the words "transmit to the memorial cell" instead of simply speaking of "remembering," its aim must have been to impress its readers by its specialized choice of terminology. A similar example reflects a metaphorical use of the theory of the impression of phantastic cells, applied to the memory cells: "The definitions of the terms, which we call syncategoreumata, are supposed to be *impressed to the mind by memory*, because they do no little service sophistically to the phantasy."[43] Thus, this introductory textbook applies the recently introduced, twelfth century ideas on the brain ventricles, and the students were exposed to the medical concept of memory processes from a very young age on.

Not only the *De disciplina scolarium* reflected the widespread popularity of these ideas, but also the near contemporary *About the mode of studying (De modo addiscendi)* of Gilbert of Tournai, which frequently referred to the work of Pseudo-Boëthius. Gilbert of Tournai was born around 1200 and entered the Franciscan order around 1240, becoming a master regent of the Paris *studium generale* after the departure of Bonaventure, his close friend.[44] His *De modo addiscendi* was written in order to help the studies of a young student from an aristocratic family in Paris at the request of the rector of the university (Bonifacio 1953). While he used the *De disciplina scolarium* and the works of Vincent de Beauvais (including his pedagogical treatise the *De eruditione puerorum*), the result was a more detailed and stylistically less overreaching introduction to university studies, written for older and more advanced students. Gilbert discussed thoroughly the moral conditions of study (Book 1), and the necessary requirements of a good professor (Book 2) in order to arrive at a thorough exploration of the actual process of studying. Evidently, memory played a central role in university studies, therefore Gilbert analyzed the physical procedure of memorizing using the medical-philosophical ideas whose influence we have already recorded above. He based his arguments on the *Nature of man* of Nemesius (attributing it to Remigius—a common misnomer in the Middle Ages) (see Brady 1948) and on the Arabic philosophical tradition—Avicenna, Averroes and Al-Ghazali (Rivers (2010). Gilbert combined the rhetorical, philosophical, and medical traditions into one continuous narrative about memory, where most memory issues have a medical background, and dedicated large space to the treatment of these problems.[45] Overzealous studying might "destroy the memorial cell," and result in insomnia; and elderly people are worse at remembering, if the humid and cold quality is preponderant in them, as memory images leak away from them just like in a ruined building, which there is no isolation anymore and the walls are putrid.[46] Moreover, he offers detailed help to students struggling with memory problems, based on the *Viaticum* of Constantine the African.[47]

Whereas there is no source collection in the field of medieval Latin, the rhetoric use of scientific terminology might be an efficient indicator of the spreading of these ideas. The example I would like to show comes from an important late thirteenth century handbook on canon law, prepared by one of the greatest canonists of the century, Guillaume Durand (the Elder) (Thibodeau 2007). Durand, who lived in Bologna, and then earned the bishopric of Mende in Southern France, compiled his enormous *Repertorium aureum*, also called *Breviarium*, after 1279 by restructuring the corpus of canon law according to recurrent problematic situations, as e.g. the elections or the translations of bishops.[48] In doing so, his purpose was to create a more user-friendly interface to the decretals, but at the same time, to avoid the necessity of memorizing the whole collection in order to solve frequently occurring legal cases. Therefore, when he dedicated his work to Cardinal Matthew of Acquasparta, he blamed the need of preparing this compilation on the finiteness of human memory:

> The human condition of the memory cell, which is contaminated by the rust of the firstly created [Adam] is so much eclipsed in its task, that it loses whatever it does not

receive often, or upon which it does not constantly meditate, exactly as a ripped sack, from which everything falls out what was put into it from another side, so that whatever is taken in through one ear, it goes out at one through the other.[49]

Although Durand's complaint about the faults of human memory were not unique at all in the age, his dedication gained a certain popularity not because of its inherent truth, but due to its extraordinary style which continued this description by citing a number of ecclesiastic canons that could be connected to the subject of memory. His witty paratextual sentences were copied out—together with the cited church canons!—in one of the earliest handbooks of chess problems, the so-called "Bonus Socius" collection, where the author introduced himself as "bonus socius," or "good company" in the prologue after the very same considerations about the errors of human memory.[50] Certainly, protracted chess endings might have borne some similarity to complicated cases of canonic lawsuits, but the reference to the mistakes of memorial cells in the fallen state of mankind is rather the result of a changing conception of memory, which reflects a biological approach to the subject. As Durand's *Repertorium* was a fundamental and popular handbook of canon law, his wording made its way into preambles of charters, as well, and surfaced a few years after its publication—even before the end of the thirteenth century—in as distant places of Europe as Brześć Kujawski in Poland, and Kättilstorp in Sweden.[51] Obviously, the medical-biological conception of memory, which emphasized the procedural aspects of memorizing, made such an impact on the intellectual audience, that speaking of memorial cells, it was acceptable not only in a scholarly milieu, but also in all kinds of written texts.

FROM PIOUS TO AGITATING MNEMONIC TECHNIQUES

How would it be possible to describe the consequences of this new, medico-philosophical approach to memory? Most importantly, the morality of memory is less than apparent in these cases: in fact, sensory perception is not guided by morality at all, and no mention is made of any morality-based preselection of the memory subject by the *vis cogitativa*. While Frances Yates had called attention to the fact that according to Albert the Great memory is also a subject of ethics and not only of rhetoric, which provided a kind of spiritual, ethically positive shelter for mnemotechnical knowledge, some scholars have justly criticized this "pious" interpretation of the art of memory in the works of Albert the Great and Aquinas.[52] One may suppose that the medical approach to memory imagery has probably paved the way for a more technicized, more instrumentalized, more mechanical conception of memory, where the memorized subjects are easily adaptable to existing structures in the memory, and their connections can accommodate new items without any moral prejudices.

As is well known, the author of the *Rhetorica ad Herennium* suggests that one should create humorous, horrible, or atrocious associations, and his late medieval followers interpreted the notion of humor widely and boldly. In my opinion, the often-reproduced illustrations of the *Figurae evangelistarum*, in which wild-looking beasts illustrate the chapters of the Gospels, already offer substantial reason to rethink the inherent connection between morality and memory in the last two centuries of the Middle Ages. However, there are several other examples where late medieval practitioners of the art of memory seemed to have completely abandoned any moral ties in creating their memory images. The humanistic commentary on the *Ad Herennium* by Francesco Maturanzio suggests remembering a clown, a fool, or a monkey playing the violin.[53] Such ridiculous or cruel images could be developed into small and rather daring scenes. A probably early version of the popular fifteenth-century treatise on the art of memory, the so-called *Memoria fecunda*, creates an entire sequence of cruel imagination: "Andrew should hold an amphora, as if he desperately wanted to drink, but he puts the bottle to his mouth clumsily and knocks out several teeth, hurting his tongue and his gums at the same time. He then spits out blood along with teeth and bits of his tongue, dripping blood on himself. This makes him angry and he throws the amphora at the wall, but it bounces back and pierces his stomach."[54] Christian Umhauser, the author of a German treatise from around 1500, proposes that to memorize a medicine we should imagine a well-known doctor, dressed in wonderful clothes, who holds an ampule of urine in his hand that he pours over an old lady.[55] "*Haec est pulchra imago*" ("This is a beautiful image!"), as the author comments. Giovanni Michele Alberto Carrara, an Italian humanist from Bergamo from the second half of the fifteenth century, advises, quoting Avicenna, that we should set up images of pretty girls whose names start with the same letter as the thing to be remembered. His example of amusing or moving images is that if we want to memorize something connected to Antonius we must imagine one of our friends named Anthony whose head is being chewed by an ass with rabies, and who, with blood spurting out, is asking desperately for help.[56] Carrara adds a curious comment at the end which hints at the process of reminiscing: "it is not possible that I would not be able to see this with the eyes of my mind, and I would not be recall Anthony to anyone asking."

This kind of instrumental, mechanic approach to memory images, and to the use of memory is opposed to earlier memory practices, guided by a strict morality, as that of the Victorine School. There might be multiple reasons why memory practices and mnemotechnic exercises became more secular, more mechanical by the fifteenth century. It could be argued that the revival of ancient rhetoric, the supposed Greek-Byzantine influences, or mass education of the late medieval universities play just as an important role in changing the metaphoric landscape of memory.[57] However, as I tried to show, from the thirteenth century, everyday mnemonic practices started to be commonly described using highly sophisticated metaphorical language, as knowledge was supposed to be "sent to the memory cell," "impressed on the mind," "elevated," or "dilated into the mental space." This mechanical-technical approach, which used medical and biological concepts, void of any moral judgments, must have significantly contributed to the "technicalization" and "encyclopedization" of memory: it has created a new concept of memory that could virtually incorporate anything and everything, be it morally good or evil, without necessarily imprinting any bad influence on the believers' soul. These tendencies had not only a temporary influence for the late Middle Ages, but also exerted a lasting effect—through the indirect or direct reception of these treatises (e.g., Johannes von Romberch, who was the main source of Lodovico Dolce's memory techniques in the sixteenth century)—on the mnemonic authors of the following centuries, several of whom—just to mention Giovanni Fontana, Giordano Bruno or Johann Heinrich Alsted—considered memory as an all-encompassing, encyclopedic faculty.

CHAPTER SIX

High Culture and Popular Culture

CAROLINE HORCH

Memoria, as understood in medieval Christianity, is remembrance and memory at the same time. As remembrance, *memoria* needs to be seen as an intentional, active and cognitive act. As memory, *memoria* is a "virtual capacity and an organic substrate," as Aleida Assmann defined it (1991: 14). Yet when remembrance and memory lead into human action it becomes commemoration.

The negative term "forgetting" complements memory and remembrance. In the *Confessiones* Augustine concisely formulates the union of remembrance and forgetting: "When I mention forgetfulness, I similarly recognize what I am speaking of. How could I recognize it except through memory?" He concludes: "Therefore memory retains forgetfulness" (Augustine, *Confessiones* 10.16; Scholz et al.).

People always knew of forgetting and the dangers it held. The book of Relevation demonstrates drastically, what is meant by eternal oblivion:

> And the books were opened: and also the book was opened, which is the book of life: and the dead were judged out of those things which were written in the books, according to their works. [. . .] This is the second death. And whosoever was not found written in the book of life was cast into the lake of fire.
>
> —Relevation 20.12–15

Apart from the intentional and deliberate act of the *damnatio memoriae*, all that has happened in the past is constantly in danger of being forgotten, which continual attempts of remembering try to counteract. Commemoration in this way becomes the present form of the past. On the one hand, a certain understanding of time is conveyed and on the other hand, it becomes apparent that past, present and future are anthropological concepts. To quote Augustine again: "without the creation no time can exist" (*Confessiones* 11.30). People create time and shape memory and commemoration, without which human existence would lose a vital meaning (Berndt 2013).

Medieval memorial culture developed various forms and possibilities of maintaining commemoration. Besides research on lists of names in special memory-books (*libri memoriales*), names were also analyzed when they appeared on other objects, pictures, and surfaces. Their appearance demonstrates that memory was not limited to the recitation of names in the liturgical context of medieval memory. As these other sources show, medieval memory was a religious, social, and historical phenomenon. It created ties and relationships over time and space, it served as means of connection in political and geographical surroundings and last not least, it brought together different groups of social status.

Essential to the effort of preserving the names of the deceased or absent was the imagination that those mentioned by name became present in the respective community. The fixation and if applicable the reading of the names guaranteed their presence and therefore the banishment of being forgotten.

In this context, the burial place of the person who was being remembered was not relevant. Augustine gives an account of the plea of his mother Monica to her sons: "Bury my body anywhere you like. [. . .] I have only one request to make of you, that you remember me at the altar of the Lord, wherever you may be" (*Confessiones* 9.11). By no means was the burial place insignificant; however, there is no necessary causal connection between the grave and the *memoria* of the deceased. Although, following the ancient Roman tradition, one could also be remembered by the grave, the culmination point of the *memoria* soon shifted to the altar where mass was celebrated. Every Eucharist repeated the order of Jesus Christ to remember:

> For I received from the Lord what I also delivered to you, that the Lord Jesus on the night when he was betrayed took bread, and when he had given thanks, he broke it, and said, 'This is my body which is for you. Do this in remembrance of me'."
> —Corinthians 11.23–25

The decisive and constitutive motive of recording names was the visualization, the *commemoratio*, among the living. The different forms of recording names, the *libri memoriales*, from the *libri vitae* laid out cumulatively and in summary to the calendrically kept necrologies will be described elsewhere in this publication. It is not surprising that records of names can also be found in liturgical books, because they were initially mentioned in the course of liturgy. This way they were brought directly before God.

The prerequisite for this visualization was an existing community, which practiced remembrance. Through the performance of the *memoria* a "community of the living and the dead" was created (Schmid and Wollasch 1967: 265; Angenendt 2001). The living and the dead also formed a community because of the mutual commitments they had made, based on the principle of reciprocal relations *do-ut-des* (*Corpus Iuris Civilis* 3, Dig. 19.5.5). The community equaled the offering, benefit, or endowment from the deceased during his lifetime after their death. It is of great importance and essential for further understanding that prayers were also seen as endowments. The certainty of receiving an endowment in return in the form of *commemoratio* and *memoria* lead the people to donations that went far beyond the mere mention of names. Thus, images, among other things, developed to serve the *memoria*: the memorial images. They give the respective *memoria* a special content and an inherently own expression. What kind of further understanding can the examination of images give us in the context of *memoria*, or more precisely: What is to be gained with the concept of memorial images? If names or name fragments are found on the altar plate of Reichenau 341 it is immediately clear that they were used for the visualization of persons before God and the praying community during the Eucharist (Geuenich, Neumüllers-Klauser, and Schmid 1983). Images visualize one or more people (or an event), but they do it substantially with greater plasticity and can transport a greater spectrum of assertions.

The German term *Memorialbild* (memorial image) was formerly often used synonymously with the rather unspecific term *Gedächtnisbild* (image for memory/souvenir). The art historian Hans Belting characterized a certain type of Byzantine images, the so-called *"Privatporträt"* as a memorial image. Subsequently, the medievalist Otto Gerhard Oexle defined the term "memorial image" as it is used today: "It does not describe a certain content or an iconographical type but a function of the image: It is used in the context of memory" (Oexle 1995a: 47; cf. Belting 1970; Oexle 1984; Althoff 1998).

Therefore, its function in the context of *memoria* is constitutive for the memorial image. The Dutch historian Truus van Bueren established the concept of memorial images in the Netherlands, especially of ones dating from the Late Middle Ages (van Bueren 1999). "Memorial images" is a term for pictorial works from various categories. Next to images it includes sculptures as well as architecture.

To declare the function as the decisive criteria for memorial images opens up a vast research perspective. Henceforth, different painted works of art could be studied in the context of *memoria*. Neither its shape, nor its contents make a pictorial work a memorial image, but rather its function, the task it had during the performance of *memoria*. This

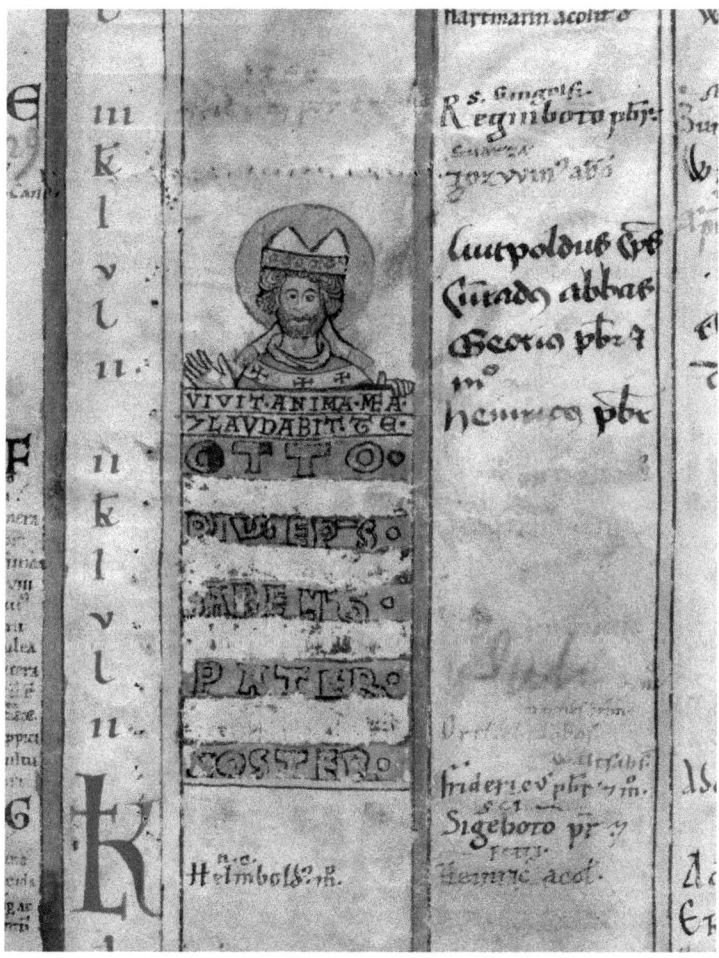

FIGURE 6.1: *Bust of Otto I of Bamberg* (1102–39). Necrology from the monastery Michelsberg in Bamberg, c. 1139 or c. 1189. Bamberg, Staatsbibliothek, Msc. Lit. 144 fol. 84v. © Staatsbibliothek Bamberg.

has decisive consequences for the scientific handling of memorial images and the formation of the hypothesis concerning the memorial function of pictorial works. On the one hand, the integration of pictorial works in the research of medieval memorial culture leads to an increase of available sources. On the other hand, it results in increased inter- and transdisciplinary research. Nevertheless, the constant referral to written sources remains essential. The concrete function of a pictorial work in the context of *memoria* has to be determined in each case; otherwise, the danger of an inflationary usage of the term "memorial image" exists. In the past decades, a variety of memorial images have been found, however, the exact inductive verification of their function remains pending. In the following, the concept of the memorial image and its potential will be outlined based on selected examples.

THE MEMORIAL IMAGE OF OTTO OF BAMBERG

Due to its position, it might seem obvious that the picture of Otto, bishop of Bamberg (d. 1139), inserted in a necrology, is a memorial image. Nevertheless, the question arises, what function the miniature fulfilled: Why did the small, unusual picture get into the

FIGURE 6.2: Tomb of presbyter Bruno, Hildesheim cathedral, today the southern outer wall of the choir, after 1194. © Creative Commons (Public Domain).

necrology of the monastery Michelsberg and not into the cathedral's records? The half-length portrait is situated above the name entry of the June 30, the anniversary of the death of the bishop, in the arcade for the members of the convent in Michelsberg. Below the portrait there is an inscription: *"Vivit anima mea [et] laudabit te"* (Appuhn 1973; Horch 2013; Horch 2014 / Ps 119.175, cf. Nospickel 2004). Only then does the name entry follow in majuscule: *"Otto pius eps. Babenb. pater noster."* An annotation describes the merits of the bishop. These are also highlighted in his vita (Herbordi dialogus, 1974, I.30: 32f; Notae sepulcrales Babenbergenses 1990: 641). Apart from his function in the court chapel, his efforts to mediate between emperor and pope, the bishop's position in Bamberg and the missionary work in Pomerania, Otto cared for the monasteries in his diocese. Among them special attention was given to the monastery of Michelsberg. He gave attention to reform the monastery and he organized the reconstruction of the church. One *vita* expresses this special connection. It reports the bishop's reputed wish to join the monastery when he was still alive. Moreover, Bishop Otto was buried in the choir of the monastery, not in the cathedral. He had honored the monastery and in turn, they admitted him posthumously into their community. Therefore, the small, exceptional picture of the bishop can be explained as being a memorial image.

Extraordinary and in need of explanation is the nimbus, with which the image of the bishop has been honored. In the year of his death in 1139, his canonization was still far away and did not occur until 1189. The nimbus can be read as a postulate, provided it was not added to the picture in 1189. Here, the principle of *do-ut-des* received an extension: First, Otto was commemorated in the monastery in return for his support and benefactions. Later, the monastery campaigned for Otto's canonization, as this ensured them a holy advocate. These different efforts of remembrance are conveyed in the small image of the bishop Otto of Bamberg with his nimbus in the necrology of the monastery of Michelsberg.

THE TOMB OF BRUNO OF HILDESHEIM AS MEMORIA

An example that ensures, cultivates, and maintains the remembrance of a specific person is the tomb of Bruno in the cathedral of Hildesheim, which, today, is positioned on the outer wall of the choir (Schuffels 2012). Bruno (d. 1197/98), a member of the cathedral chapter, left the cathedral considerable endowments. In the necrology of the cathedral, the anniversary of his death is recorded as December 17. His tomb is a singular testimony of *memoria*. As stated by Christian Schuffels, writing and image should be related to one another, as it is only through this interdependence that the memorial image is given its specific meaning. Three deepened fields with images of different sizes, divided by bridges show, starting from the bottom to the top: the corpse of Bruno, the *elevatio animae* by two angels, and in the last field a consecrating Christ. The bridges as well as the frame carry inscriptions. The reference to the *memoria* of the deceased Presbyterian is especially pronounced by the lower field, where two clerics are arranging the death cloth with loving gestures. Two further figures on the right and two on the left-hand side are also trying to touch the dead. Through their attributes they are characterized as paupers. They are wearing ragged clothing, carrying crutches, and their posture signals their frailty. These are the recipients of alms, whom the benefactor Bruno wanted to be remembered and who, in return, are praying for Bruno's salvation. The tomb of Bruno in Hildesheim shows the conditions and the performance of medieval *memoria* in a concise way (in image and word). Additionally, and not less importantly, it admonished the living in its

FIGURE 6.3: Atzmann (lectern in human form) from the church of St. Kilian in Korbach/Hassia. © Creative Commons (Public Domain).

function of remembering to fulfil their obligations towards the deceased Bruno in future. The paupers, who had received his alms, returned prayers, the clerics of the cathedral were able to repay in elaborate liturgical commemoration.

However, the person whom the commemoration was applied to, did not have to be featured in the image themselves; the name, fastened to a donated object, could be enough to represent and visualize them. In this way, an object that originally and independently did not necessarily have a memorial function, can become a memorial image. Ideal for this purpose were *vasa sacra* and other objects used in the church's interior. The attaching of names to goblets, patens and such or on the altar itself secured the *memoria* of the named. Well-known examples are the *patena aurea maiore cum gemmis diversis, legente Karolo* (the bigger golden paten with diverse gems and Charles reading) recorded in the

Liber Pontifacalis or the antependium of the altar in Basel with small pictures and the names of the Holy Roman Emperor Henry II and his wife Kunigunde (Liber Pontificalis 2, 1892: 8; Wollasch 1980a; Weinfurter 2002). Additionally, fabrics, especially liturgical garments, are focused upon, as it is not uncommon to find names embroidered in them.

THE ANONYMOUS MEMORIAL IMAGE: THE ATZMANN

An interesting subject is the so-called *Atzmann*, a genre of life-sized sculptures in churches with the function to hold the Holy Scriptures for reading. "As the Atzmann had an exposed position in the area of the altar, a distinct purpose in liturgy and iconographic prominence, this kind of statues was an ideal form of donations for the soul [. . .]" (Lempges 2017: 15). Through the addition of the benefactor's name or emblem they are ideal as memorial images because the donor is at a central position in the liturgical space and present in the commemorating community.

Therefore, the contents and form of a memorial image do not need a direct iconographic connection corresponding to the person whose *memoria* it should ensure. The commemoration of respective people was a supplementary, but often central function. In reference to the initially mentioned differentiation between memory and remembrance, the former serves as the form and the latter as the content in the context of pictorial works.

FIGURE 6.4: Bayeux Tapestry, second half of the eleventh century. Figure 4a: Depiction of King Edward ("*Edward rex*"). Figure 4b: Depiction of duke William ("*hic Willem dux*"). Figure 4c: Depiction of Harold getting the crown ("*hic dederunt Haroldo coronam regis*"). Figure 4d: Death of Harold ("*hic Haroldus rex interfectus est*"). (Bayeux, Centre Guillaume le Conquérant). © Wikimedia Commons (Public Domain).

FIGURE 6.4: *(Continued).*

THE BAYEUX TAPESTRY AS AN EMBROIDERED MEMORIA

The Bayeux Tapestry is a testimonial of political *memoria*, as it shows the Norman conquest of England by William, Duke of Normandy (d. 1087) in 1066 (Baagø and Wamers 2009). The sequence of, today, fifty-eight images starts off with a meeting between the English King Edward and Harold, the Earl of Wessex, and continues with Harold traveling to the continent to see William. He follows William on his military campaigns and swears an oath to him. After Edward's death (January 5, 1066), the crown is offered to the returned Harold. Two scenes depict him on the throne. The second half of the work describes the annexation of England by William, the Battle of Hastings (October 14, 1066) and in the second last of the still existing scenes, the death of Harold. At the beginning of the image sequence, King Edward is represented on the throne as is Harold in the middle of the sequence. Following (the logic of) this analogy, the last, now missing, scene would probably have shown the Duke William, the victor of the Battle of Hastings, on the throne. Continuously embroidered texts explain the action and name some of the people depicted. For example, in the beginning: *Edward rex, hic Willem dux* (Edward, King. Here is William the duke); in the middle: *hic dederunt Haroldo coronam regis* (here they gave the royal crown to Harold) and at the end: *hic est dux Wilelmus* (here is Duke William) and *hic Harold rex interfectus est* (here King Harold is being killed).

In current research, there is disagreement over its place of origin: England or Bayeux. An equally controversial discussion is held over the client who commissioned the tapestry; some possible candidates are Bishop Odo of Bayeux (d. 1097), the half-brother of William, Edith (d. 1075), the wife of the deceased King Edward, Eustache II (d. *c.* 1085), the Count of Boulogne or Mathilde (d. 1083), the wife of Duke William. A written source only exists from the second half of the fifteenth century in which it is reported that the tapestry was shown every year in the church of Bayeux.

So far, two interpretative approaches are being discussed in scholarly research, both of which have arguments that cannot be ignored. One approach sees the tapestry as evidence of William's legitimate accession to the throne, the other as the opposite, namely as a document for Harold's equally rightful claim to the throne. Due to their relationships to the deceased King Edward, both of them could have seen themselves as pretenders to the throne. However, Harold's oath, given to William in the twenty-third scene, can be seen as constituting a vassal relationship. It required general acceptance that Harold would have forfeited his right to the throne.

Even though the tapestry of Bayeux showcases, not to say stages, the conquest of the English throne by Duke William of Normandy, it also serves the *memoria* of Harold, who, from an Anglo-Saxon perspective, is the legitimate successor of Edward to the throne and who is described in various accompanying texts as *rex*. Modern efforts to reach a distinct assignment and monocausal interpretation remain unsuccessful.

A memorial image can appear in various forms and *vice versa*; almost every memorial image can have more than one function. Form, function, and content of a pictorial work are in an interdependent relationship that must not remain static. In relation to the difference between memory and remembrance mentioned at the beginning, one can describe the form, the shape of a memorial image as a memory in the sense of the material substrate and its contents as remembrance in the sense of a mental process. Both are subject to change, meaning that memory as well as remembrance is variable.

FIGURE 6.5: Bust of Emperor Frederick Barbarossa (so-called Cappenberg head). Mid-twelfth century (Cappenberg, Pfarrkirche St. Johannes Ev.). © Bischöfliches Generalvikariat Münster, Kunstpflege, Foto: Annkatrein Löw.

AN IMPERIAL MEMORIAL IMAGE: THE CAPPENBERG HEAD OF BARBAROSSA

An example of such a modification is the so-called "Cappenberger Barbarossakopf" (Cappenberg head of Barbarossa), a bronze head of Emperor Frederick I Barbarossa (Appuhn 1973; Horch 2013; Horch 2014), which has been located in Cappenberg for over 850 years. The *caput* measures almost 32 centimeters in height and consists of two parts, the head and stand. The head did not wear a crown, but used to wear a diadem, which no longer exists, but it can reasonably be assumed to have existed, as indicated by a knot in the nape of the neck. There are two bands around the neck. The top one is also tied with a knot, its end lies over the lower band. Over time, the hollow head was filled with a great number of small relics, wrapped in fabric. Two small pins attach the head to the stand, which is made up of an octagonal base plate, carried by four dragons, with a wall on which kneeling angels and turrets are placed alternatively in the corners. There used to be four angels but one is now missing; the four battlements carry the inscription "OTTO." Battlements surround the plate on which the head is attached, which is carried on the outstretched palms of angels. The two neckbands of the head and the battlements carry inscriptions, stating that relics of John the Evangelist were kept inside the head and that this saint's advocacy is requested for Otto. His name is also mentioned on the pinnacles as Provost Otto of Cappenberg, one of the founders of Cappenberg and at the same time godfather to the emperor. It is probably this relationship between Otto and Frederick that led this iconographically highly complex *caput* to come to Cappenberg shortly after its creation in the middle of the twelfth century. The *patronus* of the emperor and the community in Cappenberg were predestined, so to speak, to care for his *memoria*. That this happened, even after the function of the *caput* changed, is verified by written sources in Cappenberg. Initiated by Otto, the work was simultaneously used as a reliquary. A further role was given to it when the inscription OTTO was added to the rearward pinnacles. It then also served the commemoration of one of the two highly esteemed benefactors of the community. The *"caput ... formatum ad imperatoris effigiem,"* however, remained in the memory. The previously quoted line is from the will of Otto of Cappenberg, who died 1171 (Horch, forthcoming).

Modifications and shifts of accent in connection with form, function, and content cannot always be as clearly determined as with the Cappenberg head of Barbarossa. These three components interact in numerous ways, which means that different factors can affect the function of a memorial image. The example of the Cappenberg head shows how confusing and multilayered the spectrum of possible meanings and functions of such

FIGURE 6.6: Gravestone of the Counter-King Rudolf von Rheinfelden, *c.* 1180, choir of Merseburg Cathedral. © G. Schwedler.

works can be in relation to *memoria*. Intentions and functions of sculptures during the performance of remembrance must be tested anew in every case, as no fixed rules regarding the usage and reception of memorial images can be created. Neither can the possible repercussions on the performance of *memoria* be fixed.

IMAGE—INSCRIPTION—MEMORIA: THE GRAVESTONE OF RUDOLF OF RHEINFELDEN

The aforementioned principles and functional mechanisms of medieval *memoria* (the recalling of names, visualization, creation of the community of the living and the dead, foundations, and the duty of returning a favor of compensation) initially need to be considered in order to question the effects and consequences of the usage of memorial images for commemoration (in a further step). This approach can trigger a very interesting process. Where, to begin with, the function of the pictorial work in the context of *memoria* was the main focus, the perspective is shifted and the pictorial work itself is suddenly seen in a different light. Subsequently, it is not only about the function of the images in a memorial context, but also about the insights that can be gained through the memorial function of the images. If the memorial function of a pictorial work can validly be discerned—which is not always the case—then a rich variety of further perspectives can be developed from it. In such an ideal case the work with memorial images becomes a bipolar approach.

To truly work successfully with memorial images means to examine them in two different ways. How did they serve the *memoria* and what kind of effects did *memoria* have on the pictorial work? The danger of a *circulus vitiosus* must be conceded here and can only be banned by working closely with the sources, by searching for additional references and through continual reflection of one's scientific thesis and research.

As an example, the gravestone of the Rudolf of Rheinfelden (d. 1080) in the choir of the cathedral of Merseburg shall be mentioned here (Hinz 1996). It was erected directly after the death of the Swabian Duke, who died from a wound he suffered in battle against Emperor Henry IV (d. 1106); he had lost his right hand. This earliest preserved full-figure grave plate is without precursor and remained this way for more than 200 years. Why did it develop? Why was it located in such an unusual position in the cathedral? How was it possible that a usurper of the crown, who had fallen in battle, was given such a unique monument? The frame of the plate carries the inscription:

> King Rudolf, overtaken by death for the law of the fathers and rightfully lamented, is buried here. As king there was—had he reigned in times of peace—to him no one similar since Charles [Charlemagne] in the capacities of mind and sword. There, where his party won, he was slain as holy victim of the war. Death was life to him because he fell for the church.[1]

This inscription alone carries a vast potential for analysis which cannot be expanded here. It is striking that his name is mentioned (*rex hoc Rodulfus*), but that neither the date nor the year of his death are. Whereas the year was not a common addition, the day was important as it determined the day on which the deceased should be commemorated. This is unusual for a gravestone and one must ask oneself why this was done—particularly as the inscription emphasizes the day of death as the point where eternal life is obtained: "death was life to him." A possible explanation could be that the image does not necessarily refer to the person Duke Rudolf, but that the gravestone is a memorial image in remembrance of the demonstration of resistance against Emperor Henry IV. In fact, the royal insignia are clearly shown: crown, imperial orb (in form of a disc), scepter, and in addition one could add the closed chlamys on the shoulder. The gravestone of Merseburg is, next to its function as memorial image, also an image full of political messages and ambitions. If one not only views the gravestone under the formal aspect of *memoria*, but also with regard to its function in the context of *memoria*, answers to previously unanswered questions can be found. Bishop and chapter of the cathedral set a political monument marking their resistance against the emperor by presenting Rudolf as a more suitable pretender to the throne, legitimized by, in the Medieval Ages essential, the successor of Charlemagne ("to him no one similar since Charles"). A further dimension is opened when one views the unusual position of the grave and gravestone: They were in the choir of the church, where the community of the cathedral gathered to pray and to remember. Rudolf, fallen in battle, was present in the community, namely with his royal insignia.

Here it is shown that an inversion of the original question can offer new explanations and approaches. Firstly, the question must be raised whether a certain pictorial work has a memorial function and what this fact says about the *memoria*. The image complements and elaborates on the knowledge of the *memoria*. In a further step, the perspective can be altered and one can ask which meaning and consequences this special function had and what kind of additional knowledge about the image the *memoria* is able to give.

FIGURE 6.7: Charlemagne, equestrian statuette of Metz. Second half of ninth century. Paris, Musée du Louvre. © Creative Commons (Public Domain).

CHARLEMAGNE AND THE EQUESTRIAN STATUETTE OF METZ

Another example that showcases the further potential an interpretation as a memorial image can offer is the equestrian statuette of Metz (Mütherich 1965; Horch 2010). It is unclear whether this small statue was created during Charlemagne's time or if it was commissioned by his grandson Charles the Bald. It shows a horse rider whose two raised legs indicate a forward motion. The rider is equipped with a ruler's insignia: crown and orb in the left hand and, once, a sword or scepter in the right hand. His legwear resembles the Franconian traditional dress of the ninth century. Written sources from the cathedral substantiate that the statuette was placed on the rood screen on the anniversary of Charlemagne's death (January 28) and surrounded by candles. Hence, it was part of the liturgy. One saw and can see Charlemagne in the image based on this date and the fact that certain facial features and hairstyle of the rider have similarities with other contemporary images of the Franconian king. However, there are also arguments indicating that his grandson Charles the Bald is the rider. Regardless of the claims of others, he let himself be crowned in Metz only a few weeks after the death of Lothair II on August 8, 869. The coronation was setting a trend: Even though the Lothringian kingdom of Charles the Bald only existed for a few months, the mise-en-scène of an ordination of a king in Metz was the model for the future—as well as the equestrian statuette of Metz (Staubach 1981; Horch 2010).

The historic as well as the art historic research struggles to see the rider as Charles the Bald, whose political failure one could not bring together with such an unusual work and its iconographic meaning. Recently, Horst Bredekamp rightly pointed out the problem of dating the equestrian statuette based on earlier equestrian images. If one considers the memorial function of the pictorial work, a number of dating possibilities (Bredekamp: 46–9) are opened up, ranging from the first up to the second half of the ninth century. In this context, it is important to remember that Charles the Bald put a lot of effort into the field of *memoria*. This covered not only his own commemoration, but also that of his family members. In addition, a pronounced need for commemorating special days is found with this ruler.

The focus on the memorial function of the statuette creates a certain distance between the question of identifying the rider and the connected problem of it being a portrait or not. The rider is no individual in a modern understanding of the term, as he is neither Charlemagne nor Charles the Bald. The pictorial work rather creates a memorial link that connects the past (the rule of Charlemagne) with the present (the goals of Charles the Bald) and that, at the same time, is oriented toward the future. The equestrian statuette of Metz shifts between the personal commemoration (Charlemagne or Charles the Bald) and the memory of the event, the coronation of Charles the Bald.

A spectacular misunderstanding and resulting abuse of the statue lies in its use by the National Socialists. During the Second World War, eighty decorative plates were produced by the porcelain manufacturer Sévres at the behest of Hitler. On the front was a golden depiction of the statuette of Metz. On the reverse was the text: "*Imperium Caroli magni divisum per nepotes anno DCCCXLIII defendit Adolphus Hitler una cum omnibus Europae populis anno MCMXLIII*" (Werner 1995: 26f; Horch 2010: 36f.): The empire of Charlemagne, divided in 843, should be reinstalled in 1943 under Adolf Hitler with reference to the great emperor. To use the image of Charles the Bald in the form of his grandfather as an award for officers of the "Légion des Volontaires français contre les

FIGURE 6.8 Memorial image of the "Covenant of Nuns" in the *Hortus deliciarum* of Herrad of Hohenburg. The manuscript dates from the last third of the twelfth century, yet the original burned in 1870 in Strasbourg. The image is taken from a facsimile of the ninth century. Herrad of Hohenburg Hortus deliciarum; fol. 322^r. © Public Domain.

Bolschewismes" (the later SS-division "Charlemagne") is a paradoxical perversion of the memorial contents of the image.

MEMORIA AND INDIVIDUALITY: THE *HORTUS DELICIARUM* OF HERRAD OF LANDSBERG

When dealing with medieval memorial images one keyword is mentioned again and again: individualism. Firstly, one must consider that the modern understanding and idea of individualism does not do justice to the medieval one (on the following issues see Horch 2018). Often, the medieval understanding of *individuum* is misunderstood because modern categories are used. The occupation of medieval theologians and philosophers with the *individuum* took place on a level that was, in parts, not reached anymore later on. Originating from Aristotle's "categories" of being Gilbert de la Porrée (d. 1155), Thomas Aquinas (d. 1274), and William of Ockham (d. 1349) thought about the definition of the *individuum*. Even though modern criteria such as self-determination, autonomy or subjectivity were not central to them, reflections and discourses on people's non-interchangeability were put into the main sphere of attention. The modern debate about individualism in the Middle Ages is always in danger of projecting post-Enlightenment ideas onto the Middle Ages. A possibility of getting closer to the specific form of medieval individualism is given by the memorial sources of the Middle Ages. Record and recitation of names mean a certain, in a sense unique person, hence *memoria* is essentially individualizing. The different sources of medieval *memoria* carry a vast potential for the research on individualism as they are predestined to transport the image of a person (Cardelle de Hartmann and Uhl 2013). Additionally, they are innately focused on a certain person. Of course, this does not mean that memorial images or memorial sources transmit or convey likenesses the way photography does of what people actually looked like. An example of individualism through *memoria* is the miniature depicting the convent of nuns of the monastery Hohenburg in the *Hortus deliciarum* of Herrad (Green, Evans, Bischoff, and Curschmann 1979). It shows the busts of sixty nuns who do not differ in physiognomy, only in the color of their veils and robes. Nevertheless, it is not true to speak of schematic types as every person is marked by their name, making the respective depiction an individual one. Furthermore, it should be noted that at the same time the image demonstrates a collective in its homogeneity. The active turning of every nun to the founding of her community, which is depicted on the opposite side and the commitment to this, can only be shown in an image. The memorial image differs in time and content and covers a wider spectrum than the pure mentioning of names could. A community formed by individuals constitutes the own *memoria* in an act of remembering the founder, the founding act and the first convent.

CONCLUSION

Works of art also have a function to serve *memoria*, which they pass to the next generations. In this, they are not static and immutable but rather flexible. Given the fact that research perspectives change, they become an inexhaustible treasure.

We started by stating the characteristics of medieval memory concerning time, space, strata, and contexts, and discovered that each example was able to manifest these characteristics in a different way. The interpretation of each individual work of art demonstrates anew that past, present and future are mental constructions that only exist in relation to one another. Unsurpassed, Augustine reflects in the Book 11 of the *Confessiones*: "Perhaps it would be exact to say: there are three times, a present of things past, a present of things present, a present of things to come. [. . .] The present considering the past is the memory, the present considering the present is immediate awareness, the present considering the future is expectation" (cf. Flasch 1993). The characteristics connoted with the times (*praeteritum, praesens, futura*) characterize the *memoria*. Memorial images remind the present illustratively of the past and at the same time refer to a historically based and projected future.

CHAPTER SEVEN

The Social: Rituals, Faith, Practices, and the Everyday

RAINER HUGENER

Most major religions are based upon acts of remembrance. Their beliefs center on events that are said to have taken place at specific times in history. Therefore, their respective liturgies are constituted by certain holidays which mark, structure, and segment the circle of the year, celebrating the acts of God as well as the deeds and deaths of saints and martyrs. With their examples in mind, many of the faithful felt that their own souls could benefit from commemoration, so they took measures for being remembered forever, such as founding or supporting temples, synagogues, churches, mosques, hospitals, poorhouses, and hostels, or by donating to one of these institutions (Borgolte 2014–17). In return, they expected perpetual prayers to be said for intercession on their behalf. While such practices can be found in Judaic and Islamic cultures as well, they were most prevalent in Latin Christendom (Oexle 1976). Therefore, the following chapter will focus chiefly on religious rituals of commemoration among Christians in Western Europe but will also peek at the influence and exchange with the Jewish communities embedded within these societies.

The purpose of this chapter is to provide a comprehensible overview on how different rituals of liturgical commemoration evolved throughout the Middle Ages and how they depended on changing attitudes toward the afterlife, the individual, and the community. To accentuate the developments and shifts that took place from the fifth to the late fifteenth century, the study will proceed in a chronological order. At the same time, it will examine the source material very closely, and not just for heuristic reasons, but because continuous commemoration is first and foremost an administrative task and therefore dependent on keeping records in the form of registers or lists (Eco 2009; Goody 1977). Thus, it is my methodological premise that we have to analyze the media of memory in order to understand how the communities who produced them remembered.

Several distinct forms of registering those who were to be remembered for eternity evolved from early medieval times onwards that could be seen as prototypical for the methods of book-keeping which started to blossom toward the end of the Middle Ages. In this sense, it is justified to claim that religious practices of commemoration have been at the core of what has been described by medievalist scholars as the proliferation of pragmatic literacy (Britnell 1997; Clanchy 1979; Keller 1992). While this term has been coined primarily for the use of writing for profane causes, the argument can be made that to the faithful, nothing is more pragmatic than taking measures for saving their souls.

It should be noted that the subject of this study has little to do with the cognitive capacities of the human brain which might be implied by the terminology of memory studies. Instead, this chapter is concerned with highly ritualized manifestations of remembrance which are more aptly referred to as commemoration—a term that implies a more solemn, ceremonial, and official form of remembering and emphasizes its procedural as well as its public aspects (Brenner et al. 2013: 2). Some of these elements have been covered by theorizations about the social, collective, or cultural memory (Assmann 2011; Burke 1989; Fentress and Wickham 1992; Halbwachs 1950). Yet, in this context, I think it would be safer to just refrain from the memory metaphor altogether in order to avoid confusion (Algazi 2013). What happens in individual minds is quite different from how communities evoke the past, although the two are certainly interwoven in the sense that public ceremonies of commemoration are triggering and shaping people's perception of history (Cubitt 2007).

Since the late 1960s, there has been an entire field of research dedicated to medieval commemoration, focusing mostly on the scarce evidence from the early Middle Ages. Predominantly based in Germany, scholars such as Karl Schmid, Joachim Wollasch, and Otto Gerhard Oexle have rediscovered the traces of memorial practices and demonstrated their importance for medieval societies (Oexle 1976; Schmid 1985; Schmid and Wollasch 1967). Embedded within the wider context of a growing interest in social aspects of death, burial, and the afterlife (Ariès 1974; Le Goff 1984; Schmitt 1998), their studies have abundantly pointed out that rituals of religious remembrance aimed at keeping the dead present among the living and helped creating a sense of community or group identity (Oexle 1983; Schmid 1985; Wagner 2010). Moreover, they were described as a gift exchange, in which material goods were being reciprocated with suffrage for the soul (Oexle 1976; Geary 1994; Gordon and Marshall 2000). Since this did not only involve religious aspects, but economical, political, and legal matters as well, forming a creative power of vast cultural influence, such practices were duly stipulated as a "total social phenomenon" (Oexle 1995a: 39).

Over the past decades, it has become fashionable to refer to this phenomenon with the Latin term *memoria* (Borgolte 2003; Lauwers 2003). However, just as the memory metaphor mentioned above, the use of this buzzword may bear its risks. For one, using Latin implies a phenomenon which is specific and exclusive to the medieval Occident. While it is true that commemorative practices played an eminent role in this period of history, I don't see why it should be terminologically separated from other eras or cultures. Instead, I think it would be more productive to use a term which can be applied to the phenomenon of ritualized commemoration in general and, thereby, help comparing and analyzing its different manifestations across the boundaries of time and space. After all, I would claim that these rituals, which were meant to outlast generations and are sometimes still performed today, can and should be studied in the *longue durée*, transcending common concepts of periodization.

Another concern with the term is of semantic nature. Of course, the ability to remember has been referred to as *memoria* since antiquity, much like in modern English. But in the sources studied here, the term is rarely applied to liturgical commemoration, and never as a superordinate concept. According to the sources, these rituals did not serve *pro memoria*, but *pro redemptione* or *pro remedio animae*, i.e. for the redemption or salvation of the soul (Davies 2005; Magnani 2003). If we confine our search to occurrences of the term *memoria*, we end up with the wrong impression that commemorative rituals diminished during the late Middle Ages, whereas in fact, the opposite is true: As this chapter will demonstrate, more and more people wanted to be remembered with ecclesiastical ceremonies—they just did not, or hardly ever, refer to them with the term *memoria* (Hugener 2014a: 23–8).

COMMUNITIES AND GROUPS: FROM DIPTYCHS TO CONTRATERNITY BOOKS

It has been rightfully stated that the commemoration of the dead is the most primordial manifestation of cultural memory (Assmann 2011: 19, 45). Christian memorial rites did not arise out of nothing, but were based on ancient Roman as well as Jewish customs. Romans had a long tradition of honoring their ancestors, including meals at the family shrines on certain days in the year. Christians under Roman rule carried on with meals at the graves of their deceased, but they had a different understanding of how this would affect those involved, both the living and the dead. Whereas the Romans invoked their ancestors for honor and protection, the Christians were praying for their souls to be saved (Constable 2000: 172–5; Oexle 1995a: 32–3). This is an indication for the second root already mentioned: that of Jewish belief manifest in the old testament and further processed in the new testament of the Christian Bible.

Both testaments assert that God is keeping a list of the faithful and righteous who will join him in heaven and awake to everlasting life, whereas those whose names are not included or erased are destined for eternal punishment (Ex. 32:31–3; Ps. 69:29; Dan. 12:1; Mal. 3:16; Luke 10:20; Phil. 4:3; Rev. 3:5, 17:8, 20:12–5, 22:19). In several biblical verses, this register is referred to as the "book of life" (*liber vitae*) or "book of the living" (*liber viventium*) (Koep 1952). In the hope of being included in this heavenly book, the belief was formed that the deceased could benefit from intercessory prayers from the living, so their souls would be saved. In this sense, it was God who was to be remembered of a person in order to be put on the list of those bound for salvation.

Early on in post-messianic time, Christian communities started to collect the names of those who had lived with a reputation of sanctity or who had died for their belief. Over time, these lists of saints and martyrs were canonized and became known as martyrologies (Dubois 1978; Lifshitz 2000: 169–77; McCulloh 1983: 114–31). Some of these compilations were attributed to famous authors such as the Venerable Bede (d. 735), Rabanus Maurus (d. 856), or Ado of Vienne (d. 874), and were based on the Roman calendar, with the name of each saint or martyr written next to the date of his or her death, sometimes accompanied by a brief account of their deeds, and special services were held to remember them each year on that day. In return for commemorating the "very special dead," Christians were hoping for protection, mediation, and intercession on their own behalf (Brown 1981: 69–85).

But the saints and martyrs were not the only ones to be remembered in religious services. Communities would also pray for high-ranking officials of the church as well as for emperors, kings, and local lords. By reciting their names, it was felt that these persons, despite being absent or dead, would participate in the divine service (Oexle 1976: 82–3). Their memento took place during the offertory, when alms were gathered from benefactors who wished to be included in prayers. To remember them all, their names were sometimes scratched on apse walls, like in the Euphrasian Basilica in Parenzo/Poreč on Croatia's west coast, or engraved onto an altar, as was the case in the church of Reichenau-Niederzell in Southern Germany (Geuenich et al. 1983; Petrucci 1998: 45; Treffort 1996: 128).

More common, however, was the use of so-called diptychs. As their Greek name indicates, they typically consisted of two foldable boards of wax (Jakobi 1986; Taft 1991). The two opposite tablets could be used for distinguishing between different categories of addressees, such as spiritual and secular dignitaries or the living and the dead, as the Roman liturgy stipulated separate places and different formulas for their

FIGURE 7.1: Front cover of the Barberini diptych, first half of the sixth century, containing a list of officials on the back. Paris, Musée du Louvre, OA 9063. © Paris, Musée du Louvre.

commemoration (Baldovin 2011: 251–3; Constable 2000: 185). A famous example is the Barberini diptych from the first half of the sixth century, now preserved in the Musée du Louvre in Paris (OA 9063).[1] Mostly known for its precious cover, an ivory panel with scenes of the triumphant emperor carved into it, the back of the diptych contains a list of officials from the kingdom of Austrasia, collected for liturgical commemoration (Cutler 1991).

While being listed in a diptych would ensure commemoration and thus salvation, erasure or deletion was used as a drastic measure of punishment, symbolizing the exclusion from the communion of the saints (Ohly 1984). This practice was used in the conflict between western Christendom and eastern orthodoxy which eventually led to the Great Schism: Among many other things, the breach between the two churches manifested itself in the fact that Byzantine patriarchs refused to add the Roman popes to their diptychs, and vice versa (Hugener 2014b: 212; Koep 1952: 110–1).

The commemoration of the dead was sanctioned by church officials from the eighth century onward (Dix 1945: 498–511; King 1959: 168–70). In 732, Pope Gregory III recommended in a letter to St. Boniface that "everyone should offer oblations for his dead ... so the priest would celebrate their memory and intercede for them" (Tangl 1916: 50). Around the same time, a special memento for the dead is starting to appear in liturgical manuscripts such as the Bobbio Missal (Paris, Bibliothèque nationale de France, Lat. 13246; Lowe 1917). At the synods of Attigny (762) and Dingolfing (770), the attending bishops and abbots drew up a contract for a prayer league obligating its members to celebrate a number of masses at the notification of each other's death (Lemaître 2001: 228; McKitterick 2004: 163). Charlemagne (d. 814) and Louis the Pious (d. 840) decreed that all royal abbeys should pray for the emperor, his family, and for the welfare of the empire (Schmid and Oexle 1974: 72–6).

Subsequently, many actual contracts were drawn up by single individuals as well as entire groups and communities in order to be included in monastic prayers, either in exchange for a donation of material goods or by mutually praying for one another. Such associations of "friends" or "brothers" and "sisters" became known as confraternities and spread all across the Carolingian empire (McLaughlin 1994: 55–101). Monasteries exchanged the names of deceased members of their brotherhoods via scrolls or *rotuli*, some of which are still existing, revealing the long routes they have travelled (Dufour 2005–8).

As the lists of those who were to be included in prayers continuously grew, they were bound to outgrow the boards of a simple diptych. Moreover, wax was obviously not durable enough for long-term commemoration. Hence, a more permanent and extensible method of documentation was devised by using parchment and ink, marking the transition from the inscription culture of antiquity to the medieval book culture. Bound together in sturdy codices with covers made of wood or leather, there are several documents of this type that have survived the passing of time (Butz and Zettler 2013; Geuenich 2004; Geuenich and Ludwig 2015; Lemaître 2001).

The oldest of them is the confraternity book from the abbey of St. Peter in Salzburg, started in 784 (Archiv der Erzabtei St. Peter, Cod. A 1; Herzberg-Fränkel 1904: 3–60).[2] Its structure gives us an idea of the distinction between different social groups already mentioned above: prophets, saints, and martyrs, followed by the members of the convent, kings, and dukes with their families, finally bishops, abbots, and priests as well as monks and nuns from other monasteries, thoroughly divided into living and dead (McKitterick 2004: 25, 163–4, 174–85). The book is introduced by a short prayer asking God to "remember his servants who desired to be included in the prayers of the monks and gave their alms to the church, whose names were written in the book of life and put onto the altar" (Herzberg-Fränkel 1904: 6). At the end, a similar prayer is repeated for the faithful departed listed in this book, hoping that God would "grant them his eternal memory ... and keep them in the book of the living" (Herzberg-Fränkel 1904: 42).

Not only do these prayers refer to the codex as the book of life known from the Bible, they actually predicate a connection between this document and the one in heaven: Being enlisted in its earthly counterpart was presented as a guarantee for salvation. For the ones who looked for perpetual commemoration by joining the confraternity and giving their alms, this must have been a comforting thought and a great selling point. On the subject of memory, however, another detail is noteworthy: While the words *memoria, memorare,* and *commemorare* dominate these prayers, it was not the convent nor the families of the deceased who were asked to remember, but God. This explains why these records provide nothing more than names. As frustrating as this may be for the modern historian yearning for more details, even the monks themselves could not identify all of the names in their book, nor was this its purpose. Instead, it was completely sufficient when God knew who they were.

At the beginning of the ninth century, similar registers were begun in the monasteries around Lake Constance. In the abbey of Saint Gall, one such list was initiated sometime before 817, with a second portion added around 890 (Stiftsarchiv, C3 B55; Piper 1884: 1–133; Borgolte 1986). In Reichenau, a scribe started to collect names in a fascicle around 824 (Zürich, Zentralbibliothek, Ms. Rh. hist. 27; Piper 1884: 156–325; Autenrieth et al. 1979).[3] And in the abbey of Pfäfers, in the mountainous region upriver from Lake Constance, lists of names were inserted between the gospels of an evangelistary that was written and carefully illustrated around 830 (Saint Gall, Stiftsarchiv, Cod. Fab. 1; Piper 1884: 353–98; Bruckner and Sennhauser 1973). By inserting the names into the Holy Scripture, they were as close to God as they could get, making it a true *liber viventium* (McKitterick 2004: 164–5).

With the notable exception of the Pfäfers evangelistary, most of these confraternity books were not started as a codex, but bound together from single sheets, fascicles or quires over time. Being expandable was precisely one of the many advantages these codices had over the diptychs that were used before. In the most extensive of these codices, the one from Reichenau, almost 40,000 names, fifty-two communities, and four cathedral chapters have been gathered, spreading from northern Italy and Rhetia in the south to Bavaria in the east, and Francia, Hesse, and Alemannia in the northwest (McKitterick 2004: 165).

In all of these lists, certain social groups or *ordines* can be identified, such as the abbots and monks of the convent, members from other monasteries who had joined the confraternity, or benefactors of the respective church. Some of the books differentiated between members of the clergy and lay people, between the living and the dead, or between male and female. In Saint Gall, for instance, the "laymen" (*nomina laicorum*) were listed separately from the "lay women" (*nomina feminarum laicarum*), while the Reichenau codex distinguished between the "living friends" (*nomina amicorum viventium*) and the "dead friends" (*nomina amicorum defunctorum*). Such a differentiation may have been necessary because the memento of the living had another place in Roman liturgy than the intercession for the dead (Baldovin 2011: 251–3; Constable 2000: 185).

Just like in the diptychs, the names were listed in columns, sometimes explicitly introduced by a title labeling the following group. In some of these books, such as Salzburg, Saint Gall, and Pfäfers, actual columns headed by arcades were drawn in order to delimit each group (Hugener 2013: 126; McKitterick 2004: 176). Ornamented with architectural elements, plants, or mysterious creatures, these arcades could be interpreted as the gates to the heavenly Jerusalem described in the book of revelation, and those whose names were written within are about to enter God's kingdom (Neiske 2009: 131; Ross 1996: 51, 115–6). As a matter of fact, the bible foretells that only the ones who are written in the book of life will see the city of God (Rev. 21:27).

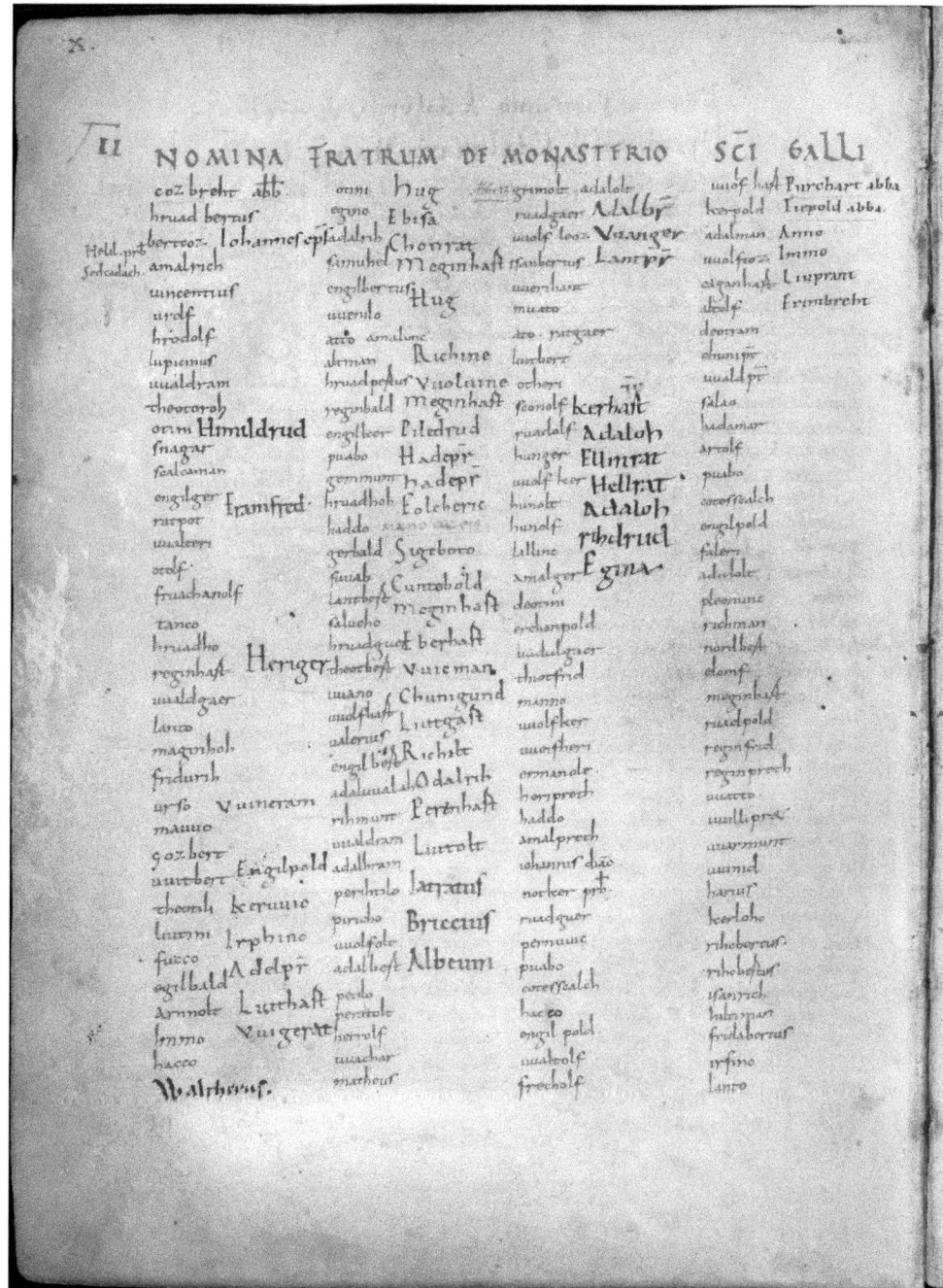

FIGURE 7.2: The Reichenau confraternity book from around 824 contains almost 40,000 names from associated communities such as the abbey of Saint Gall. Zürich, Zentralbibliothek, Ms. Rh. hist. 27, f. 18v. © Zürich, Zentralbibliothek.

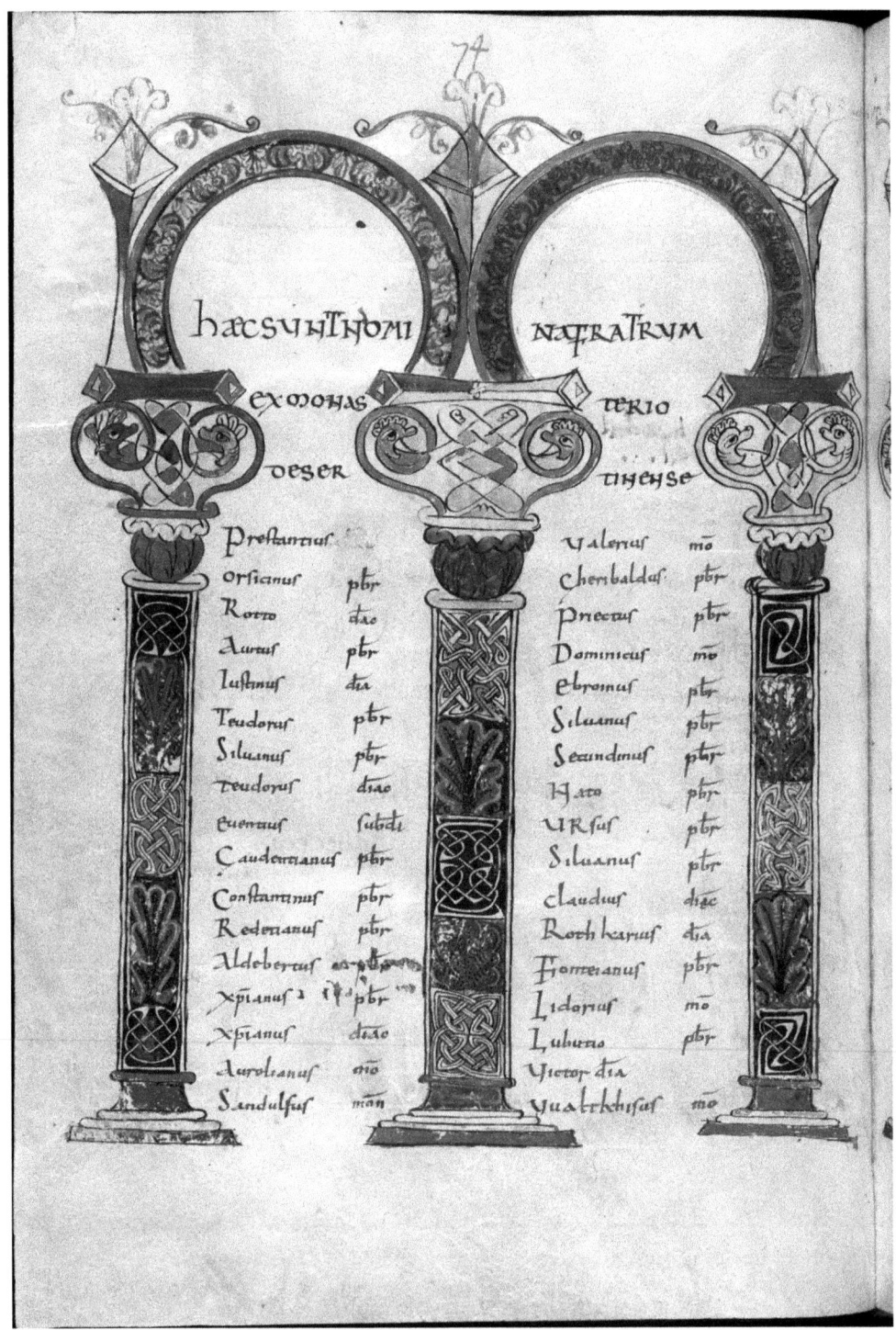

FIGURE 7.3: In the *liber viventium* of Pfäfers, created around 830, associated groups like the monks of Saint Gall are delimited by columns and arcades. Zürich, Zentralbibliothek, Cod. Fab. 1, p. 38. © Zürich, Zentralbibliothek.

Next to the codices mentioned above, only a few more memorial books from the Carolingian period have survived, proving that the confraternity movement spread across the alps to Italy (Frank 1991) as well as to Francia (Lemaître 2001) and to the British Isles (Gerchow 1988). At the royal nunnery of San Salvatore/Santa Giulia in Brescia, some 7,000 names were inserted in a liturgical codex which also contained formulae for votive masses and benedictions (Biblioteca Queriniana, Cod. G. VI. 7; Geuenich et al. 2000). In Cividale, an important intersection between the West and the East, an old Gospel manuscript (Cividale, Museo Archeologico Nazionale, Cod. XXXXVIII) was used for inserting the names of pilgrims in the ninth and tenth century (Ludwig 2009).

The *liber memorialis* from the Benedictine abbey of Remiremont in eastern France has survived in a copy that was started in 862/3, but incorporated older materials from around 821 (Rome, Biblioteca Angelica, Cod. 10; Hlawitschka et al. 1970). Distinguishing between the members of the community and external benefactors, it contains prayer instructions for both groups (Butz and Zettler 2013). Furthermore, it features a copy from a diptych of the royal family with columns drawn to separate the Merovingian kings from the Carolingian majordomos (Jakobi 1986). Included are two calendars where deceased members and benefactors have been added on the dates of their deaths, thus incorporating a new form of listing the dead which will be discussed in the following chapter.

The *liber vitae* of Durham has been started at the end of the 830s in north-eastern England (London, British Library, MS Cotton Domitian A. VII; Rollason and Rollason 2007).[4] Originally, there were 3,000 names listed, alternately written in gold and silver ink, which expresses both the material and the symbolic value that was given to being listed in this book. Several pages were left empty for names to be added in the future, which has sporadically been done until the sixteenth century, when the Reformation changed the way people wanted to remember the dead (Rollason et al. 2004).

Other memorial books may reach back to the Carolingian era, but have only survived in later copies, such as the *liber vitae* of New Minster in Winchester which dates from 1031/2 (London, British Library, Stowe 944; Keynes 1996).[5] In a rare amount of detail, its preface explains the purpose of the book: The names of brethren and benefactors were "recorded for commendation to God during daily mass" in the hope that "when memorized by writing on earth, they would be inserted into the heavenly book as well." As the preface concretizes, the list of names was to be "presented every day in front of the sacred altar," while they were only to be recited when the deacon "had time to do so" (Keynes 1996: 11–12). At the beginning of the book, there is a drawing which illustrates the result of being commemorated by the monks: Angels conduct the benefactors into the heavenly Jerusalem, the portal of which is opened by St. Peter, while others are judged and then thrown into the jaws of hell by Satan at the bottom of the page. The drastic scene was certainly understood by potential benefactors, and it supports our thesis that the arcades in the aforementioned books represented the gates of heaven.

Studying the structure of the memorial books from the early Middle Ages gives us an idea of how religious commemoration was conceived during that era. In the liturgical rituals that accompanied the use of these books, people were not so much remembered as an individual person, but as a member of a specific institution, region, or rank, monastic or lay, male or female, and last but not least: living or dead. This latter distinction, however, was merely impossible to maintain over time, since consequently, any person who was noted among the living would have had to be migrated to the list of the dead after he or she passed away. Moreover, as time passed and the lists grew, most of these

FIGURE 7.4: A drawing in the *liber vitae* of New Minster illustrates how benefactors from the left page are led directly into Heaven, while others are thrown into the jaws of hell below. London, British Library, Stowe 944, f. 7r. © London, British Library.

FIGURE 7.4: *(Continued)*.

classification systems were disturbed because new names where simply added in any free spot, without paying attention to the order that was originally intended.

It is evident that with thousands of names, these lists were not meant to be read out loud. Instead, the respective books were simply placed upon the altar during service, and a prayer was said asking God to remember the people whose names were written therein. Again, this indicates that it was not the purpose of these rituals to keep the memory of those listed alive among the living. Instead, they were collectively commended to God. He was the one who had to remember who they were—not the priests who celebrated their masses, the monks and nuns who prayed for them, or their relatives who may have had different and more individualistic ways of mourning for their lost ones altogether, without leaving any traces for posterity.

THE SAINTS AND THE DEAD: FROM MARTYROLOGIES TO NECROLOGIES

In the confraternity books of the early Middle Ages, people were listed as members of a social group, and they were only commemorated globally. Almost simultaneously, however, there was a growing desire to be prayed for individually. Presumably, this honor was first reserved to high dignitaries such as bishops and abbots, emperors and kings. But as time passed, more and more people were striving for this kind of commemoration. With pious foundations to religious institutions, they demanded for prayers to be said annually on their obit, the date of their death, hoping for intercession on their behalf. Consequently, their names were added to the martyrologies mentioned above, next to the names of the saints (Constable 2000: 178–9). In their company, people could feel assured of their salvation.

The same urge to be close to the sacred drove people to wish for a burial in church, a privilege officially reserved for saints and high-ranking clerics (Petrucci 1998; Scholz 1999). Just as an entry into a martyrology, the funeral sites in churches were meant to remind the priests to pray for the deceased and therefore, inscriptions on medieval tombstones are very often almost identical to the entries made in martyrologies (Lemaître 1980: 33; Neumüllers-Klauser 1997: 258–9; Scholz 1999: 42–3): Both indicate the date of death, the name, the social status, and sometimes the profession or the provenience of the person, introduced by the word *obiit* ("has died") or *obitus* ("death of"). An early example can be seen on the tomb of Meginbraht by the sanctuary in the monastery of Fulda in Hesse whose epitaph provides nothing but his name, his rank, and the date of his death on the second none of January: *II non[as] ianuarii ob[iit] Meginbraht diaconus [et] mo[nachus]* (Sturm 1984: 29, 240).

Again, the Benedictine abbeys around Lake Constance were the first to commemorate people on their obits by inserting their names into calendars. Traces of this new practice can be found from the mid-ninth century onward (Autenrieth 1984: 610–1; Rappmann and Zettler 1998: 281–3; Wollasch 1980b: 63–5). In Reichenau, for instance, the calendar in an old sacramentary was filled with names of deceased bishops, abbots, kings, and dukes, but also simple monks and benefactors (Vienna, Österreichische Nationalbibliothek, Cod. 1815; Baumann 1888: 271–82).[6] While in this case, an existing calendar has been converted to serve a new purpose, others were clearly made for it in the first place, such as the ones in the memorial book of Remiremont. As mentioned above, this codex did not only contain confraternity lists, but also two calendars with the names of dead members and benefactors.

RITUALS, FAITH, PRACTICES, AND THE EVERYDAY 135

Such calendars with notes about obits have become known as necrologies, although this term is a neologism from the seventeenth century; in the Middle Ages, they were still referred to as *liber vitae*. Other contemporary descriptions were *liber mortuorum*, *calendarium*, or *catalogus defunctorum* (Hugener 2014a: 31–2; Huyghebaert 1972: 34; Lemaître 1980: 5–11; Neiske 1997: 116–7). Or they were simply referred to as

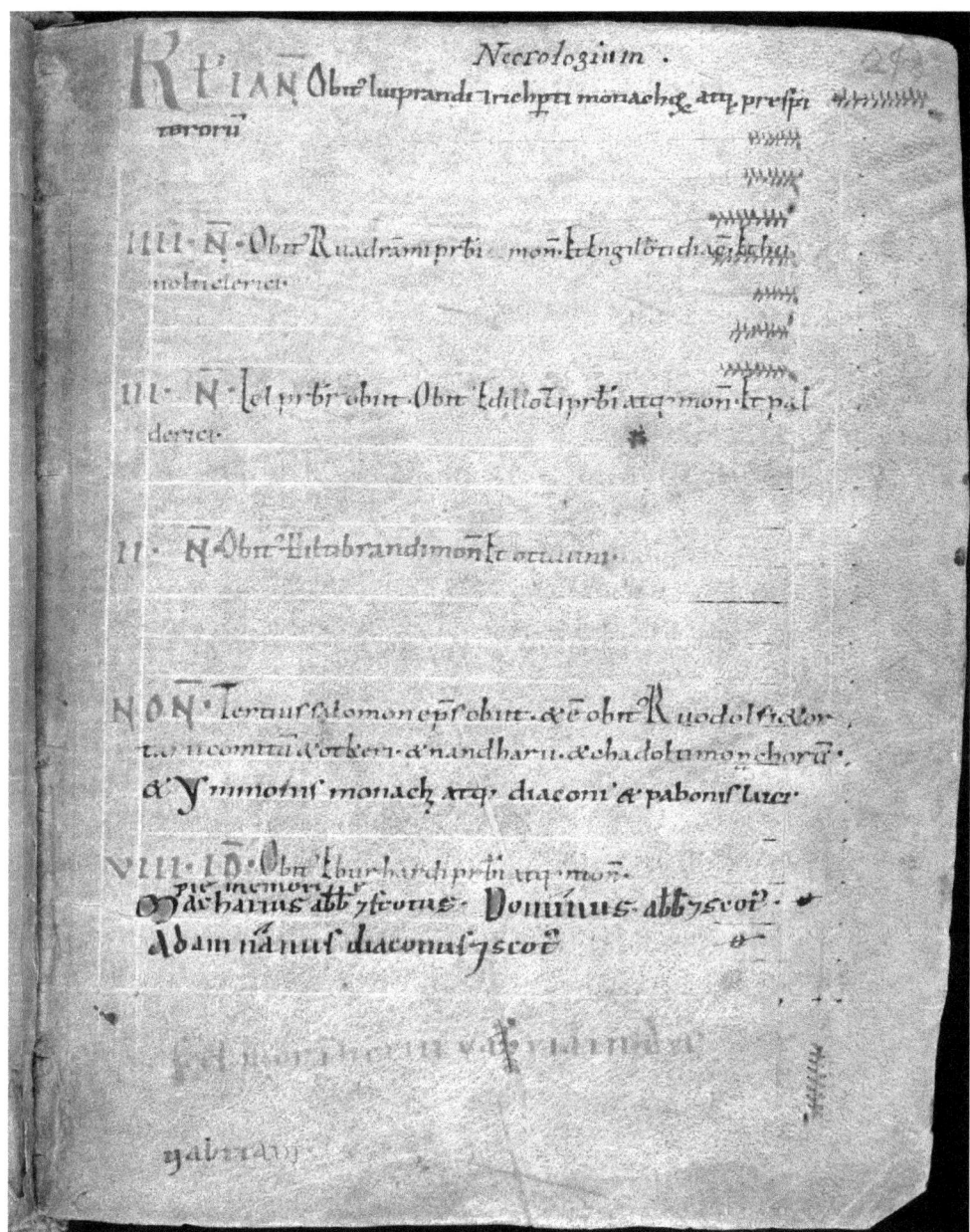

FIGURE 7.5: The chapter office book of Saint Gall contains a calendar with obit notes similar to inscriptions on tombstones. The title *Necrologium* on the first page of January is a modern addition. Saint Gall, Stiftsbibliothek, Cod. Sang. 915, p. 298. © Stiftsbibliothek Sankt Gallen.

martyrologium or *regula*, because they were often joined together with a martyrology and the monastic rule, indicating their place in liturgy: All of these writings were used during the office of the chapter, after the first hour of prayer called Prime, when the monks or nuns joined together for the lecture of a chapter of their order's rule. Before assigning tasks to each member of the community, the saints of the day were honored with a recital of the martyrology, and a prayer was said for the people whose names were written in the necrology on that date (Palazzo 1998: 161–8).

The basic framework of a necrology was the Roman calendar, with or without the names of the saints and other temporal indications, such as the "dominical letters" and the "golden numbers" used for calculating moving holidays (Lemaître 1980: 37–40). Sometimes, the highest ranked feasts were indicated by rubricated letters or standard formulas (*summum, duplex, semiduplex*). Usually, a month took up a page or two, leaving some space between each date, where the names of the deceased could be entered progressively. Most of these books were used over several decades, with several consecutive writers adding new names. This means that the names of people from very different times were written next to each other, sharing nothing but the date of their death. Usually, there is no way of telling in what year a person died. In this case, the entries can only be dated by paleographic assessment or with evidence from other sources.

Most of the time, only the names were noted, occasionally accompanied by an indicator of social status, profession or relationship to the respective community. Often, those indicators were simple letters, like "p" for *presbyter*, "l" for *laicus*, or "m.n.c." for *monachus* or *monacha nostrae congregationis* (Hugener 2013: 131–2). The customs from Cluny, in a single version surviving from the monastery of Farfa in central Italy, dictate a clear hierarchical order in the proclamation of names, starting with the highest dignitaries, emperors or kings, followed by the members of the respective community and lastly, associated "friends" (*amici, familiares*) of the community (Lemaître 1980: 15–6, 21–3).

Other monasteries, such as the abbey of Remiremont, made the same distinction by keeping two separate necrologies, one for their members and the other one for benefactors. Another way of accomplishing this separation can be found in a necrology that was probably drawn up at the Cluniac nunnery of Marcigny-sur-Loire in eastern France around 1100 (Wollasch 1971), but was later used at the order's priory in Villars-les-Moines, on the shore of Lake Morat in western Switzerland (Paris, Bibliothèque nationale de France, Fonds Lat. Nouv. Acq. 348; Schnürer 1909). This necrology features only one calendar, but there was a broad column for the monastery's members and a narrow column for lay benefactors.

Some necrologies even adapted the layout of confraternity books by adding vertical columns with colorfully ornamented arcades to the horizontal framework of the calendar (Hugener 2013: 131–3). This is the case with the necrology in the chapter office book from the Benedictine abbey at Muri, founded in 1027 by the counts of Habsburg in central Switzerland, and its female branch at Hermetschwil (Aarau, Staatsarchiv Aargau, AA/4530; Baumann 1888: 423–36).[7] Another example can be found in a necrology from the Benedictine abbey in Petershausen, near Constance in southern Germany that was drawn up shortly after 1159 (Heidelberg, Universitätsbibliothek, Cod. Sal. IX 42; Baumann 1888: 664–78).[8]

A close inspection of these examples indicates that columns were meant to represent a specific social order and structure society according to the viewpoint of the respective community, as the monastery's members were to be inserted into the first column at the left, followed by the monks and nuns from other institutions in the middle, and simple lay

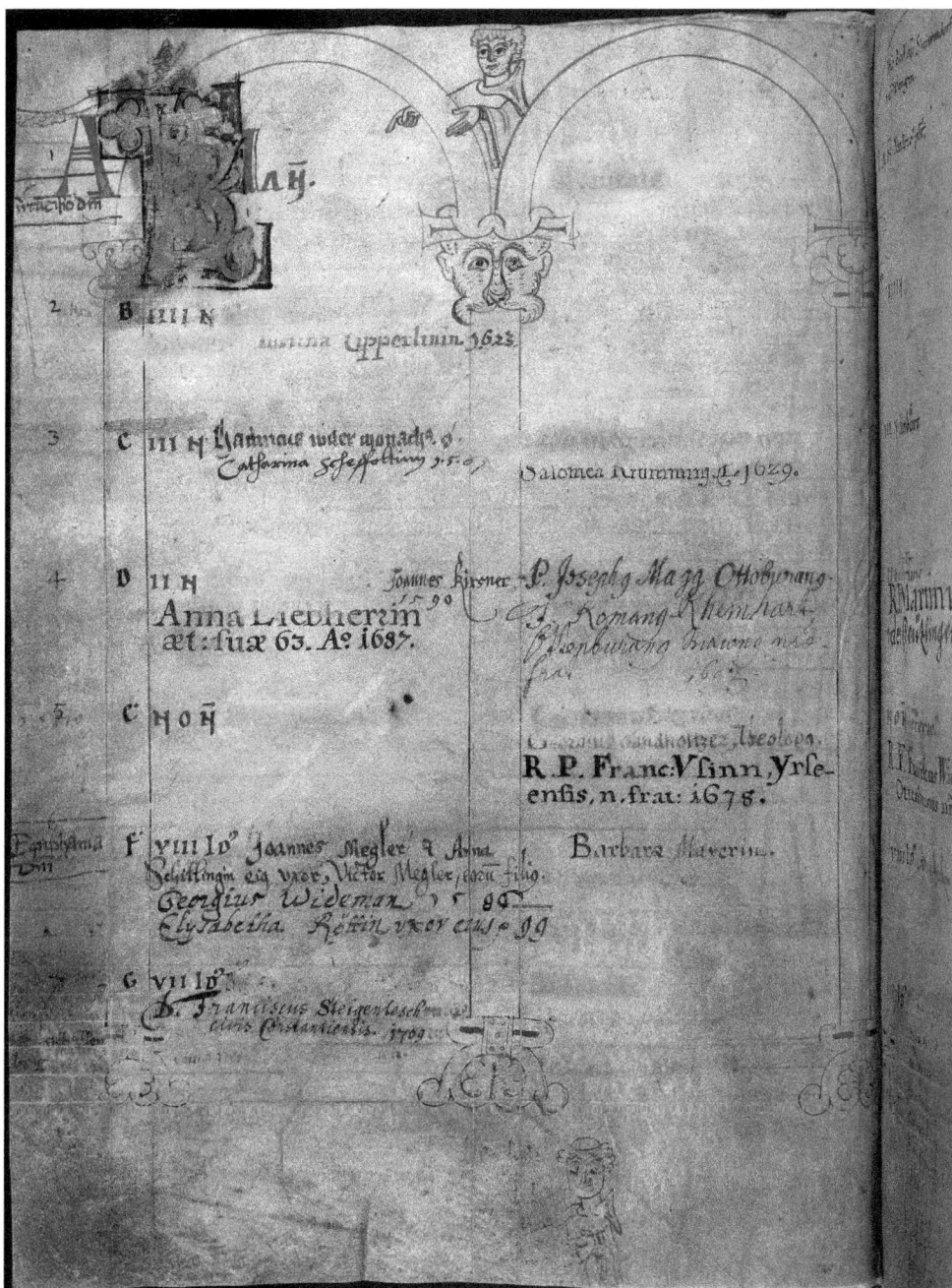

FIGURE 7.6: The necrology of Petershausen features arcades whose original purpose was to sort the members of the convent from lay benefactors, as indicated by the monk drawn on top of the first page. Heidelberg, Universitätsbibliothek, Cod. Sal. IX 42, fol. 4v. © Creative Commons (Public Domain).

people, knights, and peasants, in the last column to the right, or even outside grid. In an iconographic sense, read from left to right, this layout could express a growing distance from God. This interpretation is supported by the fact that on the first page of the Petershausen necrology, the arches are headed by the drawing of a monk pointing with both hands toward the first column, while on the opposite page, a woman in a noble dress points at the fourth column. Thus, the arcades created an architecture with a specified place for each individual much like the imaginary rooms of the ancient *ars memoriae* which were adapted by medieval scholars (Carruthers 1990; Coleman 1992; Yates 1966).

However, later writers often ignored the intended structure and inserted new names wherever there was a free spot on the respective date. Nevertheless, the samples show that there was a need for social distinction, just like there was in the confraternity books. It seems very likely that a deceased bishop or abbot was commemorated with greater honor than a simple monk or priest, and that there were different formulas for clergy members and lay people. A possible way to transgress this order was for noble laymen to join a religious congregation on their deathbed, and thus enjoying the full status of a monk (*monachus ad succurendum*).

Individual commemoration of this kind grew to be much more popular and widespread than the rituals mentioned in the previous chapter and thus, there are by far more necrologies preserved than confraternity books. Archival evidence suggests that from the twelfth century onward, most religious institutions in Europe owned some sort of necrological documents for listing dead members and benefactors. A comprehensive repertory from all dioceses in France has produced the impressive number of approximately 3,500 documents (Lemaître 1980), while extensive research for Switzerland has brought to light more than 1,000 books from nearly as many different churches, spread across small archives in the country (Hugener 2014a). Comparative surveys of this scale have yet to be conducted for other regions, but it seems very likely that they will find thousands of books as well, if they haven't been destroyed by wars or other misfortunes.

The congregation of Cluny, expanding quickly across France, Italy, Spain, Germany, Switzerland, England, and southern Scotland in the eleventh and twelfth centuries, was particularly successful in promoting their memorial services (Constable 2010: 313–38). In Cluniac liturgy, a firm connection was established between commemoration and charity (Iogna-Prat 1998; Wollasch 1979). Abbot Odilo of Cluny decreed that those requesting a mass for their souls should offer alms for the poor. In analogy to All Saints' Day on November 1, the Cluniac monasteries chose the consecutive date, November 2, for the Commemoration of All the Faithful Departed or All Souls' Day, as suggested by Odilo in the eleventh century. This new holiday provided an opportunity for the collective commemoration of the widest group possible, while at the same time giving room to relatives to mourn specifically for their lost ones.

The appeal of Cluniac commemoration is reflected by the order's necrologies, which list more than 30,000 names (Wollasch 1982). This means that next to the regular obligations of liturgy, up to a hundred masses were to be celebrated for dead members and benefactors on each day of the year. Since it was promised that for each mass for a dead member or benefactor, a poor person would receive a meal, this meant huge expenses for the community. Therefore, Peter the Venerable limited these meals to fifty per day with the justification that otherwise, "the dead would expel the living" (Bünz 2003: 265; Harvey 1993: 14; Wollasch 1971: 154).

Among other things, it was the criticism of Cluny's involvement in earthly dealings that led to a monastic reform movement at the wake of the twelfth century. A faction critical to Cluny established the Cistercian order which objected the idea of individual commemoration. At least, this was their official dogma. According to their constitutions from 1183, the members and benefactors were only to be commemorated globally on four special dates, including All Souls' Day (Wollasch 1973; Neiske 1996). Later rulings allowed the commemoration of abbots and kings. Benefactors were only to be commemorated individually upon approval of the General Chapter. Nevertheless, there are plenty of necrologies from Cistercian monasteries to prove that they accepted just as many donations as other religious institutions (Hugener 2014a: 65; Kaczmarek 1994). Even one of the Cistercians' primary reformers, Bernard of Clairvaux, had preached about the benefits of prayer as a remedy for the souls of the dead (Leclerq and Rochais 1970: 145–9, 276–7). And Caesarius of Heisterbach, another famous white monk, popularized the legend of a deceased relative who appeared in a vision to let the people know that his soul was saved only by the masses of the Cistercian order (Strange 1851: 343).

Despite their renunciation of earthly wealth, the mendicant orders of the Franciscans and Dominicans which spread across Europe in the thirteenth century widely accepted donations in return for their prayers. Several necrologies from convents of the friars and preachers bear testimony to this (Andenmatten 2009; Hugener 2014a: 67–8; Robson 2002: 116; 2006: 142). Their convents, often based in urban centers, were specialized in spiritual administration and burial services, so it was only consequent that they took care of the souls of the deceased, too. As a matter of fact, their preaching about purgatory, propagated by none other than Thomas Aquinas, may have raised people's fears about the afterlife and pressed them to take measures for the redemption of their souls (Le Goff 1984: 316–20). The growing number of tales about ghosts and revenants asking for prayers for their souls may reflect this common concern (Schmitt 1998). Henceforth, there was a flood of foundations for this very purpose that exceeded previous eras by far.

CONNECTING MEMORIES TO GIFTS: FROM NECROLOGIES TO ANNIVERSARY BOOKS

From the twelfth century onward, parallel to spreading the doctrine of purgatory and a new movement of popular piety instigated by it, there is an exponential augmentation of documents concerning religious commemoration. A multitude of charters as well as the newly revived genre of testaments or wills suggest that it became very common not just for members of the clergy and the nobility, but also for merchants, artisans, and peasants, to take precautions for the redemption of their souls by donating vast amounts of goods to the church (Bijsterveld 2007: 168–9, 190–2; Chiffoleau 1980: 336; Brown 2011: 106–8; Burgess 1991: 71–2; Hugener 2014a: 78–81; Keyser 2003: 806, 809–11; Lauwers 1997: 376–7, 474–7; Lusiardi 2000: 171–88). In return, benefactors did no longer content themselves with simply being included in prayers but demanded for special masses or private offices to be celebrated perpetually on their behalf (Angenendt 1983). Some of these services were meant to be held on a daily or weekly basis, but most founders opted for annual commemoration on the date of their death. Hence, these services were called anniversaries or years-minds (the German equivalent is *Jahrzeit* or *Jahrtag*).

This new type of commemoration was no longer exclusive to monastic institutions. Instead, donators also chose cathedrals, collegiate and parish churches, hospitals and poorhouses as a stage for being remembered. When their masses were being celebrated at local institutions, they reached a much greater audience and presence in everyday life, as there were not just the monks or nuns attending, but the names of the founders were proclaimed when the entire population gathered for worship—certainly a great way of being remembered by a crowd as large as possible in the pre-modern era before mass media. Thus, anniversaries became a vehicle of self-representation and even a status symbol. Unlike the antecedent rituals, these commemorative practices were not only directed towards God, but also aimed at being remembered for posterity and prolonging earthly fame (Oexle 1995b).

Many donators intended to improve their anniversaries by asking for extra priests to assist the service, for a specific number of prayers to be said or candles to be lit, for ringing the bells or for a choir, for dispensing alms to the poor, for a visitation of their grave, or for a hearse or catafalque to be placed in front of the altar, representing the body of the deceased, repeating the performance of the funeral (Burgess 1991: 71–2). In many cases, close relatives such as spouses, parents, or children were included in these anniversaries, manifesting a growing interest in the nuclear family as a dynastic ensemble. This development went along with the creation of surnames, starting with members of the nobility who were referred to by their ancestral seat. Other surnames were created from provenance, occupation, physical or mental characteristics, and nicknames.

With such clear specifications as to how the funds were to be used, they were no longer just plain donations, but foundations in the sense of a permanent fund to fulfill a particular purpose (Borgolte 2012, 2014–17). Usually, the endowment consisted of an annual rent from a piece of land or a house which would create a regular income for the priests who were to execute the service. Others donated material objects such as religious paintings, liturgical vessels and vestments. Some wealthy families even endowed their own altar, chapel, or chantry. Essentially, the latter was an ecclesiastical benefice endowed to perform the desired masses for the souls of the founders (Burgess 1991: 72; Wood-Legh 1965: 128–9). The priests were threatened with pecuniary punishment, should they forget to celebrate an anniversary. In this case, the revenues were to be transferred to a different institution or fall back to the founders' families (Burgess 1991: 83). Interestingly, the charters documenting such foundations often state that potential offenders would be erased from the heavenly book of life, if they jeopardized the wellbeing of the souls trusted to them (Hugener 2014b; Neiske 1997: 117–8).

Archetypally, such instructions were drawn up in a charter and after the founder's passing, he or she was inserted into a necrology, under the date of his or her death or burial (Wagner 2000). However, these entries were no longer limited to a simple name; instead, information was added regarding the founders' family and provenance, their endowment and advice for the liturgical execution, like the number of candles or specific prayers. This trend for more detailed notes can be observed in many necrologies. In the Benedictine abbey of Saint Gall, for instance, entries in an old necrology were enriched by a single scribe in the middle of the thirteenth century (Stiftsbibliothek, Cod. Sang. 453; Baumann 1888: 462–87). Systematically, he tried to attribute each name to a specific family, most of which were still important clients of the monastery. Moreover, he added marginalia or glosses in small letters to almost every entry, listing the goods which were donated by the respective person (Hugener 2014a: 116–31).

Of course, such extensive additions would fill up the pages quickly, making it necessary to draw up a new book with more space between each date. While earlier necrologies often displayed an entire month on one single page, the calendars which were drawn up from the thirteenth century onward featured only one to four days per page which, of course, resulted in much thicker books. They usually were in huge folio size, protected by solid wooden boards covered with leather, and their pages were made of parchment long after

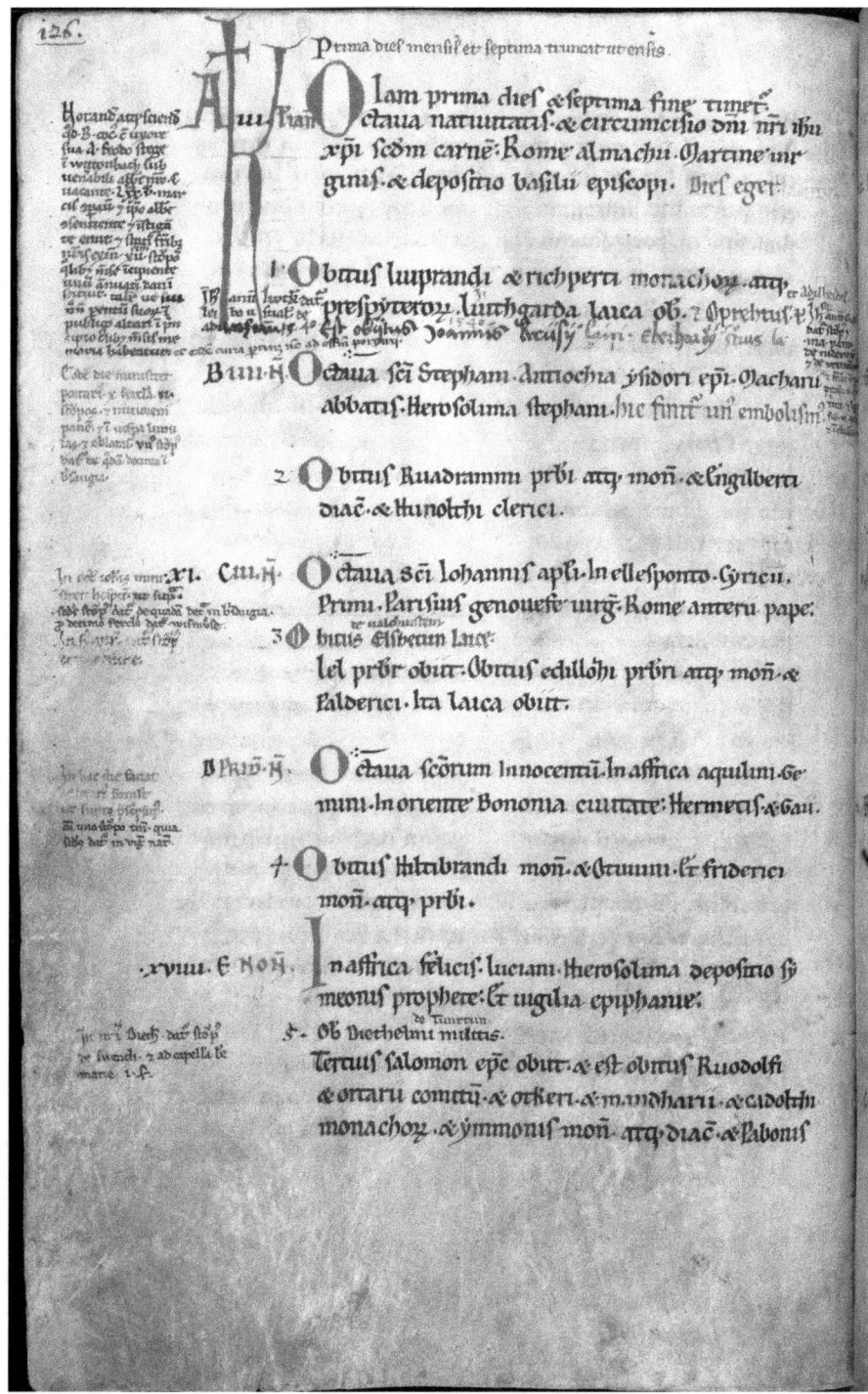

FIGURE 7.7: In the second version of the chapter office book from Saint Gall, a scribe has tried to connect each entry to a donation by adding marginal notes about the gifted goods. Saint Gall, Stiftsbibliothek, Cod. Sang. 453, p. 126. © Stiftsbibliothek Sankt Gallen.

most other documents had switched to paper; everything about them was literally made to last for eternity (Gamper 2010; Hugener 2014a: 30–1; Lemaître 1980: 37–53). Of course, as each of these books was unique, they were never published in print, but retained their manuscript character, with dozens of hands adding new entries, making them the prototype of a "living text" or "living book" (Lemaître 1988; Petrucci 1998: 46–7).

With more details added to each entry, these documents were no longer pure necrologies, but actual anniversary books or *libri anniversariorum*, an appellation that became popular in the fourteenth century (Schuler 1987). The corresponding German term is *Jahrzeitbuch*, whereas in Romance languages and English, this type of book is called obituary (Hugener 2014a: 31–3; Lemaître 1980: 12–5). However, the most common reference was still that of the *liber vitae*. Like their predecessors, these books were being considered an equivalent of the heavenly book of life; they were being used in liturgy and placed upon the altar for reciting the special masses that were to be held on each day. But in addition to that, they also fulfilled a more profane, economic purpose. Not only were they a mnemonic aid to help remember the anniversaries of the benefactors, but also the goods they gave to the church. In fact, for most institutions, these books were the first ones to systematically list the sources of income (Hugener 2014a). And for many places, especially in rural areas, these books are the earliest documents reaching back to the Middle Ages.

Starting from the second half of the thirteenth century, the first institutions to set up such hybrid books were the collegiate churches. Other than the members from most religious orders, the secular canons with their prebends were allowed to own and accumulate individual property (Crouch 2001; 159–80). Therefore, the distribution of income among the chapter's members was a key feature of the collegiate lifestyle, and their statutes are filled with rules about how each canon was to be rewarded when he attended a mass. As a matter of fact, most entries into their anniversary books regulate the portion each canon should get for attending the mass. A well-known example is the so-called book of donors from the cathedral of Strasbourg in Alsace, started in 1320 (Stanford 2011: 199).

For the same reason, celebrating anniversaries became an important source of income for the priests and chaplains at parish churches (Burgess 1987b, 1991, 2000; Brown 2003: 129–31, 2011: 100–32; Bünz 2003). It can safely be assumed that by the end of the fourteenth century, most people, no matter how modest their wealth, invested in such an assurance for their salvation. Perhaps, the experience of mass mortality during the Black Death (first in 1348) has raised awareness of the necessity to take precautions for the afterlife (Andenmatten 2009: 161; Brown 2011: 107–8; Oexle 1983: 65–8).

The promise of eternal commemoration bore its risks. Not only was it likely that priests might forget about their duties or that the documents that were kept as a reminder of these duties were lost or destroyed. Another problem was that the rents which paid for the services would no longer be paid, or at least diminish in the course of inflation. In such cases, the priests often refused to celebrate an anniversary which was no longer paid for, and they even erased the respective entries in their books, which sometimes caused heated conflicts (Hugener 2014b: 219–22). A more official procedure for this was to reduce the number of foundations officially, by approbation of the bishop or pope. This meant that the respective masses were reduced to one general anniversary for all benefactors (Bünz 2003: 278; Hugener 2014a: 105–6). But even well-established celebrations such as the royal foundations in Goslar (Lohse 2011) or Quedlinburg, Speyer, and Königsfelden (Moddelmog 2012) were likely to undergo drastic changes over time.

While anniversaries were meant to be held eternally until Judgment Day, they were sometimes accompanied by a cumulative, but only temporal form of memorial services, when citizens, accustomed to a more mercantile way of thinking, demanded for thirty, fifty, hundred or more masses to be said immediately within a week or a month after their death (Chiffoleau 1980; Lusiardi 2000). Mostly, the two different types of commemoration were combined in order to guarantee a maximal benefit, both instantly and in the long term (Marshall 2002: 20). While perpetual anniversaries were directed toward the ultimate Judgment Day, the immediate accumulation of masses was probably meant to shorten one's time in purgatory. Unlike the former, these cumulative masses did little to establish a lasting memory and can only be mentioned briefly here.

Along with the emergence of surnames, families were also identified by their coats of arms, providing dynastic cohesion over time, a phenomenon which spread from the top of society downwards during the late Middle Ages. From late in the fourteenth century onward, entries in some anniversary books were complemented with coats of arms. One of the most beautiful examples is the anniversary book from the parish of Uster in eastern Switzerland, featuring dozens of colorfully painted coats of arms—not just of the lords of Landenberg who ruled the area, but also of local peasants and craftsmen, many of which were given canting arms: The Miller family was represented by a millwheel, the Blacksmith's family by a pincer (Zürich, Zentralbibliothek, Ms. C 1).[9]

These drawings were not only an embellishment of the book, making it even more impressive than it already was, but they also had a more practical purpose, as they could help identify the donors' graves which were to be visited when celebrating their anniversaries, since the tombstones often bore their coats of arms, too. Beyond that, heraldic signs were omnipresent in medieval churches: altars, paintings, liturgical vessels and vestments, colored windows, pillars, and archways—all bore emblems of sponsors. An impressive example can still be seen in the church of Greifensee, belonging to the parish of Uster mentioned above. The unique triangular chapel was built in the middle of the fourteenth century by the noble family of Landenberg whose coats of arms are prominently featured in Uster's anniversary book, but also on the ceiling of the chapel, along with images of saints. Symbolically, the Landenberg family was placed in heaven, and when people looked up, they were physically reminded of who their lords were and where their own position was.

Families were not the only ones to manifest their identity with anniversary services. Throughout the late Middle Ages, guilds and lay fraternities started to celebrate anniversaries for all their members, ostentatiously expanding into public space by large processions. Even entire communities were celebrating anniversaries. The city of Berne, for instance, founded by duke Berchtold of Zähringen in 1191, commemorated the act of its foundation each year on the date of Berchtold's death. Priests in all monasteries and churches of the city had to celebrate his anniversary, his coat of arms was posted, candles were burnt, alms were given to the poor, and a procession was held through the streets and to the central fountain which featured a monumental figure representing the founder—all paid for by the city's council. Apparently, its members were trying to present themselves as the legitimate heirs of the duke (Hugener 2014a: 177–90).

Similar intentions were associated with the commemoration of battles, raids, and wars. Celebrations of this kind were mostly organized by city states and rural republics such as the members of the Swiss confederation or the highly autonomous marshland villages of Dithmarschen in northern Germany, but occasionally also by kings and princes (Brachmann 2006; Graf 1991, 2003; Hugener 2014a). Usually, the date of the event was turned into

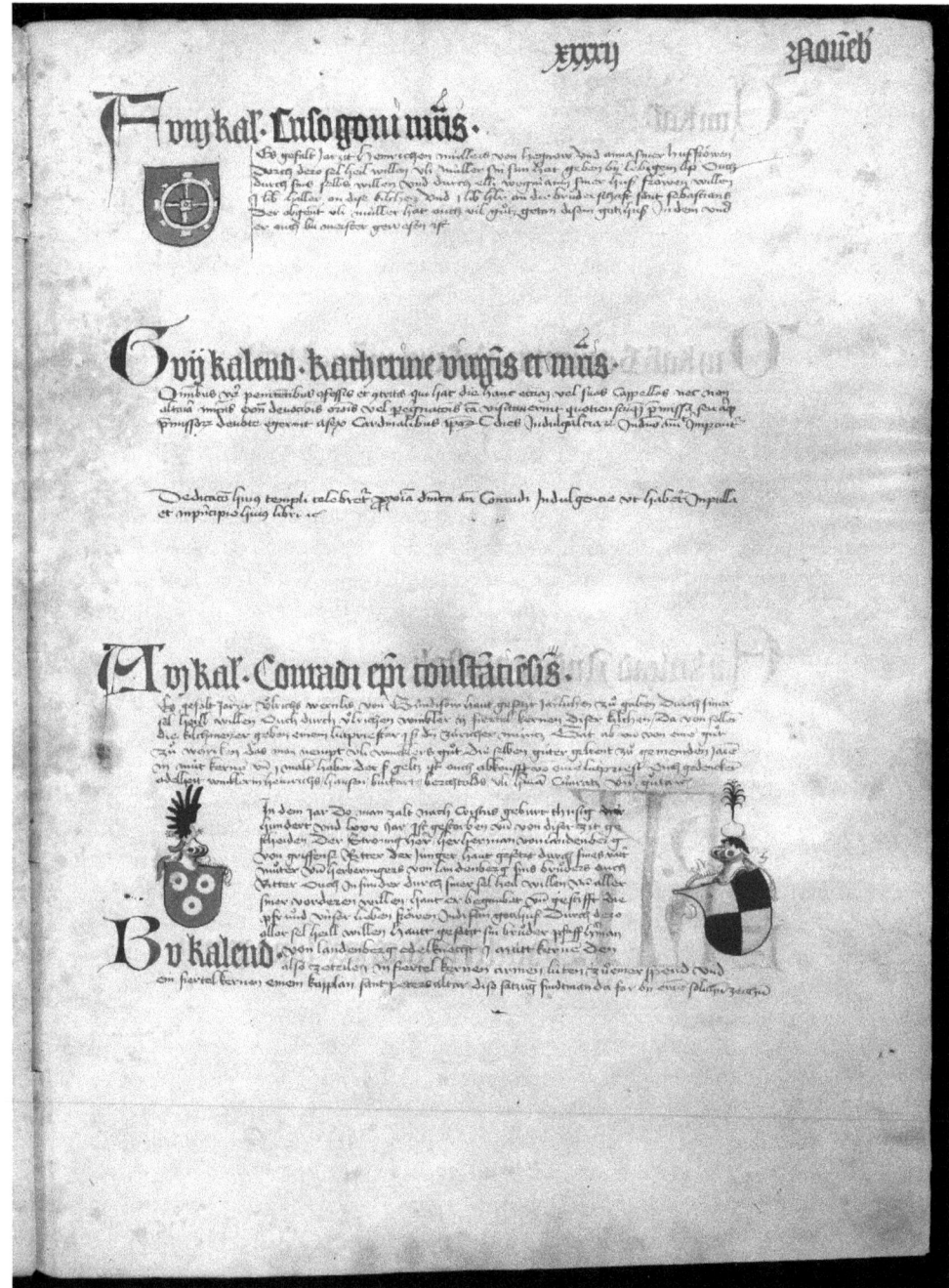

FIGURE 7.8: Many entries in the anniversary book of Uster are embellished with coats of arms of noble families as well as local craftsmen like the Millers who were represented by a millwheel (Zürich, Zentralbibliothek, Ms. C 1, fol. 42r). © Zürich, Zentralbibliothek.

a public holiday by decree and each year, when the whole population attended church, chronicles were read out and the names of the victims were recited, providing an example of sacrifice for the greater good. Often, pieces of captured goods such as flags or the enemy's armor were publicly put on display. In other cases, processions were held to commemorate disasters such as earthquakes, floods, or the Black Death (Graf 2003: 264–5). Sometimes, these commemorative celebrations were directly linked to public elections and oath-taking ceremonies, thus connecting the community's future to the past, creating a sense of unity and identity which transcended the passing of time.

The idea of annual commemoration on the date of death was also picked up by Jewish communities in Europe, particularly in Germany. Hence, the German term *yahrzeit* was introduced in Yiddish. On the date of death of a relative, candles were lit, the grave was to be visited, and special prayers such as the *kaddish* or *yizkor* were to be said (Galinsky 2005: 195–200). According to a twelfth century prayer book (*machzor*) written by rabbi Simchah of Vitry, the names of the deceased were recited on Shabbat and Yom Kippur, after reading the Torah (Hurwitz 1889: 173). Similar to Christian practice, some synagogues listed the martyrs of pogroms as well as famous scholars and local donors in what became known as memorbooks (*sefer sikaron*). It's unclear whether this word was adapted from Latin or if it hinted at where these books were placed, namely on the central lectern for the Torah called Almemor (Barzen 2011: 4; Weinberg 1924: 314–8).

Only one such book has survived from the Middle Ages. It was started in the synagogue in Nuremberg towards the end of the thirteenth century, but listed the names of Jewish victims from the First Crusade in 1096 to the pogroms during the years of the Black Death in 1349, along with the names of donors contributing to the synagogue, the cemetery, the school, the hospital, and the poor (Pomerance 2000: 33–53; Yuval 2006: 136–7). Most other Jewish memorbooks emerged in the seventeenth and eighteenth centuries, but many of them were destroyed during the Holocaust (Bell 2007: 72–82; Pomerance 2012: 95–114). While some scholars have zealously tried to show that these rites were of purely Jewish origin, others have argued that the similarities to the practices of their Christian environment are too evident to be neglected (Barzen 2011: 1).

CONCLUSION

Religious commemoration was stimulated from below as much as from above, melting popular beliefs with scholarly reflections about the afterlife. The anthropological constraint of coping with death and the desire to remember the deceased were met by the church with rituals offering salvation and thus comfort for both the living and the dying. A vivid exchange evolved, transforming material goods and immaterial services, making commemoration one of the church's largest bases of income—a common theme for criticism in the Reformation era (Marshall 2002: 94–5). While anniversaries, obits, and chantries were abolished in Protestant areas, they flourished in Catholic regions, some of which still celebrate annual masses for the deceased today.

In the course of the Middle Ages, religious commemoration underwent several characteristic changes which can be identified from a diachronic survey of the sources: The period of confraternity books from the early Middle Ages (roughly from the eighth to the tenth century) was followed by the necrologies from the central Middle Ages (eleventh and twelfth centuries) and the anniversary books from the late Middle Ages (thirteenth to fifteenth centuries). These different media types manifest a shift in how religious commemoration was conceived: Early medieval prayer leagues and confraternities were focusing on social networks; individuals were mainly of interest as a part of their specific community or group. In contrast to this, the structure of necrologies and anniversary books follows a very different approach: Here, the individual is singled out and identified by his or her date of death—at first only known to God, but later well identifiable by adding attributes such as surnames, provenance, and even coats of arms. In this sense, they were again attributed to a group, but now as members of a dynastic family.

This development may reflect the fact that individuality in a modern sense gained importance in the course of the Middle Ages (Bedos-Rezak 2011). At the same time, the proliferation of individual commemoration from the ninth century onward contests the exaggerative thesis of Colin M. Morris (1972) that individuality was not "discovered" before the middle of the eleventh century. Certainly, it is more than a coincidence that the later concept of commemoration, which focused on the individual, was much more successful over time.

CHAPTER EIGHT

Remembering and Forgetting

KAI-MICHAEL SPRENGER AND GERALD SCHWEDLER

Damnatio memoriae is the perpetual manifestation of shame through deletion of the name, titles, dignities, statues, destruction of houses, removal of images as well as the prohibition to the successors to carry the name.

—Rebhan, Hodegeta Iuris, 1656[1]

History and memory are both meaningful constructions of the past. What appears obvious in the context of history is bound to be more unexpected in the case of memory as this was considered more authentic, more approximate and more directly associated with the events, personalities, and media. History and memory are based on a connection and use of texts, images, and objects that is open to manipulation. These sources are particularly relied upon to support and legitimize power. Moreover, they form the basis for the historical recollections which apply in each case. Ultimately, they constitute or guarantee stability and security for the individuals or groups who are generally in positions of power and control the discourse. In the interplay between the meaningful construction of the past (history) and memory or the deliberate transfer of information about the past, inevitably there is a selection of information. This also involves the suppression, deletion, and destruction of other, alternative memories that would be suitable to question the primary legitimations and foundations of governance. The process involves the conscious intervention in collective historical knowledge, because what is not firmly anchored through written text or monuments becomes irretrievably forgotten in orally transmitted contexts, usually at the latest after three generations. In general, deliberate suppression and distortion of memory from collective historical consciousness is defined as *damnatio memoriae* (Gerlach 1689; Vittinghoff 1936; Flower 2006; Sprenger 2012; Rigon 2010). While the concept of *memoria damnata* was used in antiquity, the term *damnatio memoriae* is a neologism of the late medieval period and refers specifically to the forms and practices of memory sanctions in antique Rome (Schwedler 2017).

Probably the most characteristic aspect of *damnatio memoriae* is that it not only involves the destruction of memory media which trace an unwanted picture of the past. Rather, a new, supposedly congruent and clear narrative of history is actively constructed that leaves little space for alternative interpretations. Therefore, *damnatio memoriae* is a deletory and simultaneously creative form of dealing with information about the past and the meaningful construction of the past (history). The initiators and agents of this parallel destructive and creative process are always individuals and groups of individuals who themselves claim authority over the narrative from a position of power and can decide what counts for others as valid history. As Peter Burke has described it, the focus is always on the question of "who wants whom to forget what and why" (Burke 1989: 108).

Following the enormous interest in memory as a research subject, Memory Studies became established in the 1980s and 1990s (Algazi 2014: 25). Numerous studies also emerged in the field of medieval research about the techniques of memory and *memoria* (Oexle 1995a; literature review in Hugener 2013). Almost as a reversal of perspective, research into *damnatio memoriae* requires other methods, sometimes even forensic instinct, to uncover those traces that were deliberately deleted in the past and to reclassify them in their original contexts before they were manipulated. The rulers and their accomplices—whose actions often anticipated their mission—proceeded with the utmost sophistication whenever they deleted not only media about unwanted history, but also intended to conceal the act of deletion. Since multiple factors must optimally interplay to accomplish a perfect *damnatio memoriae*, and since this rarely occurs in societies where there is a broad textual as well as object-focused legacy of information about the past, in many cases it still proves possible to follow these traces and to make the subject of *damnatio memoriae* a specialist individual research topic.

Medieval *damnatio memoriae* can thus be defined as a group of individual sanctions where memory media are destroyed, distorted or re-coded both demonstrably as well as in secret. This specific definition of medieval *damnatio memoriae* by no means focuses on the complete destruction of memory. Rather, it implies a counter-construction of memory by means of the targeted re-coding—usually with negative connotations—of positively nuanced traditions and memories. This often arises due to an exemplary stigmatization and defamation of those individuals—mostly inferior political opponents—who stood as guarantors or even protagonists of an alternative historical narrative, or at least had the potential to do so. Related to this is the claim to interpretative authority and the definition of which specific preconditions, general parameters, and on behalf of which target groups' memories are supposed to be modified, forged, re-coded, or even not handed down at all. The agents and media as well as contexts and instances in which forms of medieval *damnatio memoriae* are manifested are accordingly multifaceted. They range from liturgical *memoria* and burial cult to historiography as well as iconographic traditions and public rituals that are used in the context of the *damnatio memoriae* (Sprenger 2009; Landwehr 2015).

The following observations are intended to give a brief account based on the exemplary description of recurring forms of medieval memory destruction. Selected examples then demonstrate the interplay at times of contradictory memorial manipulations within the historical context.

FORMS OF *DAMNATIO MEMORIAE*

The techniques of *damnatio memoriae* are widely divergent depending on the historical situation. However, several general principles can be discerned from the source material of medieval history.

Delete

Deletion is probably the most radical form of *damnatio memoriae* with the aim of eradicating memory media. This should prevent the ability later to rely on these as a source of information about the past and therefore potentially to reconstruct past knowledge as well as meaningfully to construct the past. This targeted destruction assumes manifold characteristics: on the level of the written record, the usual forms are burning, tearing up, cutting up, or drenching entire libraries, books or pages as well as cutting or scraping out material, re-coding or blackening out passages and names. Familiar forms usually for the object-focused, material handing down of memory media are deletion, chiselling away, removing, overturning inscriptions, toppling statues, or the removal of commemoration plaques including the demolition of buildings or entire cities. The aim was not to leave behind any traces that could convey memories.

This radical form of *damnatio memoriae* did not even stop at grave sites. The numerous deliberate desecrations of graves and destruction of corpses are a powerful testament to this. The aim was to avoid the corpse being used as a medium for remembering or even for founding a cult after the death of the person in question. One prominent example is the case of Arnold of Brescia (1090–1155), one of the most controversial figures of the twelfth century. He was excommunicated by the Pope for his radical, idiosyncratic doctrine. Due to a citizens' uprising in Rome, at the height of his power he became the leader of the Roman civic commune. However, in 1155 during Emperor Frederick Barbarossa's campaign to capture Rome he was taken prisoner, handed over to the Pope, and executed in Rome. The consensus of the few reports is that he was burned. Gerhoh of Reichersberg, who was obviously well informed, describes this as follows:

> For this teaching he was not only excommunicated from the church of god, but moreover killed by hanging and *post mortem* burned by fire and thrown into the River Tiber, so that the Roman people, whom he had seduced with his doctrine, would not be devoted to him as a martyr.[2]

Obviously, the intent here was the utter destruction of several levels and media of memory. Burning the body and the refusal of a burial site by scattering the ashes into the River Tiber were intended to prevent any opportunities for liturgical *memoria* by the grave and probably also the potential worship of relics. The texts and sermons of Arnold of Brescia also consistently became an object of *damnatio memoriae*. Thus, it is certainly no accident that not a single manuscript or text by Arnold has survived. Not even single positive comments are preserved about him–his story is only known from the texts of his opponents and persecutors (Schmitz-Esser 2007: 80–5).

A similar situation applied for so-called antipapists who were generally also refused a burial place as a site of a liturgical *memoria*. The few exceptional cases where more prominent burial places were preserved for deceased antipapists confirm this rule. These cases mostly concern unpopular traditions that can be appreciated not least from the example of the second Hohenstaufen antipope Paschal III. We know from the Appendix of Gesta Rahewini that Paschal was buried by the canons of St. Peter's in Rome. However, today we search in vain on the plaque set up by the entrance to the catacombs of St. Peter's Basilica with its list of all the successors of St. Peter who are buried here. There is no mention of the name Paschal III who was the rival to Pope Alexander III from 1164 to 1168 and claimed the antipapist St. Peter's Basilica. The verdict of the official church is that the antipopes did not count among the prominent group of lawful successors of Peter. Instead, they stood outside the Christian community as excommunicated schismatics. There was no place for them as pope in the collective memory culture of the *Sancta Apostolica Ecclesia*. Nor was there any motive to distinguish their burial places or to pass on their exact location for posterity (Ziese 1982: 271–3; Sprenger 2012).

In this context, the target of deliberate destruction might not only be graves, but also other personal memory media such as the residences and other representative or identifying buildings for the person or persons in question. Such a targeted razing of the houses of those individuals, who were sanctioned with a *damnatio*, seems to indicate the example of the antique practice of *damnatio memoriae*, particularly in the context of civic Rome. For example, there is evidence of such a sanction imposed by Pope Paschal II (1099–1118) against the Roman Corsi family who were amongst the most influential supporters of the Emperor and of the (anti)Pope Clement (III) (1084–1100). The demolition of the fortified houses of the Corsi close to the Capitol at a symbolically significant location inside the city is hardly to be interpreted as an exclusively military action.[3] Instead, it marks a deliberate belittling of the status and the social *memoria* of that family. Only the ruined building and the gaping hole made the defeat and loss of prestige of the Corsi visible for all Romans and in a complementary way represented the victory of the supporters of Pope Paschal II in the city that was still contested under the schism. A similar "semantics of building demolition" has been discerned by more recent studies on object-focused memory practices as well as on historic culture in republican Rome as a "historical and political [sophisticated] [. . .] kind of deletion" and a specific form of *damnatio memoriae* (Walter 2004: 170f.; Hartmann 2010: 142f.). It is plausible that people may still have remembered these antique law practices at the time of Paschal II in Rome, even if it was only as a schematic model, especially as they were also used by later popes such as Gelasius II (1118–19) or Innocent III (1198–1216) in similar crisis-ridden contexts against their opponents (Duchesne 1955: 323).

The targeted destruction of entire cities followed a similar motivation of making a visible example, although in practice this was much more difficult to implement. A well-known example at least for the intended complete demolition of a city was Emperor Frederick Barbarossa's plan to raze the Lombardian metropolis of Milan as his potentially most dangerous opponent among the cities of the upper Italian mainland after the defeat and unconditional surrender of 1162. However, the plan failed. Yet, even given the actual scale of the destruction this punitive strike must and should naturally imply a highly symbolic and deterrent character for the Emperor's remaining opponents (Berwinkel 2007).

The antique tradition of the destruction of burial sites and houses not only has a counterpart in the medieval period. The same applies for the deletion of names on inscriptions, although due to the changing "epigraphical habits" comparatively fewer inscriptions were erected in medieval times. Special significance was granted to the use of lists in the religious and political domain, whether these were official lists, diptychs of the priests and bishops or the so-called memory books referring to the books of life (*libri vitae*) that were mentioned in the Bible. Here, we also discover numerous individual examples where the names of individuals and families were deleted (Hugener 2014b: 203f.; Geary 1994b).

Conceal and Ignore

The technique of concealing and ignoring is considerably less radical than active destruction, since this form of *damnatio memoriae* can at least theoretically be reversed. This category ultimately also includes all forms of censorship where texts and images are not generally destroyed, but where a unique system of access rules is imposed. Memory media are removed from the active field of perception; they are no longer directly available to influence the formation of memory and tradition through their presence and immanence (Margalit 2002: 208). A good example of this is the very early canon of the early Christian statutes *Statuta ecclesiae antiqua*. This statute of rules emerged between 475 and 485 probably in southern France and adopted numerous older documents that are no longer known today. The fifth canon explicitly regulates the use of the unacceptable content for Christians of pagan literature and heretical Christian doctrines: "The bishop should not read the books of the pagans or those of heretics except out of necessity and at the appropriate time."[4] This means that while pagan texts were available in the diocesan towns, they were not allowed to be read. Bishops should therefore attempt even more to be familiar with the arguments in Christian heretical texts to refute them if required. However, these books should not be accessible for ordinary priests or laypeople. In the medieval period, this passage gained enormous influence when it was initially adopted in the significant collection of canon law the *Vetus Gallica*. Later, it was incorporated in the *Decretum Gratini* (D.37 C.1, cf. ed. Friedberg and Richter), the canon law that was used by the Catholic Christian Church.

Concealing and ignoring through such manipulation on the material level of objects and texts also applies to the field of oral language. Unwanted information is suppressed. The spiral of silence is a fitting term to describe this process—namely, that keeping silent leads to silence and permanent silence ultimately leads to forgetting. The subject, person or incident is gradually less spoken about, until it no longer actively exists in the conversational context. What is silenced is conserved in the status of latency, but the discourse of the next generation goes beyond this and the prolonged continuation of this practice lets it slide into oblivion.

Belittle and neutralize

Belittling and neutralizing represent the downgrading of the importance of an event or cultural practice from the past. This involves reducing the effectiveness of individual statements or elements. Particularly effective strategies include classification within a new value context, annotation, and connotations. These lead to downgrading which can be associated with devaluation. For the purposes of maintaining power, the achievements and successes of an opponent are skilfully denied or belittled as inadequate and neutralized, while one's own successes are emphasised much more vigorously.

Belittling already applies to the polemical use of distorting titles of rulers in contemporary and later historical estimation. In the centuries-long conflicts between the pope and emperor—for example, many times in the conflict between Emperor Frederick Barbarossa and Pope Alexander III—repeated reference was made only to the so-called emperor (*dictus imperator*) or in the conflict between Emperor Louis IV of Bavaria and Pope John XXII of "he who calls himself emperor" (*qui imperatorem se dicit*). The papal curia therefore negated the imperial claim and the associated imperial rights of its opponents, even if there was a clear perception of the authority of the individual as a counterpart or historical personality. In this context, we can observe an intensification of this targeted denial and modification of titles in the case of Pope John XXII (1245–1334), who did not even grant Emperor Louis IV of Bavaria (1281–1347) a title as emperor or king, and not even grant other titles as duke, prince, or earl, but instead simply referred to him merely as "the Bavarian" (*Bavarus*). In return, Louis only referred to the pope as *Iacobus de Caturco, falso se papam nominantis*, so he denied him the papal title and reduced him to his origin from Cahors, which was denounced as a merchants' town. An irony of history is that even though no self-descriptions of Emperor Louis are preserved, later this strategy used by the pope was not even perceived as belittling. Instead, the initial polemical intent and belittling regional description was used as *epitheton ornans*, as an honorary title. Today, this is perceived as the positive and exclusive title of the emperor: "Louis of Bavaria."

Re-code and re-write

The technique of re-coding and re-writing is one of the most effective strategies of *damnatio memoriae*. While existing forms and contexts are adopted, they are instilled with new or changed content. Intensive and primarily literary research into *réécriture* succeeded in showing that in the guise of an apparently faithful reworking of texts about the past, the substantial amendments and forgeries of history resembled a process of forgetting (Goullet 2003; Goullet 2005). The philological and historical perspective of *réécriture* research could prove a deliberate, classifying, selective, and suppressive consciousness of the past on the part of individual editors and copyists. Such text modifications can be classified in the contradictory sphere of confirmatory "revised-writing" (*Wiederschrift*) and refuting "counter-writing" (*Widerschrift*) (Reimitz 2004: 206). In the medieval period, hundreds of chronicles were revised, reworked, and rewritten at the copyist stage. A meticulous philological approach can especially show that this method subjected countless individuals, events, and practices to a *damnatio memoriae*. A special example of this on the material level are the forms of re-use like a palimpsest, where for the sake of saving materials, what seem to be older and insignificant texts on parchment were scraped and shaved off to enable use later, apparently for more important texts.

A typical example of *réécriture* is the rather curious story of the preservation of a charter of (anti)Pope Clement (III) for the municipality of Bologna in the year 1084. After the end of the schism there was no longer any reason to hand down a charter of Clement (III), who was now considered the antipope, since this document had forfeited any kind of legal force. However, the recipients did not want to forego the privileges once handed down by Clement (III) and *post schism* revised the antipapist original to a harmless pseudo-original record of Pope Gregory VII. However, the original document bearing the signature and seal of (anti)Pope Clement (III) was destroyed. This presumably original charter of Pope Gregory VII for the municipality of Bologna, pre-dated to the year 1074, was for a long time considered as fake due to content and textual inconsistencies. However, only the meticulous philological arguments of Antonio Pini could prove that this content was in fact a charter issued by (anti)Pope Clement (III) dating from the year 1084. This proves the extent of the intricacies involved in changing the name and re-coding to attain a non-contradictory position (Pini 1997: 345–86).

However, not only the individual records could become the target of such skilful and focused re-coding strategies. Entire cities were supposed to change their names according to the will of those in power to obscure any positive association with the original city founders and political opponents or to let it fall into oblivion. Two widely known examples should suffice to illustrate this case.

The upper Italian Piedmontese city of Alessandria was founded in 1168 as a military action in the conflict between Emperor Frederick I Barbarossa and the upper Italian cities. The Lombard League accepted the city and named it after Pope Alexander III who supported the Lombard League. In 1174, the city was under siege for six months by Frederick Barbarossa, but to no avail. After the Peace of Constance treaty between the

Lombard League and the emperor in 1183, the city was formally newly established and given the name Cesaria (imperial city). However, the city did not become established. The example of the Apulian city of Manfredonia also indicates the prominent conflict scenario of the disputes between the Hohenstaufen and the papal curia.

In 1256, Manfred (1232–66), son of the Hofenstaufen Emperor Frederick II, laid the foundation stone of the city that he named after himself. The ruins of neighboring antique Siponto were integrated into the new city plan. Manfred died in 1266 in the Battle of Benevento against Charles of Anjou, so he did not live to see the city's completion. To erase the memory of the unpopular Hofenstaufen Manfred, the Anjou, his victors, renamed the city that they completed as Sypontum Novellum (Nuova Siponto). However, ultimately, this name could not become established.

Forms of a *damnatio memoriae* also appear through re-coding in architecture and individual representative buildings. The Basilica Santa Maria in Trastevere in Rome is an extremely well-known case. Its rebuilding is comparable to creative destruction which makes it eminently eligible to be regarded as an act of *damnatio memoriae* (Stroll 1987: 125–7). Regarding the antipopes, it is significant that it was the titular church of Pope Anacletus II (Pietro Pierleoni 1130–8) that to all intents and purposes he had richly decorated so it was adequate to serve his *memoria*. Due to his death in 1138, the rival Pope Innocent II (1130–43) gained political influence. He seized the building project to publicize his own ambition and to rebuild and complete the church according to his ideas. He commissioned an impressive apse mosaic of himself as a benefactor on a golden background, thus deleting any trace of Anacletus and his initiative to decorate the church so lavishly. He therefore not only re-coded the initiative to construct this place as a general memorial for Anacletus, but also the real image of Anacletus, which was replaced by the extravagant apse mosaic. However, a unique feature was that the creation of the form language of the mosaic on a golden background was not at all typical of the contemporary style. Rather, thanks to its Byzantine resonance it referred instead to the pre-Christian period. The re-coding is almost concealed in the old, virtually antiquarian style (Sible de Blaauw 2014; Kinney 2016: 337–47).

Victors' history

A famous motto attributed to Marcus T. Cicero is: *Galli victi silent, canunt victores:* "the defeated Cocks/Gauls are silent, but the victors sing." Those who obviously lose a war, battle, or conflict are not only defeated with the loser's flaw but henceforth are subjected to the vocal narrative of the triumphant victor. Furthermore, the often-inconclusive story is reconstructed retrospectively as though no other options were plausible than the downfall. To this end, mementos, texts, or even objects are manipulated so that there no longer seems to be any doubt about the legitimacy of the victor. In this case, a *damnatio memoriae* mainly involves creating a caricature of and vilifying the vanquished as predestined for defeat. The purpose here is not the destruction of the memory of the person as such, but merely the positive aspects. The public announcement of the demise and the negative implications of the verdict made the opponent a condemned person and an outcast. A special variation is the *pittura infamante*, the image of shame, which is widespread in upper Italy (Ortalli 2013).

At the same time, one's own story is exaggerated and represented as more glorious—and justifiably favoured by "God and history." This is especially evident in the later exaggerated status of generals and rulers like Charlemagne. The voices describing this identity-making king as a brutal power broker and slaughterer were set aside (Hergemöller 2007). Yet, is styling as a saint not equally a manipulation of history, a *damnatio memoriae*? Here, personal preferences and specific character attributes are falsified and distorted in sacrifice to the unlikely foil of the immaculate hero. While *divinatio* is deemed as far more positive than *damnatio*, nevertheless, both are interpretations, which require the substantial historiographical reinterpretation of events.

FAMOUS EXAMPLES OF OBLIVION AND *DAMNATIO MEMORIAE* IN THE MIDDLE AGES

Theodoric the Great

There are now strong indications that Theodoric (451–526), the king of the Ostrogoths, was subjected to *damnatio memoriae*. As a skilful military leader, he united the many regions of Italy to a kingdom and occupied the old imperial residence in Ravenna. He had an enormous palace built and an impressive palace church that is still preserved today. After his death, his successors could not maintain power, whether this was because from the year 527 the Eastern Roman Emperor Justinian I sought to conquer the kingdom of the Visigoths, or because the outbreak of the plague afflicted the kingdom. The battles between Byzantium and the Goths for nominal rule also led to the use of culture and history as media of self-representation. Churches and monuments were re-dedicated or completely removed. In the year 552, on behalf of Emperor Justinian I, General Narses destroyed numerous monuments and inscriptions that commemorated the rule of the Goths. Alongside the demonstration of political power another religious aspect emerged

FIGURE 8.1: The *damnatio memoriae* of King Theodoric (451–526). After the death of Theodoric his palace in Ravenna was converted into the basilica Sant' Apollinare Nuovo and memories of him were removed. Some traces of hands and feet in the mosaics show that the *damnatio memoriae* was only carried out to some extent. © S. Schwedler.

as a motif: while the Ostrogoths were Arians, or believers of the homoios creed, the Byzantines were Catholics. Therefore, a deliberate campaign was to delete any reference to a heretical practice of cult and image. While large areas of the palace were destroyed, the palace chapel was rededicated as a Catholic church, known today as the Basilica of Sant'Apollinare Nuovo in Ravenna. The mosaics now reveal that the *damnatio memoriae* did not entirely succeed in erasing all traces. The mosaic with Theodoric's palace was remodeled and several of the depicted figures were replaced with curtains. However, some of the hands were still visible. The once heretical space of Theodoric's palace chapel was transformed by the rededication of the basilica to a new patron saint (St. Martin) and cleansing the images within a "Catholic" space. Here, the incumbent Archbishop Agnellus played a special and prominent role as an obliterative and re-coding actor. However, precisely because inscriptions and dedications of Theodoric remained intact in so many other places, it becomes clear how at least an intended complete *danmatio memoriae* was implemented in a quite uncomprehensive and unsystematic manner. The antique practice already reveals that *memoria damnata* should have been carried out like a wide-ranging administrative act, however, in politically insignificant regions and locations it was not always forcefully pursued.

Rudolf of Rheinfelden

The case of King Rudolf of Rheinfelden (1028–80) shows rather well how *damnatio memoriae* worked in the high Middle Ages. He was the rival of King Henry IV (1050–1106). Henry was of the Salian dynasty and had already been German king within the Empire for twenty-one years. As a result of his constant hostilities with Pope Gregory VII, it was only a matter of time before enough important princes came together and formed an opposition. On March 15, 1077, Rudolf of Rheinfelden, Duke of Swabia, was declared king. For three years neither side was willing to give in and the decision as to who was to be called rightful king had to be made on the battlefield. After fierce combat, close to the River Elster in Saxony on October 15, 1080, the supporters of Rudolf of Rheinfelden proved successful in battle, but Rudolf was severely injured and died the following day (Althoff 2006: 173–7). The imperial Salian side, in particular, publicized the outcome of the battle as an ordeal or judgment of God, favoring Henry. The historiographer Bishop Otto of Freising (*c.* 1112–58) describes how Henry IV reacted when he visited the tomb of Rudolf.

> Not long after that, Rudolf was killed by the followers of the Emperor [Henry IV] in open battle and buried in the church of Merseburg [in Saxony] like a king. It is said of the Emperor that, after the [Saxon] uprisings were suppressed, he once visited the church in Merseburg and saw Rudolf buried like a king. *Cuidam dicenti*—someone who was speaking, asked why he would permit a person who was not king to be buried like a king. The emperor answered: Would that all my enemies lie buried so honourably.[5]

This narration was formulated by Bishop Otto of Freising probably between 1156 and 1158 (Schmale 1965: 12f). Although Otto used older documents and chronicles and may have come across that story in writings that are lost today, it could be argued that Otto's narration is an anecdote. He gave a plausible explanation for the elaborate bronze plate on the tomb that had survived relatively unscathed. The historian Otto of Freising gives an insight into a world of memory-makers who were familiar with the intellectual purging of the past. Writers like him produced up-to-date history that confirms their own party. It is very easy to conclude that, for Otto, writing history also meant excluding "deviant" behavior and unpleasant "flaws" as far as possible. Cleansing the past was done by cleansing or rewriting books that contain history (Schmale 1988: 1, 132). Although in general it is difficult to prove intentional silence, or deliberate over- or underestimation, it is often possible to discern certain tendencies. In the work of Otto of Freising, too, one can discover a certain readiness on the part of Otto to adapt his perspective according to the circumstances.

What is particularly striking about this episode is that Otto records how at the imperial court reflections were made quite openly about the potential risk of a burial site with the presumptuous and false title. Thus, the ruler is always granted initiatives to cleanse history in his sense, and in this case to erase monuments with a strong sacred impact. Evidently, it was deemed to be a potential risk for the present ruler. That Henry rejected the *damnatio memoriae* provides a good example of how under certain circumstances not deleting the history of losers serves to further enhance the celebrity of the victors.

Antipopes: Formosus, Clement (III) and Victor (IV)

"As a holy and deceased antipope one lives dangerously"—this motto lends itself well to the description of the deliberate destruction of the burial sites of presumably illegitimate or so-called antipopes like Formosus, Clement (III) (Wibert of Ravenna) and Victor (IV). The case of the so-called "Cadaver Synod" against Pope Formosus is notorious and comparatively well documented (Scholz 1992: 216–42). After extremely diffused conflicts surrounding the papal office, Pope Stephen VI was undeterred from the devious form of exhumation and setting up on a throne before the assembled judges to subject the corpse of Formosus to a legal judgment. Even if the *damnatio memoriae* judgment and declaring the deceased as unworthy—a legal element from Antiquity—was not permanent, it demonstrates the contemporary importance, which prevailed at the curia in the ninth century, of consensual (and here conciliar) judgment (*senatus consultum*) and sanction—even against a deceased person. The case of Formosus firstly highlights that it was not a question of later throwing the corpse into the River Tiber, but rather of proving in public—here represented by the synod—that he was an antipope. The "Cadaver Synod," which appears "gruesome" to the modern onlooker (Zimmermann 1968: 55), corresponded to the view that the legal personality outlives death. The deceased person was still regarded as the owner of rights; he could be accused, like Formosus, and yet also file a law suit in his own right. Precisely this *vis vegetans*, which deceased persons and their decomposing corpses were meanwhile trusted as being capable of, should be prevented by the measures of a *damnatio memoriae*, including the deletion of memory and posthumous mutilations.[6]

When the rumor was spread by the supporters of the schismatic Pope Clement (III) (Wibert of Ravenna), who passed away in the year 1100, that miracles occurred at his grave in Civita Castellana, Pope Paschal II ordered the city to be conquered and his former rival for the Cathedra Petri to be disinterred and thrown into the Tiber.[7] The deliberate destruction of the corpse of Wibert of Ravenna points here to a highly specific form of treating the corpse of the inferior opponent of church politics. As an act, which one could classify as *damnatio* or rather as *deletio memoriae*, it records the fundamental claim of the victors to seize authority over the narrative about the crisis of the schism, which was still by no means overcome at the time of the destruction of the grave. The message of this measure to the still influential and dangerous supporters of Wibert of Ravenna was unmistakeable: in the opinion of Paschal II and his supporters, Wibert of Ravenna was an antipope and certainly did not count among the lawful successors of St.

Peter. Thus, in the collective, positive memory culture of the Sancta Romana Ecclesia there was no place in the foremost ranks of Roman bishops. Moreover, there was no motive whatsoever to distinguish his burial place or even to pass on his legacy.

Since in the eyes of the victorious Pope Paschal II he had passed away in *statu excommunicationis* or as a heretic, there was no question of a burial in consecrated ground or even inside a church, nor was there any chance of passing on his individual Christian liturgical *memoria* according to the strict rules of church law (Scholz 1998: 270–306). Moreover, a prominent burial place in a cathedral was totally unacceptable. However, basically the desecration of a grave signified in medieval terms an outrageous act and the graves even of former political adversaries were usually left in peace. However, in individual cases and in politically explosive circumstances the burial places of so-called antipopes were deliberately destroyed.

Such radical measures were particularly urgent when a localized veneration of saints of former rivals began to be established at these graves. This was the case for Clement (III) or Wibert of Ravenna who even after his death could still become a serious potential danger for Pope Paschal II and his supporters. Even a grave of "Pope Clement III"—and not Archbishop Wibert of Ravenna—had to be a mark of contention, for he had never lived as legitimate Pope Clement—at least from the perspective of his victorious rival Paschal II. However, a saint and "Pope Clement III" was not allowed. Any veneration as a miracle-working saint had to posthumously legitimize his canonical choice, so degrading his victorious adversary Paschal II as the real schismatic, as the genuine pseudo- or antipope. Inevitably, this would have resulted in, and ultimately did lead to a dangerous perpetuation and consolidation of the contemporary schism. However, precisely this point was the specific motivation to spread his cult of sainthood among determined supporters of Wibert. For the effective prevention of this veneration of an unheard of "saint and antipope," there was a pressing need to destroy the grave, to get rid of the mortal remains as potential relics as well as the epitaph and any material basis of any kind of liturgical memorial in prayer and any hagiographical *memoria*, so almost turning these into a utopia. The waves of the River Tiber should not only wash away the corpse of Wibert, but also the presumed virtue of his "relics" and therefore any kind of positive memory of Pope Clement or ultimately any doubt about his illegitimacy. On the other hand, Paschal, as the legitimate pope, was to shine even more brightly as the victorious successor of the apostle princes. Such acts to prevent a cult of sainthood surrounding a schismatic antipope were no isolated case. A similar situation as for Clement (III) applied in the late twelfth century for the rival Pope Alexander III, Victor (IV), who died in 1164 in Lucca and was buried in the cathedral. In December 1187—more than a decade after the end of the Alexandrine schism—the prominent burial place of (anti)Pope Victor (IV) in Lucca provoked Pope Gregory VIII to intervene personally. He broke open the grave of the Octavian and is said to have thrown out of the church the mortal remains of the former schismatic rival Pope Alexander III.[8] In this case, the special prominence of the burial place inside the cathedral in Lucca as well as the local legacy of miracles and the presumptuous epitaph, which counted Pope Victor among the saints, might be regarded as decisive for this act of *deletio memoriae* by Pope Gregory VIII (Sprenger 2012b: 308–36).

Petrus Flota/Pierre Flote (d. 1302)

Under Pope Boniface VIII the idea of *memoria damnata* or *damnatio memoriae* also gained importance as a political instrument of law alongside what at first was the more influential eschatological and spiritual sanction *post mortem* which was linked with salvation. An exemplary case here is the *damnatio memoriae* of Petrus Flota and the bull of November 1302, "*Ad malefactorum vindictam*," whereby Pope Boniface was supposed to condemn the *memoria* of Petrus Flota, his family and his ancestors up to the fourth generation (Schmidt 2006: 109–22). Petrus Flota (Pierre Flote) (d. July 1302) was considered one of the most influential political advisors of King Philip IV of France, Philip the Fair (1285–1314). He and his family also maintained close relations with the papal curia. In 1301, in the pope's correspondence the family's *sincera devotio* towards the pope and the Church of Rome is still praised. During 1302, these loyal relations broke down when Petrus Flota accepted a fatal key position in the conflicts between the French monarchy and Pope Boniface. In a public assembly, he officially affronted the curia with a deliberately provocative translation of a papal bull "*Clericis laicos*." Boniface VIII's reaction was correspondingly fierce. In summer 1302, he announced: "That is the devil or one possessed by the devil. Pierre Flote, a person full of fire and brimstone, is to be chastised and condemned as a heretic . . ." The purpose was to warn the French king of the diabolical whisperings of Pierre Flote. Since the conflict could not be laid to rest, in November 1302 there followed the previously mentioned *damnatio*.

The *damnatio memoriae* of Petrus Flota by Pope Boniface is formally interpreted as the direct consequence of the defamation of Flota as a heretic and the related excommunication. However, politically it must be considered as an instrument of conflict, whereby division is to be spread among the supporters of the French King Philip IV. The statements of Pope Boniface VIII's papal bull integrate two ideas that were key for the medieval practice of *damnatio memoriae*. Firstly, there is the eschatological intention of this sanction whose direct allusion to the relevant sections of the Old Testament regarding salvation emphasized the final judgment of God.[9] Secondly, it concerns the actual measures to be implemented and in view of the real impact of more effective legal rulings such as the confiscation of goods, loss of benefices and the extension of sanction to the fourth generation. In the bull of 1297 "In excelso throno," the same Pope had already applied this in a comparable form against the Roman Colonna family.

However, the relative accumulation of evidence for the term *memoria damnata*, and not least the bull for the *damnatio* of Petrus Flota indicate that here—in direct reference to the antique practices of condemnation over and above the question of salvation—there was an expedient and practically useful option in the conflict with those who threatened the papal primacy. This applied to the living as well as the deceased parties or their families.

From the perspective of the papal curia, a conceptually defined idea of *memoria damnata* was generally applied to deceased persons, whose activities had represented a *de facto* or even potential threat to the legitimacy of the pope and his exclusive agency, or still suggested such a potential threat. In this case, it served as a tool of overcoming the conflict and the past and to define how such rivalry should be commemorated in the future. As a sanction *post mortem* it was therefore not exclusively aimed at the individual person, but rather at their real or presumed illegitimate claims that certainly continued to have an effect and could also be kept alive *post mortem* among their supporters who were still living. It was important to counteract this threat. Moreover, it was paramount to motivate the still existing or potential political support by identifying the individuals and persuading them to switch political sides with a warning about the eschatological as well as—at the latest since Boniface VIII—implicit consequences for their legal ownership rights. From the perspective of the curia, these were due to their mistaken political partisanship.

Doge Marino Faliero in Venice (1274–1355)

The case of the Venetian Doge Marino Faliero attracts a certain notoriety and enjoys a rich reception in art and literature. The Doge was said to have conspired to carry out a *coup d'etat* and was beheaded on April 17, 1355 on the *Scala Foscara* (*Scala del Piombo*), where one year earlier he had been crowned as doge. His portrait in the Doge's Palace was shrouded by a black curtain and was re-coded with the inscription *"Hic est locus Marini Faletri decapitati pro criminibus"* ("This is the space reserved for Marino Faliero, beheaded for his crimes"). This emphasizes that it was not about the complete destruction of the memory of Marino Faliero, but about the memory of him as the *past* doge, as the public enemy and condemned criminal in those rooms that played a special representative role in social life and the public interest (Ortalli 1979).

The actual and obvious parallels to the antique practice of *damnatio memoriae* are interesting. The execution of the disgraced doge on the staircase of the Doge's Palace has an analogy, which is certainly no coincidence, with the practice of the Roman republic and the imperial period. The corpses of those emperors and public personalities who were condemned with a *damnatio memoriae* were put on show on the Gemonian Steps on the edge of the Capitol. This was then followed by a refusal of a conventional burial place as a site of individual, family and social *memoria* by later throwing the bodies into the River Tiber (Sprenger 2012a).

The greatest possible publicity of such demonstrations of power offered the victor a high degree of legitimation that could be useful in the future for the permanent guarantee of his individual claims and for the eternal defamation of the memory of the inferior opponent. Moreover, the staging of such public acts in places of great political symbolism (like the Doge's Palace) and in architectural contexts that were formally places for the promotion to the highest honors of the later delinquents, such as for Roman emperors at the Capitol or the Venetian doge at the Doge's Palace, does not seem in the medieval period to have been an accidental analogy to the antique practice. This includes the deliberate demolition of the family houses of the condemned persons, and publicly showcasing the ruins to underline and serve as a reminder of the social condemnation of the once famous and highly esteemed families.[10] Nevertheless, this aspect merits further detailed analysis.

Louis the Bavarian

The special case of the *damnatio memoriae* of Emperor Louis IV of Bavaria carried on for decades and continued well beyond the emperor's death. At the height of the conflict between the pope and the emperor in the 1330s reciprocal threats were made as well as judgments and vilifications. The explicit *damnatio memoriae* was made by Pope Clement VI who used the deletion of the memory of Louis as a weapon in the context of a public act. On Maundy Thursday, April 13, 1346, he had the final sentence read out of the condemnation of Emperor Louis of Bavaria in Avignon (Schunk 1788: 341–52):

> Thus, we fervently beseech the power of God that the aforenamed Louis [...] be cursed as one who enters and departs. God strike him with madness, blindness and spiritual confusion. Heaven above him send lightning bolts to him. The rage of the Almighty and Saint Peter and Paul, whose church he claimed for himself and tried

diligently to do harm to, flare up against him now and in future. May the whole world fight against him and the earth open up and swallow him alive. Let his name be destroyed in a generation and the memory of him vanish from the earth
—Schwedler 2011: 165–201, lines 160–173.

These drastic words were accompanied by an incredibly impressive symbolic act—the lit candles were extinguished and thrown to the floor. The statement that the name "Louis" was forgotten and his memory was to be scattered on the earth seems to be a rhetorical climax in the lengthy speech. Not only the enemy of the church himself, but also his influence and afterlife should be destroyed. The metaphor of forgetting is taken from Psalm 109, the curse psalm of David. The section of the psalm *"in generatione altera deleatur nomen eius"*[11] ("and in the generation following let their name be blotted out") is rephrased in the papal text as: *"In generatione una deleatur nomen eius et dispereat de terra memoria eius."* This reference is not about oblivion, as shown by the far superior power of communication with which this curse is proclaimed. The text came with the obligation to read it out publicly both on Sundays and in the bishop suffragans and main churches and was addressed to a long list of dioceses— Bamberg, Toul, Paderborn, Bresslau, Regensburg, Chambéry, Basel, Utrecht, Passau, Lüttich, Osnabrück, Kammin, Chur, Brixen, Verdun, as well as the archbishops of Besançon, Cologne, Magdeburg, Mainz, Milan, Lalosca-Bács, Trier, Bremen, and Salzburg (cf. Hoberg 1972).

The pope lay claim with the judgment to the *memoria* of Louis not only to decide whose *memoria* was worthy of public esteem, and whose was not. He also claimed to be the representative of St. Peter and to be able to make statements about his state of mind. However, as impressive as this papal suggestion was it gained little resonance among contemporaries. This was particularly so because it did not concern a heretic, but rather an elected and crowned emperor who still ruled very effectively. The emperor could survive the polemics and diplomatic attacks of several popes. Irrespective of the unverifiable implied harm on the part of the pope for Louis' soul, the commemoration of his worldly status was not entirely unscathed. Even decades after his death there was defamatory blacking out of his images in books by individual scribes' offices or the destruction and rewriting of his charters. A few copies of these documents that are preserved to this day still bear testimony to this kind of polemically ordered form of *damnatio memoriae* (Schwedler 2017: 129–46). The widely publicised papal letter was a request constantly to remember that Louis' salvation was lost and that one could "forget" him and his followers. The fact that servants later actually followed this suggestion of "making forgotten" with acts of deletion only shows the long-lasting influence of institutions like the papacy when it is a question of forming and re-forming history and its source material for future generations.

PERSPECTIVES

Memory is not innocent, as has been demonstrated. The respective historical image crucially depends on the extent to which previous generations consciously or unconsciously manipulated mementos, and therefore influenced the narrative. The purpose of the endeavors to uncover the practice of *damnatio memoriae* is not only to concentrate on material damage to monuments and documents. Rather, it is also important to be aware of forms of re-coding and counter-constructions.

Further in-depth studies must be conducted to show the extent to which the forms and contexts of medieval *damnatio memoriae* are differentiated in terms of their basic understanding from the antique practice, or to consider how the antique examples were continued and further developed in a living tradition and in different social conditions (such as religion and rule) during the medieval period.

NOTES

Introduction

1. Cic. inv.1.,9: *memoria est firma animi rerum ac uerborum ad inuentionem perceptio*. Analogously Rhet. Her.1.,3: *memoria est firma animi rerum et uerborum et dispositionis perceptio*.
2. Isidori Hispalensis Episcopi 1962, XI.i.12: *Mens autem vocata, quod emineat in anima, velquod meminit. Vnde et inmemores amentes. Quapropter non anima, sed quod excellit in anima mens vocatur, tamquam caput eius vel oculus.*
3. Alcuinus (Alkuin of Tours), Disputatio de rhetorica et de virtutibus sapientissimi regis Karoli et Albini magistri, PL 101.941: *CAR. Quid dicis de nobilissima, ut reor, rhetoricae parte, memoria?[. . .] CAR. Suntne aliqua eius praecepta, quomodo vel illa adhibenda vel augenda sit?— ALB. Non habemus eius alia praecepta, nisi dicendi [Ms., discendi] exercitationem et scribendi usum, et cogitandi studium; et ebrietatem cavendam, quae omnibus bonis studiis nocet maxime; quae non solum corporis aufert sanitatem, sed etiam mentis [Ms., menti] adimit integritatem.*
4. Hincmarus Rhemensis, De una et non trina deitate, PL 125.516: *Haec ergo tria, memoriam, intellectum, voluntatem, haec, inquam, tria animadverte separatim pronuntiari, inseparabiliter operari. Et item post plurima (cap. 10): Credo Patrem et Filium et Spiritum sanctum, per signa quaedam visibilia, per species quasdam assumptae creaturae, posse et separabiliter demonstrari, et inseparabiliter operari.*
5. Bernhard, Ad clericos de conversatione, Par. 4, Sancti Bernardi Opera IV: 74f.: *Transiit enim velociter totus ille pruritus delectationis iniquae, et voluptatis illecebra tota brevi finita est; sed amara quaedam impressit signa memoriae, sed vestigia foeda reliquit. In illud siquidem repositorium, velut in sentinam aliquam, tota decurrit abominatio, immunditia tota defluxit.*
6. John of Salisbury, Polycraticus Prol 12.1–17: *Siquidem vita brevis, sensus hebes, negligentiae torpor, inutilis occupatio, nos paucula scire permittunt, et eadem iugiter excutit et avellit ab animo fraudatrix scientiae, inimica et infida semper memoriae noverca, oblivio.*
7. Luhmann 1997: 579: "Die Hauptfunktion des Gedächtnisses liegt also im Vergessen, im Verhindern der Selbstblockierung des Systems durch ein Gerinnen der Resultate früherer Beobachtungen."

Chapter One

1. Guenée 2011; Goetz 2008; Deliyannis 2003; Kempshall 2011.
2. Thélamon 2001; Fédou 2004; Morlet 2012; Blaudeau 2015; van Nuffelen 2018.
3. Translation: Gerald Schwedler.

Chapter Three

1. The publications to which we will refer in this chapter by no means form the complete bibliography of the subject. They have been chosen because they provide access to the wide-ranging scholarly literature.

2. Being able to use a pen was not necessarily seen as an intellectual ability, but rather as a technical craft. Several examples are known of semi-literate scribes who, when copying texts, had made mistakes suggesting that they did not quite understand the context of the text they were writing down.
3. The expense of parchment led, for instance, to the creation of palimpsests: the practice of erasing text from the pages of a manuscript to write down a new text. In many cases, the imperfect effacement of the original text proved to be a blessing for modern scholars, who were able to reconstruct important works dating from classical Antiquity, some of them presumed lost (Declercq 2007).
4. We cannot present here in any detail the discussion the process of the separation of the Romance languages from Latin (Wright 1991).
5. The practice of making short notes about memorable events in the margins of Easter tables in liturgical calendars, which led to the historiographical genre of annals, in a way imposed the linear order of the succession of years onto the ever-returning cycle of ecclesiastical feasts (Lake 2014: 346).

Chapter Four

1. Lucie Doležalová's research leading to this study was supported by the Czech Science Foundation, through project "Creative Copying": Miscellanies of Ulricus Crux de Telcz (d. 1504), no. 17-06326S, carried out at the Faculty of Humanities, Charles University. Tamás Visi's research was supported by IGA project carried out at the Faculty of Arts, Palacky University in Olomouc (IGA_FF_2017_039).
2. An example of a late medieval reception of Augustine's and later theologians' ideas on this "trinity of the mind" is a treatise Three points of Christian Religion (*De tribus punctis Christianae religionis*) compiled by Thomas Hibernicus, here copied by Crux de Telcz (d. 1504) in Žďár in 1454, in which the three, memory, intelligence, and will are presented as the best example of how Holy Trinity works: *Item optimum exemplum habemus ad hoc in anima nostra. Nam videmus quod in anima sunt tria, scilicet memoria et intelligencia ac voluntas. Memoria que memoratur preteritorum, intelligencia quia intelligit bonum a malo, voluntas quia hoc vult hoc non vult. Et tamen est una anima et una substancia. Nam memoria est tamquam pater a nullo generatus, intelligencia tamquam filius a memoria generatus, voluntas tamquam spiritus sanctus procedens a memoria et an intelligencia. Nec tamen memoria fuit antequam intelligenciam, nec intelligencia fuit antequam voluntas. Et sic patet quomodo ista tria, scilicet memoria et intelligencia et voluntas, sunt in una anima et una substancia, et unum generatur ab alio.* (We have the best example in our soul. We see that there are three [components] in our soul: memory and intelligence and will. Memory which remembers the past, intelligence which distinguishes good from bad, will because it wants this and does not want that. And yet there is one soul and one substance. Since memory is like the father not generated by anyone, intelligence like the son generated by memory, will like the Holy Spirit coming from memory and intelligence. Yet memory did not originate before intelligence, nor intelligence before the will. And thus it is clear in which way these three, that is memory and intelligence and will are in one soul and one substance and one is generated by another, Třeboň, Státní oblastní archiv, A 6, fol. 12r). The English translations here and elsewhere, unless noted otherwise, are ours.
3. *Scriptum est eciam de eo universitatibus nostris, quod omne scibile et omne operabile sciat. Quapropter aliqui iudicant eum fore bonum, aliqui vero malum. Alii dicunt, quod a dyabolo sit edoctus, alii a deo; unde quidem multis videtur, quod fuerit precursor Antichristi vel unus*

de discipulis, vel angelum dei vel dyabolum in effigie hominis fuisse. Nunquam enim fuit a seculo auditum de simili, nec videtur possibile, quod tanta potuisset legisse, quanta memorie commendavit, si eciam haberet quam plurimam etatem sive annos seniles. Cf. Zürich, Zentralbibliothek, MS C 101, fol. 148r-v; cf. Werner 1979: 169 f. The manuscript was written by Gallus Kemli from Sankt Gallen, digital facisimile is available on e-codices.unifr. ch. The beginning of the text describes in detail the vast memory of this person: *Epistula de quodam, qui censebatur Antichristus vel eius figura. Apparuit temporibus nostris videlicet modernis sub annis Domini M° CCCC XLVI die septimo a Ianuario hec presens copia gardiana in Colonia venerando Cardanensi valde docto puero per gardianum Parisiensem missa, per quam totam urbem Parisiensem pre amiracione conmotam vidimus et mirabilibus refertam, nec credimus; audivimus et non intelligimus. Venit ad nos quidam iuvenis cum octo equis nomine Venerandus Cardanensis, nacione Hyspanus de civitate Cardanensi Castello oriundus, annorum uno de XX. Tytulus eius: miles in armis, magister in artibus, in utroque iure doctor, magister in medicinis, doctor in theolya [!] et in omnibus perfectus et in omnibus eque promptus, in omnibus compositus, valde affabilis et multum humilis. Memoriter tenet quasi totam bibliam et Nycolaum de Lyra, et scripta beati Thome, Alexandrum de Hallis, Bonamventuram, Scoti et aliorum multorum. Prompte allegat omnes leges, decretales cum glosa et scit totum decretum; similiter totum Avicennam, Ypocratem, Galienum et cum hoc plures alios libros in medicina; et in artibus vix credibile est Aristotilem plura scivisse. Scit etiam omnes textus, omnia commenta commentatorum et Alberti et aliorum multorum. Scit etiam totam metaphisicam, ut dicitur, et rethoricam. Novit etiam quinque ydiomata legere, scribere et pronunciare. Expertus est Latinum, Hebraicum, Grecum, Caldaicum et Arabicum, et fuit in multis locis, in quibus hoc scripsit et legit. Consequenter audivimus eum respondere pluribus doctoribus diversarum facultatum et scienciarum omnibus interrogationibus et arguere volentibus de omni materia. Et hoc idem fecit in Haidelberga feria 3ᵃ et feria 4ᵃ ante festum annunciacionis, ad sanctum Iacobum et in pluribus aliis locis. Et fuerunt duo anni quod recessit de Hyspania missus a rege Castelli; et fuit in Ytalia et respondit publice in omnibus universitatibus quasi ad omnia. Quare et met fatetur, quod didicerit Doctrinale in 7 diebus, quod adhuc memorie comendavit. Quidque legit quamvis cursorie, totum intelligit et totum retinet. Tam etiam scripsit gesta Ptolomei et super magnam partem Biblie et maxime super Apocalipsim et super plures alios libros composuit. Scit etiam musicam non solam, sed et in omni instrumento musicali ludere et ipsum componere.* [fol. 148v] *Item in presencia regis Francie conposuit quandam epistulam utique pulcherrimam, que de pace multa concludit; et dicitur quod sciverit omnem praticam videlicet artium mechanicorum et ea emendare et proclamare.*

4. In a different context, there was the practice of "beating the bounds"—it was frequent in medieval parishes and among medieval land owners to beat children while going through with them and showing them the borders of the parish's or family's land property—the memory of physical pain would be more efficient than calm repetition, cf. e.g. Homans 1975.
5. Aquinas, *Sententia libri Metaphysicae*, I, 1, 15: *Experimentum enim est ex collatione plurium singularium in memoria receptorum. Huiusmodi autem collatio est homini propria, et pertinet ad vim cogitativam, quae ratio particularis dicitur: quae est collativa intentionum individualium, sicut ratio universalis intentionum universalium.* English translation Rowan 1961.
6. Cf. Robinson et al. 1985: 93, 113 f.; Agrimi and Crisciani 1994; Agrimi and Crisciani 1988.
7. *Ut autem scias melius confiteri, studeas saltem semel in die examinare, quomodo tempus expendisti, et discurre per singulas horas cogitando loca, in quibus fuisti, cum quibus personis, quid cogitasti, quid dixisti, quid audivisti, quid fecisti, ut cognoscas relaxaciones lingue, cordis,*

et sensuum, in quibus et quotiens offendisti, aut dedisti aliis materiam offendendi . . . et ordinate repete in mente tua, nec te pigeat in tali examinacione exercere . . . (cap. 16 *Erudicio utilis ad omnia supradicta*, p. 242).

8. Among the most wide-spread ones, there are Thomas à Kempis' *De imitatione Christi* (à Kempis 1848), or Henry Suso's *Horologium sapiencie* (Künzle 1977).
9. On similar concerns in Islamic mysticism, see al-Ghazali 1995.
10. Petrarch, *Secretum meum* 1.1.1: *Quid agis, homuncio? quid somnias?* [. . .] *An non te mortalem esse meministi?* See Petrarca 2016: 10 [Latin], 11 [English tr.].
11. *Minime mirareris, nisi quia animum invasit oblivio. Ceterum brevi admonitione in multorum malorum memoriam revocandus es.* Petrarca 2016: 178 [3.7.1, Latin], 179 [English tr.].
12. Augustine, *Confessions* 10,8. The Latin original reads: *Ibi quando sum, posco, ut proferatur quidquid volo, et quaedam statim prodeunt, quaedam requiruntur diutius et tamquam de abstrusioribus quibusdam receptaculis eruuntur, quaedam catervatim se proruunt et, dum aliud petitur et quaeritur, prosiliunt in medium quasi dicentia: ne forte nos sumus? et abigo ea manu cordis a facie recordationis meae, donec enubiletur quod volo atque in conspectum prodeat ex abditis* (http://faculty.georgetown.edu/jod/latinconf/latinconf.html).
13. *Nunquam tam subito evigilo, quin animus meus te intra se locatam inveniat* (EDA 6, Vir; Newman 2016: 92).
14. *Dilectissime domine sue, cuius memoriam nulla intercipere potest oblivio, fidelissimus eius tunc primum tui nominis oblivionem, cum mei nominis memor non ero* (EDA 8, Vir; Newman 2016: 93).
15. *Vale summa spes mea in qua sola michi conplaceo, quam nunquam reduco ad memoriam, quia nunquam amitto a memoria* (EDA 20, Vir; Newman 2016: 105).
16. Moses Maimonides, Mishneh Torah, Hilkhot Yesodei ha-Torah 2:2. English tr. quoted from D. Goldstein, F. Lachower, and Isaiah Tishby, *The Wisdom of the Zohar*, vol. 3, 978.
17. In medieval Jewish literature any person who died a violent death could be referred to as a "saint."
18. *Integram vix non noctem traduxi insomnem, continuo imago Ioannis Hus oculis meis representabat sese, diem consuetis in laboribus transegi, nunc quiescere volo, nequeo autem. Hus enim a concilio Constantiensi ad me appellat, et gravamina exhibet, quo igitur pro equo et iusto decretoriam ferre sententiam, et deinceps quiete dormire valeam suppliciter oro mihi commodari.* Brno, Moravský zemský archiv, fund G12, inventory number 387, Cerroni II, book number 263, fol. 192v—the codex is a miscellany of different formats dating from the fifteenth to the eighteenth century.
19. Maimonides' autograph manuscripts were preserved by his descendants who held important positions in the Jewish communities of Egypt for over two centuries after Maimonides' death, cf. Ben-Sasson 2007: 1–17.
20. Translation Altmann 1967: 231–2, Arabic original Maimonides 1957: 200f. [nr. 117].
21. Introduction to the commentary on *Pereq Heleq* of tractate Sanhedrin: "The circle would have to be extended to include a discourse on the forms which the prophets mentioned in connection with the Creator and the angels; into this enters the *Shiur Qoma* and its subject matter. For [a treatment of] this subject alone, even if shortened to the utmost degree, a hundred pages would be insufficient . . ." English translation Altmann 1967: 231.
22. Cf. Altmann 1967: 225–80; the relevant discussion is on pages 231f. A facsimile edition of the manuscript: Sassoon 1956. The clause "into this enters the *Shiur Qoma* and its subject matter" is erased; cf. previous note. Most of the medieval manuscripts do not contain the passage about *Shiur Qoma*; however, four further manuscripts do contain it–their ancestors were probably copied from MS Pococke 295 *before* Maimonides deleted the sentence.

23. Cf. Bayle 1713: 71.
24. On medieval Jewish autobiographies, see Yuval 1994.
25. Lines 379–83; in the original Middle English, it reads: *But—Lord Crist!—whan that it remembreth me/ Upon my yowthe, and on my jolitee,/ It tikleth me aboute myn herte roote./ Unto this day it dooth myn herte boote/ That I have had my world as in my tyme.*
26. A possible exception is Petrarch, who claimed that he remembered his childhood as a happy time when his religious sentiments were especially strong. See Petrarca 2016: 171 [3.5.7–8].
27. The letter begins: *Salutem plurimam et veritatis catholice ageracionem. Mentibus humanis insita est cupido veritatis. A te autem, qui cathedram regiminis teneas in Thabor, et a tuis coadiutoribus cupio certificari de duabus dubiis. Unum si magister Iohannes Hus incineratus sit pro communione utriusque speciei et an tenuit quod sit de precepto vel mandavit, vel pro aliis articulis sibi ascriptis utraque in condempnacione. Secundum si eclipsis, que eodem anno erat, fuit miraculosa vel naturalis, et an eodem die incineracionis sit facta ut quasi communiter ab omnibus vestre ymmo eciam et ab aliquibus nostre partis refertur. Puto quod totus mundus abiret post tam magnum miraculum et neque me contradictorem amplius habebitis in hiis. An dum fuit in vinculis constitutus ante Viti feria sexta post Marcelli, ante Bonifacii naturalis sit facta eclipsis, ut a fide dignis personis accepi* (Praha, Národní knihovna, XI C 8, fol. 226r).

Chapter Five

1. The first "Blockbuch" editions of the *Ars memorandi notabilis per figuras ewangelistarum* are dated to around 1465–70, but some manuscripts were copied earlier, around 1455. See Susanne Rischpler (2013), "Gedruckt und gezeichnet. Das Blockbuch 'Ars memorandi' und seine handschriftlichen Zeugen," in Bettina Wagner (ed.), *Blockbücher des 15. Jahrhunderts. Eine Experimentierphase im frühen Buchdruck. Beiträge der Fachtagung in der Bayerischen Staatsbibliothek München am 16. und 17. Februar 2012*, 215–54, Wiesbaden: Harrassowitz. See also Rafał Wójcik (2012), "Masters, Pupils, Friends and Thieves. A Fashion of ars memorativa in the Environment of Early German Humanists," *Daphnis*, 41: 399–418. For an English translation of this text, with the title "A Method for Recollecting the Gospels," see Mary Carruthers, and Jan M. Ziolkowski (eds), (2002), *The Medieval Craft of Memory. An Anthology of Texts and Pictures*, Philadelphia: University of Pennsylvania Press, 255–93.
2. On the concept of the *imago agens*, see the Introductory chapter by Gerald Schwedler and Frances A. Yates (1966), *The Art of Memory*, London: Routledge and Kegan Paul, 10–13.
3. See the fundamental study by Georg Lakoff and Mark Johnson (1980), *Metaphors We Live By*, Chicago: University of Chicago Press. For reasons of clarity, I will avoid using the specific terminology of cognitive linguistics, where fundamental conceptual structures behind metaphors are called "image schemas." See Beate Hampe, (2005), "Image schemas in cognitive linguistics. Introduction," in Beate Hampe and Joseph E. Grady, *From Perception to Meaning. Image Schemas in Cognitive Linguistics*, 1–12, Berlin: Mouton de Gruyter
4. On Capuanus, see John R. Martindale (1980), *The Prosopography of the Later Roman Empire*, vol. 2, Cambridge: Cambridge University Press, 260.
5. My translation from Cassiodorus, *Variae*, 5, 22: "*Illa vero memoria, quae oratorum thesaurus iure vocitatur, tanta in eum firmitate consedit, ut semel audita scripto apud eum putes esse recondita. Magnum beneficium oblivionis nescire defectum: et quaedam similitudo vere caelestium est tempore decursa semper habere praestantia.*" Theodor Mommsen (ed.) (1894), *Cassiodorus Senator, Variae* (Monumenta Germaniae Historica, Auctores antiquissimi 12), Berlin: Weidmann, 157.

6. On the interpretation of contemplation, see Joachim Gruber (2006), *Kommentar zu Boethius, De consolatione philosophiae*, 2nd edn, Berlin: De Gruyter, 375 and John F. Magee, (2009), "The Good and Morality. Consolatio 2–4," in John Marenbon (ed.), *The Cambridge Companion to Boethius*, Cambridge: Cambridge University Press, 194.
7. Cf. his words "*patitur in simplicibus rebus linguae retinacula*": "he suffered from a blocked speech when he speaks about simple matters," but he was all the more frightening/fluent, when he had to deliver a speech: "*eo tamen terrentior [variant: torrentior] cum perorat.*"
8. *Variae*, 5, 22: "*Illa vera memoria, quae oratorum thesaurus iure vocitatur, tanta in eum firmitate consedit, ut semel audita scripto apud eum putes esse recondita.*" Theodor Mommsen, ed. (1894), *Cassiodorus Senator, Variae* (Monumenta Germaniae Historica, Auctores antiquissimi 12), Berlin: Weidmann, 157.
9. Gusztáv Wenzel (ed.), (1860), *Codex Diplomaticus Arpadianus continuatus. Árpádkori Új Okmánytár*, vol. I, Budapest: Eggenberger, 102–3 (DF 206834): "*Inestimabile beneficium est obliuionis nescire defectum, et quedam uere similitudo celestium, tempore decursa habere in memória*" and Richard Marsina, ed. (1971), *Codex diplomaticus et epistolaris Slovaciae*, vol. I, Bratislava: SAV, 164 (DF 273236). See Richard Marsina (1971), "Die Arengen in ungarischen Urkunden bis zum Jahre 1235," *Folia diplomatica*, 1: 215–25, here 223.
10. This common place occurs in countless variations in arengas of the high Middle Ages. Just to quote a few: "*Quoniam labilis est hominum memoria et facile traduntur oblivioni, que scriptorum vel testium auctoritate non firmantur . . .*" (Beaune, 1179; Auguste Bernard and Alexandre Bruel (eds.), (1894), *Recueil des chartes de l'abbaye de Cluny*, vol. 5, Paris: Imprimerie nationale, 630); "*Quoniam labilis est hominum memoria, necesse est humanos actus litterarum testimonio confirmari*" (Wilten/Tirol, 1234; Joseph Rapp (1827), "Über das vaterländische Statutenwesen," *Beiträge zur Geschichte, Statistik und Naturkunde und Kunst von Tirol und Vorarlberg*, 3, 104); "*Quoniam labilis est hominum memoria et rerum turbe non sufficit, congruum est et ad cautelam futurorum expediens, quod ea, que geruntur in tempore tam in rebus ecclesiaticis quam mundanis, ne propter oblivionem labantur cum tempore . . .*" (Pannonhalma, 1237–40; László Erdélyi, (1902), *A Pannonhalmi Főapátság története (History of the Pannonhalma Archabbey)*, vol. 1, Budapest: Stephaneum, 771); "*Quoniam memoria hominum labilis est et caduca, perutile visum est . . .*" (Osnabrück, 1251/1253/1254/1264/1267/ 1268/1272/1273/1277, in several variants; Friedrich Filippi and Max Bär (eds), (1899), *Osnabrücker Urkundenbuch*, vol. 3. *Die Urkunden der Jahre 1251–1280*, Osnabrück: Historischer Verein zu Osnabrück, 2, 12, 62, 87, 218, 251, 324, 325, 330, 412); "*Quia labilis est hominum memoria, et rerum turbe non sufficit, inuentum fuit scripture remedium*" (Lisbon, 1255; Leontina Ventura and António Resende de Oliveira (eds), (2006), *Chanceleria de D. Afonso III. Livro 1*, vol. 2, Coimbra: Universidade de Coimbra, 289); "*Quoniam hominum memoria labilis esse dinoscitur, auctore teste qui ait quod 'labitur occulte fallitque volatilis etas'* [Ovid. Met. 10, 519]" (Borken, 1264; *Osnabrücker Urkundenbuch . . .* (as above), 372); "*Memoria labilis est res et rerum turbe non sufficit*" (Vienna, 1276; Wilhelm Karlin (ed.), (1855), *Saal-Buch des Benediktiner-Stiftes Göttweig* (Fontes rerum Austriacarum II/8), Vienna: Staatsdruckerei, 324); "*Quia labilis est hominum memoria, ne, quod bona fide inter contrahentes agitur, lapsu temporis et mentis oblivione depereat, consuetum est placita hominum . . .*" (Lünen, 1291; Roger Wilmans (ed.), (1871), *Die Urkunden des Bisthums Münster von 1201–1300*, Münster: Regensberg, 745); "*quum labilis memoria hominum sopitur oblivionis caligine, certis est sigillorum indiciis recordacio*" (Vyskyth, 1297; Jan T. Lubomirski (ed.), (1863), *Kodeks dyplomatyczny księstwa Mazowieckiego*, Warsaw: Gazeta Polska, 33); "*Labilis est hominum memoria ut sapientes testantur . . .*" (Jean de Saint-Victor, *Memoriale historiarum*, around 1330–5; see Isabelle

Guyot-Bachy (2000), *Le "Memoriale historiarum" de Jean de Saint-Victor*, Turnhout: Brepols, 530). See also Zofia Wilk-Wos,"Memoriae commendare. Memorative Arengen in den Urkunden der Gnesener Erzbischöfe im 14. Jahrhundert," in Sébastien Rossignol and Anna Adamska (eds), *Urkundenformeln im Kontext. Formen der Schriftkultur im Ostmitteleuropa des Mittelalters*, 149–64, Vienna: Böhlau.

11. For a recent survey on the study of charter preambles (arengas), see Sébastien Rossignol (2016), "Introduction: Text and Context—Preamble and Formulary," in Sébastien Rossignol and Anna Adamska (eds), *Urkundenformeln im Kontext. Formen der Schriftkultur im Ostmitteleuropa des Mittelalters*, 19–34, Vienna: Böhlau.

12. "*Quoniam fragilis est memoria et rerum turbe non sufficit . . .*" (Münster, 1217). Wilmans, Roger (ed.), (1871), *Die Urkunden des Bisthums Münster von 1201–1300*, Münster: Regensberg, 53.

13. See Arnaldus de Villa Nova (1585), *Opera omnia. Cum Nicolai Tavrelli medici et philosophi in quosdam libros annotationibus. Indice item copiosissimo*, Basileae: ex Officina Pernea per Conradum Waldkirch: *Aphorismi*: 243–4, *De bonitate memoriae*: 837–8. The authenticity of the *De bonitate memoriae* has been questioned: Juan A. Paniagua and Pedro Gil-Sotres (eds), (1993), *Arnaldus de Villa Nova, Commentum in quasdam parabolas et alias aphorismorum series. Aphorismi particulares, Aphorismi de memoria, Aphorismi extravagantes* (Opera medica omnia, vol. VI/2), Barcelona: Universitat de Barcelona, 374. Nevertheless, it was extremely popular in manuscripts and prints. See also Mary Carruthers (1990), *The Book of Memory*, Cambridge: Cambridge University Press, 50.

14. "*humanis mentibus inscripsit potentis nature digitus, ut ea que ab hominibus geruntur in tempore, taliter humana maturentur industria, et maturata scripto commendantur, ne defluente tempore oblivionis simul cum tempore defluant in profundum*" (Bremen, 1235; Wilhelm von Hodenberg (ed.), (1848), *Hoyer Urkundenbuch*, 2. vol., *Archiv des Stiftes Bassum*, Hannover: Jännecke, 19). Some other examples: "*Dum sit cautum, pias et providas hominum actiones scripture testimonio roborare, ne vel hominum malicia infirmentur, vel oblivionis caligine ab humana memoria processu temporis elabantur*" (Eppenstein, 1245; Wilhelm Sauer (ed.), (1886), *Nassauisches Urkundenbuch*, vol. 1, *Die Urkunden des ehemals Kurmainzischen Gebiets*, Wiesbaden: Niedner, 335); "*ut ea, quae geruntur in tempore, ne cum tempore defluant, et labantur, dignum est, ut que memorie posterorum sunt commendanda, litterarum patrocinio perhennentur*" (Nitra, 1258; Georgius Fejér (ed.), (1831), *Codex diplomaticus Hungariae*, vol. 7 (1), Buda: Typis universitatis, 507;); "*Labilis est hominum memoria et ea, que fiunt ab hominibus, in oblivionem defluunt ex facili, nisi scripture testimonio perhennentur*" (Münster, 1260; Steinfurt, 1270; Roger Wilmans (ed.), (1871), *Die Urkunden des Bisthums Münster von 1201–1300*, Münster: Regensberg, 349, 447); "*ne ea, que sub tempore [fiunt] digna memorie, simul cum tempore defluant, expedit, ut eis scripture remedio succurratur*" (Boizenburg, 1297, Verein für Mecklenburgische Geschichte und Altertumskunde (ed.), (1867), *Mecklenburgisches Urkundenbuch*, vol. 4. *1297–1300*, Schwerin: Hofbuchhandlung Stiller, 29).

15. "*Quia cellule memorialis capacitas ad memoriter retinendum multigenam contractuum prolixitatem nequid (=nequit) sufficere, rerum circumstancias necesse est litterarum serie perhennare*" (Reichenbach, Silesia, 1310), Gustav A. Stenzel (ed.), (1854), *Liber fundationis claustri sanctae Mariae virginis in Heinrichow*, Breslau: Stenzel, 209. Some other examples: "*humane nature fragilitatem oculo mentis inspiciens, testamentum quoddam, ne a cellula memorie excludatur, scripto commendare ... dignum duxi*" (Seitenstetten?, 1225?; Isidor Raab (ed.), (1870), *Urkundenbuch des Benediktiner-Stiftes Seitenstetten*, Vienna: Holzhausen, 40); "*queque gesta hominum in decursu temporum obliuionis caligine obducuntur et a cellula*

memorie continuoque preconio prorsus euanescunt, si non clare ac solenniter sint disposita" (Sącz, 1292; Franciszek Piekosiński (1886), *Kodeks dyplomatyczny małopolski*, vol. 2, Cracow: Akademia umiejętności, 183).

16. The earlier edition (Carl I. Burkhard, ed. (1917), *Nemesius of Emesa, Premnon Physicon a N. Alfano in Latinum translatus*, Leipzig: Teubner) is now superseded by Irene Chirico (ed.), (2011), *Alfano I, Premnon physicon. Versione latina del Peri physeos anthropou di Nemesio*, Rome: Storia e Letteratura.
17. See Michaud-Quentin, Pierre (1949), "La classification des puissances de l'âme au XIIe siècle," *Revue du Moyen Âge latin*, 5: 15–34, here 18.
18. Verbeke, Gérard, and José R. Moncho (eds.), (1975), *Némésius d'Émèse, De natura hominis, traduction de Burgundio de Pise*, Leiden: Brill, 77. "*Quae vero antea visa erant, memoria servat, coniungit autem utraque mens, et quod sensibile et quod memorabile.*"
19. "*Rememoratio vero dicitur, cum oblivio mediaverit memoriam.*" Ibid., 87.
20. Ibid., 88.
21. Ibid., 88. See also Tullio Manzoni (1998), "The cerebral ventricles, the animal spirits and the dawn of brain localization of function," *Archives Italiennes de Biologie*, 136 (2): 103–52. Manzoni proves that Nemesius was the ultimate source of the tripartite ventricular localization in the Latin West.
22. See Hasse, "The Soul's Faculties," 308. For the immense influence of his *On the Soul* (*De Anima*) in the Latin West, see Dag N. Hasse (2000), *Avicenna's De Anima in the Latin West. The Formation of a Peripatetic Philosophy of the Soul, 1160–1300*, London and Turin: Warburg Institute-Nino Aragni.
23. See Oskar C. Gruner (ed.), (1973), *Ibn-Sina, The Canon of Medicine of Avicenna*, New York: AMS Press, 135–9. See also ibid., 471.
24. Gerrit Bos (ed.), (1995), *Ibn Al-Jazzar, On Forgetfulness and its Treatment, Critical edition of the Arabic text and the Hebrew translations with commentary and translation into English*, London: Royal Asiatic Society. See also Gerrit Bos (1994), "Ibn Al-Gazzar's Risala Fin-Nisyan and Constantine's 'liber de oblivione'," in Charles Burnett and Danielle Jacquart (eds.), *Constantine the African and Ali ibn al-Abbas al-Magusi. The "Pantegni" and Related Texts*, 203–32, Leiden: Brill. As it was shown by Bos, Constantine the African's *De oblivione* abbreviated several sections of the description of the brain by Al-Gazzar. For a dated, but still useful overview of the history of brain ventricles in the eleventh and twelfth centuries, see Walther Sudhoff (1913), "Die Lehre von Hirnventrikeln in textlicher und graphischer Tradition des Altertums und Mittelalters," *Archiv für Geschichte der Medizin*, 7: 149–205, here 165–72.
25. The Latin text of this treatise is edited in the obsolete edition of Franz Redeker (1917), *Die "Anatomia magistri Nicolai physici" und ihr Verhältnis zur Anatomia Cophonis und Richardi*, Leipzig: Noske, who suggests that the *Anatomia magistri Nicolai* and the *Anatomia Richardi* are not derivative of each other, but rather they contain different notes taken about the same, or similar lectures in Salerno during the twelfth century. On the other hand, Karl Sudhoff published another, more recent version of the *Anatomia Richardi*, which later became part of the so-called *Micrologus* by Richardus Anglicus. Sudhoff—who dates these texts to *c.* 1210— claimed that the two versions of the *Anatomia Richardi* were composed by the same author, whereas the *Anatomia magistri Nicolai* was written by his student, perhaps in Paris. See Karl Sudhoff (1927), "Der Micrologus-Text der Anatomia Richards des Engländers," *Archiv für Geschichte der Medizin*, 19: 209–39, here 237. For the ms. tradition, see Ernest Wickersheimer (1979), *Dictionnaire biographique des médecins en France au Moyen Age*, vol. 1, Geneva: Droz, 694–8. The text of Richardus Anglicus became very popular and was translated into

Occitan, French, and Catalan: Corradini, Maria Sofia (2012), "La letteratura medica medievale in lingua d'oc fra tradizione antica e Rinascimento europeo," in Anna Alberni et al. (eds.), *El saber i les llengües vernacles a l'època de Llull i Eiximenis*, 147–70, Barcelona: Publicacions de l'Abadia de Montserrat.

26. Richardus Salernitanus (1907), "Anatomia," in Ignaz Schwarz (ed.), *Die medizinischen Handschriften der K. Universitätsbibliothek in Würzburg*, 77–92, Würzburg: Scheiner, here 71. "*Dividitur itaque caput secundum unam divisionem scilicet in proram et puppim, et secundum hoc prora dicitur pars anterior capitis scilicet loco, quo memorialis cellula conjungitur relique parti capitis. Puppis vero dicitur pars illa in qua continetur memorialis cellula. Dividitur item caput secundum aliam divisionem in III partes vel cellulas scilicet in fantasticam seu anteriorem cellulam, racionem seu mediam, memorialem seu postremam*" (edited from the thirteenth century Italian ms., Würzburg, M. p. med. q. 1., originating from the Cistercian abbey of Ebrach).

27. Richardus Salernitanus, (1907), "Anatomia," in Ignaz Schwarz (ed.), *Die medizinischen Handschriften der K. Universitätsbibliothek in Würzburg*, 77–92, Würzburg: Scheiner, here 82. My translation. "*Item cerebrum dicitur templum anime vel sapiencie vel sciencie. Sicut enim in templo sunt tres partes principales, scilicet vestibulum, consistorium, apotheca, sic in cerebro. Anima igitur in fantastica cellula quasi in vestibulo diverse imaginantur forme. In logistica quasi in consistorio de imaginativis discernitur. In memoriali quasi in apotheca autem ea que imaginacio suscipit, racio decernit [et] memorie commendat conservanda Notandum autem est quod vestibulum anime id est fantastica cellula V partes id est V sensus habet ante se.*" On its relationship to other versions of the text, similarly ascribed to Richardus Anglicus, see Sudhoff, "Der Micrologus-Text," 235–7.

28. Italo Ronca, ed. (1977), *William of Conches, Dragmaticon philosophiae*, Turnhout: Brepols, 240–1 (VI, 18, 4). For a translation, see Italo Ronca and Matthew Curr, trans. (1997), *William of Conches, A Dialogue on Natural Philosophy*, Notre Dame, IN: University of Notre Dame Press, 156. See also Sudhoff, "Die Lehre von Hirnventrikeln," 169–70, and Tanja Klemm (2013), *Bildphysiologie. Wahrnehmung und Körper in Mittelalter und Renaissance*, Berlin: Akademie, 40–1.

29. "*Item medici ponunt cerebrum esse templum sive sedem animae, et hoc maxime quantum ad illam partem anime, quae est cognitiva. Sicut enim in templo tres sunt partes principales, scilicet vestibulum, consistorium et apotheca, ita fantastica cellula, logistica et memorialis partes sunt cerebri principales. Anima ergo fantastica cellula quasi in vestibulo diversas per imaginationem suscipit formas, in logistica cellula quasi in consistorio de imaginatis ratione discernit, in memoriali vero cellula quasi in apotheca anima ea, quae imaginatio recipit, ratio discernit, per memorium conservat.*" Vincent de Beauvais (1591), *Speculum maius*, vol. 1, Venice: Dominicus Nicolinus, 298v. (book 24, ch. 47). My translation. In the *Anatomia magistri Nicolai physici*, it is claimed that the ancient churches (not Christian ones!) were divided into these three parts. Corner, *Anatomical Texts*, 72.

30. On the *Speculum maius*, see Mary Franklin-Brown (2013), "The Speculum Maius, Between Thesaurus and Lieu de Mémoire," in Elma Brenner et al. (eds.), *Memory and Commemoration in Medieval Culture*, 143–62, Farnham: Ashgate; Mary Franklin-Brown (2012), *Reading the World. Encyclopedic Writing in the Scholastic Age*, Chicago and London: The University of Chicago Press, and Hans Voorbij (2014), "An updated list of surviving manuscripts of the Speculum Maius," *Vincent of Beauvais Newsletter*, 38: 4–17.

31. This section was verbatim taken over from Vincentius by the late fifteenth century Hungarian Franciscan Pelbartus of Temesvár in his alphabetically organized commentary on the

Sentences by Peter Lombard (1576), *Aureum sacrae theologiae rosarium*, vol. 1, Venice: Ziletti, 347v.

32. Paola Bernardini, ed. (2009): *Anonymi magistri artium Quaestiones super librum de anima (Siena, Biblioteca Comunale, ms. L.III.21, ff. 134ra-174va)*, Florence: Sismel. The text also includes the metaphor of the brain as a church of the soul ("*cerebrum dicitur quasi templum anime*"), where memory is the storage room (*apotheca*). For a recent survey of the Medieval Latin commentary tradition of the De anima, see Sander W. De Boer, (2013), *The Science of the Soul. The Commentary Tradition on Aristotle's De anima, c. 1260–c. 1360*, Leuven: Leuven University Press. Even in animal psychology, the question was raised whether animals are capable of remembering and recollecting past memories, and if so, which animals are best at it. See Anselm Oelze (2017), *Animal Rationality. Later Medieval Theories, 1250–1350*, Leiden: Brill, 164–202.

33. Cf. Al-Ghazali, *Metaphysica*, p. II, 4, 4. See the late twelfth century Latin translation of Dominicus Gundissalinus and his collaborator in Toledo: Joseph T. Muckle, ed. (1933), *Al-Ghazali, Algazel's Metaphysics. A Mediaeval Translation*, Toronto: St. Michael's College, 170-1. For a new critical edition of this part of the *Metaphysica*, see Eva St. Clair (2005), "Algazel on the Soul. A Critical Edition," *Traditio*, 60: 69–70.

34. *Anonymi magistri artium Quaestiones . . .*, 11–2. Similarly, Al-Ghazali's *Metaphysics* was the source of the tripartite division of the brain in Jacques de Thérine's *Quodlibet* in the early fourteenth century: Palémon Glorieux, ed. (1958), *Jacques de Thérines, Quodlibets I et II— Jean Lesage, Quodlibet I*, Paris: Vrin, 270–1.

35. "*Archam intencionum vocat primam partem postreme concavitatis cerebri in qua est virtus estimativa, unde recta eius diffinicio est ista, quod est vis anime sensibilis ordinata in celula ad inquirendum nunc que sunt in archa <nunc> ad componendum et dividendum ea que sunt apud ymaginacionem et estimacionem. [. . .] Virtus memorativa est vis anime sensibilis ordinata in posteriori parte posterioris concavitatis cerebri, retinens quod apprehendit estimacio de intencionibus insensatis, unde memoria se habet ad estimacionem sicut ymaginativa ad sensum communem. Eius instrumentum est, sicut dictum*" *Anonymi magistri artium Quaestiones*, 11–2. The latter comparison between imagination and memory goes back to Avicenna's *Liber de Anima*, pars I, 5. See Simone van Riet, ed. (1972): *Avicenna, Liber de anima seu Sextus de naturalibus*, Leiden: Brill, 89. (Avicenna Latinus 1.1.)

36. John of Głogów, or Glogovia was a professor and "dominated the arts faculty for four decades" at the University of Cracow in the late fifteenth and early sixteenth century. See Paul Knoll (2016), *"A Pearl of Powerful Learning". The University of Cracow in the Fifteenth Century*, Leiden: Brill, 343–4, 358–9, 392–5 (here 358), and Marian Zwiercan (1963), "Jan z Głogowa," in *Polski Słownik Biograficzny*, vol. 10, 450–2, Cracow: PAN. On this commentary, see Zdzisław Kuksewicz (1962), "Le prolongement des polémiques entre les Albertistes et les Thomistes vu à travers le Commentaire du De anima de Jean de Głogów," *Archiv für Geschichte der Philosophie*, 44: 151–71. As Kuksewicz demonstrated, John of Głogów remained relatively independent of Jean Versor, and based several arguments of his on the commentary of Jean de Jandun.

37. For example, John of Głogów, *Questiones*, x6^v On Mondino and his *Anatomy*, see Franco Bacchelli (2005), "Mondino de' Liuzzi," in *Dizionario Biografico degli Italiani*, vol. 65, 309–14, Rome: Istituto dell'Enciclopedia Italiana.

38. John of Głogów, *Questiones*, x8^v. The textbook was targeted at the audience of the bachelor arts course according to the title page ("pro Juniorum in philosophie studiis institutione ad laudem dei resolute").

39. For a discussion of the use of brain diagrams in textbooks of late medieval natural philosophy, see Annemieke R. Verboon (2010), *Lines of Thought. Diagrammatic Representation and the Scientific Texts of the Arts Faculty, 1200–1500*, Diss. Leiden, 200–22. For later derivatives of the same image, see Karl Sudhoff (1916), "Ein unbekannter Druck von Johann Peyligks aus Zeitz 'Compendiosa capitis physici declaratio', auch 'Anatomia totius corporis humani' genannt," *Archiv für Geschichte der Medizin*, 9: 309–14.
40. Not only scholastic, but also Augustinian anthropology was exposed to the influence of Arabic philosophical and medical knowledge. For a neat summary about Augustine's Trinitarian concept of memory, and its critics in the thirteeenth century, see Magdalena Bieniak (2010), *The Soul-Body Problem at Paris, ca. 1200–1250. Hugh of St. Cher and His Contemporaries*, Leuven: Leuven University Press, 151–5.
41. On the *Disciplina scolaris*, see below. The *Moralium dogma philosophorum* is a very popular twelfth-century anthology, transmitted in more than hundred manuscripts, which has been variously attributed to William of Conches, Alan of Lille, and Walter of Châtillon. See René A. Gauthier (1953), "Les deux recensions du Moralium dogma philosophorum," *Revue du Moyen Age latin*, 9: 171–260, and John R. Williams (1957), "The Quest for the Author of the Moralium dogma philosophorum (1931–1956)," *Speculum*, 32: 736–47.
42. "Senece tradicio, Lucani inexplecio, Virgilii prolixitas, Stacii urbanitas, dura Flacci translacio, durior Persii edicio, Marcialis indigna lesio, Nasonis discrecio, sunt indaganda et memoriali cellule commendanda." Pseudo-Boèce, *De disciplina scolarium*, 96.
43. "*Terminorum autem determinaciones quas sincategoreumata appellamus*, memorialiter menti imprimende, *utpote que sophistice non parum deserviunt fantasie*." Pseudo-Boèce, *De disciplina scolarium*, 97. For the use of the word "*imprimere*" in a similar sense, see also ibid., 117.
44. On Gilbert, see Marjorie Burghart (2012a), "Du sermon-modèle aux paroles d'un saint. Le remploi du sermon In synodis, 3 de Guibert de Tournai dans la Vita Braulionis, indice pour la datation des sermones ad status?" *Medieval Sermon Studies*, 56: 9–29 and Marjorie Burghart (2012b), "In corde prudentis requiescit sapientia. Le sermon pour la fête de saint Antoine de Padoue de Guibert de Tournai, OMin (d. 1284)," *Il Santo*, 52: 45–105.
45. Gilbert, *De modo*, 193–222.
46. Gilbert, *De modo*, 191 ("per immoderationem applicationis animi ad studendum inde cellula memorialis destruitur"); 201 ("Senes autem in quibus abundat frigidum, et per consequens accidentale humidum et extrinsecum quod defluit in detrimentum, sigillari non permittit imaginem, sed fit in eis sicut ruinosis edificiis, in quibus non fit sigillatio propter putrefactionem").
47. Gilbert, *De modo*, 206–8.
48. The dating to after 1279 is based on Thibodeau, *The Rationale Divinorum Officiorum*, 121, who says that Durand refers in the *Repertorium* (Guillaume Durand the Elder (1497), *Aureum repertorium super toto corpore iuris canonici*, Venice: Paganino de Pagininis, c. 5., 60v–61v) to his short work on *Penance*, finished around 1279, while earlier he dated its second redaction to 1274–9: Timothy M. Thibodeau (2000), "Canon law and liturgical exposition in Durand's Rationale," *Bulletin of Medieval Canon Law*, 22: 41–52, here 43. Fasolt dates the *Repertorium* to the time before Durant left Italy for Mende (1291): Constantin Fasolt (1991), *Council and Hierarchy. The Political Thought of William Durant the Younger*, Cambridge, Cambridge University Press, 70.
49. "Protoplasti rubigine humana contaminata condicio sic cellule memorialis eclipsatur officio ut perdat quod non sepe perspicit, vel iugiter meditatur, quinimmo velut de pertuso sacculo aliunde excidit quod aliunde immittitur, sic profecto quod aure una ingeritur, altera protinus

egeritur. Ut accedat quod legitur de peni. di. iiii. de pertuso et de conse. di. v. ne tales. vers. unde et morbi. Et veluti vicine speculator imaginis secedens a speculo considerate iam effigiei non meminit, sic profecto quod oculata lectio tribuit momentanei actus interpositio intercipit et excludit ut accedat de pe. di. ii. si enim inquit. circa medium vers. estote, et probatur de pe. di. iii. iudas. in fine. iuxta illud: quantum disco, tantum dedisco. Mens ergo humana fluxum patitur cum in cauta opportune levigatur vel immunda veridice iudicatur." Durand, *Aureum repertorium*, 3r.

50. "Protoplasti rubigine humana condicio sic cellule memorialis eclipsatur officio [. . .] Idcirco ego bonus socius sociorum meorum precibus acquiescens partita que videram, queque per studium de novo inveneram [. . .] in hoc libello redigere procuravi." Magee, James F., ed. (1910), *Good Companion (Bonus socius). XIIIth Century Manuscript Collection of Chess Problems*, Florence: Tipografia Giuntina, facsimile between p. 8 and 9. The text cannot be dated with security, but it cannot have been written earlier than 1274/1279, because of the clear reference to the *Aureum repertorium*.

51. "Prothoplasti rubigine humana contaminata condicio sic cellule memorialis officio eclipsatur, quod successu temporis novercante diu gestorum non valeat recordari; quinimo, tanquam in speculo native ymaginis speculator ab eo secedens, qualis fuerit, minime recordatur, sic profecto quod temporaliter agitur continuo ab humana labitur noticia si non fuerit scripture testimonio roboratum"; Brześć Kujawski, 1297 (*Kodeks dyplomatyczny wielkopolski*, vol. 2, 1288-1349, (Poznan: Kraszewski, 1878), 138 ; reused later on in Wielichow, 1304, *Kodeks*, 234) "Quoniam prothoplasti rubigine memorialis cellula sic suo eclipsatur oficio, quod raro vel breviter servat que percipit, et quia frequenter eciam pie vel iuste et legaliter gesta subvertere nititur, et sepe satis ad hoc insidias parat excogitata malicia perversorum ad hec igitur sane consulere vias precludere et occasiones multas perimere sapientum pericia scripture remedio provide adinvenit", Kettilstorp (Sweden), 1291; Liljegren, Johann Gustav, ed. (1834), *Svenskt diplomatarium. Åren 1286-1299, no. 903-1300*, vol. II (1), Stockholm: Norstedt, 111.

52. Coleman, *Ancient and medieval memories*, 455; Nikulin, *Memory*, 117.

53. Maturantius Perusinus, Franciscus, ed. (1496), *M. T. Cicero, Rhetoricorum libri cum tribus commentis*, Venice: Philippus Pincius, f. 82^r.

54. "Andreas capiat amforam volens vehementer bibere et eam cum tanta importunitate in os suum trudat ut plures dentes evellat linguamque cum dentina crudeliter vulneret, quo facto expuat sanguinem cum dentibus et partibus linguae ita ut seipsum turpiter maculet, et sic iratus proiciat anforam contra murum, que resiliens intret ventrem suum." Berlin, SB, ms. germ. qu. 1522, f. 282^v. This manuscript contains a probably early variant of the *Memoria fecunda* treatise, which significantly differs from the version published by Pack, Roger A. (1980), "An Ars Memorativa," *Archives d'Histoire Doctrinale et Littéraire du Moyen Âge*, 46: 221–75.

55. "Imago (ut antea dixi) est similitudo et figura et significatio rei, quam volumus locis tradere. Verbi gratia, si vellem commemorare medicinam, ad locum constituo medicum mihi cognitum mirabili veste indutum urinale in manu habens et urina vetulam respergens. Hec est pulchra imago. In ordine regula: Imagines debent esse rarae, mirabiles, inusitatae, ridiculae, quia natura usitata re non exsuscitatur et debemus eis attribuere egregiam pulchritudinem aut unicam turpitudinem si aliquas exornabimus aut corona aut veste, tunc cruentam aut steno oblitas inducamus." Munich, BSB, clm. 4417f, f. 3^{r-v}. Interestingly, this quotation does not appear in the printed, significantly altered edition of the text, cp. Umhauser, Christian (1501), *Ars memoratiua S. Thome, Ciceronis, Qunitiliani, Petri Rauenne*, Nürnberg: Ambrosius Hueber, f. 2^r.

56. Giovanni M.A. Carrara (1491), *De omnibus ingeniis augendae memoriae*, Bologna: Plato de Benedictis, f. a5ʳ: "*Ut risum moveat figura, aut misericordiam aut admirationem, haec enim facit etiam puellas recordari, ut inquit Avicenna sexto naturalium particula quarta. Facile enim invenitur quaesita figura quae affectum animae commoverit. Exemplum hoc est: in ore asini rabidi caput Antonii constituam morsibus fere ossa confringi, cruorem effluere, illum auxilia petere, et passis palmis vociferare. Fieri non poterit, ut cum voluero, non videam hunc oculis mentis meae, et reddere Antonium nesciam repetenti.*"
57. For these reasons of the late medieval revival of memory culture, see Frances Yates (1976), "Ludovico da Pirano's Memory Treatise," in Cecil H. Clough (ed.), *Cultural Aspects of the Italian Renaissance. Essays in Honour of P.O. Kristeller*, 111–22, Manchester and New York: Manchester University Press and Zambelli (Byzantine influence); Heimann-Seelbach, Sabine (2000); *Ars und Scientia. Genese, Überlieferung und Funktionen der mnemotechnischen Traktatliteratur im 15. Jahrhundert*, Berlin: De Gruyter, 417–33; Farkas Gábor Kiss (2016), "Introduction," in Farkas Gábor Kiss (ed.), *The Art of Memory in Late Medieval Central Europe*, 15–8, Paris: L'Harmattan; and Seelbach and Kemper (eds), *Zentrale Gedächtnislehren des Spätmittelalters*.

Chapter Six

1. *Rex hoc Rodulfus patrum lege peremptus/Plorandus merito conditur in tumulo/Rex illi similis si reget tempore pacis/Consilio gladio non fuit a Karolo / Qua vicere sui ruit hic sacra victima belli/Mors sibi vita fuit ecclesiae cecidit.* Translation Gerald Schwedler, in Rösch and Simon 2012: 163–83, cf. the incorrect variant of Bücking 1968: 393–5: *Rex hoc Rudolfus patri reg[is] ereptus*. Cf. Bauch 1976: 303 note 33.

Chapter Seven

1. Digitized manuscript available online: http://www.louvre.fr/en/oeuvre-notices/leaf-diptych-emperor-triumphant (accessed July 16, 2017).
2. Digitized manuscript available online: http://www.stift-stpeter.at/de/bildgalerien/detail.asp?id=11&tit=Das%2520Verbruederungsbuch%2520von%2520St.%2520Peter (accessed July 16, 2017).
3. Digitized manuscript available online: http://www.e-codices.unifr.ch/de/list/one/zbz/Ms-Rh-hist0027 (accessed July 16, 2017).
4. Digitized manuscript available online: http://www.bl.uk/manuscripts/FullDisplay.aspx?ref=Cotton_MS_Domitian_A_VII (accessed July 16, 2017).
5. Digitized manuscript available online: http://www.bl.uk/manuscripts/FullDisplay.aspx?ref=Stowe_MS_944 (accessed July 16, 2017).
6. Digitized manuscript available online: http://bibliotheca-laureshamensis-digital.de/view/onb_cod1815 (accessed July 16, 2017).
7. Digitized manuscript available online: http://www.e-codices.unifr.ch/de/list/one/saa/4530 (accessed July 16, 2017).
8. Digitized manuscript available online: http://digi.ub.uni-heidelberg.de/diglit/salIX42 (accessed July 16, 2017).
9. Digitized manuscript available online: http://dx.doi.org/10.7891/e-manuscripta-27846 (accessed July 16, 2017).

Chapter Eight

1. *Memoriae damnatio, hic est perpetuae infamiae irrogatio, cum abolitione, erasione nominis, titulorum, dignitatum, statuarum, aedium demolitione, imaginum detractione, posteris nominis interdictione.* Trans. GS (Rebhan 1656).
2. *Pro qua etiam doctrina non solum ab ecclesia Dei anathematis mucrone separatus insuper etiam suspendio neci traditus, quin et post mortem incendio crematus atque in Tybrim fluvium proiectus est, ne videlicet Romanus populus, quem sua doctrina illexerat, sibi eum martyrem dedicaret* (Reichersberg 1897: 347).
3. *Sed et adhuc fumigat sceleratorum Ethna, Paschaliciis suffocata virtutibus, tantoque frequentius interius estuat quanto solidius exterius compilatur: quoniam Corsorum domus, videlicet Stefani etr filiorum et fratrum eius atque nepotum iam per domnum papam P.omnes destructae erant . . .* (Duchesne 1955: 298).
4. *Ut episcopus gentilium libros non legat, haereticorum autem pro necessitate et tempore* (Munier 1963: 167).
5. *Non multo post tempore Rŏdulfus in publico bello a fidelibus imperatoris necatur et in ecclesia Merseburc venisset ibique prefatum Rŏdulfum velut regem humatum vidisset, cuidam dicenti cur eum, qui rex non fuerat, velut regali honore sepultum iacere permitteret, dixerit: Utinam omnes inimici mei tam honorifice iacerent.* Transl. GS (Schmale 1965: 142–4).
6. Probably when Formosus was pope (891–6), though possibly earlier, a painting was provided in a small church near the Temple of Claudius, showing Christ in the midst of SS Peter, Paul, Laurence, and Hippolytus, with at his feet a barbarian prince (Boris) on one side and Formosus on the other. The painting, found in 1689, was published by De Rossi (De Rossi 1869: 59). Formosus's figure had even then disappeared, but his name was still recognizable: FORMOSVs. Duchesne noted with regret that this interesting piece of evidence had long since become invisible.
7. ad annum 1099 (Waitz 1861: 17): *Wigbertus Romanae et apostolicae sedis invasor, moritur; [. . .] Quidam autem de fautoribus eius rumorem sparserunt in populum, ad sepulcrum eius vidisse divina micuisse luminaria. Quapropter dominus apostolicus Paschalis zelo Dei inflammatus iussit ut effoderetur et in Tyberim iacteretur. Quod et factum est* (Longo 2012).
8. ad annum 1187: *Lucam inveniens ibi confracto sepulcro Octaviani ossa deiecit extra ecclesiam* (Bethmann 1844: 474).
9. *Ad malefactorum vindictam exurgere cogimur, [. . .]. Ne ergo glorietur peccator et, quod homo sit, sciat, exurgimur et severiattem misericordia temperantes ac in ipsius die conspectu, cuius vices in terris gerimus, facientes iudicium dicti Petri tamquam ex predictis hostis publici et ivine a humane lese maiestatis rei <u>dampnamus memoriam</u> eiusque filios, [. . .]* (Schmidt 2006: 121).
10. *[. . .] quoniam Corsorum domus, videlicet Stefani et filiorum et fratrum eius atque nepotum iam per domnum papam P[aschalis] omnes destructae eran t . . .* (Duchesne 1955: 298).
11. Ps. 108,13: *fiat novissimum eius interitus in generatione altera deleatur nomen eius.*

BIBLIOGRAPHY

Adamska, Anna (2000), "From Memory to Written Record in the Periphery of Medieval Latinitas. The Case of Poland in the Eleventh and Twelfth Centuries," in Karl Heidecker, ed., *Charters and the Use of the Written Word in Medieval Society*, 83–100, Turnhout: Brepols.

Adamska, Anna (2004), "The Study of Medieval Literacy: Old Sources, New Ideas," in Anna Adamska and Marco Mostert, eds, *The Development of Literate Mentalities in East Central Europe*, 13–50, Turnhout: Brepols.

Adamska, Anna (2015), "L'*Ars dictaminis* a-t-elle été possible en langue vernaculaire? Quelques sondages," in Benoit Grévin and Anne-Marie Turcan-Verkerk, eds, *Le Dictamen dans tous ses états. Perspectives de recherche sur la théorie et la pratique de l'Ars dictaminis (XIe–XVe siècles)*, 389–414, Turnhout: Brepols.

Adamska, Anna and Marco Mostert (2010), "The Literacies of Medieval Towndwellers and Peasants: a Preliminary Investigation," in Agnieszka Bartoszewicz et al., eds, *Świat Średniowiecza. Studia ofiarowane profesorowi Henrykowi Samsonowiczowi*, 317–30, Warszawa: Wydawnictwa Uniwersytetu Warszawskiego.

Agrimi, Jole and Chiara Crisciani (1988), *Edocere Medicos: Medicina Scholastica nei Secoli XIII–XV*, Naples: Guerini.

Agrimi, Jole and Chiara Crisciani (1994), *Les "consilia" médicaux*, trans. Caroline Viola, (Typologie des sources du Moyen Age occidental 69), Turnhout: Brepols.

Al-Ghazali, Abu Hamid (1995), *The Remembrance of Death and the Afterlife*, trans. T. Winter, Cambridge: Islamic Texts Society.

Al-Isfahani, Muhammad (1932), *Kitab al-zahrah (The Book of the Flower): The First Half*, ed. A.R. Nykl and Ibrahim Tuqan, Chicago: University of Chicago Press.

Algazi, Gadi (2014), "Forget Memory. Some Critical Remarks on Memory, Forgetting and History," in Sebastian Scholz, Gerald Schwedler, and Kai-Michael Sprenger, eds, *Damnatio in memoria. Deformation und Gegenkonstruktionen in der Geschichte*, 25–34, Köln: Böhlau.

Allen, Michael, ed. (2010), *Frechulf of Lisieux, Opera Omnia* (Corpus Christianorum Continuatio Mediaevalis 169), Turnhout: Brepols.

Althoff, Gerd (1998), "Geschichtsbewusstsein durch Memorialüberlieferung," in Hans-Werner Goetz, ed., *Memoria. Der geschichtliche Zeugniswert des liturgischen Gedenkens im Mittelalter, Hochmittelalterliches Geschichtsbewusstsein im Spiegel nichthistoriographischer Quellen*, 85–100, Berlin: Akad.-Verl.

Althoff, Gerd (2006), *Heinrich IV*, Darmstadt: Thorbecke.

Altmann, Alexander (1967), "Moses Narboni's 'Epistle on *Shi'ur Qomā*'," in Alexander Altmann, ed., *Jewish Medieval and Renaissance Studies*, 225–88, Cambridge, MA: Harvard University Press.

Andenmatten, Bernard (2009), "Les frères prêcheurs et les revenus des anniversaires. Le témoignage de l'obituaire du couvent dominicain de Lausanne," in Nicole Bériou and Jacques Chiffoleau, eds, *Économie et religion: L'expérience des ordres mendiants (XIIIe–XVe siècle)*, 153–69, Lyon: Presses universitaires de Lyon.

Andrade, Amélia A. (2011), "Une source privilégiée pour l'étude de l'espace à échelle régionale dans le Portugal médiéval: les enquêtes royales. Historiographie et suggestions de recherches," *Cahiers des recherches médiévales et humanistes* 21: 9–25.
Angenendt, Arnold (1983), "Missa specialis: Zugleich ein Beitrag zur Entstehung der Privatmessen," *Frühmittelalterliche Studien*, 17: 153–221.
Angenendt, Arnold (2001), *Das Frühmittelalter. Die abendländische Christenheit von 400 bis 900*, Stuttgart, Berlin, Köln: Kohlhammer.
Angenendt, Arnold (2013), "Die liturgische Memoria—Hilfe für das Fortleben im Jenseits," in Rainer Berndt, ed., *Wider das Vergessen und für das Seelenheil. Memoria und Totengedenken im Mittelalter*, 199–226, Münster: Aschendorff.
Antonín, Robert (2017), *The Ideal Ruler in Medieval Bohemia*, Leiden: Brill.
Appuhn, Horst (1973), "Beobachtungen und Versuche zum Bildnis Kaiser Friedrichs I. Barbarossa in Cappenberg," *Aachener Kunstblätter*, 44: 121–93.
Arberry, A.J., trans. (1953), Ibn Hazm, *The Ring of the Dove*, London: Luzac.
Ariès, Philippe (1974), *Western Attitudes Toward Death from the Middle Ages to the Present*, Baltimore: Johns Hopkins University Press.
Aristotle (1924), *Aristotle's Metaphysics*, ed. W.D. Ross. Oxford: Clarendon Press.
Arvay, Susan M. (2011), *Private Passions: The Contemplation of Suffering in Medieval Affective Devotions*, Ann Arbor, Umi dissertation publishing.
Assmann, Aleida (1991), "Zur Metaphorik der Erinnerung," in Aleida Assmann and Dietrich Harth, eds, *Mnemosyne. Formen und Funktionen der kulturellen Erinnerung*, 13–35, Frankfurt a.M.: Fischer-Taschenbuch-Verl.
Assmann, Jan (1997), *Das kulturelle Gedächtnis: Schrift, Erinnerung und politische Identität in frühen Hochkulturen*, München: Ch. Beck.
Assmann, Jan (2006), *Religion and Cultural Memory*, trans. Rodney Livingstone, Stanford: Stanford University Press.
Assmann, Jan (2011), *Cultural Memory and Early Civilization: Writing, Remembrance, and Political Imagination*, Cambridge: Cambridge University Press.
Augustinus (2002), Bekenntnisse/Confessiones, übers. u. eingel. v. Joseph Bernhart, Frankfurt a.M.: Insel.
Autenrieth, Johanne (1984), "Verbrüderungsbücher der Bodenseeklöster in paläographisch-kodikologischer Sicht," in Karl Schmid and Joachim Wollasch, eds, *Memoria: Der geschichtliche Zeugniswert des liturgischen Gedenkens im Mittelalter*, 603–12, Munich: Wilhelm Fink.
Autenrieth, Johanne, Dieter Geuenich, and Karl Schmid, eds (1979), *Das Verbrüderungsbuch der Abtei Reichenau* (Monumenta Germaniae Historica, Libri memoriales N.S. 1), Hannover: Hahnsche Buchhandlung.
Baagøe, Jette and Egon Wamers, eds (2009), *Die letzten Wikinger / Les derniers Vikings. Der Teppich von Bayeux und die Archäologie / La tapisserie de Bayeux et l'archéologie. Kat. d. Ausst. in Kopenhagen 2005/2006 und Frankfurt 2009*, Frankfurt a.M.: Stadt Frankfurt Dez. Kultur u. Wissenschaft.
Bacchelli, Franco (2005), "Mondino de' Liuzzi," in *Dizionario Biografico degli Italiani*, vol. 65, 309–14, Rome: Istituto dell'Enciclopedia Italiana.
Baldovin, John (2011), "History of the Latin Text and Rite," in Edward Foley, ed., *A Commentary on the Order of Mass of The Roman Missal: A New English Translation*, 247–54, Collegeville: Liturgical Press.
Barbier, Josiane (2014), *Archives oubliées du Haut Moyen Âge, Les gesta municipalia en Gaule franque (VIe–IXe siècle)* (Histoire et archives, Vol. 12.), Paris: Honoré Champion.

Bardy, Gustave, ed. (1952), *Eusébe de Césarée, Histoire ecclésiastique I*, Paris: Les Éditions du Cerf.
Barrett, Timothy (2013), "Parchment, Paper and Artisanal Research Techniques," in Jonathan Wilcox, ed., *Scraped, Stroked and Bound. Materially Engaged Readings of Medieval Manuscripts*, 115–27, Turnhout: Brepols.
Bartlett, Robert (2013), *Why Can the Dead Do Such Great Things? Saints and Worshippers from the Martyrs to the Reformation*, Princeton: Princeton University Press.
Barzen, Rainer (2011), "Das Nürnberger Memorbuch: Eine Einführung," in Alfred Haverkamp and Jörg R. Müller, eds, *Corpus der Quellen zur Geschichte der Juden im spätmittelalterlichen Reich*, Trier/Mainz 2011. Available online: http://www.medieval-ashkenaz.org/NM01/einleitung.html (accessed July 16, 2017).
Basore, John W., trans. (1935), *Seneca. Moral Essays, Volume III. De Beneficiis* (Loeb Classical Library 310), Cambridge, MA: Harvard University Press.
Bauch, Kurt (1976), *Das mittelalterliche Grabbild. Figürliche Grabmäler des 11. bis 15. Jahrhunderts in Europa*, Berlin, New York: de Gruyter.
Baumann, Franz Ludwig, ed. (1888), *Necrologia Germaniae* (Monumenta Germaniae Historica, Necrologia Germaniae 1), Berlin: Weidmann.
Bayard, Florence (2000), *L'art du bien mourir au XVe siècle. Étude sur les arts de bien mourir au bas Moyen Age à la lumière d'un "ars moriendi" allemand du XVe siècle*, Paris: Presses de l'université de Paris-Sorbonne.
Bayle, Pierre (1713), *Letters of Abelard and Heloise*, London: J. Watts.
Bazell, Dianne M., ed. (1993), *Arnoldus de Villa Nova, De esu carnium*, Barcelona: Universitat de Barcelona.
Beauvais, Vincent de (1591), *Speculum maius*, vol. 1, Venice: Dominicus Nicolinus.
Bedell, John (1999), "Memory and Proofs of Age in England, 1272–1327," *Past & Present*, 162: 3–27.
Bedos-Rezak, Brigitte Miriam (2011), *When Ego Was Imago: Signs of Identity in the Middle Ages*, Leiden/Boston: Brill.
Bedos-Rezak, Brigitte Miriam (2016), "S'inscrire tant dans le temps. Les chartes et l'éternité (IXe–XIIIe siècle)," *Memini*, Available online: http://journals.openedition.org/memini/840; DOI: 10.4000/memini.840 (accessed January 19, 2018).
Behrmann Thomas (1995), "Einleitung. Ein neuer Zugang zum Schriftgut der oberitalienischen Kommunen," in Hagen Keller and Thomas Behrmann, eds, *Kommunales Schriftgut in Oberitalien. Formen, Funktionen, Überlieferung*, 1–16, München: Wilhelm Fink Verlag.
Bell, Dean Phillip (2007), *Jewish Identity in Early Modern Germany: Memory, Power and Community*, Aldershot: Ashgate.
Belting, Hans (1970), *Das illuminierte Buch in der spätbyzantinischen Gesellschaft. Heidelberg*, Heidelberg: Winter.
Ben-Sasson, Menahem (2007), "The Maimonidean Dynasty: Between Conservatism and Revolution," in Jay M. Harris, ed., *Maimonides after 800 Years: Essays on Maimonides and His Influence*, 1–17, Cambridge, MA: Harvard University Press.
Bernard, Auguste and Alexandre Bruel, eds (1894), *Recueil des chartes de l'abbaye de Cluny*, vol. 5, Paris: Imprimerie nationale.
Bernardini, Paola, ed. (2009), *Anonymi magistri artium Quaestiones super librum de anima (Siena, Biblioteca Comunale, ms. L.III.21, ff. 134ra–174va)*, Florence: Sismel.
Berndt, Rainer (2013), "Tuet dies zu meinem Gedächtnis. Die Eucharistie als Grundlage christlicher *memoria* in Kirche und Theologie des Mittelalters," in Rainer Berndt, ed., *Wider das Vergessen und für das Seelenheil. Memoria und Totengedenken im Mittelalter*, 21–39, Münster: Aschendorff Verlag.

Bernhardus Claravallensis (Bernhard of Clairvaux) (1966), "Ad clericos de conversione / In festivitate omnium sanctorum," in Dom Jean Leclercp, ed., *Sancti Bernardi Opera vol. IV*, 70–116, Romae: Editiones Cistercienses.

Berns, Jörg Jochen and Wolfgang Neuber, eds (1993), *Ars memorativa. Zur kulturgeschichtlichen Bedeutung der Gedächtniskunst 1400–1750*, Tübingen: Niemeyer.

Berns, Jörg Jochen and Wolfgang Neuber, eds (1998), *Documenta Mnemonica. Text- und Bildzeugnisse zu Gedächtnislehren und Gedächtniskünsten von der Antike bis zum Ende der Frühen Neuzeit*, Tübingen: Niemeyer.

Bertrand, Paul (2015), *Les Écritures ordinaires. Sociologie d'un temps de révolution documentaire (1250–1350)*, Paris: Publications de la Sorbonne.

Berwinkel, Holger (2007), *Verwüsten und Belagern. Friedrich Barbarossas Krieg gegen Mailand (1158–1162)*, Tübingen: De Gruyter.

Bethmann, Ludwig Konrad, ed. (1844), *Sigebertus Gemblacensis Chronica, Continuatio Aquicinctina, Auctarium Nicolai Ambienensis*, 405–38, Hannover.

Bijsterveld, Arnaud-Jan (2007), *Do ut des: Gift Giving, Memoria, and Conflict Management in the Medieval Low Countries*, Hilversum: Verloren Publishers.

Bischoff, Bernhard (1989), *Latin Palaeography: Antiquity and the Middle Ages*, trans. by Dáibhí Ó Cróinín and David Ganz, Cambridge: Cambridge University Press.

Blaauw, Sible de (2014), "Kirchenbau und Erinnerung in Rom unter Anaklet II. und Innozenz II.," in Sebastian Scholz, Gerald Schwedler, and Kai-Michael Sprenger, eds, *Damnatio in memoria. Deformation und Gegenkonstruktionen in der Geschichte*, 129–52, Köln: Böhlau.

Black, Deborah L. (2017), "Avicenna and Averroes," in Sven Bernecker and Kourken Michaelian, eds, *The Routledge Handbook of Philosophy of Memory*, 448–60, London: Routledge.

Blaudeau, Philippe and Peter van Nuffelen, eds (2015), *L'historiographie tardo-antique et la transmission des savoirs*, Berlin: De Gruyter.

Blum, Herwig (1969), *Die antike Mnemotechnik*, Hildesheim, New York: Georg Olms.

Boitani, Piero et al., eds (1992–2006), *Lo Spazio letterario del Medioevo*, part II: *Il Medioevo volgare*, 3 vols., Roma: Salerno Editrice.

Bolgar, Robert R. (1954), *The Classical Heritage and its Beneficiaries*, Cambridge: Cambridge University Press.

Bonifacio, Enrico, ed. (1953), *Gilberto de Tournai, De modo addiscendi*, Turin: Società editrice internazionale.

Borgolte, Michael (2003), "Memoria: Bilan intermédiaire d'un projet de recherche sur le moyen âge," in Jean-Claude Schmitt and Otto Gerhard Oexle, eds, *Les tendances actuelles de l'histoire du Moyen Age en France et en Allemagne: Actes des colloques de Sèvres (1997) et Göttingen (1998)*, 53–69, Paris: Publications de la Sorbonne.

Borgolte, Michael (2012), *Stiftung und Memoria*, Berlin: Akademie.

Borgolte, Michael (2014–17), *Enzyklopädie des Stiftungswesens in mittelalterlichen Gesellschaften. Grundlagen*, 3 vols., Berlin: De Gruyter

Borgolte, Michael, Dieter Geuenich, and Karl Schmid, eds (1986), *Subsidia Sangallensia: Materialien und Untersuchungen zu den Verbrüderungsbüchern und zu den älteren Urkunden des Stiftsarchivs Sankt Gallen*, Sankt Gallen: Buchhandlung am Rösslitor.

Borst, Arno, Gerhard von Graevenitz, Alexander Patschovsky, and Karlheinz Stierle, eds (1993), *Tod im Mittelalter*, Konstanzer Bibliothek 20, Konstanz: Universitätsverlag.

Bos, Gerrit (1994), "Ibn Al-Gazzar's Risala Fin-Nisyan and Constantine's 'liber de oblivione'," in Charles Burnett and Danielle Jacquart, eds, *Constantine the African and Ali ibn al-Abbas al-Magusi. The "Pantegni" and Related Texts*, 203–32, Leiden: Brill.

Bos, Gerrit, ed. (1995), *Ibn Al-Jazzar, On Forgetfulness and its Treatment, Critical Edition of the Arabic text and the Hebrew Translations with Commentary and Translation into English*, London: Royal Asiatic Society.

Bossy, John (2002), "Moral Arithmetic: Seven Sins into Ten Commandments," in Edmund Leites, ed., *Conscience and Casuistry in Early Modern Europe*, 213–44, Cambridge: Cambridge University Press.

Bouchard, Constance Brittain (2014), *Rewriting Saints and Ancestors. Memory and Forgetting in France, 500–1200*, Philadelphia: University of Pennsylvania Press.

Brachmann, Christoph (2006), *Memoria—Fama—Historia: Schlachtengedenken und Identitätsstiftung am lothringischen Hof (1477–1525) nach dem Sieg über Karl den Kühnen*, Berlin: Gebrüer Mann.

Brady, Ignatius OFM (1948), "Remigius–Nemesius," *Franciscan Studies*, 8: 275–84.

Bredehoft, Thomas A. (2011), "Multiliteralism in Anglo-Saxon Verse Inscriptions," in Elisabeth M. Tyle, ed., *Conceptualising Multilingualism in England, c. 800–c. 1250*, 15–32, Turnhout: Brepols.

Bredekamp, Horst (2014), Der schwimmende Souverän. Karl der Große und die Bildpolitik des Körpers. Eine Studie zum schematischen Bildakt, Berlin: Verlag Klaus Wagenbach.

Brenner, Elma, Meredith Cohen, and Mary Franklin-Brown, eds (2013), *Memory and Commemoration in Medieval Culture*, Farnham: Ashgate.

Bresc, Henri and Isabelle Heullant-Donat (2007), "Pour une réévaluation de la 'révolution du papier' dans l'Occident médiéval," *Scriptorium*, 61 (2): 354–83.

Britnell, Richard H., ed. (1997), *Pragmatic Literacy: East and West, 1200–1330*, Woodbridge: Boydell Press.

Brown, Andrew (2003), *Church and Society in England, 1000–1500*, Basingstoke/New York: Palgrave Macmillan.

Brown, Andrew (2011), *Civic Ceremony and Religion in Medieval Bruges c. 1300–1520*, Cambridge: Cambridge University Press.

Brown, Peter (1981), *The Cult of the Saints: Its Rise and Function in Latin Christianity*, Chicago: University of Chicago Press.

Brown, Warren et al., eds (2013), *Documentary Culture and the Laity in the Early Middle Ages*, Cambridge: Cambridge University Press.

Bruckner, Albert and Hans Rudolf Sennhauser, eds (1973), *Liber Viventium Fabariensis*, Basel: Alkuin.

Brunner, Thomas (2009), "Le passage aux langues vernaculaires dans les actes de pratique en Occident," *Le Moyen Age*, 115: 29–72.

Bueren, Truus van (1999), *Leven na de dood. Gedenken in de late Middeleeuwen. Katalog der Ausstellung in Utrecht 1999*, Turnhout: Brepols.

Bunčić, Daniel et al., eds (2016), *Biscriptality. A Sociolinguistic Typology*, Heidelberg: Universitätverlag Winter.

Bünz, Enno (2003), "Memoria auf dem Dorf: Pfarrkirche, Friedhof und Beinhaus als Stätten bäuerlicher Erinnerungskultur im Spätmittelalter," in Werner Rösener, ed., *Tradition und Erinnerung in Adelsherrschaft und bäuerlicher Gesellschaft*, 261–306, Göttingen: Vandenhoeck & Ruprecht.

Burckhardt, Jacob (1878), *The Civilization of the Renaissance in Italy*, trans. S.G.G. Middlemore, London: Kegan Paul & Co.

Burgess, Clive (1987a), "Late Medieval Wills and Pious Conventions: Testamentary Evidence Reconsidered," in Michael Hicks, ed., *Profit, Piety, and the Professions in Later Medieval England*, 14–33, Gloucester: Alan Sutton.

Burgess, Clive (1987b), "A Service for the Dead: The Form and Function of the Anniversary in Late Medieval Bristol," *Transactions of the Bristol and Gloucestershire Archaeological Society*, 105: 183–221.

Burgess, Clive (1991), "The Benefactions of Mortality: The Lay Response in the Late Medieval Urban Parish," in David Michael Smith, ed., *Studies in Clergy and Ministry in Medieval England*, 65–86, York: University of York.

Burgess, Clive (2000), "Longing to be Prayed For: Death and Commemoration in an English Parish in the later Middle Ages," in Bruce Gordon and Peter Marshall, eds, *The Place of the Dead: Death and Remembrance in Late Medieval and Early Modern Europe*, 44–65, Cambridge: Cambridge University Press.

Burghart, Marjorie (2012a), "Du sermon-modèle aux paroles d'un saint. Le remploi du sermon In synodis, 3 de Guibert de Tournai dans la Vita Braulionis, indice pour la datation des sermones ad status?" *Medieval Sermon Studies*, 56: 9–29.

Burghart, Marjorie (2012b), "In corde prudentis requiescit sapientia. Le sermon pour la fête de saint Antoine de Padoue de Guibert de Tournai, OMin (d. 1284)," *Il Santo*, 52: 45–105.

Burke, Peter (1989), "History as Social Memory," in Thomas Butler, ed., *Memory. History, Culture and the Mind*, 97–113, Oxford: Basil Blackwell.

Burke, Peter (1991), "The Social History of Language," in Peter Burke, *The Art of Conversation*, 1–33, Ithaca, NY: Cornell University Press.

Burkhard, Carl I., ed. (1917), *Nemesius of Emesa, Premnon Physicon a N. Alfano in Latinum translatus*, Leipzig: Teubner.

Brno, Moravský zemský archiv, fund G12, inventory number 387, Cerroni II, book number 263.

Buttimer, Charles H., ed. (1939), *Hugues de Saint Victor, Didascalicon de studio legendi (Studies in Medieval and Renaissance Latin)*, Washington, DC: The Catholic University Press.

Butz, Eva-Maria and Alfons Zettler (2013), "The Making of the Carolingian Libri Memoriales," in Elma Brenner, Meredith Cohen, and Mary Franklin-Brown, eds, *Memory and Commemoration in Medieval Culture*, 79–92, Farnham: Ashgate.

Butzer, Günter and Manuela Günter (2004), *Kulturelles Vergessen. Medien—Rituale—Orte*, Göttingen: Vandenhoeck & Ruprecht.

Campbell, Jeffrey (1995), *The Ars Moriendi. An Examination, Translation, and Collation of the Manuscripts of the Shorter Latin version*, PhD diss., School of Graduate Studies, University of Ottawa.

Cardelle de Hartmann, Carmen and Susanne Uhl, eds (2013), *Heilige Bücher*, Berlin: Akad.-Verl.

Carrara, Giovanni M.A. (1491), *De omnibus ingeniis augendae memoriae*, Bologna: Plato de Benedictis.

Carruthers, Mary (1990), *The Book of Memory. A Study of Memory in Medieval Culture*, Cambridge: Cambridge University Press.

Carruthers, Mary (1992), "Thomas Bradwardine, 'De memoria artificale adquirenda'," *Journal of Medieval Latin*, 2: 25–43.

Carruthers, Mary (1996), "Boncompagno at the Cutting Edge of Rhetoric. Rhetorical Memory and the Craft of Memory," *Journal of Medieval Latin*, 6: 44–64.

Carruthers, Mary (1998), *The Craft of Thought: Meditation, Rhetoric, and the Making of Images: 400–1200*, Cambridge: Cambridge University Press.

Carruthers, Mary and Jan M. Ziolkowski, eds (2002), *The Medieval Craft of Memory. An Anthology of Texts and Pictures*, Philadelphia: University of Pennsylvania Press.

Carson Pastan, Elisabeth and Stephen D. White (2014), *The Bayeux Tapestry and its Contexts: A Reassessment*, Woodbridge: Boydell & Brewer.

Casagrande, Carla and Silvana Vecchio (1994), "La classificazione dei peccati tra settenario e decalogo (secoli XIII–XV)," *Documenti e studi sulla tradizione filosofica medieval,* 5: 331–95.

Cassiodorus (1894), *Variae,* ed. Theodor Mommsen (Monumenta Germaniae Historica, Auctores antiquissimi 12), Berlin: Weidmann.

Cassiodorus (1992), *Variae,* transl. S.J.B. Barnish (Translated Texts for Historians 12), Liverpool: Liverpool University Press.

Chazan, Mireille (1999), *L'idée d'Empire de Sigebert de Gembloux à Jean de Saint-Victor (XIIe–XIVe siècle),* Paris: Champion.

Chibnall, Marjorie, ed. (1986), *The Historia Pontificalis of John of Salisbury,* Oxford, Clarendon Press.

Chiffoleau, Jacques (1980), *La comptabilité de l'au-delà: Les hommes, la mort et la religion dans la région d'Avignon à la fin du Moyen Age (vers 1320–vers 1480),* Rome: École française de Rome.

Chirico, Irene, ed. (2011), *Alfano I, Premnon physicon. Versione latina del Peri physeos anthropou di Nemesio,* Rome: Storia e Letteratura.

Clanchy, Michael T. (1979), *From Memory to Written Record: England 1066–1307,* Oxford: Blackwell.

Clanchy, Michael (1993; 2013), *From Memory to Written Record: England 1066–1544,* Chichester: Wiley-Blackwell.

Clark, Andrew, ed. (1914), *Lincoln Diocese Documents, 1450–1544* (Early English Text Society, 149), 37–44, London: Kegan Paul.

CDM I (1876): Piekosiński, Franciszek, ed. (1876), *Codex Diplomaticus Poloniae Minoris,* vol. 1, Kraków: Akademia Umiejętności.

Coleman, Janet (1992; 2005), *Ancient and Medieval Memories. Studies in the Reconstruction of the Past,* Cambridge: Cambridge University Press.

Coleman, Joyce (1996), *Public Reading and Reading Public in Late Medieval England and France,* Cambridge: Cambridge University Press.

Connerton, Paul (1989), *How Societies Remember,* Cambridge: Cambridge University Press.

Constable, Giles (2000), "The Commemoration of the Dead in the Early Middle Ages," in Julia M.H. Smith, ed., *Early Medieval Rome and the Christian West: Essays in Honour of Donald A. Bullough,* 169–95, Leiden/Boston/Cologne: Brill.

Constable, Giles (2010), *The Abbey of Cluny: A Collection of Essays to Mark the Eleven-Hundredth Anniversary of its Foundation,* Berlin: Lit.

Corner, George W. (1927), *Anatomical Texts of the Earlier Middle Ages,* Washington, DC: Carnegie Institute; NY: AMS Press Reprint.

Corpus Iuris Civilis (1999), Text und Übersetzung, Vol. 3, Digesten 11–20, trans. and eds, Okko Behrends, Rolf Knüttel, Berthold Kupisch, and Hans-Hermann Seiler, Heidelberg.

Corradini, Maria Sofia (2012), "La letteratura medica medievale in lingua d'oc fra tradizione antica e Rinascimento europeo," in Anna Alberni et al., eds, *El saber i les llengües vernacles a l'època de Llull i Eiximenis,* 147–70, Barcelona: Publicacions de l'Abadia de Montserrat.

Cressy, David (1993), "Purification, Thanksgiving and the Churching of Women in Post-Reformation England," *Past & Present* 141: 106–46.

Croenen, Godfried (2018), "La guerre en Normandie au XIVe siècle et le problème de l'évolution textuelle des chroniques de Jean Froissart," in Anne Curry and Véronique Gazeau, eds, *La guerre en Normandie (XIe–XVe siècle),* 111–47, Caen: Presses Universaires de Caen.

Crouch, D. (2001), "The Origins of the Chantry: Some Further Anglo-Norman Evidence," *Journal of Medieval History,* 27: 159–80.

Cubitt, Catherine (2000), "Monastic Memory and Identity in Early Saxon England," in William O. Frazer, ed., *Social Identity in Early Medieval Britain*, 253–76, London: Leicester University Press.

Cubitt, Geoffrey (2007), *History and Memory*, Manchester: Manchester University Press.

Cutler, Anthony (1991), "Barberiana: Notes on the Making, Content, and Provenance of Louvre, OA. 9063," in Ernst Dassmann and Klaus Thraede, eds, *Tesserae: Festschrift für Josef Engemann*, 329–39, Münster: Aschendorff.

Damian-Grint, Peter (1999), *The New Historians of the Twelfth-Century Renaissance: Inventing Vernacular Authority*, Woodbridge: The Boydell Press.

Davies, Wendy (2005), "Buying with Masses: Donation pro remedio animae in 10th Century Galicia and Castile-León," in François Bougard, Cristina La Rocca, and Régine Le Jan, eds, *Sauver son âme et se perpétuer: Transmission du patrimoine et mémoire au haut Moyen Âge*, 401–16, Rome: École française de Rome.

Davies, Wendy and Paul Fouracre, eds, (1986), *The Settlement of Disputes in Early Medieval Europe*, Cambridge: Cambridge University Press.

De Boer, Sander W. (2013), *The Science of the Soul. The Commentary Tradition on Aristotle's De anima, c. 1260–c. 1360*, Leuven: Leuven University Press.

De La Roncière, Charles (1983), "Conclusions: de la mémoire vécue à la tradition, perception et enregistrement du passé," in *Temps, mémoire, tradition au Moyen-Age: Actes du XIIIe Congrès de la Société des historiens médiévistes de l'Enseignement supérieur public, Aix-en-Provence, 4–5 juin 1982*, 267–79, Aix-en-Provence: Université d'Aix-en-Provence.

De Rossi, Giovanni Battista (1869), *Bullettino die archeologia cristiana*, 2, Roma: Tipografia Salviucci.

De Vincentiis, Amedeo (2004), "Memorie bruciate. Conflitti, documenti, oblio nelle città italiane del tardo medioevo," *Bullettino dell'Istituto storico italiano per il Medio Evo*, 106 (1): 167–98.

De Vivo, Filippo (2010), "Ordering the Archive in Early Modern Venice," *Archival Science*, 10: 231–48.

Declercq, Georges (2000), "Originals and Cartularies: The Organization of Archival Memory (Ninth–Eleventh Centuries)," in Karl Heidecker, ed., *Charters and the Use of the Written Word in Medieval Society*, 147–70, Turnhout: Brepols.

Declercq, Georges, ed. (2007), *Early Medieval Palimpsests*, Turnhout: Brepols.

Dejoux, Marie (2014), "Gouverner par enquête en France de Philippe Auguste aux derniers Capétiens," *French Historical Studies*, 37 (2): 271–302.

Delisle, Léopold, ed. (1872), *Chronique de Robert de Torigni, abbé de Mont-Saint-Michel*, Rouen.

Denzel, Markus A. et al., eds (2002), *Kaufmannsbücher und Handelspraktiken vom Spätmittelalter bis zum beginnenden 20. Jahrhundert / Merchant's Books and Mercantile "Pratiche" from the late Middle Ages to the Beginning of the 20th century*, Stuttgart: Franz Steiner Verlag.

Derolez, Albert (2003), *The Palaeography of Gothic Manuscript Books: From the Twelfth to the Early Sixteenth Century*, Cambridge: Cambridge University Press.

Diringer, David (1982), *The Book before Printing. Ancient, Medieval and Oriental*, New York: Dover.

Dix, Gregory (1945), *The Shape of the Liturgy*, London: Dacre Press.

Doležalová, Lucie (2014), "Passion and Passion: Intertextual Narratives in Late Medieval Bohemia between Typology, History, and Parody," in Marek Thue Kretschmer, ed., *Biblical Typology as a Mode of Thinking in Medieval Historiography*, 245–65, Turnhout: Brepols.

Doležalová, Lucie and Tamás Visi (2010), "Revisiting Memory in the Middle Ages," in Lucie Doležalová and Tamás Visi, eds, *The Making of Memory in the Middle Ages* 1–8, Leiden: Brill.
Dubois, Jacques (1978), *Les martyrologes du moyen âge latin* (Typologie des sources du moyen âge occidental 26), Turnhout: Brepols.
Duchesne, Louis, ed. (1892), *Le Liber pontificalis. Texte, introduction et commentaire par L. Duchesne*, vol. 2, Paris: Ernest Thorin.
Dufour, Jean, ed. (2005–8), *Recueil des rouleaux des morts (VIIIe siècle–vers 1536)*, 4 vols., lettres (Recueil des historiens de la France, obituaires 8), Paris: Académie des inscriptions et belles.
Duffy, Eamon (2001), *The Voices of Morebath: Reformation and Rebellion in an English Village*, New Haven: Yale University Press.
Durand the Elder, Guillaume (1497), *Aureum repertorium super toto corpore iuris canonici*, Venice: Paganino de Pagininis.
Eco, Umberto (1988), "An Ars oblivionalis? Forget it!" *PMLA*, 103 (3): 254–61.
Eco, Umberto (2009), *The Infinity of Lists*, New York: Rizzoli.
Eisenstein, Elisabeth (1979), *The Printing Press as an Agent of Change: Communications and Cultural Transformations in Early-Modern Europe*, 2 vols., Cambridge: Cambridge University Press.
El Tayyib, Abdulla (1983), "Pre-Islamic Poetry," in A.F.L. Beeston et al., eds, *Arabic Literature to the End of the Umayyad Period*, 27–112, Cambridge: Cambridge University Press.
Elias, Norbert (1991), "Changes in the We-I Balance (1987)," in Norbert Elias, *Society of Individuals*, ed., Michael Schröter, trans. Edmund Jephcott, 153–237, New York and London: Continuum.
Erdélyi, László (1902), *A Pannonhalmi Főapátság története (History of the Pannonhalma Archabbey)*, vol. 1, Budapest: Stephaneum.
Everard, Judith (2001), "Sworn testimony and memory of the past in Brittany, c. 1100–1250," in Elisabeth van Houts, ed., *Medieval Memories. Men, Women and the Past, 700–1300*, 72–91, Harlow: Longman.
Faini, Enrico (2008), "Alle origini della memoria comunale. Prime ricerche," *Quellen und Forschungen aus italienischen Archiven und Bibliotheken*, 88: 61–81.
Fasolt, Constantin (1991), *Council and Hierarchy. The Political Thought of William Durant the Younger*, Cambridge, Cambridge University Press.
Favreau, Robert (1997), *Épigraphie médiévale*, Turnhout: Brepols.
Fédou, Michel (2004), "L'écriture de l'histoire dans le christianisme ancient," *Recherches de Science Religieuse*, 92 (4): 539–68.
Fejér, Georgius, ed. (1831), *Codex diplomaticus Hungariae*, vol. 7 (1), Buda: Typis universitatis.
Fentress, James and Chris Wickham (1992), *Social Memory*, Oxford: Blackwell.
Ferguson, Charles A. (1959), "Diglossia," *Word*, 15: 325–40.
Fichtenau, Heinrich (1957), *Arenga. Spätantike und Mittelalter im Spiegel von Urkundenformeln*, Graz, Köln, Innsbruck: Wagner.
Filippi, Friedrich and Max Bär, eds (1899), *Osnabrücker Urkundenbuch*, vol. 3. *Die Urkunden der Jahre 1251–1280*, Osnabrück: Historischer Verein zu Osnabrück.
Flasch, Kurt (1993), *Was ist Zeit? Augustinus von Hippo. Das XI. Buch der Confessiones. Historisch-philosophische Studie. Text—Übersetzung—Kommentar*, Frankfurt a.M.: Klostermann.
Flower, Harriet Isabel (2006), *The Art of Forgetting. Disgrace and Oblivion in Roman Political Culture,* Chapel Hill: University of North Carolina Press.

Fontaine, Jacques, ed. (1968), *Sulpice Sèvére, Vie de Saint Martin*, Paris: Les Éditions du Cerf.
Foot, Sarah (1999), "Remembering, Forgetting and Inventing: Attitudes to the Past in England at the End of the first Viking Age," *Transactions of the Royal Historical Society*, 9: 185–200.
Foot, Sarah and Chase F. Robinson, eds (2012), *The Oxford History of Historical Writing*, vol. 2: *400–1400*, Oxford: Oxford University Press.
Frank, Thomas (1991), *Studien zu italienischen Memorialzeugnissen des XI. und XII. Jahrhunderts*, Berlin/New York: De Gruyter.
Franklin-Brown, Mary (2012), *Reading the World. Encyclopedic Writing in the Scholastic Age*, Chicago and London: University of Chicago Press.
Franklin-Brown, Mary (2013), "The Speculum Maius, Between Thesaurus and Lieu de Mémoire," in Elma Brenner et al., eds, *Memory and Commemoration in Medieval Culture*, 143–62, Farnham: Ashgate.
Fried, Johannes (2001), "Erinnerung und Vergessen. Die Gegenwart stiftet die Einheit der Vergangenheit," *Historische Zeitschrift*, 273: 561–93.
Fried, Johannes (2012), *Der Schleier der Erinnerung. Grundzüge einer historischen Memorik*, München: Beck.
Friedberg, Emil and Emil Ludwig Richter, eds (1879), *Decretum magistri Gratiani*, Leipzig.
Fudge, Thomas A. (2011), "Jan Hus at Calvary: The Text of an Early Fifteenth-Century *Passio*," *Journal of Moravian History*, 11: 45–81.
Frank, Thomas (1991), *Studien zu italienischen Memorialzeugnissen des XI. und XII. Jahrhunderts*, Berlin/New York: De Gruyter.
Galinsky, Judah D. (2005), "Commemoration and Heqdesh in the Jewish Communities of Germany and Spain during the 13th Century," in Michael Borgolte, ed., *Stiftungen in Christentum, Judentum und Islam vor der Moderne: Auf der Suche nach ihren Gemeinsamkeiten und Unterschieden in religiösen Grundlagen, praktischen Zwecken und historischen Transformationen*, 191–204, Berlin: De Gruyter.
Gamper, Rudolf (2010), "Die Gestaltung der Jahrzeitbücher," in Peter Erhart and Jakob Kuratli Hüeblin, eds, *Bücher des Lebens—Lebendige Bücher: Katalog zur Ausstellung im Regierungsgebäude des Kantons Sankt Gallen*, 268–73, Sankt Gallen: Stiftsarchiv.
Gantner, Clemens, Rosamond McKitterick, and Sven M. Meeder, eds (2015), *Cultural Memory and the Resources of the Past: Europe c. 400–1000*, Cambridge: Cambridge University Press.
Garipzanov, Ildar, ed. (2011), *Historical Narratives and Christian Identity on a European Periphery: Early History Writing in Northern, East-Central, and Eastern Europe (c. 1070–1200)*, Turnhout: Brepols.
Gauthier, René A. (1953), "Les deux recensions du Moralium dogma philosophorum," *Revue du Moyen Age latin*, 9: 171–260.
Geary, Patrick J. (1994a), *Living with the Dead in the Middle Ages*, Ithaca, NY/London: Cornell University Press.
Geary, Patrick J. (1994b), *Phantoms of Remembrance. Memory and Oblivion at the End of the First Millennium*, Princeton, NJ: Princeton University Press.
Geary, Patrick J. (1999), "Land, Language and Memory in Europe 700–1100," *Transactions of the Royal Historical Society*, 9: 169–84.
Geary, Patrick J. (2002), "Oblivion Between Orality and Textuality in the Tenth Century," in Gerd Althoff, ed., *Medieval Concepts of the Past: Ritual, Memory, Historiography*, 111–122, Washington, DC: German Historical Institute.
Gerchow, Jan (1988), *Die Gedenküberlieferung der Angelsachsen: Mit einem Katalog der Libri Vitae und Nekrologien*, Berlin/New York: De Gruyter.
Gerlach, Johann Heinrich (1689), *De damnatione memoriae*, Lipsiae.

Geuenich, Dieter (2004), "A Survey of the Early Medieval Confraternity Books from the Continent," in David Rollason, A.J. Piper, and Margaret Harvey, eds, *The Durham Liber Vitae and its Context*, 141–8, Woodbridge: Boydell Press.

Geuenich, Dieter and Uwe Ludwig, eds (2015), *Libri vitae. Gebetsgedenken in der Gesellschaft des Frühen Mittelalters*, Cologne/Weimar/Vienna: Böhlau.

Geuenich, Dieter, Renate Neumüllers-Klauser, and Karl Schmid, eds (1983), *Die Altarplatte von Reichenau-Niederzell* (MGH Libri Memoriales et Necrologia N. S., I Supp.), 20–9, Hannover: Hahn.

Geuenich, Dieter, Uwe Ludwig, and Arnold Angenendt, eds (2000), *Der Memorial- und Liturgiecodex von San Salvatore/Santa Giulia in Brescia* (Monumenta Germaniae Historica, Libri memoriales N.S. 4), Hannover: Hahnsche Buchhandlung.

Glorieux, Palémon, ed. (1958), *Jacques de Thérines, Quodlibets I et II—Jean Lesage, Quodlibet I*, Paris: Vrin.

Goody, Jack (1977), "What's in a List?" in id.: *The Domestication of the Savage Mind*, 74–111, Cambridge: Cambridge University Press.

Goetz, Hans Werner (2008), *Geschichtsschreibung und Geschichtsbewusstsein im hohen Mittelalter*, 2nd edn, Berlin: Akademie Verlag.

Goitein, Shlomo D. (2015), *Letters of Medieval Jewish Traders*, Princeton: Princeton University Press.

Goldstein, David (1989), Yeruḥam Fishel Lachower Isaiah Tishby, *The Wisdom of the Zohar*. Oxford: Oxford University Press.

Gordon, Bruce and Peter Marshall, eds (2000), *The Place of the Dead: Death and Remembrance in Late Medieval and Early Modern Europe*, Cambridge: Cambridge University Press.

Goullet, Monique (2003), "Vers une typologie de réécritures hagiographiques, à partir de quelques exemples du Nord-Est de la France. Avec une édition synoptique des deux Vies de saint Èvre de Toul," in Monique Goullet and Martin Heinzelmann, eds, *La réécriture hagiographique dans l'Occident médiéval. Transformations formelles et idéologiques*, 109–44, Ostfildern: Thorbecke.

Goullet, Monique (2005), *Écriture et réécriture hagiographiques. Essai sur les réécritures de Vies de saints dans l'Occident latin medieval (VIIIe–XIIIe s.)*, Turnhout: Brepols.

Graf, Klaus (1991), "Schlachtengedenken im Spätmittelalter: Riten und Medien der Präsentation kollektiver Identität," in Detlef Altenburg, Jörg Jarnut, and Hans-Hugo Steinhoff, eds, *Feste und Feiern im Mittelalter. Paderborner Symposion des Mediävistenverbandes*, 63–9, Sigmaringen: Thorbecke.

Graf, Klaus (2003), Erinnerungsfeste in der Stadt," in Hanno Brand, Pierre Monnet, and Martial Staub, eds, *Memoria, Communitas, Civitas. Mémoire et conscience urbaines en occident à la fin du Moyen Age*, 263–73, Ostfildern: Thorbecke.

Green, Rosalie et al., eds (1979), *Hortus deliciarum. Herrad of Hohenbourg*, 2 vols., London, Leiden: Brill.

Greenway, Diana, ed. (1996), *Henry Archdeacon of Huntingdon, Historia Anglorum, The History of the English People*, Oxford: Clarendon Press.

Greenway, Diana (1999), "Dates in History: Chronology and Memory," *Historical Research*, 72 (178): 127–39.

Gruber, Joachim (2006), *Kommentar zu Boethius, De consolatione philosophiae*, 2nd edn, Berlin: De Gruyter.

Gruner, Oskar C., ed. (1973), *Ibn-Sina, The Canon of Medicine of Avicenna*, New York: AMS Press.

Guenée, Bernard (1985), "L'historien et la compilation au XIIIe siècle," *Journal des savants*, 1–3: 119–35.
Guenée, Bernard (2011), *Histoire et culture historique dans l'Occident medieval*, 3rd edn, Paris: Aubier Montaigne.
Guyot-Bachy, Isabelle (2000), *Le 'Memoriale Historiarum' de Jean de Saint-Victor—Un historien et sa communauté au début du XIVe siècle*. Turnhout: Brepols.
Guyotjeannin, Olivier (1997), "Super omnes thesauros rerum temporalium: les fonctions du Trésor des chartes du roi de France (XIVe–XVe siècles)," in Koku Fianu and D.J. Guth, eds, *Écrit et pouvoir dans les chancelleries médiévales: espace français, espace anglais*, 109–31, Louvain-la-Neuve: Brepols.
Hajdu, Helga (1936), *Das mnemotechnische Schrifttum des Mittelalters*, Budapest: Deutsches Institut der königlich Ungarischen Peter Pazmany Universität.
Halbwachs, Maurice (1950), *La mémoire collective*, Paris: Presses universitaires de France.
Halbwachs, Maurice (1952), *On Collective Memory*, ed. and tr., Lewis A. Coser, Chicago: University of Chicago Press.
Hale, Rosemary Drage (1995), "Taste and See, for God is Sweet: Sensory Perception and Memory in Medieval Christian Mystical Experience," in Anne Clark Bartlett, Thomas H. Bestul, Janet Goebel, and William F. Pollard, eds, *Vox Mystica: Essays on Medieval Mysticism in Honor of Professor Valerie M Lagorio*, 3–14, Rochester: D.S. Brewer.
Hampe, Beate (2005), "Image schemas in cognitive linguistics. Introduction," in Beate Hampe and Joseph E. Grady, eds, *From Perception to Meaning. Image Schemas in Cognitive Linguistics*, 1–12, Berlin: Mouton de Gruyter.
Harris, Joseph (2010), "Old Norse Memorial Discourse between Orality and Literacy," in S. Ranković et al., eds, *Along the Oral-Written Continuum. Types of Texts, Relations and their Implications*, Turnhout: Brepols.
Harris-Stoertz, Fione (2015), "Remembering Birth in the Thirteenth and Fourteenth Centuries," in Elizabeth Cox et al., eds, *Reconsidering Gender: Time and Memory in Medieval Culture*, 25–59, Rochester, NY: D.S. Brewer.
Hartmann, Andreas (2010), *Zwischen Relikt und Reliquie. Objektbezogene Erinnerungspraktiken in antiken Gesellschaften*, Berlin: Vandenhoeck & Ruprecht.
Harvey, Barbara (1993), *Living and Dying in England 1100–1540: The Monastic Experience*, Oxford: Oxford University Press.
Haskins, Charles Homer (1927), *The Renaissance of the Twelfth Century*, Cambridge, MA and London: Harvard University Press.
Hasse, Dag N. (2000), *Avicenna's De Anima in the Latin West. The Formation of a Peripatetic Philosophy of the Soul, 1160–1300*, London and Turin: Warburg Institute-Nino Aragni.
Hasse, Dag N. (2010), "The Soul's Faculties," in Robert Pasnau and Christina van Dyke, eds, *The Cambridge History of Medieval Philosophy*, 305–19, Cambridge: Cambridge University Press.
Hayes, Zachery, ed. (2000), *Bonaventure, Works of Saint Bonaventure 3. Disputed Questions on the Mystery of the Trinity*, New York: The Franciscan Institute.
Hazm, Ibn (1981), *Ṭawq al-Ḥamāmah*, chapter 27, ed. Ihsan Abbas, *Rasa'il Ibn Hazm al-Andalusi*, vol. 1, Beirut: Dar al-Kitab al-Arabi.
Heebøll-Holm, Thomas Kristian (2014), "Apocalypse then? The First Crusade, Traumas of War and Thomas de Marle," in Lars Kjær, Niels Lund, and Kerstin Hundahl, eds, *Denmark and Europe in the Middle Ages, c. 1000–1525: Essays in Honour of Professor Michael H. Gelting*, 237–54, Farnham: Ashgate.

Heimann-Seelbach, Sabine (2000), *Ars und scientia. Genese, Überlieferung und Funktionen der mnemotechnischen Traktatliteratur im 15. Jahrhundert. Mit Edition und Untersuchung dreier deutscher Traktate und ihrer lateinischen Vorlagen*, Tübingen: Niemeyer.

Heinzelmann, Martin (1994), *Gregor von Tours (538–594). Zehn Bücher Geschichte: Historiographie und Geschichtskonzept im 6. Jahrhundert*, Darmstadt: Wissenschaftliche Buchgesellschaft.

Herbordi dialogus de vita s. Ottonis episcopi Babenbergensis (1974), eds Jan Wikarjak and Kazmierz Liman, Warszawa, 1974 (Monumenta Poloniae historica, Ser. Nova 7,3).

Hergemöller, Bernd-Ulrich (2007), *Die Freunde des Bösen. Malographie, schwarze Legende und Hate Crime im Mittelalter (Hergemöllers historiographische Libelli)*, Hamburg: HHL-Verlag.

Herrmann, Douglas J. and Roger Chaffin, eds (1988), *Memory in Historical Perspective: The Literature before Ebbinghaus*, New York and Berlin: Springer Verlag.

Herzberg-Fränkel, Siegmund (1904), *Dioecesis Saliburgensis* (Monumenta Germaniae Historica, Necrologia Germaniae 2), Berlin: Weidmann.

Hinz, Berthold (1996), *Das Grabdenkmal Rudolfs von Schwaben. Monument der Propaganda und Paradigma der Gattung*, Frankfurt a.M.: Fischer-Taschenbuch-Verl.

Hlaváček, Ivan (2004), "Dreisprachigkeit im Bereich der Bömischen Krone: Zum Phänomen der Sprachbenutzung im bömischen diplomatischen Material bis zur hussitischen Revolution," in Anna Adamska and Marco Mostert, eds, *The Development of Literate Mentalities in East Central Europe*, 289–310, Turnhout: Brepols.

Hlawitschka, Ernst, Karl Schmid, and Gerd Tellenbach, eds (1970), *Liber Memorialis von Remiremont* (Monumenta Germaniae Historica, Libri memoriales 1), Berlin: Weidmann.

Hoberg, Hermann (1972), *Die Einnahmen der apostolischen Kammer unter Innozenz VI.*, Paderborn: Schöningh.

Hodenberg, Wilhelm von, ed. (1848), *Hoyer Urkundenbuch*, 2. vol., *Archiv des Stiftes Bassum*, Hannover: Jännecke.

Holford, Matthew (2008), "Testimony (To Some Extend Fictitious): Proof of Age in the First Half of the Fifteenth Century," *Historical Research*, 82: 1–25.

Holford, Matthew, ed., (2009), *Vol. xxvi (21–25 Henry VI) (1442–1447)*, London & Woodbridge.

Holford, Matthew, S.A. Mileson, C.B. Noble, and Kate Parkin, eds, (2010), *Vol. xxiv (11–15 Henry VI) (1432–1437)*, London & Woodbridge.

Homans, George Caspar (1975), *English Villagers of the Thirteenth Century*, New York: W.W. Norton.

Horch, Caroline (2001), *Der Memorialgedanke und das Spektrum seiner Funktionen in der Bildenden Kunst des Mittelalters*, Königstein im Taunus: Langewiesche.

Horch, Caroline (2010), "Die Metzer Reiterstatuette als Memorialbild," *Rhein-Maas. Studien zur Geschichte, Sprache und Kultur*, 1: 17–46.

Horch, Caroline (2013), *Nach dem Bild des Kaisers. Funktionen und Bedeutungen des Cappenberger Barbarossakopfes*, Köln: Böhlau.

Horch, Caroline (2014), "*caput argenteum ad imperatoris formatum effigiem* und *crux aurea qua Sancte Johannis nuncupare solebat*. Der Cappenberger Barbarossakopf in seiner Funktion als Reliquiar," in Imgard Siede and Annemarie Stauffer, eds, *Textile Kostbarkeiten staufischer Herrscher. Werkstätten, Bilder, Funktionen. Tagungsband zum internationalen Kolloquium im Rahmen der Ausstellung "Die Staufer und Italien"* Mannheim, 116–31, Petersberg: Imhof.

Horch, Caroline (2018): "Individuum inefffabile est. Individualität und Identität im Mittelalter," in Guido Meyer, Marco A. Sorace, Clara Vasseur, and Johannes Bündgens, eds, *Identitätsbildung. Spiritualität der Wahrnehmung und die Krise der Moderne*, 244–80, Freiburg i.B., München: Herder.

Hugener, Rainer (2013), "Lebendige Bücher: Materielle und mediale Aspekte der Heilsvermittlung in der mittelalterlichen Gedenküberlieferung," in Carmen Cardelle de Hartmann and Susanne Uhl, eds, *Heilige Bücher im Mittelalter*, 122–40, Berlin: Akademie.

Hugener, Rainer (2014a), *Buchführung für die Ewigkeit. Totengedenken, Verschriftlichung und Traditionsbildung im Spätmittelalter*, Zürich: Chronos.

Hugener, Rainer (2014b), "Gestrichen aus dem Buch des Lebens: Tilgungen in der mittelalterlichen Gedenküberlieferung," in Sebastian Scholz, Gerald Schwedler, and Kai Michael Sprenger, eds, *Damnatio in Memoria: Konstruktion und Gegenkonstruktion von Geschichte*, 203–24, Cologne/Weimar/Vienna: Böhlau.

Hughes, John, trans. (1818), *Letters of Abelard and Heloise*, London: Dean and Munday.

Hurwitz, Simeon (1889), *Machsor Vitry*, Berlin: Itzkowski.

Huyghebaert, Nicolas (1972), *Les documents nécrologiques* (Typologie des sources du moyen âge occidental 4), Turnhout: Brepols.

Ilievsky, Petar Hr. (2002–3), "An Iconic Script for Visual Evangelic Preaching," *Illinois Classical Studies*, 27/28: 153–64.

Innes, Matthew (2012), "Historical Writing, Ethnicity, and National Identity: Medieval Europe and Byzantium in Comparison," in Sarah Foot and Chase F. Robinson, eds, *The Oxford History of Historical Writing*, vol. 2: 400–1400, 539–75, Oxford: Oxford University Press.

Iogna-Prat, Dominique (1998), "The Dead in the Celestial Bookkeeping of the Cluniac Monks Around the Year 1000," in Lester K. Little and Barbara H. Rosenwein, eds, *Debating the Middle Ages: Issues and Readings*, 340–62, Malden: Blackwell.

Isidore of Seville ([1911] 1962), *Isidori Hispalensis Episcopi Etymologiarum sive Originum libri XX*, ed. Wallace Martin Lindsay, Oxford: Clarendon Press.

Iwanami, Atsuko (2004), *Memoria et oblivio. Die Entwicklung des Begriffs memoria in Bischofs- und Herrscherurkunden des Hochmittelalters*, Berlin: Duncker & Humblot.

Jacob, Christian (2007), "Introduction: Faire corps, faire lieu," in Christian Jacob, ed., *Lieux de savoir. Espaces et communautés*, 17–41, Paris: Albin Michel.

Jakobi, Franz-Josef (1986), "Diptychen als frühe Form der Gedenk-Aufzeichnungen: Zum Herrscher-Diptychon im Liber Memorialis von Remiremont," *Frühmittelalterliche Studien*, 20: 186–212.

Janeczek, Andrzej (2014), "Urban Communes, Ethnic Communities, and Language Use in Late Medieval Red Ruthenian Towns," in Marco Mostert and Anna Adamska, eds, *Uses of the Written Word in Medieval Towns. Medieval Urban Literacy II*, 19–35, Turnhout: Brepols.

John of Głogów, (1501), *Questiones libror[um] de anima magistri Johannis Versoris*, Metz: Caspar Hochfeder impensis Johannis Haller.

Jungmann, Josef Andreas (1958), *Missarum sollemnia. Eine genetische Erklärung der Römischen Messe*, 2 vols., Freiburg: Herder.

Jussen, Bernhard (2002), "Challenging the Culture of Memoria. Dead Men, Oblivion, and the 'Faithless Widow' in the Middle Ages," in Gerd Althoff, Johannes Fried, and Patrick J. Geary, eds, *Medieval Concepts of the Past. Ritual, Memory, Historiography*, 215–31, Cambridge: Cambridge University Press.

Kaczmarek, Michal (1994), "Rozwój liturgii memoratywnej u cystersów od form prostych do w pełni wykształconego nekrologu." *Nasza prezeszlosc*, 83: 281–93.

Kadlec, Jaroslav (1986), "*Planctus super civitatem Pragensem* a jeho autor," *Studie o rukopisech,* 25: 47–73.
Karlin, Wilhelm, ed. (1855), *Saal-Buch des Benediktiner-Stiftes Göttweig* (Fontes rerum Austriacarum II/8), Vienna: Staatsdruckerei.
Keller, Hagen (1992), "Vom heiligen Buch zur Buchführung: Lebensfunktionen der Schrift im Mittelalter," *Frühmittelalterliche Studien,* 26: 1–31.
à Kempis, Thomas (1848), *De imitatione Christi: Libri quatuor,* Oxford: J.H. Parker.
Kempshall, Matthew (2011), *Rhetoric and the Writing of History: 400–1500,* Manchester: Manchester University Press.
Kervyn de Lettenhove, M., ed. (1867–77), *Œuvres de Froissart, Chroniques,* Bruxelles: Closson; reprint Osnabrück 1967.
Keynes, Simon, ed. (1996), *The Liber vitae of the New Minster and Hyde Abbey Winchester,* British Library Stowe 944, Copenhagen: Rosenkilde & Bagger.
Keyser, Richard (2003), "La transformation de l'échange des dons pieux: Montier-la-Celle, Champagne, 1100–1350," *Revue Historique,* 628: 793–816.
Kilpatrick, Hilary (1991), "Autobiography and Classical Arabic Literature," *Journal of Arabic Literature,* 22: 1–20.
King, Archdale (1959), *The Liturgies of the Past,* London: Longman.
Kinney, Dale (2016), "Managed memory in S. Maria in Trastevere," in Mariette Verhoeven, Lex Bosman, and Hanneke van Asperen, eds, *Monuments & Memory. Christian Cult Buildings and Constructions of the Past. Essays in honour of Sible de Blaauw,* 337–47, Turnout: Brepols.
Kirby, John L., ed. (1970), *Calendar of Inquisitions Post Mortem Vol. xv (1–7 Richard II),* London.
Kirby, John L., ed. (1974), *Vol. xvi (7–15 Richard II),* London.
Kirby, John L., ed. (1987), *Vol. xviii (1–6 Henry IV) (1399–1405),* London.
Kirby, John L., ed. (1988), *Vol. xvii (15–23 Richard II),* London.
Kirby, John L., ed. (1992), *Vol. xix (7–14 Henry IV) (1405–1413),* London.
Kirby, John L., ed. (1995), *Vol. xx (1–5 Henry V) (1413–1418),* London.
Kirby, John L. and Janet A. Stevenson, eds (2001), *Vol. xxi (6–10 Henry V),* London & Woodbridge.
Kiss, Farkas Gábor (2012), "Performing from Memory and Experiencing the Senses in Late Medieval Meditative Practice," *Daphnis,* 41: 419–52.
Kiss, Farkas Gábor et al. (2016a), Paulinus of Skalbmierz (d. 1498). "Populus meus captivus ductus est (before 1498)," in Farkas Gábor Kiss, ed., *The Art of Memory in Late Medieval Central Europe,* Budapest and Paris: L'Harmattan.
Kiss, Farkas Gábor (2016b), "Introduction," in Farkas Gábor Kiss, ed., *The Art of Memory in Late Medieval Central Europe,* 15–8, Paris: L'Harmattan.
Klaniczay, Gábor (2004), "Speaking about Miracles: Oral Testimony and Written Record in Medieval Canonization Trials," in Anna Adamska and Marco Mostert, eds, *The Development of Literate Mentalities in East Central Europe,* 365–95, Turnhout: Brepols.
Klapisch-Zuber, Christiane (2000), *L'ombre des ancêtres. Essai sur l'imaginaire médiéval de la parenté,* Paris: Fayard.
Klemm, Tanja (2013), *Bildphysiologie. Wahrnehmung und Körper in Mittelalter und Renaissance,* Berlin: Akademie.
Knoll, Paul (2016), "A Pearl of Powerful Learning": The University of Cracow in the Fifteenth Century, Leiden: Brill.

Knoll, Paul W. and Frank Schaer, eds (2003), *Gesta principum Polonorum/ The Deeds of the Princes of the Poles*, Budapest, New York: Central European University Press.

Koep, Leo (1952), *Das himmlische Buch in Antike und Christentum: Eine religionsgeschichtliche Untersuchung zur altchristlichen Bildersprache*, Bonn: Hanstein.

Koziol, Geoffrey (2012), *The Politics of Memory and Identity in Carolingian Royal Diplomas: The West Frankish Kingdom (840–987)*, Turnhout: Brepols.

Kraemer, Joel L. (1986), *Humanism in the Renaissance of Islam: The Cultural Revival during the Buyid Age*, Leiden: Brill.

Kranz, Horst and Walter Oberschelp (2009), *Mechanisches Memorieren und Chiffrieren um 1430. Johannes Fontanas Tractatus de instrumentis artis memorie*, Stuttgart: Franz Steiner Verlag.

Krynen, Jaques (1992), "Sur la culture historique des rois: Louis XI et le Rosier des guerres," in Pierre Jaubert and Gérard Aubin, eds, *Liber amicorum*, 399–409, Talence: Presses universitaires de Bordeaux.

Krynen, Jaques (1993), *L'Empire du roi—Idées et croyances politiques en France, XIIIe–XVe siècles*, Paris: Gallimard.

Kuksewicz, Zdzisław (1962), "Le prolongement des polémiques entre les Albertistes et les Thomistes vu à travers le Commentaire du De anima de Jean de Głogów," *Archiv für Geschichte der Philosophie*, 44: 151–71.

Künzle, Pius, ed. (1977), *Heinrich Seuses Horologium sapientiae erste kritische Ausgagbe*, Freiburg: Universitätsverlag.

Kuznetsova, Anna (2006), "New religion, new Letters: Invention of Alphabets in the Lives of Holy Missionaries," in Michael Richter and Ernst Bremer, eds, *Langauge of Religion—Language of the People*, 311–20, München: Wilhelm Fink Verlag.

Kytzler, Bernhard, ed. (1993), *Rom als Idee*, Darmstadt: Wissenschaftliche Buchgesellschaft.

Laager, Jacques, ed. (1996), *Ars moriendi. Die Kunst, gut zu leben und gut zu sterben: Texte von Cicero bis Luther*, Zürich: Manesse Verlag.

Ladurie, Emmanuel Le Roy (1978), *Montaillou: The Promised Land of Error*, trans. Barbara Bray, New York: G. Braziller.

Lake, Justin (2014), "Authorial Intention in Medieval Historiography," *History Compass* 12 (4): 344–360.

Lakoff, Georg and Mark Johnson (1980), *Metaphors We Live By*, Chicago: University of Chicago Press.

Lalou, Élisabeth, ed. (1992), *Les tablettes à écrire de l'antiquité à l'époque moderne*, Turnhout: Brepols.

Landwehr, Achim (2015), "Kulturelles Vergessen. Erinnerung an eine historische Perspektive," *Merkur*, 69/795: 84–92.

Lapidge, Michael and Pierre Monat, eds (2005), *Beda Venerabilis, Histoire ecclésiastique du peuple anglais*, Paris: Les Éditions du Cerf.

Larsson, Inger (2013), "Nordic digraphia and diglossia," in Mary Garrison et al., eds, *Spoken and Written Language. Relations between Latin and the Vernacular Languages in the Earlier Middle Ages*, 73–85, Turnhout: Brepols.

Lauer, Philippe, ed. (1926), *Histoire des fils de Louis le Pieux*, Paris: Les Belles Lettres.

Lauwers, Michel (1997), *La mémoire des ancêtres, le souci des morts: Morts, rites et société au Moyen Âge (diocèse de Liège, XIe–XIIIe siècles)*, Paris: Beauchesne.

Lauwers, Michel (2003), "Memoria: A propos d'un objet d'histoire en Allemagne," in Jean-Claude Schmitt and Otto Gerhard Oexle, eds, *Les tendances actuelles de l'histoire du Moyen Age en France et en Allemagne: Actes des colloques de Sèvres (1997) et Göttingen (1998)*, 105–26, Paris: Publications de la Sorbonne.

Le Goff, Jacques (1984), *The Birth of Purgatory*, Chicago/London: University of Chicago Press.
Le Goff, Jacques (1992), *History and Memory*, New York: Columbia University Press.
Leclerq, Jean, Henri Rochais, eds (1970), *Sancti Bernardi Opera*, vol. VI/1, Rome: Editiones Cistercienses.
Lemaître, Jean-Loup (1980), *Répertoire des documents nécrologiques français* (Recueil des historiens de la France, obituaires 7), Paris: Imprimerie Nationale.
Lemaître, Jean-Loup (1988), "Un livre vivant: l'obituaire," in Jean Glénisson, ed., *Le livre au Moyen Age*, 92–4, Paris: Presses du CNRS.
Lemaître, Jean-Loup (2001), "Des Libri memoriales aux obituaires," in Olivier Dumoulin and Françoise Thelamon, eds, *Autour des morts: Mémoire et identité*, 221–31, Rouen: Publications de l'Université de Rouen.
Lempges, Anja (2017), *Der Atzmann. Stummer Diener für lautes Lob*, Regensburg: Universität Mainz
Liber Pontificalis (1892), Vol. 2, ed. Louis Duchesne, Paris.
Lifshitz, Felice (2000), "Bede, Martyrology," in Thomas Head, ed., *Medieval Hagiography: An Anthology*, 169–77, New York: Garland.
Liljegren, Johann Gustav, ed. (1834), *Svenskt diplomatarium. Åren 1286–1299, no. 903–1300*, vol. II (1), Stockholm: Norstedt.
Lindsay, Wallace, ed. (1911), *Isidore de Séville, Etymologiae*, Oxford: Oxford University Press.
Little, Lester K. (1975), "Formules monastiques de malédiction au IX et X siècles," *Revue Mabillon*, 58: 377–99.
Lobrichon, Guy (1998), *1099—Jérusalem Conquise*, Paris: Seuil.
Lohse, Tillmann (2011), *Die Dauer der Stiftung: Eine diachronisch vergleichende Geschichte des weltlichen Kollegiatstifts St. Simon und Judas in Goslar*, Berlin: Akademie.
Lombard, Peter (1576), *Aureum sacrae theologiae rosarium*, vol. 1, Venice: Ziletti.
Longo, Umberto (2012), "A Saint of Damned Memory. Clement III. (Anti)Pope," in Umberto Longo and Lila Yawn, eds, *Framing Clement III (anti)pope, 1080–1100, Reti Medievali Rivista*, 13 (1): 1–119.
Lowe, Elias Avery (1917), *The Bobbio Missal: A Gallican Mass-Book*, London: Harrison & Sons.
Lubomirski, Jan T., ed. (1863), *Kodeks dyplomatyczny księstwa Mazowieckiego*, Warsaw: Gazeta Polska.
Luce, Siméon, ed. (1869), *Jean Froissart, Chroniques, 1*, Paris: Librairie Renouard.
Ludwig, Uwe (2009), "L'Evangeliario di Cividale come liber vitae: Osservazioni sulle note commemorative nel Codex Forojuliensis," in Gilberto Ganzer, ed., *L'Evangeliario di San Marco*, 107–34, Udine: Gaspari.
Luhmann, Niklas (1997), "Gedächtnis," in Niklas Luhmann, ed., *Die Gesellschaft der Gesellschaft*, 576–94, Frankfurt a. M.: Suhrkamp.
Lusiardi, Ralf (2000), *Stiftung und städtische Gesellschaft: Religiöse und soziale Aspekte des Stiftungsverhaltens im spätmittelalterlichen Stralsund*, Berlin: De Gruyter.
MacLuhan, Marshall (1962), *The Gutenberg Galaxy: The Making of Typographic Man*, Toronto: University of Toronto Press.
Magee, James F., ed. (1910), *Good Companion (Bonus socius). XIIIth Century Manuscript Collection of Chess Problems*, Florence: Tipografia Giuntina.
Magee, John F. (2009), "The Good and Morality. Consolatio 2–4," in John Marenbon, ed., *The Cambridge Companion to Boethius*, Cambridge: Cambridge University Press.
Magnani Soares-Christen, Eliana (2003), "Transforming Things and Persons: The Gift pro anima in the Eleventh and Twelfth Centuries," in Gadi Algazi, Valentin Groebner, and

Bernhard Jussen, eds, *Negotiating the Gift: Pre-Modern Figurations of Exchange*, 269–84, Göttingen: Vandenhoeck & Ruprecht.

Maierù, Alfonso (1987), *Grafia e interpunzione del Latino nel Medioevo*, Roma: Olschiki.

Maimonides (1957), *Teshuvot ha-Rambam*, ed. Joshua Blau, vol. 1, Jerusalem: Mekize Nirdamim.

Manzoni, Tullio (1998), "The cerebral ventricles, the animal spirits and the dawn of brain localization of function," *Archives Italiennes de Biologie*, 136 (2): 103–52.

Marache, René and Yvette Julien, eds (1967), *Aulu-Gelle, Nuits Attiques*, Paris: Les Belles Lettres.

Marchal, Guy P. (2001), "De la mémoire communicative à la mémoire culturelle: Le passé dans les témoignages d'Arezzo et de Sienne (1177–1180)," *Annales. Histoire, Sciences Sociales*, 56 (3): 563–89.

Margalit, Avishai (2002), *The Ethics of Memory*, London: Harvard University Press.

Marshall, Peter (2002), *Beliefs and the Dead in Reformation England*, Oxford: Oxford University Press.

Marsham, Andrew (2012), "Universal Histories in Christendom and the Islamic World c. 700–c. 1400," in Sarah Foot and Chase F. Robinson, eds, *The Oxford History of Historical Writing*, vol. 2: *400–1400*, 431–56, Oxford: Oxford University Press.

Marsina, Richard (1971), "Die Arengen in ungarischen Urkunden bis zum Jahre 1235," *Folia diplomatica*, 1: 215–25.

Marsina, Richard, ed. (1971), *Codex diplomaticus et epistolaris Slovaciae*, vol. I, Bratislava: SAV.

Martindale, John R. (1980), *The Prosopography of the Later Roman Empire*, vol. 2, Cambridge: Cambridge University Press.

Martínez Pizarro, Joaquín (2003), "Ethnic and National History, ca. 500–1000," in Deborah M. Deliyannis, ed., *Historiography in the Middle Ages*, 44–87, Leiden: Brill.

Martinez-Gros, Gabriel (2013), "Ibn Hazm on History: A Few Remarks," in Camilla Adang, Maribel Fierro, and Sabine Schmidtke, eds, *Ibn Hazm of Cordoba: The Life and the Works of a Controversial Thinker* (Handbook of Oriental Studies, Series 1, vol. 103), 87–94, Leiden: Brill.

Martino, Carla di (2006), "Memoria dicitur multipliciter. L'apporto della scienza psicologica araba al medioevo latino," in Maria M. Sassi, ed., *Tracce nella mente. Teorie della memoria da Platone ai moderni*, 119–37, Pisa: Edizioni della Normale.

Martino, Carla di (2008), *Ratio particularis. La doctrine des sens internes d'Avicenne à Thomas d'Aquin*, 123–38, Paris: Vrin.

Maturantius Perusinus, Franciscus, ed. (1496), *M.T. Cicero, Rhetoricorum libri cum tribus commentis*, Venice: Philippus Pincius.

Mauskopf Deliyannis, Deborah, ed. (2003), *Historiography in the Middle Ages*, Leiden: Brill.

McCulloh, John (1983), "Historical Martyrologies in the Benedictine Tradition," in William Lourdaux and Daniel Verhelst, eds, *Benedictine Culture, 750–1050*, 114–31, Louvain: Louvain University Press.

McGlynne, Margaret (2009), "Memory, Orality and Life Records: Proofs of Age in Tudor England," *Sixteenth Century Journal*, 40 (3): 679–97.

McKitterick, Rosamond (1989), *The Carolingians and the Written Word*, Cambridge: Cambridge University Press.

McKitterick, Rosamond (2004), *History and Memory in the Carolingian World*, Cambridge: Cambridge University Press.

McKitterick, Rosamond (2015), "Transformations of the Roman Past and Roman Identity in the early Middle Ages," in Clemens Gantner et al., eds, *The Resources of the Past in Early Medieval Europe*, 225–44, Cambridge: Cambridge University Press.
McLaughlin, Megan (1994), *Consorting with Saints: Prayer for the Dead in Early Medieval France*, Ithaca, NY: Cornell University Press.
McNamer, Sarah (2009), *Affective Meditation and the Invention of Medieval Compassion*, Philadelphia: University of Pennsylvania Press.
Meyer, Jesse (2013), "Parchment Production: a Brief Account," in Jonathan Wilcox, ed., *Scraped, Stroked and Bound: Materially Engaged Readings of Medieval Manuscripts*, 93–6, Turnhout: Brepols.
Michaud-Quentin, Pierre (1949), "La classification des puissances de l'âme au XIIe siècle," *Revue du Moyen Âge latin*, 5: 15–34.
Minnis, Alaister (2005), "Medieval Imagination and Memory," in Alaister Minnis and Ian Johnson, eds, *The Cambridge History of Literary Criticism*, vol. 2: *The Middle Ages*, 239–74, Cambridge: Cambridge University Press.
Moddelmog, Claudia (2012), *Königliche Stiftungen des Mittelalters im historischen Wandel: Quedlinburg und Speyer, Königsfelden, Wiener Neustadt und Andernach*, Berlin: Akadamie.
Moeglin, Jean-Marie (1993), *Dynastisches Bewußtsein und Geschichtsschreibung. Zum Selbstverständnis der Wittelsbacher, Habsburger und Hohenzollern im Spätmittelalter*, München: Stiftung Historisches Kolleg.
Moeglin, Jean-Marie (2002), "Hat das Mittelalter europäische *lieux de mémoire* erzeugt?" *Jahrbuch für Europäische Geschichte*, 3: 17–37.
Moeglin, Jean-Marie (2005), "La mémoire d'un héros fondateur. Lidéric forestier et comte de Flandre," in Agostino Paravicini Bagliani, ed., *La mémoire du temps au moyen âge*, 87–116, Firenze: SISMEL.
Moeglin, Jean-Marie (2006), "Froissart, le métier d'historien et l'invention de la guerre de cent ans," *Romania* 124: 429–70.
Moeglin, Jean-Marie (2012), "Von Hermann von Niederalteich zu Aventin," in Alois Schmid and Ludwig Holzfurtner, eds, *Studien zur bayerischen Landesgeschichtsschreibung in Mittelalter und Neuzeit—Festgabe für Andreas Kraus zum 90. Geburtstag* (Zeitschrift für bayerische Landesgeschichte 41), 117–49, München: Beck.
Mommsen, Theodor, ed. (1894), *Cassiodorus Senator, Variae*, (Monumenta Germaniae Historica, Auctores antiquissimi 12), Berlin: Weidmann.
Monumenta Germaniae Historica. All editions can be accessed online: <https://www.dmgh.de>.
Moos, Peter von (1996), *Geschichte als Topik. Das rhetorische Exemplum von der Antike zur Neuzeit und die historiae im 'Policraticus' Johanns von Salisbury*, Köln, Hildesheim: Olms.
Morlet, Sébastien and Lorenzo Perrone, eds. (2012), *Eusèbe de Césarée. Histoire ecclésiastique. Commentaire, 1. Études d'introduction* (Anagôgé 6), Paris: Les Belles Lettres.
Morris, Colin M. (1972), *The Discovery of the Individual, 1050–1200*, New York: Harper & Row.
Mosley, James (2013), "The Technologies of Print," in Michael F. Suarez, ed., *The Book. A Global History*, 130–53, Oxford: Oxford University Press.
Mostert, Marco (1995), "What happened to literacy in the Middle Ages? Scriptural evidence for the history of the western literate mentality," *Tijdschrift voor Geschiedenis*, 108: 323–35.
Mostert, Marco (2008), "Forgery and Trust," in Petra Schulte et al., eds, *Strategies of Writing: Studies on Text and Trust in the Middle Ages. Papers from 'Trust in Writing in the Middle Ages*, 37–59, Turnhout: Brepols.
Mostert, Marco (2011), "Using and Keeping Written Texts: Reading and Writing as Forms of Communication in the Early Middle Ages," *Scrivere et leggere nell'alto Medioevo*, vol. 1

(Settimane di Spoleto 2011), 71–94, Spoleto: Fondazione Centro Italiano di Studi su'll Alto Medioevo.
Mostert, Marco (2012), *A Bibliography of Works on Medieval Communication*, Turnhout: Brepols.
Mostert, Marco and Paul S. Barnwell, eds (2011), *Medieval Legal Process Physical, Spoken and Written Performance in the Middle Ages*, Turnhout: Brepols.
Mostert, Marco and Anna Adamska, eds. (2014a), *Writing and the Administration of Medieval Towns. Medieval Urban Literacy I*, Turnhout: Brepols.
Mostert, Marco and Anna Adamska, eds. (2014b), *Uses of the Written Word in Medieval Towns. Medieval Urban Literacy II*, Turnhout: Brepols.
Muckle, Joseph T., ed. (1933), *Al-Ghazali, Algazel's Metaphysics. A Mediaeval Translation*, Toronto: St. Michael's College.
Munier, Charles, ed. (1963), *Concilia Galliae 314–506*, Turnhout: Brepols.
Mütherich, Florentine (1965), "Die Reiterstatuette aus der Metzer Kathedrale," in Kurt Martin et al., eds, *Studien zur Geschichte der europäischen Plastik. Fs. f. Theodor Müller z. 80. Geb.*, 9–16, München: Hirmer.
Nagy, Balázs and Frank Schaer, eds (2001), *Autobiography of Emperor Charles IV; And, His Legend of St. Wenceslas: Karoli IV Imperatoris Romanorum Vita Ab Eo Ipso Conscripta; Et, Hystoria Nova de Sancto Wenceslao Martyre*, Budapest: Central European University Press.
Neiske, Franz (1996), "Cisterziensische Generalkapitel und individuelle Memoria," in Gert Melville, ed., *De ordinae vitae: Zu Normvorstellungen, Organisationsformen und Schriftgebrauch im mittelalterlichen Ordenswesen*, 260–83, Münster: Lit.
Neiske, Franz (1997), "Funktion und Praxis der Schriftlichkeit im klösterlichen Totengedenken," in Clemens M. Kasper and Klaus Schreiner, eds, *Viva vox und ratio scripta: Mündliche und schriftliche Kommunikationsformen im Mönchtum des Mittelalters*, 97–118, Münster: Lit.
Neiske, Franz (2009), "Die Ordnung der Memoria. Formen necrologischer Tradition im mittelalterlichen Klosterverband," in Franz J. Felten, Annette Kehnel, and Stefan Weinfurter, eds, *Institution und Charisma: Festschrift für Gert Melville*, 127–38, Cologne: Böhlau.
Neuber, Wolfgang (2001), "Memoria," in Gert Ueding, ed., *Historisches Wörterbuch der Rhetorik, 5*: 1037–78, Tübingen: Niemeyer.
Neumüllers-Klauser, Renate (1997), "Von der Memoria zum Grabdenkmal: Zum Bedeutungswandel des Totengedenkens im 13. Jahrhundert," in Hans-Joachim Krause, ed., *Festschrift für Ernst Schubert: Zur Kunst des 13. Jahrhunderts in Mitteldeutschland*, 257–86, Weimar: Böhlau.
Newman, Barbara (2016), *Making Love in the Twelfth Century. "Letters of Two Lovers" in Context*, Philadelphia: University of Pennsylvania Press.
Niemeyer, Jan F. and Co van de Kieft (2002), *Mediae Latinitatis lexicon minus*, Darmstadt Wissenschaftliche Buchgesellschaft.
Nikulin, Dmitri (2015), *Memory. A History*, Oxford: Oxford University Press.
Noble, Claire, ed. (2004), *Vol. xxiii (6–10 Henry VI) (1427–1432)*, London & Woodbridge.
Noble, Claire, ed. (2009), *Vol. xxv (16–20 Henry VI) (1437–1442)*, London & Woodbridge.
Nospickel, Johannes, ed. (2004), *Das Necrolog des Klosters Michelsberg in Bamberg*, Hannover: Hahn.
Notae sepulcrales Babenbergenses, in MGH SS 17, ed. Heinrich Pertz, Stuttgart 1990, 640–2.
Novikoff, Alex J., ed. (2016), *The Twelfth Century Renaissance: A Reader*, Toronto: University of Toronto Press.

Nuffelen, Peter van (2012), *Orosius and the Rhetoric of History*, Oxford: Oxford University Press.
Nuffelen, Peter van (2018), "Ecclesiastical historiography," in Scott McGill and Edward Watts, eds, *A Companion to Late Antique Literature*, 161–75, New York: Wiley Blackwell.
O'Donnell, James (2004), "Memoria," *Augustinuslexikon*, 3: 1249–57, Basel: Schwabe AG.
Odstrčilík, Jan (2013), "Poučení o správném způsobu studia ve středověkém traktátu De modulo studendi (VK Olomouc, M I 357)," (Teaching the correct was of studying in medieval treatise De modulo studendi), *Acta Universitatis Carolinae: Historia Universitatis Carolinae Pragensis: Příspěvky k dějinám Univerzity Karlovy*, 53 (2): 23–39.
Oelze, Anselm (2017), *Animal Rationality. Later Medieval Theories, 1250–1350*, Leiden: Brill.
Oexle, Otto Gerhard (1976), "Memoria und Memorialüberlieferung im früheren Mittelalter," *Frühmittelalterliche Studien*, 10: 70–95.
Oexle, Otto Gerhard (1983), "Die Gegenwart der Toten," in Herman Braet and Werner Verbeke, eds, *Death in the Middle Ages*, 19–77, Louvain: Louvain University Press.
Oexle, Otto Gerhard (1984), "Memoria und Memorialbild," in Karl Schmid and Joachim Wollasch, eds, *Memoria. Der geschichtliche Zeugniswert des liturgischen Gedenkens im Mittelalter. Sonderforschungsbereich Mittelalterforschung. Colloquium*, 384–440, München: Fink.
Oexle, Otto Gerhard (1995a), "Memoria als Kultur," in Otto Gerhard Oexle, ed., *Memoria als Kultur*, 9–78, Göttingen: Vandenhoeck und Ruprecht.
Oexle, Otto Gerhard (1995b), "Fama und Memoria: Legitimationen fürstlicher Herrschaft im 12. Jahrhundert," in Jochen Luckhardt, Franz Niehoff, and Gerd Biegel, ed., *Heinrich der Löwe und seine Zeit: Herrschaft und Repräsentation der Welfen 1125–1235*, vol. 2, 62–8, Munich: Hirmer.
Oexle, Otto Gerhard (1996), "Individuum und Erinnerungskultur im 13. Jahrhundert, oder: Wie man eine moderne Biographie schreibt," *Rechtshistorisches Journal*, 15: 44–50.
Oexle, Otto Gerhard (2009), "Memoria. Institutionalisierung und Kulturelles Gedächtnis," in Birgit Lodes and Laurenz Lütteken, eds, *Institutionalisierung als Prozeß—Organisationsformen musikalischer Eliten im Europa des 15. und 16. Jahrhunderts*, 15–54, Laaber: Laaber-Verlag.
Ohly, Friedrich (1984), "Bemerkungen eines Philologen zur Memoria," in Karl Schmid and Joachim Wollasch (eds), *Memoria: Der geschichtliche Zeugniswert des liturgischen Gedenkens im Mittelalter*, 9–68, Munich: Wilhelm Fink.
Ohly, Friedrich (2005), "A philologist's remarks on memoria," in Samuel Peter Jaffe, ed., *Sensus spiritualis. Studies in Medieval Significs and the Philology of Culture*, 285–369, Chicago: University of Chicago Press.
Olick, Jeffrey K. et al., eds (2011), *The Collective Memory Reader*, New York: Oxford University Press.
Orme, Nicholas (1995), "The Culture of Children in Medieval England," *Past and Present*, 148 (1): 48–88.
Ortalli, Gherardo (1979), "*. . . pingatur in Palatio . . .*". *La pittura infamante nei secoli XII–XVI*, Rome: Jouvence.
Ortalli, Gherardo (2013), *La pittura infamante nei secoli XIII–XVI*, Rome: Viella.
Oxford, Bodleian Library, MS Pococke 295.
Pack, Roger A. (1980), "An Ars Memorativa," *Archives d'Histoire Doctrinale et Littéraire du Moyen Âge*, 46: 221–75.
Page, Raymond I. (2014), "Runes," in Michael Lapidge, et al., eds, *The Wiley Blackwell Encyclopedia of Anglo-Saxon England*, 414–15, Hoboken: Wiley.

Palazzo, Éric (1998), *A History of Liturgical Books from the Beginning to the Thirteenth Century*, Collegeville: Liturgical Press.

Paniagua, Juan A. and Pedro Gil-Sotres, eds (1993), *Arnaldus de Villa Nova, Commentum in quasdam parabolas et alias aphorismorum series. Aphorismi particulares, Aphorismi de memoria, Aphorismi extravagantes* (Opera medica omnia, vol. VI/2), Barcelona: Universitat de Barcelona.

Parkin, Kate, ed. (2003), *Vol. xxii (1–5 Henry VI)(1422–1427)*, London & Woodbridge.

Parshall, Peter (1999), "The Art of Memory and the Passion," *Art Bulletin*, 81: 456–72.

Pethes, Nicolas (2008), *Kulturwissenschaftliche Gedächtnistheorien zur Einführung*, Hamburg: Junius-Verlag.

Petrarca, Francesco (2016), *My Secret Book*, ed. and trans. Nicholas Mann, Cambridge, MA: Harvard University Press.

Petrucci, Armando (1998), *Writing the Dead: Death and Writing Strategies in the Western Tradition*, Stanford: Stanford University Press.

Piekosiński, Franciszek (1886), *Kodeks dyplomatyczny małopolski*, vol. 2, Cracow: Akademia umiejętności.

Piper, Paul, ed. (1884), *Libri confraternitatum Sancti Galli, Augiensis, Fabariensis* (Monumenta Germaniae Historica, Necrologia Germaniae, Suppl.), Berlin: Weidmann.

Pini, Antonia Ivan (1997), "Le bolle di Gregorio VII (1074) e di Pasquale II (1114) alla chiesa Bolognese," *Atti e memorie (Romagna)*, 48: 345–86.

Plassmann, Alheydis (2007), "Mittelalterliche *origines gentium*. Paulus Diaconus als Beispiel," *Quellen und Forschungen aus italienischen Archiven und Bibliotheken*, 87: 1–35.

Plummer, Charles, ed. (1892–9), *Two of the Saxon Chronicles Parallel. With Supplementary Extracts from the Others*, 2 vols, Oxford: Oxford University Press.

Pohl, Walter (2008), "Rome and the Barbarians in the Fifth Century," *Antiquité Tardive*, 16: 93–101.

Pomerance, Aubrey (2000), "Bekannt in den Toren: Name und Nachruf in Memorbüchern," in Sabine Hödl and Eleonore Lappin, eds, *Erinnerung als Gegenwart: Jüdische Gedenkkulturen*, 33–53, Berlin/Vienna: Philo.

Pomerance, Aubrey (2012), "Die Memorbücher der jüdischen Gemeinden in Franken," in Michael Brenner and Daniela F. Eisenstein, eds, *Die Juden in Franken*, 95–114, Munich: Oldenbourg.

Praha, Národní knihovna České republiky, MS XI C 8.

Prinz, Otto (1936–66), "Memoria," *Thesaurus Linguae Latinae*, 8: 665–84, Lipsiae: Teubner.

Raab, Isidor, ed. (1870), *Urkundenbuch des Benediktiner-Stiftes Seitenstetten*, Vienna: Holzhausen.

Raesaenen, Marika, Gritje Hartmann, and Earl J. Richards, eds (2016), *Relics, Identity, and Memory in Medieval Europe*, Turnhout: Brepols.

Rapp, Joseph (1827), "Über das vaterländische Statutenwesen," *Beiträge zur Geschichte, Statistik und Naturkunde und Kunst von Tirol und Vorarlberg*, 3: 1–116.

Rappmann, Roland and Alfons Zettler (1998), *Die Reichenauer Mönchsgemeinschaft und ihr Totengedenken im frühen Mittelalter*, Sigmaringen: Thorbecke.

Rebhan, Johann (1656), *Hodegeta Ivris, Chartis brevibus viam scientiæ legitimæ simplicem atque rectam designans & edocens*, Strasburg.

Recueil des Historiens des croisades, Historiens occidentaux, III, 1866, Paris: Académie des Inscriptions et Belles-Lettres.

Redeker, Franz (1917), *Die "Anatomia magistri Nicolai physici" und ihr Verhältnis zur Anatomia Cophonis und Richardi*, Leipzig: Noske.

Reichersberg, Gerhoch von (1897), *De investigatione Antichristi* I,40, ed. Sackur, Vol. 3, Hannover.

Reik, Theodor (1920), "Über kollektives Vergessen," *Intern. Zeitschrift für Psychoanalyse*, 6: 202–15.

Reimitz, Helmut (2004), "Die Konkurrenz der Ursprünge in der fränkischen Historiographie," in Walter Pohl (ed), *Die Suche nach den Ursprüngen. Von der Bedeutung des frühen Mittelalters*, 191–209, Wien: Verlag der österreichischen Akademi der Wissenschaften.

Remensnyder, Amy G. (1995), *Remembering Kings Past: Monastic Foundation Legends in Medieval Southern France*, Ithaca, NY: Cornell University Press.

Rexroth, Frank (1994), "Armut und Memoria im spätmittelalterlichen London," in Dieter Geuenich and Otto Gerhard Oexle, eds, *Memoria in der Gesellschaft des Mittelalters*, 336–60, Göttingen: Vandenhoeck & Ruprecht.

Reynolds, Dwight F., Kristen E. Brustad, Michael Cooperson, et al. (2001), *Interpreting the Self: Autobiography in the Arabic Literary Tradition*, Berkeley: University of California Press.

Richard, Jean (2002), "Le plurilinguisme dans les actes de l'Orient latin," in Olivier Guyotjeannin, ed., *La langue des actes. Actes du XI Congrès international de la diplomatique (Troyes, jeudi 11–samedi 13 septembre 2003)*: no pagination. Available online: http://elec.enc.sorbonne.fr/CID2003/richard (accessed January 1, 2019).

Rider, Jeff (2000), "Like Lambs to the Slaughter: Improvising Murder in the Twelfth Century," unpublished paper delivered at IMC Leeds.

Riet, Simone van, ed. (1972): *Avicenna, Liber de anima seu Sextus de naturalibus*, Leiden: Brill.

Rigon, Antonio, ed. (2010), *Condannare all'oblio. Pratiche della damnatio memoriae nel Medioevo. Atti del convegno di studio svoltosi in occasione della XX edizione del Premio internazionale Ascoli Piceno*, Rome: Istituto storico italiano per il Medio Evo.

Rischpler, Susanne (2004), "Le cœur voyant. Mémoriser les Sentences de Pierre Lombard," in Frank Willaert et al., eds, *Medieval Memory. Image and Text*, 3–40, Turnhout: Brepols.

Rischpler, Susanne (2013), "Gedruckt und gezeichnet. Das Blockbuch 'Ars memorandi' und seine handschriftlichen Zeugen," in Bettina Wagner, ed., *Blockbücher des 15. Jahrhunderts. Eine Experimentierphase im frühen Buchdruck. Beiträge der Fachtagung in der Bayerischen Staatsbibliothek München am 16. und 17. Februar 2012*, 215–54, Wiesbaden: Harrassowitz.

Rivers, Kimberly (2010), *Preaching the Memory of Virtue and Vice: Memory, Images and Preaching in the Late Middle Ages*, Turnhout: Brepols.

Robinson, Olivia F., T. David Fergus, and William M. Gordon (1985), *An Introduction to European Legal History*, Abingdon: Professional Books Ltd.

Robson, Michael (2002), "The Grey Friars in York, c. 1450–1530," in James G. Clark, ed., *The Religious Orders in Pre-Reformation England*, Woodbridge: Boydell Press.

Robson, Michael (2006), *The Franciscans in the Middle Ages*, Woodbridge: Boydell Press.

Roffe, David (2016), "Talking to Others and Talking to Itself: Government and the Changing Role of the Records of the Domesday Inquest," in David Roffe, ed., *Domesday Now: New Approaches to the Inquest and the Book*, 289–303, Woodbridge: The Boydell Press.

Rollason, David, A.J. Piper, and Margaret Harvey, eds (2004), *The Durham Liber Vitae and its Context*, Woodbridge: Boydell Press.

Rollason, David, Lynda Rollason, eds (2007), *The Durham Liber Vitae*, 3 vols., London: British Library.

Romberch, Johannes (1520), *Congestorium artificiose memorie*, Venice: Georgius de Rusconibus.

Ronca, Italo, ed. (1977), *William of Conches, Dragmaticon philosophiae*, Turnhout: Brepols.
Ronca, Italo and Matthew Curr, trans. (1997), *William of Conches, A Dialogue on Natural Philosophy*, Notre Dame, IN: University of Notre Dame Press.
Rosenthal, Joel T. (2018), *Social Memory in Late Medieval England: Village Life and Proofs of Age*, New York: Palgrave-Macmillan.
Ross, Leslie (1996), *Medieval Art: A Topical Dictionary*, Westport/London: Greenwood Press.
Rossignol, Sébastien (2016), "Introduction: Text and Context—Preamble and Formulary," in Sébastien Rossignol and Anna Adamska, eds, *Urkundenformeln im Kontext. Formen der Schriftkultur im Ostmitteleuropa des Mittelalters*, 19–34, Vienna: Böhlau.
Rowan, John P., trans. (1961), St. Thomas Aquinas, *Commentary on the Metaphysics of Aristotle*. Chicago: Henry Regnery.
Rück, Peter (1971), "Die Ordnung der herzoglich savoyischen Archive unter Amadeus VIII. (1398–1451)," *Archivalische Zeitschrift*, 67: 11–101.
Rück, Peter, ed. (1991), *Pergament: Geschichte, Struktur, Restaurierung, Herstellung*, Sigmaringen: Thorbecke.
S. Augustine (1981), *Aureli Augvstini Confessionum libri XIII*, ed. Martin Skutella, ed. corr. curaverunt H. Juergens and W. Schaub, Studgardiae, Bibliotheca scriptorum Graecorum et Romanorum Teubnerianae.
Salernitanus, Richardus (1907), "Anatomia," in Ignaz Schwarz, ed., *Die medizinischen Handschriften der K. Universitätsbibliothek in Würzburg*, 77–92, Würzburg: Scheiner.
Sassoon, Solomon D., ed. (1956), *Maimonidis Commentarius in Mischnam*, Copenhagen: E. Munksgaard.
Sauer, Wilhelm, ed. (1886), *Nassauisches Urkundenbuch*, vol. 1., *Die Urkunden des ehemals Kurmainzischen Gebiets*, Wiesbaden: Niedner.
Schaeken, Jos (2012), "The Birchbark Documents in Time and Space—Revisited," in Kristel Zilmer and Judit Jesch, eds, *Epigraphic Literacy and Christian Identity*, 201–24, Turnhout: Brepols.
Schmale, Franz-Josef, ed. (1965), *Otto episcopi Frisingensis et Rahewini, Gesta Friderici seu rectius Cronica*, Darmstadt: Wissenschaftliche Buchgesellschaft.
Schmale, Franz-Josef (1988), "Fälschungen in der Geschichtsschreibung," in *Fälschungen im Mittelalter*, Vol. 5, 121–32, Hannover: Hahn.
Schmid, Karl, ed. (1985), *Gedächtnis, das Gemeinschaft stiftet*, Munich/Zürich: Schnell & Steiner.
Schmid, Karl and Joachim Wollasch (1967), "Die Gemeinschaft der Lebenden und der Verstorbenen in den Zeugnissen des Mittelalters," *Frühmittelalterliche Studien*, 1: 365–405.
Schmid, Karl and Otto Gerhard Oexle (1974), "Voraussetzungen und Wirkung des Gebetsbundes von Attigny," *Francia*, 2: 71–122.
Schmidt, Tilmann (2006), "La condamnation de Pierre Flote par le pape Boniface VIII," *Mélanges de l'Ecole française de Rome. Moyen Âge*, 118: 109–22.
Schmitt, Jean-Claude (1993), "Bilder als Erinnerung und Vorstellung. Die Erscheinungen der Toten im Mittelalter," *Historische Anthropologie*, 1: 347–58.
Schmitt, Jean-Claude (1998), *Ghosts in the Middle Ages: The Living and the Dead in Medieval Society*, Chicago: University of Chicago Press.
Schmitt, Jean-Claude (2013), "Images and the Work of Memory, with Special Reference to the Sixth-Century Mosaic of Ravenna, Italy," in Elma Brenner, Meredith Cohen, and Mary Franklin-Brown, eds, *Memory and Commemoration in Medieval Culture*, 13–32, Farnham: Ashgate.

Schmitz-Esser, Romedio (2007), *Arnold von Brescia im Spiegel von acht Jahrhunderten Rezeption. Ein Beispiel für Europas Umgang mit der mittelalterlichen Geschichte vom Humanismus bis heute*, Münster: LIT.

Schnürer, Gustav, ed. (1909), *Das Necrologium des Cluniazenser-Priorates Münchenwiler*, Fribourg: Collectanea Friburgensia.

Scholz, Sebastian (1992), *Transmigration und Translation. Studien zum Bistumswechsel der Bischöfe von der Spätantike bis zum hohen Mittelalter*, Köln: Böhlau.

Scholz, Sebastian (1998), "Das Grab in der Kirche. Zu seinen theologischen und rechtlichen Hintergründen in Spätantike und Frühmittelalter," *Zeitschrift der Savigny-Stiftung für Rechstgeschichte: Kanonistische Abteilung*, 84: 270–306.

Scholz, Sebastian (1999), "Totengedenken in mittelalterlichen Grabinschriften vom 5. bis zum 15. Jahrhundert," *Marburger Jahrbuch für Kunstwissenschaft*, 26: 37–59.

Scholz, Sebastian, Gerald Schwedler, and Kai Michael Sprenger, eds (2014), *Damnatio in memoria: Deformation und Gegenkonstruktionen in der Geschichte. Tagung am Historischen Seminar der Universität Zürich vom 23. September bis 25. September 2010*, Köln, Weimar, Wien: Böhlau.

Schuffels, Christian (2012), *Das Brunograbmal im Dom zu Hildesheim. Kunst und Geschichte einer romanischen Skulptur*, Regensburg: Schnell and Steiner.

Schuler, Peter-Johannes (1987), "Das Anniversar: Zu Mentalität und Familienbewusstsein im Spätmittelalter," in Peter-Johannes Schuler, ed., *Die Familie als sozialer und historischer Verband: Untersuchungen zum Spätmittelalter und zur frühen Neuzeit*, 67–117, Sigmaringen: Thorbecke.

Schulte, Petra et al., eds (2008), *Strategies of Writing. Studies on Text and Trust in the Middle Ages*, Turnhout: Brepols.

Schunk, Johann Peter, ed. (1778–80), *Beyträge zur Mainzer Geschichte mit Urkunden*, Book I–III, Mainz.

Schutz, Herbert (2004), *The Carolingians in Central Europe, their History, Arts, and Architecture: A Cultural History of Central Europe, 750–900*, Leiden: Brill.

Schur, Yechiel Y. (2008), *The Care for the Dead in Medieval Ashkenaz, 1000–1500*, New York: New York University.

Schuster, Beate (2000), "Comment comprendre les récits de la première croisade? À propos de 1099—Jérusalem Conquise, de Guy Lobrichon," *Médiévales* 39: 153–68.

Schwarz, Ignaz, ed. (1907), *Die medizinischen Handschriften der K. Universitätsbibliothek in Würzburg*, Würzburg: Scheiner.

Schwedler, Gerald (2011), "'dampnate memorie Ludovici de Bavaria'. Erinnerungsvernichtung als metaphorische Waffe im Konflikt zwischen der Kure und Kaiser Ludwig dem Bayern," in Claudia Garnier, ed., *Sterben über den Tod hinaus. Politische, soziale und religiöse Ausgrenzung in vormodernen Gesellschaften*, 165–201, Münster: Ergon.

Schwedler, Gerald (2012), "Purifying Memory in the Middle Ages. Cleansing Soul, Deleting Remembrances and the Example of the Attempted Purge of Rudolf of Rheinfelden," in Petra Rösch and Udo Simon, eds, *How Purity is made—Persistence and Dynamics of the Purity Mindframe*, 163–83, Frankfurt a.M.: Harrassowitz.

Schwedler, Gerald (2014), "Bindungen lösen. Die Anleitung des Bernhard von Clairvaux zum Vergessen," in Kerstin Hitzbleck and Klara Hübner, eds, *Die Grenzen des Netzwerks 1200–1600*, 239–58, Ostfildern: Thorbecke.

Schwedler, Gerald (2017), "Karl IV. als Stratege des Vergessens," in Jan Royt and Jiří Kuthan, eds, *Emperor Charles IV., Lands of the Bohemian Crown and Europe*, Praha: Karolinum Press, S. 129–46.

Seelbach, Sabine and Angelika Kemper, eds (2018), *Zentrale Gedächtnislehren des Spätmittelalters*, De Gruyter: Berlin.

Sennis, Antonio (2004), "Omnia tollit aetas et cuncta tollit oblivio. Ricordi smarriti e memorie costruite nei monasteri altomedievali," *Bullettino dell'Istituto storico italiano per il Medio Evo*, 106: 93–135.

Shaw, Philipp A. (2013), "Adapting the Roman Alphabet for Writing Old English: Evidence from Coin Epigraphy and Single-Sheet Charters," *Early Medieval Europe*, 21: 115–39.

Small, Jocelyn Penny (1997), *Wax Tablets of the Mind: Cognitive Studies of Memory and Literacy in Classical Antiquity*, London: Routledge.

Sot, Michel (2003), "Local and Institutional History, 300–1000," in Deborah. M. Deliyannis, ed., *Historiography in the Middle Ages*, 89–114, Leiden: Brill.

Sot, Michel and Christiane Veyard-Cosme, eds. (2014), *Eginhard, Vie de Charlemagne*, Paris: Les Belles Lettres.

Spiegel, Gabrielle M. (2002), "Memory and History. Liturgical Time and Historical Time," *History and Theory*, 41 (2): 149–62.

Sprenger, Kai-Michael (2009), "Damnatio memoriae oder Damnatio in memoria? Überlegungen zum Umgang mit so genannten Gegenpäpsten als methodisches Problem der Papstgeschichtsschreibung," *Quellen und Forschungen aus italienischen Archiven und Bibliotheken*, 89: 31–62.

Sprenger, Kai-Michael (2012a), "The Tiara in the Tiber. An Essay on the Damnatio in Memoria of Clement III (1084–1100) and Rome's River as a Place of Oblivion and Memory," *Reti Medievali*, 13 (1): 153–74.

Sprenger, Kai-Michael (2012b), *Zwischen den Stühlen. Studien zur Wahrnehmung des Alexandrinischen Schismas in Reichsitalien (1159–1177)*, Berlin: De Gruyter.

Spufford, Margareth (1971), "The Scribes of Villagers' Wills in the Sixteenth and Seventeenth Centuries and their Influence," *Local Population Studies*, 7 (7): 28–43.

Spurkland, Terje (2004), "Literacy and 'Runacy' in Medieval Scandinavia," in Jonathan Adams, ed., *Scandinavia and Europe, 800–1350: Contact, Conflict and Coexistence*, 333–44, Turnhout: Brepols.

Sroka, Stanisław A. (2011), "Villains, Merchants and the Written Word: A Document of Highland Outlaws from the Polish-Hungarian Border Area from 1493," in Marco Mostert and Paul S. Barnwell, eds, *Medieval Legal Process Physical, Spoken and Written Performance in the Middle Ages*, 267–80, Turnhout: Brepols.

St. Clair, Eva (2005), "Algazel on the Soul. A Critical Edition," *Traditio*, 60: 69–70.

Stanford, Charlotte A. (2011), *Commemorating the Dead in Late Medieval Strasbourg: The Cathedral's Book of Donors and Its Use (1320–1521)*, Farnham: Ashgate.

Staubach, Nikolaus (1981), *Das Herrscherbild Karls des Kahlen. Formen und Funktionen monarchischer Herrschaft im früheren Mittelalter*, Duisburg: Universitätsverlag.

Steinmann, Martin (2013), *Handschriften im Mittelalter. Eine Quellensammlung*, Basel: Schwabe Verlag.

Stenzel, Gustav A., ed. (1854), *Liber fundationis claustri sanctae Mariae virginis in Heinrichow*, Breslau: Stenzel.

Stock, Brian (1983), *The Implications of Literacy: Written Language and Models of Interpretation in the Eleventh and Twelfth Centuries*, Princeton: Princeton University Press.

Stock, Brian (1985), *The Implications of Literacy: Written Language and Models of Interpretation in the Eleventh and Twelfth Centuries*, Princeton: Princeton University Press.

Strange, Joseph, ed. (1851), *Cesarii Heisterbacensis monachi ordinis Cisterciensis Dialogus miraculorum*, Cologne: Heberle.

Straube, Benjamin (2012), "An Overview of the Neuro-Cognitive Processes Involved in the Encoding, Consolidation, and Retrieval of True and False Memories," *Behavioral and Brain Functions*, 8: Art. 35.

Stroll, Mary (1987), *The Jewish Pope. Ideology and Politics in the Papal Schism of 1130*, Leiden: Brill.

Stubbs, William, ed. (1879), *The Historical Works of Gervase of Canterbury*, Rerum Britannicarum medii aevi Scriptores, Rolls Series 73/1, London: Longmans.

Sturm, Erwin (1984), *Die Bau- und Kunstdenkmale der Stadt Fulda*, Fulda: Parzeller.

Sudhoff, Walther (1913), "Die Lehre von Hirnventrikeln in textlicher und graphischer Tradition des Altertums und Mittelalters," *Archiv für Geschichte der Medizin*, 7: 149–205.

Sudhoff, Karl (1916), "Ein unbekannter Druck von Johann Peyligks aus Zeitz 'Compendiosa capitis physici declaratio', auch 'Anatomia totius corporis humani' genannt," *Archiv für Geschichte der Medizin*, 9: 309–14.

Sudhoff, Karl (1927), "Der Micrologus-Text der Anatomia Richards des Engländers," *Archiv für Geschichte der Medizin*, 19: 209–39.

Sutton, Edward and Harris Rackham, eds. (1967), *Marcus Tullius Cicero, De Oratore*, Cambridge, MA: Harvard University Press.

Taft, Robert F. (1991), *A History of the Liturgy of Saint John Chrysostom*, vol. 4: The Diptychs, Rome: Oriental Institute Press.

Tangl, Michael, ed. (1916), *Die Briefe des heiligen Bonifatius und Lullus* (Monumenta Germaniae Historica, Eppistolae selectae 1), Berlin: Weidmann.

Thélamon, Françoise (2001), "Écrire l'histoire de l'Église: d'Eusèbe de Césarée à Rufin d'Aquilée," in Bernard Pouderon and Yves-Marie Duval, eds, *L'historiographie de l'Église des premiers siècle*, 207–35, Paris: Beauchesne.

Thibodeau, Timothy M. (2000), "Canon law and liturgical exposition in Durand's Rationale," *Bulletin of Medieval Canon Law*, 22: 41–52.

Thibodeau, Timothy M. (2007), *The Rationale divinorum officiorum of William Durand of Mende. A New Translation of the Prologue and Book One*, New York: Columbia University Press.

Thomson, Rodney, Nigel Morgan, Michael Gullick, and Nicholas Hadgraft (2008), "Technology of Production of the Manuscript Book," in Nigel J. Morgan and Rodney M. Thomson, eds, *The Cambridge History of the Book in Britain*, vol. 2, 75–84, Cambridge: Cambridge University Press.

Tinti, Francesca (2018), "Writing Latin and Old English in Tenth-Century England: Patterns, Formulae and Language Choice in the Leases of Oswald of Worcester," in Rory Naismith and David A. Woodman, eds, *Writing, Kingship and Power in Anglo-Saxon England*, 303–27, Cambridge: Cambridge University Press.

Tobi, Yosef (2004), *Proximity and Distance: Medieval Hebrew and Arabic Poetry*, trans. Murray Rosovsky, Leiden: Brill.

Tombeur, Paul, ed. (2013), *Rodulfus Trudonensis, Gesta Abbatum Trudonensium I–VII*, Turnhout: Brepols.

Tóth, István G. (2000), *Literacy and Written Culture in Early Modern Central Europe*, Budapest: Central European University Press.

Tracy, Kisha G. (2015), "Memory, Recollection, and Forgetting," in Albrecht Classen, ed., *Handbook of Medieval Culture: Fundamental Aspects and Conditions of the European Middle Ages*, vol. 2, 1020–38, Berlin: De Gruyter.

Tracy, Kisha G. (2017), *Memory and Confession in Middle English Literature*, Palgrave Macmillan.

Třeboň, Státní oblastní archiv, MS A 6.

Třeboň, Státní oblastní archiv, MS A 7.

Treffort, Cécile (1996), *L'église carolingienne et la mort: Christianisme, rites funéraires et pratiques commémoratives*, Lyon, Presses Universitaires de Lyon.

Umhauser, Christian (1501), *Ars memoratiua S. Thome, Ciceronis, Qunitiliani, Petri Rauenne*, Nürnberg: Ambrosius Hueber.

Van der Gouw, Jaap (1980), "Munimenta et Monumenta," *Nederlands Archivenblad*, 84 (4): 497–514.

Van Houts, Elisabeth, ed. (1992–5), *The Gesta Normannorum ducum of William of Jumièges, Orderic Vitalis and Robert of Torigni*, Oxford: Oxford University Press.

Van Houts, Elisabeth (2001), "Medieval Memories," in Elisabeth van Houts, ed., *Medieval Memories. Men, Women and the Past, 700–1300*, 1–16, Harlow: Longman.

Vansina, Jan (1985), *Oral Tradition as History*, Oxford: James Currey.

Ventura, Leontina and António Resende de Oliveira, eds (2006), *Chanceleria de D. Afonso III. Livro 1*, vol. 2, Coimbra: Universidade de Coimbra.

Verbeke, Gérard and José R. Moncho, eds (1975), *Némésius d'Émèse, De natura hominis, traduction de Burgundio de Pise*, Leiden: Brill.

Verboon, Annemieke R. (2010), *Lines of Thought. Diagrammatic Representation and the Scientific Texts of the Arts Faculty, 1200–1500*, Diss. Leiden.

Verein für Mecklenburgische Geschichte und Altertumskunde, ed. (1867), *Mecklenburgisches Urkundenbuch*, vol. 4. *1297–1300*, Schwerin: Hofbuchhandlung Stiller.

Villa Nova, Arnoldus de (1585), *Opera omnia. Cum Nicolai Tavrelli medici et philosophi in quosdam libros annotationibus. Indice item copiosissimo*, Basileae: ex Officina Pernea per Conradum Waldkirch.

Visi, Tamás (2010), "Remembering and Forgetting the Sabians. Moses Maimonides, Moses Narboni, and Eleazar Eilenburg," in Lucie Doležalová, ed., *The Making of Memory in the Middle Ages*, 415–40, Leiden: Brill.

Vittinghoff, Friedrich (1936), *Der Staatsfeind in der römischen Kaiserzeit. Untersuchungen zur "damnatio memoriae,"* Berlin: Junker und Dünnhaupt.

Voorbij, Hans (2014), "An updated list of surviving manuscripts of the Speculum Maius," *Vincent of Beauvais Newsletter*, 38: 4–17.

Wagner, Wolfgang Eric (2000), "Von der Stiftungsurkunde zum Anniversarbucheintrag: Beobachtungen zur Anlage des Liber oblationum et anniversariorum im Wiener Schottenkloster," in Michael Borgolte, ed., *Stiftungen und Stiftungswirklichkeiten: Vom Mittelalter bis zur Gegenwart*, 145–70, Berlin: Akadamie.

Wagner, Wolfgang Eric (2010), Die liturgische Gegenwart des abwesenden Königs: Gebetsverbrüderung und Herrscherbild im frühen Mittelalter, Leiden: Brill.

Waitz, Georg, ed. (1861), *Annales S. Disibodi*, Hannover.

Wallis, Faith (1995), "The Ambiguities of Medieval 'Memoria'," *Canadian Journal of History*, 30: 77–83.

Walsham, Alexandra and Julia Crick (2004), "Introduction: Script, Print and History," in Alexandra Walsham and Julia Crick, eds, *The Uses of Script and Print, 1300–1700*, 1–26, Cambridge: Cambridge University Press.

Watkins, Oscar D. (1920), *A History of Penance*, vol. 2, London: Longmans, Green.

Weijers, Olga, ed. (1976), *Pseudo-Boèce, De disciplina scolarium*, Leiden: Brill.

Weinberg, Magnus (1924), "Untersuchungen über das Wesen des Memorbuches," *Jahrbuch der jüdisch-literarischen Gesellschaft*, 16: 253–320.
Weinfurter, Stefan (2002), *Heinrich II. (1002–1024). Herrscher am Ende der Zeiten*, 3rd edn., Regensburg: Pustet.
Weinrich, Harald (1997), *Lethe. Kunst und Kritik des Vergessens*. München: C.H. Beck.
Welzer, Harald, Christian Gudehus and Ariane Eichenberg, eds (2010), *Erinnerung und Gedächtnis. Ein interdisziplinäres Handbuch*, Stuttgart: Metzler.
Wenzel, Gusztáv, ed. (1860), *Codex Diplomaticus Arpadianus continuatus. Árpádkori Új Okmánytár*, vol. I, Budapest: Eggenberger.
Werner, Jakob (1979), *Beiträge zur Kunde der lateinischen Literatur des Mittelalters*, Hildesheim: Georg Olms Verlag.
Werner, Karl Ferdinand (1995), *Karl der Große oder Charlemagne? Von der Aktualität einer überholten Fragestellung*, München: Beck.
Wickersheimer, Ernest (1979), *Dictionnaire biographique des médecins en France au Moyen Age*, vol. 1, Geneva: Droz.
Wilk-Woś, Zofia, "Memoriae commendare. Memorative Arengen in den Urkunden der Gnesener Erzbischöfe im 14. Jahrhundert," in Sébastien Rossignol and Anna Adamska, eds, *Urkundenformeln im Kontext. Formen der Schriftkultur im Ostmitteleuropa des Mittelalters*, 149–64, Vienna: Böhlau.
Williams, Henrik (2008), "Runes," in Stefan Brink and Neil Price, eds, *The Viking World*, 281–90, London: Routledge.
Williams, John R. (1957), "The Quest for the Author of the Moralium dogma philosophorum (1931–1956)," *Speculum*, 32: 736–47.
Wilmans, Roger, ed. (1871), *Die Urkunden des Bisthums Münster von 1201–1300*, Münster: Regensberg.
Winterbottom, Michael, ed. (1978), *Gildas De Excidio Britanniae, The Ruin of Britain and other Works*, London: Phillimore.
Wójcik, Rafał (2012), "Masters, Pupils, Friends and Thieves. A Fashion of ars memorativa in the Environment of Early German Humanists," *Daphnis*, 41: 399–418.
Wollasch, Joachim (1971), "A Cluniac Necrology from the Time of Abbot Hugh," in Noreen Hunt, ed., *Cluniac Monasticism in the Central Middle Ages*, 143–90, London: Palgrave Macmillan.
Wollasch, Joachim (1973), "Neue Quellen zur Geschichte der Cistercienser," *Zeitschrift für Kirchengeschichte*, 84: 188–232.
Wollasch, Joachim (1979), "Les obituaires: Témoins de la vie clunisienne," *Cahiers de civilisation médiévale*, 1979, 139–71.
Wollasch, Joachim (1980a), "Bemerkungen zur Goldenen Altartafel von Basel," in Christel Meyer and Uwe Ruberg, eds, *Text und Bild. Aspekte des Zusammenwirkens zweier Künste in Mittelalter und früher Neuzeit*, 383–407, Wiesbaden: Reichert.
Wollasch, Joachim (1980b), "Zu den Anfängen liturgischen Gedenkens an Personen und Personengruppen in den Bodenseeklöstern," *Freiburger Diözesanarchiv*, 100: 59–78.
Wollasch, Joachim, ed. (1982), *Synopse der Cluniazensischen Necrologien*, 2 vols., Munich: Wilhelm Fink.
Wood, Ian (2013), *The Modern Origins of the Early Middle Ages*, Oxford: Oxford University Press.
Wood-Legh, Kathleen L. (1965), *Perpetual Chantries in Britain*, Cambridge: Cambridge University Press.

Wright, Roger, ed. (1991), *Latin and the Romance Languages in the Early Middle Ages*, London: Routledge.

Yates, Frances A. (1966), *"The Art of Memory,"* Chicago: University of Chicago Press.

Yates, Frances (1976), "Ludovico da Pirano's Memory Treatise," in Cecil H. Clough, ed., *Cultural Aspects of the Italian Renaissance. Essays in Honour of P.O. Kristeller*, 111–22, Manchester and New York: Manchester University Press and Zambelli.

Yuval, Israel Y. (1994), "A German-Jewish Autobiography of the Fourteenth Century," *Binah*, 3: 79–99

Yuval, Israel Jacob (2006), *Two Nations in Your Womb: Perceptions of Jews and Christians in Late Antiquity and the Middle Ages*, Berkeley/Los Angeles/London: University of California Press.

Zajic, Andreas (2014), "Texts on Public Display: Strategies of Visualising Ephigraphic Writing in Late Medieval Austrian Towns," in Marco Mostert and Anna Adamska, eds, *Uses of the Written Word in Medieval Towns. Medieval Urban Literacy II*, 389–426, Turnhout: Brepols.

Ziese, Jürgen (1982), *Wibert von Ravenna. Der Gegenpapst Clement III. (1084–1100)*, 271–3, Stuttgart: Hiersemann.

Zilmer, Kristel (2012), "Epigraphic Literacy and the Communication of Christian Culture in Northern Europe," in Kristel Zilmer and Judit Jesch, eds, *Epigraphic Literacy and Christian Identity*, 1–24, Turnhout: Brepols.

Zimmermann, Harald (1968), *Papstabsetzungen des Mittelalters*, Graz: Böhlau.

Zürich, Zentralbibliothek, MS C 101.

Zwiercan, Marian (1963), "Jan z Głogowa," in *Polski Słownik Biograficzny*, vol. 10, 450–2, Cracow: PAN.

CONTRIBUTORS

Anna Adamska is an affiliated scholar in the Institute for the History and Culture at Utrecht University, The Netherlands. Her research and publications focus on medieval (pragmatic) literacy and communication, and encompass forms and functions of charters, the social history of language, source criticism, and the methodology of Medieval Studies. She is also interested in the cultural and socio-religious history of East Central Europe, as well as in the history of the humanities in this region. She co-edited several volumes in the series *Utrecht Studies in Medieval Literacy* published by Brepols Publishers.

Lucie Doležalová got her PhD in Medieval Studies at the Central European University in Budapest, Hungary, in 2005 and is currently working as an Associate Professor of Medieval Latin at the Charles University in Prague, Czech Republic. In her research, she focuses on late medieval manuscript culture (forthcoming monograph on "creative copying" in late medieval Bohemia), medieval libraries, Latin opuscula, obscurity, and the art of memory. Among others, she edited *The Making of Memory in The Middle Ages* (2009).

Farkas Gábor Kiss studied Medieval Studies, Hungarian and Latin Language and Literature in Budapest, Hungary, and finished his dissertation on "Imitation and imagination in the epic poem of Nicholas Zrínyi" in 2006. After research visits in Innsbruck and Paris, he is now lecturer at the Eötvös Loránd University, Budapest, Hungary. He has published widely in the field of medieval and renaissance theory and art of memory, recently: "The art of memory in East Central Europe in the late Middle Ages" (2014).

Caroline Horch studied History, Philosophy and Art History at the universities of Münster, Hannover, Munich, Aix-en-Provence, and Nijmegen. She earned state examination in History and Philosophy at Universität Münster in 1987, received a Ph.D. in Art History at Katholieke Universiteit Nijmegen in 2002, and a Habilitation degree in Medieval History at Universität Duisburg-Essen in 2007 (Der Cappenberger Barbarossakopf). She taught medieval history at the universities of Düsseldorf, Duisburg-Essen, Halle/Saale and Oldenburg. In various articles, she combines the disciplines of History and Art History.

Rainer Hugener has gained his doctoral degree from the University of Zürich with his ground-breaking work on documents of medieval commemoration. His studies also comprise publications on Swiss historiography and sightings of ghosts. He is currently working at the State Archive of Zürich, Switzerland, preparing the publication of a selection of documents crucial to the process of state building from the thirteenth to the eighteenth century.

Jean-Marie Moeglin studied at the École normale supérieure in Paris, became Directeur d'études an der Ecole pratique des Hautes Etudes in 1995 and is professor for medieval

History at the Sorbonne Université, France. His research focus lies on medieval historiography, the Hundred Years' War, medieval diplomacy and medieval Germany. He authored and edited various volumes, and recently he published Diplomatie et "relations internationales" au Moyen Age (2017) together with Stéphane Péquignot.

Joel T. Rosenthal is a Distinguished Professor Emeritus, Stony Brook University, USA. He co-edits *Studies in Medieval and Renaissance History* and *Medieval Prosopography*. He has published on various aspects of social history and has recently (2017) written *Social Memory in Medieval England* and co-edited and contributed to (2019) a volume of essays on T.F. Tout, the Manchester medieval historian of the early twentieth century.

Gerald Schwedler is professor for medieval History at the Christian-Albrechts Universität Kiel, Germany. His research areas include medieval historiography, European diplomacy, memory culture, and economic history. He published various books and articles on medieval strategies of memory and forgetting (*damnatio memoriae*, forthcoming). He currently works on cultural inflation and imitation in the Middle Ages (Nachahmen im Mittelalter 2018) as well as medieval patterns to deal with cultural degeneration (Exzerpieren—Kompilieren—Tradieren, 2017).

Kai-Michael Sprenger published his dissertation on "Perception and Coping with the Alexandrian Schism in Imperial Italy (1159–1177)" and remains research associate at the German Historical Institute in Rome, Italy, with the project on the memory of Emperor Friedrich Barbarossa. Since January 2016, he has been an advisor in the Ministry of Science, Further Education and Culture, and has authored numerous publications, mainly on medieval church and regional history (Italy, Mainz, Upper Swabia), memory and *damnatio memoriae*, on the history of books and printing, on contemporary art as well as on the reception history of the Middle Ages.

Tamás Visi is an Associate Professor at the Kurt and Ursula Schubert Centre for Jewish Studies at Palacky University, Czech Republic. He earned his doctorate with a dissertation on the early Ibn Ezra supercommentaries at the Central European University in Budapest in 2006. In 2012, he was a Fellow of the Institute for Advanced Studies at the Hebrew University of Jerusalem. His main interests are Moravian Jewish history (especially rabbinic literature and other Hebrew sources), medieval Jewish philosophy and intellectual history. He has recently co-edited the volume *Berechiah ben Natronai ha-Naqdan's Works and Their Reception* published by Brepols (2019).

INDEX

Aachen 17
Abelard 82–6
Adalbert of Bamberg 18
Adam of Bremen 19
Ado of Vienne 125
Aimoin of Fleury 36, 69
Albericus de Rosate 11
Albert Behaim 18
Albertus Magnus 14, 98
Alcuin 13
Alessandria, Italy 152
Alexander III, pope 149, 151, 157
Al-Ghazali 103
Al-Jazzar, Ibn 99
al-Isfahani, Abu Bakr Muhammad Abi Sulayman Dawud 81–2
Alsted, Johann Heinrich 105
al-Muqaffa, Ibn 86
Anacletus 153
Andreas of Regensburg 37
anniversary books 142–5
Aquinas, Thomas 14, 75, 98, 122, 138
Archive 62, 69, 70, 138
Aristotle 12, 14, 41, 75, 84, 98, 100
Arnald of Villanova 97
Arnold of Brescia 149
Arras 20
ars memoriae 2, 7, 8, 9, 12, 14, 88, 95
Ashkenaz 3, 83, 125, 145
Attigny 127
Atzmann 112, 113
Augustine 3, 12, 13, 74, 80, 81, 107, 108
Augustodunensis, Honorius 5
Aulus Gellius 22
Averroes 84, 103
Avicenna 94, 100, 103

Baghdad 81
Barbarossa, Frederick, emperor 116, 117, 149, 150, 152
Barberini diptych 126
Bede, the Venerable 7, 21, 33, 68, 125
Le Bel, Jean 38
Benedict XIII, pope 5

Berchtold of Zähringen 143
Bergamo 105
Berne 143
Bernhard of Clairvaux 14
Bible 1, 3, 5, 108
  Deut. 25.17 1
  Ps. 109 160
  Lk. 22.19 1, 5
  John 11.25 3
  1 Cor. 11.23–45 5, 108
Black Death 145
Boëthius 96, 102
Bonaventure 76, 77, 13
Boniface VIII, pope 157
Bouvines 19
Bradwardine, Thomas 9
Bremen 19, 97, 160
Bruno, Giordano 105
Bruno of Hildesheim 110, 111
Brześć Kujawski 104
Buckland, Joan 53–5
Burckhardt, Jacob 73
Burgundio of Pisa 98
Buridan, Jean 14
Burke, Peter 41
Burzoe 86

Caesarius of Heisterbach 139
Cambrai 20
Cambridge 47, 64
Cappenberg 116–18
Carpet from Bayeux 113–15
Carrara, Giovanni Michele Alberto 105
Carruthers, Mary 15, 75
Cassiodorus (485–c. 580) 7, 94
Charlemagne 17, 21, 118–20, 127
Charles IV 86, 87
Charles the Bald 31, 120
Chaucer, Geoffrey 87
Cicero 9, 22, 25, 26, 41, 153
Clanchy, Michael 15, 57
Clement III, (anti) pope 150, 152, 156, 157
Clement VI, pope 159
Cluny 5, 136, 138

Coleman, Janet 15
collective memory 59
Cologne 91
Comenos, Manuel, emperor 28
Constance 26, 27, 84, 136
Constantine the African 103
Cornwall 45
Cosmas of Prague 25

damnatio memoriae 8, 147–54
Dante Alighieri 8
Decretum Gratini 151
Devon 45, 50
Dingolfing 127
Diptych 128
Dolce, Lodovico 105
Domesday Book 68, 69
Durand, Guillaume 103–4, 173
Durham 70, 131

Easter 33, 68
Edward I, king of England 115
Edward III, king of England 38
Eginhard 20, 27
Eisenstein, Elisabeth 67
Eiximenis, Francesc 11
Erinnerungskultur 2
Essex 49
Eudes of St. Amand 28
Eusebius of Caesarea 22, 23, 24, 32, 34
Evesham 44

Faliero, Doge Marino 159
Farfa 136
Floating gap 87
Fontana, Giovanni 12, 105
Formosus, (anti-) pope 156
Fournier, Jacques 76
Freculf of Lisieux 24
Fried, Johannes 15
Froissart, Jean 17, 18, 30, 38
Frutolf from Michelsberg 36
Fulcher of Chartres 35

Galen 86, 98–100
Geary, Patrick 15
Genoa 20
Gerhoh of Reichersberg 149
Gervase of Canterbury 7, 25
Gilbert of Tournai 103
Gildas 26
Gloucestershire 51
Goslar 142

Gregory III, pope 127
Gregory VII, pope 155
Gregory of Nyssa 98
Gregory of Tours 32, 69
Guenée, Bernard 36
de Guise, Jacques 17, 19
Gutenberg, Johannes 67

Hajdu, Helga 14
Halberstadt 18
Harold, the Earl of Wessex 115
Haskins, Charles Homer 73
Hazm, Ibn 83, 87
Helmold of Bosau 20
Héloise 82
Henry I, emperor 28
Henry II, emperor 112
Henry II, king of England 18, 21
Henry IV, emperor 118–19, 155–6
Hermann of Niederaltaich 36, 37
Hermetschwil 136
Herodotus 22
Herrad of Landsberg 121
Hinkmar of Reims 13
Hohenburg 122
Honotius of Autun 102
Hugh of Fleury 18
Hugh of St. Victor 9, 17, 22, 24
Huntingdon, Henry 21
Hus, Jan 79, 84, 87, 88

Innocent II, pope 153
Ishaq, Hunayn Ibn 86
Isidore of Sevilla 13, 17
Islam 1, 9, 66, 83

Jahrzeit/Jahrtag 139, 142
Jerusalem 34
Jesus Christ 2, 5, 23, 24, 30, 59, 77–9, 88
Jewish memory 83
John of Głogów 100–2
John of Salisbury 14, 20
John of Winterthur 26
Judaism 1, 19, 83
Justinian I, emperor 154

Kättilstorp 104
de Kryspe, Johann Romberch 11, 91, 94, 105

Landenberg, family 143
Levold of Northof 26
liber vitae 15, 28, 131, 132, 140, 150
liber viventum 128, 130

INDEX 211

libri memoriales 107, 131
Liege 34
Lieu de memoire 5, 15
Lithuania 66
London 54, 55
Louis IV of Bavaria, emperor 151, 159
Louis the Pious 24, 31
Louis XI 39
Luhmann, Niklas 16

MacLuhan, Marshall 67
Magdeburg 18
Maimonides 83, 85
Manfred, son of Frederick II 153
Marcigny-sur-Loire 136
Martin of Troppau 19, 24, 37
Martyrology 134
Mathilde of Tuscia 21
Matthew of Acquasparta 103
Maturanzio, Francesco 104
Maurus, Rabanus 125
de Medici, Piero 5
Melk 94, 95
Memorik 15
memory studies 1–2, 16, 148
Merseburg 155
Metz 120
Michelsberg 111
Montaillou 76
Monte Cassino 18
Muri 136

Necrology 135
Nemesius of Emesa 98
Niederaltaich 19
Nora, Pierre 15
Norfolk 49, 52
Northampton 54

Oblivio 2
Odilo of Cluny 138
Oexle, Otto Gerhard 124
Olomouc 74
Orose 24, 32
Otloh of St. Emmeram 8
Otto I of Bamberg 109, 110, 111
Otto of Cappenberg 116
Otto of Freising 20, 21, 37
Ovid 102
Oxford 54, 86

Paderborn 27
Parenzo/Poreč 125

Paris 35
Paschal III, pope 149
Pelbárt of Temesvár 100
Peter Lombard 7
Peter the Venerable 138
Petrarch 80
Petrus Flota 157
Pfäfers 128, 130
Philip VI, king of France 38
Philippe de Commines 39
Piacenza 17
Piccolomini, Enea Silvio 25
pittura infamente 153
Pius II, pope 39
Plato 12, 41, 98
de la Porrée, Gilbert 122
Prague 84
Proofs of Age 42–51

Quintilian 9

Ramon Lull 11
Ranke, Leopold von 20
Regensburg 8, 37
Reginon of Prüm 19
Reichenau 108, 125, 129, 134
Reisch, Gregor 102
Remiremont 134
rewriting 152
Rhetorica ad Herennium 9
Richard I, king of England 26, 70
Richard II, king of England 21
Richard of Salerno 99
Ricoeur, Paul 39
Robert of Torigni 25
Rolevinck, Werner 24
Rome 59, 149, 153
Rudolf of Rheinfelden 117, 118, 155
Rufin of Aquileia 23
Rune-stick 63

Saba Malaspina 19
Saint Gall 74, 128, 141
Saint-Denis 29, 35, 36
Saint-Trond 20
Salerno 99
Schmid, Karl 124
Siegbert of Gembloux 34, 36
da Signa, Boncompagno 9
Somerset 46
St. Boniface 28
St. Jerome 23

Stock, Brian 15
Sulpicius Severus 27
Surrey 44
Sussex 48

Tertullian 3
Theoderic, king of the Ostrogoths 7, 96, 154
Thietmar of Merseburg 19, 28
Thomas of Kempen 6
Thomas, Robert 43
Thucydides 22

Victor IV, (anti) pope 156, 157
victor's history 153, 156

Vienna 134
Vincent of Beauvais 19, 100

will 53–5
William of Conches 102
William of Ockham 122
William the Conqueror 21, 70
William, Duke of Normandy 115
Wipo 26, 27
Worcester 44

Yates, Frances 14
Yorkshire 44, 45

Zürich 129, 130, 143, 165